Confirmation Bias in Criminal Cases

Confirmation Bias in Criminal Cases

MOA LIDÉN

Great Clarendon Street, Oxford, OX2 6DP,
United Kingdom

Oxford University Press is a department of the University of Oxford.
It furthers the University's objective of excellence in research, scholarship,
and education by publishing worldwide. Oxford is a registered trade mark of
Oxford University Press in the UK and in certain other countries

© Oxford University Press 2023

The moral rights of the author have been asserted

First Edition published in 2023

All rights reserved. No part of this publication may be reproduced, stored in
a retrieval system, or transmitted, in any form or by any means, without the
prior permission in writing of Oxford University Press, or as expressly permitted
by law, by licence or under terms agreed with the appropriate reprographics
rights organization. Enquiries concerning reproduction outside the scope of the
above should be sent to the Rights Department, Oxford University Press, at the
address above

You must not circulate this work in any other form
and you must impose this same condition on any acquirer

Public sector information reproduced under Open Government Licence v3.0
(http://www.nationalarchives.gov.uk/doc/open-government-licence/open-government-licence.htm)

Published in the United States of America by Oxford University Press
198 Madison Avenue, New York, NY 10016, United States of America

British Library Cataloguing in Publication Data

Data available

Library of Congress Control Number: 2023932447

ISBN 978–0–19–286764–3

DOI: 10.1093/oso/9780192867643.001.0001

Printed and bound in the UK by
TJ Books Limited

Links to third party websites are provided by Oxford in good faith and
for information only. Oxford disclaims any responsibility for the materials
contained in any third party website referenced in this work.

Preface

During my last year of law school, I had a teacher in Contemporary Jurisprudence who, on the first day of the course, would ask all students: 'Why is law legitimate?' The students would take turns and do their best to answer this question, which I believe surprised and challenged us all. Among the students who had already started doing some reading for the course, there would be answers like 'because the citizens, by voting, have given the legislator power to legislate' or 'because law builds on fundamental ethical principles with which any moral person would agree'. The teacher's question, however, steered my thoughts in a completely different direction. Listening to my fellow students' answers I became increasingly unsure whether my answer, yet unspoken, was appropriate or even relevant. I thought to myself, this answer could either come across as that from an obnoxious teenager who has not made the effort to open her books yet, or, maybe, there is just a slight chance it will hit the bull's eye and be a roaring success, impressing both my teacher and fellow students. After having turned the question inside-out and upside-down, silently to myself, multiple times, it was finally my turn to give my answer. With my pulse raising and my hands starting to sweat slightly, I decided to let go of much of what I had learned during the last couple of years and not worry, for a moment, about the reactions. I answered: 'Is law legitimate?' Following what felt like at least 10 seconds of silence, the teacher, to my great relief and content, smiled and said: 'Good, that is a very interesting thought.' Throughout the course, the teacher would keep challenging and inspiring us in similar ways, which I believe not only promoted our critical thinking but also made us more comfortable feeling that our opinions were relevant and even important.

Ever since law school I have kept asking similar questions and felt driven towards challenging assumptions in different ways. This is probably also why the combination of law and psychology was so appealing to me. Studying psychology, and specifically legal psychology, opened up endless opportunities to evaluate critically what was really going on in law, and particularly in the decision-making of practitioners operating within the context of criminal investigations and proceedings. One aspect of human decision-making that appeared especially problematic was the so-called confirmation bias, commonly referred to as 'tunnel vision'. I decided to devote my PhD research as well as much of the research I have conducted thereafter to this. Hence, this book is the result of research I have conducted since 2013 and am still conducting today. This research consists, primarily, of scenario-based experimental research studies with practitioners like police officers, crime scene investigators, forensic doctors, forensic analysts, prosecutors, and judges, as participants. Given the breadth of these practitioners' backgrounds, as well as the complex multidisciplinary nature of criminal cases, today I collaborate with other researchers in the fields of forensic genetics, forensic medicine, forensic anthropology, and computer science, among others. This book is devoted to all the researchers who faithfully and tirelessly continue to conduct research in this challenging field with the aim of improving the legitimacy of criminal law and procedure. It is also devoted to the person who has not only supported me in my research quests brilliantly but also shares my fascination for challenging assumptions. Leo, thank you for all the love, fun, conversation, and bagels.

Acknowledgements

The author would like to extend her gratitude to the following individuals for supporting the writing of this book in different ways.

Olga Tokariuk, journalist, and Cristiano Tinazzi, journalist, for providing information and relevant documents in the case against Mr Vitaly Markiv.

Lena Linderoth, archivist, the Legal section, National Archive, Sweden, for providing information and documents pertaining to the Therese Johanessen case.

Per Erling Holck, Professor, Institute of Basic Medical Sciences, Oslo University, for providing pictures pertaining to the Therese Johanessen case.

Nataraja Moorthy, professor and crime scene investigator, for providing information and photographs for one of the case studies from India ('Case Study 1: Homicide or Struck by Lightning?').

Thérèse Björkholm, for being an inspiring teacher in Contemporary Jurisprudence asking critical questions that made me practice and appreciate freedom of thought.

Xabier Agirre Aranburu, Senior Coordinator, former Head of the Investigative Analysis Section, at the International Criminal Court, for providing input, suggesting relevant sources, and encouragement, especially for research in the field of international criminal law.

Joseph Almog, for help in communication with the Israeli police authority.

Itiel Dror, Senior Researcher, Cognitive Consultants International, for providing input and encouragement.

Eli M. Rosenbaum, Director, Human Rights and Special Prosecutions Section, Criminal Division, U.S. Department of Justice, for providing guidance regarding the Ivan the Terrible case.

Table of Contents

1. The 'Human Factor' in Criminal Cases: Introduction — 1
   1.1 General — 1
2. Confirmation Bias — 6
   2.1 Introduction — 6
   2.2 Background — 7
      2.2.1 Definition of Confirmation Bias — 11
      2.2.2 Why Does Confirmation Bias Occur? — 18
         2.2.2.1 Cognitive Explanations — 19
         2.2.2.2 Emotional and Motivational Explanations — 23
         2.2.2.3 Social and Organizational Explanations — 28
3. Confirmation Bias in Criminal Investigations — 35
   3.1 Introduction — 35
   3.2 Search for Information — 37
      3.2.1 Suspect-driven Investigations — 37
   3.3 Evaluation of Information — 44
      3.3.1 Believing is Seeing — 44
      3.3.2 Asymmetrical Scepticism — 47
   3.4 Confirmation Bias, False Positives, and False Negatives — 51
   3.5 Confirmation Bias in Specific Investigative Settings — 55
      3.5.1 Interviews — 55
         3.5.1.1 Introduction — 55
         3.5.1.2 Understanding Bias—Suspect Interviews — 56
         3.5.1.3 Understanding Bias—Witness Interviews — 60
         3.5.1.4 Understanding Bias—Plaintiff Interviews — 67
         3.5.1.5 Mitigating Bias — 68
         3.5.1.6 Conclusion — 73
      3.5.2 Suspect Line-ups — 74
         3.5.2.1 Introduction — 74
         3.5.2.2 Understanding Bias — 75
         3.5.2.3 Mitigating Bias — 82
         3.5.2.4 Conclusion — 86
      3.5.3 Crime Scene Investigations — 87
         3.5.3.1 Introduction — 87
         3.5.3.2 Understanding Bias — 89
         3.5.3.3 Mitigating Bias — 98
         3.5.3.4 Conclusion — 102
      3.5.4 Forensic Analysis — 103
         3.5.4.1 Introduction — 103

	3.5.4.2 Understanding Bias—Criminalistics	104
	3.5.4.3 Understanding Bias—Forensic Medicine	112
	3.5.4.4 Understanding Bias—Forensic Anthropology	120
	3.5.4.5 Mitigating Bias	123
	3.5.4.6 Conclusion	139

4. Confirmation Bias in Criminal Litigations — 140
4.1 Introduction — 140
4.2 Prosecutorial Decision-making — 141
- 4.2.1 Introduction — 141
- 4.2.2 Understanding Bias — 142
  - 4.2.2.1 Overconfident leadership — 142
  - 4.2.2.2 Pre-trial Decisions — 148
  - 4.2.2.3 The Charging Decision — 151
- 4.2.3 Mitigating Bias — 154
  - 4.2.3.1 Changing decision-maker — 154
  - 4.2.3.2 Devil's Advocates, Red Teams, and Evidence Review Boards — 155
- 4.2.4 Conclusion — 158

4.3 Judges' Decision-making — 159
- 4.3.1 Introduction — 159
- 4.3.2 Understanding Bias — 160
  - 4.3.2.1 Pre-trial Detention, Interim Decisions, and Other Decisions Preceding the Assessment of Guilt — 160
  - 4.3.2.2 Story Construction — 167
  - 4.3.2.3 Crime Gravity and Sentencing — 175
- 4.3.3 Mitigating Bias — 177
  - 4.3.3.1 Changing Decision-maker — 177
  - 4.3.3.2 Structured Evaluations of Evidence — 179
- 4.3.4 Conclusion — 180

5. Overall Summary and Conclusion — 183
5.1 Summary and Implications — 183
5.2 Concluding Remarks — 191

Glossary — 195
Bibliography — 197
Index — 267

1
The 'Human Factor' in Criminal Cases

Introduction

1.1 General

The importance of the so-called human factor for the progress, outcome, and accuracy of criminal investigations and proceedings has been acknowledged for longer than one might think. In fact, as early as 1906, Hans Gross, an Austrian criminal jurist and criminologist, made observations of that nature. He noted the importance for criminal investigators to reflect carefully about the point at which they form definite opinions in a case since, at that stage, they would become tenaciously attached to such opinions until forced to abandon them.[1] Yet at that point, Gross noted that it would already be too late as 'the best clues will have been lost, often beyond the possibility of recovery'.[2] Today, the importance of the human factor is debated and researched, not the least in relation to wrongful convictions,[3] although its relevance for the ever-growing pile of cold cases found in many police departments across the world has also been acknowledged.[4] Occasionally, the hopes and prospects of correcting previous errors and solving seemingly unsolvable cases are renewed with innovations in forensic science such as advanced DNA technology[5] and Next Generation Identification (NGI),[6] as well as technological progresses, today often based on artificial intelligence (AI).[7] While such developments can indeed be excellent investigative tools, they all disregard one important factor which is constant and common to all jurisdictions: human decision-makers, that is, the practitioners working within the context of criminal investigations and proceedings. Since all jurisdictions do not only have the human element in common but are also fundamentally dependent on the decision-making processes

---

[1] Gross (1906). Criminal Investigation: A Practical Handbook for Magistrates, Police Officers and Lawyers.
[2] Gross (1906). Criminal Investigation: A Practical Handbook for Magistrates, Police Officers and Lawyers, p. 4.
[3] Ohio Innocence Project (2021). The Impact of Human Factors on Criminal Investigations.
[4] Roach (2017). The Retrospective Detective: Cognitive Bias and the Cold Case Homicide Investigator.
[5] Davis et al. (2014). Working Smarter on Cold Cases: Identifying Factors Associated with Successful Cold Case Investigations, pp. 375–382.
[6] Stokes (2019). Technical Note: Next Generation Identification—A Powerful Tool in Cold Case Investigations, pp. 74–49.
[7] Kureishy, LaPlante, & Meley (2019). Fighting Financial Crimes with Artificial Intelligence.

of the humans operating inside of them, understanding potential sources of error stemming from the humans is, arguably, even more essential than accurate and appropriate usage of forensic and technological developments. This raises the questions regarding what is it more specifically about the 'human factor' that may constitute a threat to the proper administration of justice, and what, if anything, can be done about it.

While the 'human factor' is indeed a broad and vague term which entails a range of potentially problematic mechanisms, one such mechanism which has been described since the beginning of the seventeenth century is confirmation bias. In fact, one of the most influential scholars examining confirmation bias, Raymond Nickerson, in 1998 stated that '[i]f one were to attempt to identify a single problematic aspect of human reasoning that deserves attention above all others, the confirmation bias would have to be among the candidates for consideration'.[8]

In line with Nickerson's observation, the relevance of understanding and mitigating confirmation bias in the context of criminal justice has also been confirmed by field-specific research beginning in the 1990s. Overall, it is easy to see how confirmation bias in criminal investigations and proceedings can make criminal justice inaccurate and inefficient, potentially resulting in great harm, both for the involved people and in terms of financial cost for unsuccessful or misguided investigations and proceedings. This is because confirmation bias can make criminal investigations and proceedings narrow, one-sided, and inaccurate. More specifically, confirmation bias connotes 'the seeking or interpreting of evidence in ways that are partial to existing beliefs, expectations, or a hypothesis in hand'.[9]

Simultaneously, the decision-maker's search for counterarguments becomes less effective and if contradicting information is considered, it is assigned only limited importance.[10] Furthermore, a crucial component of confirmation bias is that it happens more or less subconsciously.[11]

What does this mean for the administration of criminal justice? In the context of criminal justice, human decision-makers are present at every step, including a range of different practitioners such as police officers, crime scene investigators, forensic analysts, forensic doctors, prosecutors, and judges who, while they all operate within the same context, have distinctively different tasks and responsibilities. Subsequently, the more specific manifestations of confirmation bias in their decision-making, as well as possible ways to mitigate the bias, will vary. Even practitioners who are expected by law or professional standards to remain objective, who are highly motivated, competent, and intelligent, and who might even perceive of themselves as objective, can display confirmation bias.[12] Since confirmation bias

---

[8] Nickerson (1998). Confirmation Bias: A Ubiquitous Phenomenon in Many Guises, p. 175.
[9] Nickerson (1998). Confirmation Bias: A Ubiquitous Phenomenon in Many Guises, p. 175.
[10] Nickerson (1998). Confirmation Bias: A Ubiquitous Phenomenon in Many Guises, p. 175.
[11] Nickerson (1998). Confirmation Bias: A Ubiquitous Phenomenon in Many Guises, pp. 175–220.
[12] Nickerson, Confirmation Bias: A Ubiquitous Phenomenon in Many Guises, pp. 175–220.

is a largely subconscious phenomenon, the practitioners are unlikely to detect and mitigate it in themselves. Also, the primary focus of criminal case procedures per se is that of crimes and evidence rather than how practitioners best live up to standards of objectivity. Therefore, what the more specific manifestations of confirmation bias are, as well as how best to mitigate such bias, are questions that need to be answered by researchers using scientifically established methodologies.

Apart from providing a general scientific framework for understanding what confirmation bias is and why it occurs (Chapter 2), this book addresses the research already conducted into manifestations of confirmation bias in criminal investigations and litigations, including police interviews with suspects, witnesses, and plaintiffs as well as forensic doctors' assessments of cause of death and judges' determinations of a defendant's guilt (Chapters 3 and 4). For example, while police officers may display confirmation bias by asking suspects questions that are presumptive of guilt (Section 3.5.1.2), forensic doctors may instead 'see' in their observations of a deceased body signs that are primarily consistent, rather than inconsistent, with the investigative hypothesis which has been disclosed to them by investigators (Section 3.5.4.3). Such tendencies are likely to affect the evidence presented in court, impacting on the basis for judges' decision-making. Furthermore, judges can themselves develop a confirmation bias. For example, confirmation bias can be triggered by a preliminary decision about the suspect's guilt prior to the main hearing (Section 4.3.1.1). Consequently, all the assessments and decisions made throughout the course of criminal investigations and proceedings can, in one way or another, contribute to error. The different types of errors that may result from confirmation bias are discussed in Section 3.4 and may include false positives as well as false negatives. Apart from outlining manifestations and consequences, this book also illustrates how psychological research into confirmation bias can be used and converted into potential bias mitigation strategies, a field that is less well researched. Since confirmation bias acts outside conscious awareness and therefore outside practitioners' control, effective debiasing techniques require other types of measures than raising awareness. Being aware of the risk of confirmation bias may result in practitioners taking precautions, for example in how they conduct suspect interviews, work with autopsies or crime scene investigations. Awareness in itself is not, however, enough. Accordingly, effective debiasing techniques operate differently, for example by changing decision structures and implementing blinding and second opinion procedures. While the number of research studies examining debiasing techniques is growing, many questions remain regarding the more specific techniques to use and how to implement them. Some debiasing techniques have been evaluated more carefully than others, which will be pointed out in the chapters addressing such issues in each respective field of decision-making. Possible manifestations and possible debiasing techniques are summarized in Table 5.1 (Chapter 5).

The research cited in this book stems from a range of fields, including law, psychology, forensic science, medicine, biology, and computer science, as well as inter- and multidisciplinary research combining these fields. Consequently, the primary audience of this book is academics with an interest in criminal law and procedure as well as legal psychology, including cognitive, emotional and motivational, and social and organizational psychology.

In addition to the cited research, case studies shall be used to illustrate different manifestations of confirmation bias. The use of case studies merits two initial remarks. First, confirmation bias cannot be directly *observed* in the sense that the progress of the cases provides 'evidence' of confirmation bias. However, behaviours displayed by practitioners in these cases overlap with the behaviours referred to as confirmation bias. Case studies are not only conducted in hindsight but are also unable to make visible the cognitive, emotional, and other processes at play in practitioners' minds. Similarly, case studies cannot determine whether a displayed one-sidedness is conscious or subconscious. As discussed in Section 2.2.1, interpreting one-sidedness as a subconscious rather than conscious process is an interpretation that gives practitioners the benefit of doubt. Such an interpretation presupposes that practitioners are motivated to live up to professional standards and that they would have acted differently had they been aware of their one-sidedness. This will not always be true. The case studies nevertheless provide the necessary connection to real-life criminal cases and possible manifestations of confirmation bias in them. Together with the research cited throughout this book, this is likely to be the most viable way to explain the practical relevance of this bias, as well as how it can be mitigated.

Secondly, since confirmation bias is a product of the humans operating within a criminal jurisdiction, rather than a specific jurisdiction per se, the case studies originate from a wide range of jurisdictions, national as well as international. This includes France, India, Israel, Italy, Kenya, Norway, Spain, Sweden, the United Kingdom, the United States, the International Criminal Court (ICC), the Special Tribunal for Lebanon (STL), the International Criminal Tribunal for Rwanda (ICTR), and the European Court of Human Rights (ECtHR). Case studies from specific jurisdictions will be used to illustrate a specific type of manifestation. For example, the London bombings in 2005 and the subsequent fatal shooting of Mr de Menezes is used as an example of a suspect-driven investigation (Section 3.2.1), but this does not mean that suspect-driven investigations do not exist in other jurisdictions. Similarly, the Israelian Tair Rada case, the Norwegian Therese Johannessen case, as well as a few other examples from national jurisdictions, are used to illustrate the forensic confirmation bias (see Sections 3.5.4.2 and 3.5.5.5). These examples should not be interpreted as an exhaustive list or as suggestions that the named jurisdictions are unique or especially problematic. Rather than the jurisdictions themselves, it is the humans operating in the jurisdictions that are the spotlight of this book. While human decision-makers are a continuous and common denominator across all jurisdictions, relevant variations in the applicable laws, guidelines and practices across jurisdiction will be pointed out. Readers are encouraged to consider whether and how confirmation bias, as it is depicted here, may also be at play in other similar situations or situations that are more familiar to them.

2
Confirmation Bias

2.1 Introduction

The human understanding when it has once adopted an opinion ... draws all things else to support and agree with it. And though there be a greater number and weight of instances to be found on the other side, yet these it either neglects and despises, or else by some distinction sets aside and rejects; in order that by this great and pernicious predetermination the authority of its former conclusions may remain inviolate ... .[1]

Francis Bacon, 1620

The Prosecutor seems to have started from the premise that her case theory is correct and that this theory provides the necessary coherence to link the disparate evidentiary elements she relies upon. However, this is putting the cart in front of the horse. In order to prove her case, the Prosecutor must first demonstrate the aforesaid connections and coherence. This has not been done.[2]

ICC Judge Henderson in *The Prosecutor v. Laurent Gbagbo and Charles Blé Goudé*, 2019

This chapter provides a framework that enables understanding of what confirmation bias is as well as why it occurs. This entails a brief background (Section 2.2) addressing research into confirmation bias in a range of contexts other than the legal context. While this book focuses on understanding and mitigating bias in criminal cases (Chapters 3 and 4), it is essential that the reader thinks of confirmation bias as the human element it is rather than as a product of a specific context. As captured by the epigraphs above, the behaviour today referred to as confirmation bias (Section 2.2.1) is a long-recognized phenomenon and its relevance and implications for different specific contexts have become clear. One aspect of this bias which makes it particularly intricate is its largely subconscious nature. While individuals may be fully aware of what confirmation bias is and why it occurs, they will still be unable to observe the bias *as it occurs* in their

---

[1] Bacon (1620). Novum Organum, p. 36.
[2] The Prosecutor v. Laurent Gbagbo and Charles Blé Goudé, Situation in Côte d'Ivoire, ICC-02/11-01/15, Annex B, § 79 Judge Henderson's reasons.

own reasoning. There is no empirical evidence for a 'judicial exceptionalism',[3] meaning that legal actors are more resistant to confirmation bias than others, due to their training and experience. Thus, bias awareness is inadequate for effective bias mitigation, which underlines the need to implement empirically evaluated mitigation methods, here referred to as debiasing techniques. A crucial first step is to understand why the bias occurs (Section 2.2.2), a question which will be addressed from the perspectives of cognitive psychology (Section 2.2.2.1), emotional and motivational psychology (Section 2.2.2.2), as well as social and organizational psychology (Section 2.2.2.3). Explanations provided from each of these respective fields can then be converted into context-specific debiasing techniques, which will be addressed in relation to criminal cases in Chapters 3 and 4.

2.2 Background

The human inclination to form hypotheses and hold on to them tenaciously, despite contradictory evidence, was already recognized at the beginning of the seventeenth century.[4] However, the term 'confirmation bias' only began to gain acceptance in the 1960s,[5] with the work of Peter Cathcart Wason. Since then, a wealth of data has been collected on the topic, primarily using controlled psychological laboratory experiments. Much of the early research built on Wason's famous '2-4-6 task' in which participants are told that the numbers 2, 4, and 6 adhere to a rule and their task is to find out what that rule is through testing with series of three numbers.[6] Wason, as well as his colleague Johnson-Laird, who both replicated the findings with similar tasks,[7] noted that most participants generated a series of numbers that potentially could confirm their hypothesis of what the rule was, while far fewer generated numbers that were inconsistent with the rule and therefore could falsify their hypotheses. For instance, participants whose hypothesis was that the second number was twice the first number and the third number was three times the first number tended to generate sets of numbers consistent with that hypothesis (e.g. 3-6-9 or 100-200-300). Some of the participants displayed wishful thinking by repeatedly stating the same rules using different series of numbers, hoping that it was not the rule but the series of numbers that was incorrect. Only very few participants (21 per cent) got the rule right from the beginning. What characterized the

---

[3] Edmond & Martire (2019). Just Cognition: Scientific Research on Bias and Some Implications for Legal Procedure and Decision Making, p. 664.
[4] Bacon (1620). Novum Organum, p. 36.
[5] Wason (1960). On the Failure to Eliminate Hypotheses in a Conceptual Task, pp. 129–140; Popper (1935). The Logic of Scientific Discovery.
[6] Wason (1960). On the Failure to Eliminate Hypotheses in a Conceptual Task, pp. 129–140.
[7] Wason (1968). Reasoning about a Rule; Wason & Johnson-Laird (1972). Psychology of Reasoning: Structure and Content.

reasoning of these participants was that they used an exclusion method whereby they generated several series of numbers that were inconsistent with the rule and therefore could falsify their hypotheses (e.g. 1–47 or 6–42), before providing their answer. Wason and Johnson-Laird concluded that the confirmation strategy used by the majority of participants was evidence that individuals may have difficulties with abandoning their hypotheses.

While Wason and Johnson-Laird's conclusions were criticized,[8] their relevance was emphasized by research conducted in the time period 1968–1980. During this time, the research area grew quite rapidly, primarily as a result of Herbert Simon's research on so-called bounded rationality, which Simon conducted in the 1950s and for which he was awarded the Nobel Prize in 1978.[9] Specifically, Simon explained that when humans make decisions, they do not have access to all relevant information and even if they did, they would not be able to use all the information due to constraints in the environment, attention, or memory. Instead, humans use heuristics and one such heuristic is the 'satisficing' heuristic (from the words satisfactory and sufficing) which means that humans evaluate one decision alternative at the time and choose the first alternative that meets their minimum requirements.[10] Using Simon's research as a foundation, Tversky and Kahneman (1974) conducted their Nobel Prize-winning (2003) research on heuristics and biases.[11] This research suggested that people are cognitively unable or disinclined to engage in the often complex information processes implied by normative models of decision making. Due to limits in time, knowledge, and computational resources, individuals instead resort to simpler judgmental or decision-making heuristics. While these heuristics are easy to apply and allow fairly accurate performance, they come at a price; in some situations, they produce systematic and serious judgment fallacies or biases, including confirmation bias. As such, with Tversky and Kahneman's as well as Simon's research, bias as a more general topic gained attention, but their research did not address confirmation bias in any further detail.

In the 1980s, other researchers used more elaborate and realistic versions of Wason's experimental design and found evidence of confirmation bias in both day-to-day human reasoning[12] as well as in more specific contexts such as scientific testing.[13] This research illustrated, for example, that the tendency to favour

---

[8] Wetherick (1962). Eliminative and Enumerative Behavior in a Conceptual Task, pp. 246–249.

[9] Simon (1957). Models of Man: Social and Rational-Mathematical Essays on Rational Human Behavior in a Social Setting.

[10] Simon (1976). From Substantive to Procedural Rationality, pp. 129–148; Schwartz et al. (2002). Maximising Versus Satisficing: Happiness is a Matter of Choice, pp. 1178–1197; Barros (2010) Herbert A. Simon and the Concept of Rationality: Boundaries and Procedures, pp. 455–472.

[11] Tversky & Kahneman (1974). Judgment under Uncertainty: Heuristics and Biases, pp. 1124–1131.

[12] Doherty et al. (1979). Pseudodiagnosticity, pp. 111–121.

[13] Mynatt, Doherty, & Tweney (1977). Confirmation Bias in a Simulated Research Environment: An Experimental Study of Scientific Inference, pp. 85–95.

hypothesis-consistent evidence was a source of overconfidence.[14] However, this time period also entailed more critical examination of the generalizability and implications of the results found using Wason's 2-4-6 task and similar studies. Several experiments revealed that participants' responses changed, sometimes for the better and sometimes for the worse,[15] when the task characteristics were just slightly altered (such as changing the triples of numbers, using descending instead of ascending numbers, asking participants to discover two rules instead of one or to engage in disconfirmatory testing). When the task was adapted to reflect real-life decision-making somewhat better, for example simulating real scientific testing or human reasoning in a more general sense, performance improved in one study[16] but not in another study.[17]

From 1987 until today, several researchers have underlined that what was commonly described as an irrational confirmation bias might in fact be a completely rational so-called *positive test strategy*.[18] Their argument was that positive testing is more likely than negative testing to lead to falsification of incorrect hypotheses. Furthermore, whether a behaviour is rational or irrational is contingent on the environment of an individual.[19] Frequently, the so-called Bayesian model was, and still is, used to explain how supposedly irrational behaviours can in fact be fully rational, if considered from a statistical point of view.[20] This model has also been used to explicate what confirmation bias is, for example failure to update beliefs in accordance with the theorem,[21] while others have focused on how the model can be used to avoid fallacies and biases.[22] Occasionally, single books have drawn attention to the topic of human cognition and error, including, for example, those published by Kahneman, primarily *Thinking, Fast and Slow*,[23] as well as *Noise*.[24] However, the seemingly most influential research conducted during this time period when it comes to confirmation bias specifically was that of Raymond

---

[14] Koriat, Lichtenstein, & Fischhoff (1980), Reasons for Confidence, pp. 107–118.

[15] Cherubini, Castelvecchio, & Cherubini (2005). Generation of Hypotheses in Wason's 2-4-6 Task: An Information Theory Approach, pp. 309–332; Rossi, Caverni, & Girotto (2001). Hypothesis Testing in a Rule Discovery Problem: When a Focused Procedure is Effective, pp. 263–267; Tweney et al. (1980). Strategies for Rule Discovery in an Inference Task, pp. 109–123; Gale & Ball (2009). Exploring the Determinants of Dual Goal Facilitation in a Rule Discovery Task, pp. 294–315; Poletiek (1996). Paradoxes of Falsification, pp. 447–462.

[16] Vallée-Tourangeau & Payton (2008). Graphical Representation Fosters Discovery in the 2-4-6 Task, pp. 625–640.

[17] Dunbar (1993). Concept Discovery in a Scientific Domain, pp. 397–434.

[18] Klayman & Ha (1987). Confirmation, Disconfirmation, and Information in Hypothesis Testing, pp. 211–228.

[19] Gigerenzer (2008). Rationality for Mortals; Todd & Gigerenzer (2012). Ecological Rationality: Intelligence in the World.

[20] Fischhoff & Beyth-Marom (1983). Hypothesis Evaluation from a Bayesian Perspective, pp. 239–260.

[21] Fischhoff & Beyth-Marom (1983). Hypothesis Evaluation from a Bayesian Perspective, pp. 239–260.

[22] Dahlman (2019). De-Biasing Legal Fact-Finders with Bayesian Thinking, pp. 1115–1131.

[23] Kahneman (2011). Thinking, Fast and Slow.

[24] Kahneman, Sibony, & Sunstein (2021). Noise—A Flaw in Human Judgment.

Nickerson. In 1998, Mr Nickerson introduced his today widely accepted definition of confirmation bias, which is addressed in detail in the next section (2.2.1).

Following the more critical examination of Wason's experimental paradigm and the increased usage of other experimental methods, two important meta-analyses examining confirmation bias in how individuals remember and search for information were published in 1998 and 2009. The first was based on 70 studies and confirmed that attitudes influence memory,[25] that is, individuals remember information that supports their views on political, social, or personal issues, compared to information challenging their views.[26] This tendency was stronger for issues linked to important personal values,[27] which is sometimes referred to as *ego involvement*,[28] while it was weaker for controversial issues like abortion and the war in Vietnam. One possible explanation of the latter finding is *defensive processing*, that is, individuals attend to hypothesis-inconsistent information not to incorporate it into their decision-making, or to change their minds, but rather to be able to counterargue it.[29] This is particularly relevant considering the results in the second meta-analysis (based on 91 studies), according to which individuals' prior attitudes, beliefs, behaviours, and decisions influence their subsequent search for information.[30] The typical methodology in the studies was to assess attitudes and beliefs using self-report, and behaviours and decisions were operationalized by previous behaviour/decisions in the session. Participants were then asked to choose from a list of consistent and inconsistent alternatives to their attitudes and beliefs (as indicated by for instance the heading of a newspaper article).

Hence, not only do individuals remember hypothesis-consistent information better but they also tend to seek out such information more often. Clearly, this is likely to provide an effective shield against hypothesis-inconsistent information, which makes it less likely that individuals will change or even modify their views, even if there is plenty of contradicting information. The tendency to search more often for hypothesis-confirming information was also stronger when individuals had moderate or high commitment to a pre-existing belief.[31] In these studies, individuals had committed to their beliefs for example because they had to choose a view freely or had to (or anticipated having to) explain and justify the view publicly.

---

[25] See early research in Bruner & Goodman (1974) Value and Need as Organizing Factors in Perception, pp. 33–44; Fiske & Taylor (1991). Social Cognition.

[26] Eagly et al. (1999). The Impact of Attitudes on Memory: An Affair to Remember, pp. 64–89.

[27] Johnson & Eagly (1989). The Effects of Involvement on Persuasion: A Meta-analysis, pp. 290–314.

[28] Sherif & Hovland (1961). Social Judgment. Assimilation and Contrast Effects in Communication and Attitude Change; Eagly et al. (1999). The Impact of Attitudes on Memory: An Affair to Remember, pp. 64–89.

[29] Eagly et al. (1999). The Impact of Attitudes on Memory: An Affair to Remember, pp. 64–89; Pratkanis (1989). Attitude Structure and Function.

[30] Hart et al. (2009). Feeling Validated Versus Being Correct: A Meta-Analysis of Selective Exposure to Information, p. 559.

[31] Hart et al. (2009). Feeling Validated Versus Being Correct: A Meta-Analysis of Selective Exposure to Information, p. 559.

Furthermore, commitment originated in that individuals had to make some sacrifice to choose a view, for example by dedicating a great deal of time or effort to making the decision. If challenging information of moderate or high quality was presented, or if the belief had high relevance to the individuals' enduring values, the tendency was further strengthened.[32]

2.2.1 Definition of Confirmation Bias

The most commonly accepted definition of confirmation bias was provided by Nickerson in 1998. In his words, confirmation bias is 'the seeking or interpreting of evidence in ways that are partial to existing beliefs, expectations, or a hypothesis in hand'.[33] Simultaneously, the decision-maker's search for counterarguments is not as effective and if contradicting information is considered, it is only assigned limited importance.[34]

In his work, Nickerson emphasized that confirmation bias can appear 'in many guises',[35] that is, it can manifest itself in many different contexts and at different stages of human information processing. For instance, a witch hunt[36] is a brutal example of how confirmation bias can have extreme consequences on a societal level.[37] This is illustrated by the fact that many European courts had special regulations for the evidence and the standards of proof[38] when the allegations concerned sorcery.[39] To illustrate, in the opinion of the French judge Bodinus, trials regarding sorcery could not be conducted in the same way as trials regarding other crimes since proving someone guilty of sorcery was very difficult and not one out of a million witches could be convicted, had the normal rules applied. This resulted in a reversed burden of proof whereby an acquittal required that the prosecutor's malice was 'clearer than the sun'. This suggests that the French courts were barely responsive to potentially hypothesis-inconsistent information, partly due to the reversed burden of proof (as well as the seemingly very high standard of proof, 'clearer than the sun') and partly because it seems there were no other conceivable reasons for someone's innocence (such as her not being a witch at all) other than the prosecutor's malice. Furthermore, the tests which were used to establish

---

[32] Hart et al. (2009). Feeling Validated Versus Being Correct: A Meta-Analysis of Selective Exposure to Information, p. 557.
[33] Nickerson (1998). Confirmation Bias: A Ubiquitous Phenomenon in Many Guises, p. 175.
[34] Nickerson (1998). Confirmation Bias: A Ubiquitous Phenomenon in Many Guises, p. 175.
[35] Nickerson (1998). Confirmation Bias: A Ubiquitous Phenomenon in Many Guises, p. 175.
[36] Tegler Jerselius (2003). Den Stora Häxdansen, pp. 13–17; Söderberg (1999). Svartalf och Sotpacka, pp. 45–48,
[37] Nickerson (1998). Confirmation Bias: A Ubiquitous Phenomenon in Many Guises, p. 191; Söderberg (1999). Svartalf och Sotpacka, pp. 45–48; Tegler Jerselius (2003). Den Stora Häxdansen, pp. 15–17.
[38] Mackay (1932). Extraordinary Popular Delusions and the Madness of Crowds, p. 528.
[39] Nickerson (1998). Confirmation Bias: A Ubiquitous Phenomenon in Many Guises, p. 191.

whether someone was a witch offered no practical possibility to prove this hypothesis wrong. A woman would be thrown into water with her hands behind her back.[40] If the woman floated, she was considered a witch who had been saved by Satan and as such, she had to be sentenced to death.[41] If instead, the woman drowned, she was considered innocent.[42]

Within the field of medicine, there are both historical and contemporary manifestations of confirmation bias, perhaps most clearly illustrated by the fact that medical practitioners historically focused on positive results of a treatment while disregarding the possibility that a patient would have improved without the treatment, for example due to the patient's natural resilience.[43] Likewise, contemporary studies indicate that physicians and psychiatrists who are aware of a patient's medical diagnosis tend to make more diagnosis-consistent interpretations of information regarding the patient, compared to those who are unaware of the diagnosis.[44]

In science, a potentially very problematic manifestation of confirmation bias is the *file drawer problem*,[45] that is, a tendency for null findings to remain unpublished, either because the researcher does not attempt to get them published or because the journals show no interest in them.[46] Consequently, only positive results are conveyed, while the null findings remain in the file drawer, prevented from challenging or changing dominating views. A historical example of this is the US physicist Robert Milikan who in 1923 received the Nobel Prize for his work on determining the charge of electrons.[47] Out of Milikan's 107 studies, only 58 were published and all the published studies supported his hypothesis. However, the remaining 59 studies that disconfirmed his hypothesis were never published. In the odd event that negative results are published, they are often met with excessively conservative attitudes and/or claims that the results are simply due to methodological flaws.[48] Alternatively, a theory may be adjusted so that it accommodates the findings while still enabling the maintenance of the theory,[49] which, thus, is insufficiently questioned.[50] For example, in his research on the development of the telephone, Alexander Graham Bell continued to focus on undulating current and

---

[40] Nickerson (1998). Confirmation Bias: A Ubiquitous Phenomenon in Many Guises, p. 191.
[41] Nickerson (1998). Confirmation Bias: A Ubiquitous Phenomenon in Many Guises, p. 191.
[42] Nickerson (1998). Confirmation Bias: A Ubiquitous Phenomenon in Many Guises, p. 191.
[43] Nickerson (1998). Confirmation Bias: A Ubiquitous Phenomenon in Many Guises, p. 192.
[44] Eadie et al. (2011). Does Knowledge of Medical Diagnosis Bias Auditory-Perceptual Judgments of Dysphonia?, pp. 420–429; Mendel et al. (2011). Confirmation Bias: Why Psychiatrists Stick to Wrong Preliminary Diagnoses, pp. 2651–2659.
[45] Rosenthal (1979). The 'File Drawer Problem' and Tolerance for Null Results, pp. 638–641.
[46] Rosenthal (1979). The 'File Drawer Problem' and Tolerance for Null Results, pp. 638–641; Rothstein, Sutton, & Borenstein (2005). Publication Bias in Meta-analysis, pp. 1–7.
[47] Milikan (2013). The Autobiography of Robert Milikan.
[48] Nickerson (1998). Confirmation Bias: A Ubiquitous Phenomenon in Many Guises, pp. 195–196; Fugelsang et al. (2004). Theory and Data Interaction of the Scientific Mind: Evidence from the Molecular and Cognitive Laboratory, pp. 86–95.
[49] Nickerson (1998). Confirmation Bias: A Ubiquitous Phenomenon in Many Guises, pp. 195–196.
[50] Nickerson (1998). Confirmation Bias: A Ubiquitous Phenomenon in Many Guises, pp. 195–196.

electromagnets even after he and other researchers had obtained good results with liquid devices, which were used to produce the first intelligible telephone call to Bell from his assistant Watson in 1876.[51]

Two aspects of Nickerson's definition of confirmation bias which are essential in demarcating confirmation bias from other types of confirmatory reasoning are: (i) the point in time and the basis upon which a conclusion is drawn, and (ii) that confirmation bias refers to a case-building process which is subconscious and spontaneous, rather than conscious and deliberate.[52]

When it comes to the first aspect, it is essential to note that confirmation bias refers to conclusions that are premature both in terms of time and in terms of the basis of the conclusions. In essence, an individual with a confirmation bias has already drawn a conclusion, on a shaky basis, and this predetermined conclusion dictates how the individual searches for and evaluates information. This individual also maintains the conclusion independently of subsequent relevant information. Hence, the predetermined conclusion dominates the individual's information processing because it 'draws all things else to support and agree with it',[53] using Bacon's words. Somewhat ironically, this decisiveness is not because individuals have a firm basis for their views, even if the individuals themselves may feel that is the case, but in fact it is fairly unclear what the basis is. One possible basis which seems particularly relevant for the legal context is that individuals have previously been involved in the sense that they, for example, have already made some type of preliminary decision or assessment regarding a suspect.[54] While such decisions or assessments are both legally and logically separate from the question of guilt, they may well trigger a confirmation bias, as illustrated by research with for example police officers[55] and judges.[56] However, it can also have to do with attitudes, beliefs, and behaviours in a more general sense.[57] Hence, the purpose of searching for and evaluating information becomes substantially different than what was intended in a criminal case. Instead of first searching for arguments and proof for and against possible conclusions, evaluating them, and then drawing the conclusion that seems to be dictated by the information,[58] this process is aimed at finding

---

[51] Gorman (1995). Hypothesis Testing, pp. 217–238; Eysenck & Keane (2015). Cognitive Psychology, p. 538.
[52] Nickerson (1998). Confirmation Bias: A Ubiquitous Phenomenon in Many Guises, pp. 175–176.
[53] Bacon (1620). Novum Organum, p. 36.
[54] Hart et al. (2009). Feeling Validated Versus Being Correct: A Meta-analysis of Selective Exposure to Information, pp. 555–588.
[55] Lidén, Gräns, & Juslin (2018). The Presumption of Guilt in Suspect Interrogations: Apprehension as a Trigger of Confirmation Bias and Debiasing Techniques, pp. 336–354.
[56] Lidén, Gräns, & Juslin (2018). 'Guilty, No Doubt': Detention Provoking Confirmation Bias in Judges' Guilt Assessments and Debiasing Techniques, pp. 219–247.
[57] Hart et al. (2009). Feeling Validated Versus Being Correct: A Meta-analysis of Selective Exposure to Information, pp. 555–588; Eagly et al. (1999). The Impact of Attitudes on Memory: An Affair to Remember, pp. 64–89.
[58] Nickerson (1998). Confirmation Bias: A Ubiquitous Phenomenon in Many Guises, p. 175.

support for a conclusion that has already been drawn. In an applied setting, it is not necessarily noticeable whether an individual is simply using information as means to an end or is instead actively and critically evaluating what the implications of the information are. Practitioners working within the context of criminal investigations and proceedings, regardless of whether they are police officers, crime scene investigators, forensic doctors, or judges, all have discretionary tasks and also often ambiguous complex information to deal with. This means that a range of potential conclusions can be justified. There is no objective yardstick against which the conclusions can be compared and assessed to be right or wrong. For example, when forensic doctors evaluate whether a cut wound has been made using a specific type of knife, this is a visual comparison in which forensic doctors integrate their training and experience, and although some conclusions may be easier to draw than others, the forensic doctors have all the necessary skills to come to any conclusion. Similarly, judges who are interpreting a legal statute will consider the wording of the statute, the legislative history, and possibly case law, but how to integrate and prioritize these different sources of information is up to the judges. As long as the judges reason in conventionally acceptable terms, such as the wording of a statute or the legislative history, they will probably be able to articulate either interpretation. In fact, given their legal training, they are probably quite good at articulating different interpretations, whatever the interpretations are.

The one-sided nature of reasoning is not necessarily easily detectable for outside observers, but it is even less likely that individuals will notice the bias in themselves. This is because of the largely subconscious nature of confirmation bias.[59] While Nickerson himself did not address the implications of this aspect in any detail, some guidance is provided by research in cognitive psychology, a field in which it is generally accepted that humans have conscious and subconscious cognition, and that these can be distinguished by the level of brain activity.[60] While single researchers believe that consciousness is a yes/no phenomenon,[61] the absolute majority believes that consciousness comes in degrees.[62] Hence, Nickerson's notion that confirmation bias is a more or less subconscious process seems compatible with findings in cognitive neuroscience. While the distinction therefore

---

[59] Nickerson (1998). Confirmation Bias: A Ubiquitous Phenomenon in Many Guises, pp. 175–176.

[60] Kalat (2017). Biological Psychology, p. 430; Cosmelli et al. (2004). Waves of Consciousness: Ongoing Cortical Patterns During Binocular Rivalry, pp. 128–140; Dehaene (2007). Conscious and Nonconscious Processes, Distinct Forms of Evidence Accumulation, p. 22; Dehaene & Naccache (2001). Towards a Cognitive Neuroscience of Consciousness: Basic Evidence and a Workspace Framework, pp. 1–37; Dahaene (2007). Conscious and Nonconscious Processes, Distinct Forms of Evidence Accumulation? pp. 21–50.

[61] This view is supported only by a minority of researchers; see, for example, Sergent & Dehaene (2004). Is Consciousness a Gradual Phenomenon?, pp. 720–728.

[62] The majority of researchers support this view; see, for example, Pessiglione, et al. (2007). How the Brain Translates Money into Force: A Neuroimaging Study of Subliminal Motivation, pp. 904–906; Williams et al. (2004). Amygdala Responses to Fearful and Happy Facial Expression under Conditions of Binocular Suppression, pp. 2898–2904.

seems fairly straightforward on this general level it is far from clear how conscious and subconscious processes may interact in the decision-making process in an individual with a confirmation bias. The notion that conscious and subconscious decision-making processes can be distinguished, although not completely separated, finds support for example in frameworks distinguishing between two different modes of thinking referred to as *System 1* and *System 2*.[63] This distinction gains partial support from neuroscientific studies[64] and also forms the basis for *dual process theories*, for instance Kahneman and Fredricks' *dual process theory of probability judgment* describing how Systems 1 and 2 interact in the decision-making process and more specifically in a decision-maker with a confirmation bias.[65] Whereas System 1 generates an intuitive partial judgment, that judgment gains support from the analytical System 2, for instance by generating arguments for the judgment. However, the individual is not necessarily aware that the arguments have this purpose but instead experiences that he or she is reasoning back and forward on an issue and then ultimately ends up with a conclusion which, in fact, he or she had already reached. This suggests that both subconscious and conscious processes mutually support confirmatory reasoning, although most of the processing is subconscious.

While a possible starting point, the dual process theories far from provide a full account of how confirmation bias may be simultaneously conscious and subconscious. To this end, the research into so-called metacognition seems more reassuring. In essence, this research suggests that while the reasoning process as such is conscious, the consequences of the reasoning are subconscious. In other words, individuals lack the metacognitive capacity not only to detect but also to stop bias from entering their own reasoning. Put simply, metacognition is 'cognition about cognition',[66] or more specifically about monitoring and controlling cognitive functioning with regards to quality and validity criteria.[67] Metacognition, being a so-called higher executive function,[68] consists of a range of metacognitive skills such as self-regulation, in relation to which abilities to self-monitor and self-correct are

---

[63] See, for example, Evans (2008). Dual-Processing Account of Reasoning, Judgment and Social Cognition, pp. 255–278.
[64] Lieberman (2003). Reflexive and Reflective Judgment Processes: A Social Cognitive Neuroscience Approach, pp. 44–67; Lee et al. (2007). Anatomical Traces of Vocabulary Acquisition in the Adolescent Brain, pp. 1184–1189; Andreasen (1988). Brain Imaging: Applications in Psychiatry, pp. 1381–1388; Warach (1995). Mapping Brain Pathophysiology and Higher Cortical Function with Magnetic Resonance Imaging, pp. 221–235; Kalat (2017). Biological Psychology, pp. 107–11.
[65] Kahneman & Frederick (2005). A Model of Heuristic Judgment, pp. 267–294.
[66] Koriat (2002). Metacognition Research: An Interim Report. In Perfect & Schwarts (Eds). Applied Metacognition, p. 261; Flavell (1979). Metacognition and Cognitive Monitoring: A New Area of Cognitive-developmental Inquiry, pp. 906–911.
[67] Nelson (1996). Consciousness and Metacognition, pp. 102–116; Thompson, Prowse Turner, & Pennycook (2011). Intuition, Reason and Metacognition, pp. 107–140.
[68] Hogan et al. (2014). Metacognitive Skill Development and Applied Systems Science: A Framework of Metacognitive Skills, Self-regulatory Functions and Real-World Applications, p. 82; Hofmann, Schmeichel, & Baddeley (2012). Executive Functions and Self-regulation, pp. 174–180.

key.⁶⁹ For self-regulation to be effective, individuals must first be aware of their current state in relation to a desired goal and this may result in goal-correcting behaviour.⁷⁰ In addition, critical thinking (CT), including analysis, evaluation, and inference⁷¹ as well as reflective judgment (RJ), that is, to judge and make decisions in a reflective manner,⁷² are metacognitive skills. However, it is essential to remember that being a critical and/or reflective thinker is not enough to mitigate confirmation bias. Though an individual may very well possess the cognitive skills necessary for CT and RJ, the *willingness* to conduct these skills ultimately dictates how well they are performed.⁷³ Using Ku's words, 'a critical thinker must also have a strong intention to recognize the importance of good thinking and have the initiative to seek better judgment'.⁷⁴

A prosecutor may, for example, form a firm belief in a hypothesis, and also invest time, effort, and investigative resources into the hypothesis. These are all circumstances which are likely to make the prosecutor less, not more, willing to challenge the hypothesis.⁷⁵ Hence, even prosecutors who are normally excellent critical and reflective thinkers may be unwilling to challenge their hypothesis in this scenario. In line with the subconscious nature of confirmation bias, prosecutors are not necessarily aware of this motivation or how it is impacting on their reasoning. This ties closely to another related metacognitive skill, confidence judgment, which has a central role when individuals decide, for example, whether to report information externally that they retrieved from memory.⁷⁶ It is likely that prosecutors who have selectively searched for and evaluated information, and who also remember hypothesis-consistent information better than inconsistent, will feel relatively confident that their hypotheses are correct. However, confidence and

---

⁶⁹ Kuhn (2000). Metacogntive Development, pp. 178–181.
⁷⁰ Kuhn (2000). Metacogntive Development, pp. 178–181.
⁷¹ Dwyer, Hogan, & Stewart (2014). An Integrated Critical Thinking Framework for the 21st Century, pp. 43–52; Facione (1990). The Delphi Report: Committee on Pre-college Philosophy; Reeves (1990). An Application of Bloom's Taxonomy to the Teaching of Business Ethics, pp. 609–616; Dwyer, Hogan, & Stewart (2011). The Promotion of Critical Thinking Skills through Argument Mapping. In Horvart & Forte (Eds). Critical Thinking, pp. 97–122.
⁷² Dawson (2008). Metacognition and Learning in Adulthood. Prepared in Response to Tasking from ODNI/CHCO/IC Leadership Development Office; Hofer (2004). Epistemological Understanding as a Metacognitive Process: Thinking Aloud during Online Searching, pp. 43–55.
⁷³ Halpern (1998). Teaching Critical Thinking for Transfer Across Domains: Disposition, Skills, Structure Training, and Metacognitive Monitoring, p. 449; Halpern (2008). Is Intelligence Critical Thinking? Why We Need a New Definition of Intelligence. In Kyllonen, Roberts, & Stankov (Eds). Extending Intelligence: Enhancement and New Constructs, pp. 293–310; Facione et al. (2002). The California Critical Thinking Skills Test: CCTST; Ennis (1998). Is Critical Thinking Culturally Biased?, pp. 15–33.
⁷⁴ Ku (2009). Assessing Student's Critical Thinking Performance: Urging for Measurements using Multiple-response Format, p. 71.
⁷⁵ Lidén (2020). Confirmation Bias in Investigations of Core International Crimes: Risk Factors and Quality Control Techniques. In Agirre et al. (Eds). Quality Control in Criminal Investigation, pp. 461–528; Dwyer, Hogan, & Stewart (2014). An Integrated Critical Thinking Framework for the 21st Century, pp. 43–52.
⁷⁶ Koriat & Goldsmith (1996). Monitoring and Control Processes in the Strategic regulation of Memory Accuracy, pp. 490–517.

accuracy are not always well-calibrated. In fact, research shows that the accuracy of confidence judgments, including those made by professionals in a number of contexts, is poor.[77] This means that in many judgment situations, people are more confident in their performance than they are correct in that performance. In the legal context, the miscalibration between confidence and accuracy is a well-known and debated issue when it comes to eyewitnesses, who are often asked to give metacognitive judgments of their memory performance (i.e. "how confident are you that the man wore a blue shirt?")[78] Likewise, research shows that professionals involved in the process, such as the police, prosecutors, attorneys, judges, and jurors, often judge the credibility of witness testimony by how confident the witness appears.[79] Thus, such professional actors have been found to believe in confident witnesses more than less confident witnesses.[80] It is possible that confident prosecutors also, sometimes, come across as more trustworthy than those less confident. Yet, with prosecutors just as with witnesses, confidence is not necessarily an indicator of accuracy.[81] Potentially of interest in this context is the research which is currently being conducted into so-called second-order metacognitive judgments. This is sometimes referred to as meta-metacognition, that is, judgments that aim to assess the accuracy of and regulate a first-order metacognitive judgment, for example the accuracy of a confidence judgment.[82] However, it is still unclear whether some individuals have more effective meta-metacognition than others,[83] as well as whether this is in fact the same phenomenon as metacognition.[84] Hence, the research into metacognition provides one potential explanation of how confirmation bias may be conscious or subconscious. It also clearly distinguishes this subtle form of case-building process from other forms of conscious case-building processes, such as defence counsels, who, in line with their roles, consciously attempt to protect

---

[77] Griffin & Brenner (2004). Perspectives on Probability Judgment Calibration. In Koehler & Harvey (Eds). Blackwell Handbook of Judgment and Decision Making, pp. 177–198.
[78] Allwood (2010). Eyewitness Confidence. In Granhag (Ed.), Forensic Psychology in Context: Nordic and International Approaches, pp. 281–303.
[79] Cutler, Penrod, & Stuve (1988). Juror Decision Making in Eyewitness Identification Cases, pp. 41–55; Lindsay, Wells, & Rumpel (1981). Can People Detect Eyewitness-identification Accuracy Within and Across Situations? pp. 79–89; Well, Ferguson, & Lindsay (1981). The Tractability of Eyewitness Confidence and its Implications for Triers of Fact, pp. 688–696.
[80] Boyce, Beaudry, & Lindsay (2007). Belief of Eyewitness Identification Evidence. In Lindsay et al. (Eds). Handbook of Eyewitness Psychology, pp. 501–525.
[81] Wells et al. (1998). Eyewitness Identification Procedures: Recommendations for Lineups and Photospreads, pp. 603–647.
[82] Buratti & Allwood, Regulating Metacognitive Processes—Support for a Meta-metacognitive Ability, p. 18.
[83] Buratti & Allwood (2012). The Accuracy of Meta-metacognitive Judgments: Regulating the Realism of Confidence, pp. 243–253, Buratti, Allwood, & Kleitman (2013). First-and Second-order Metacognitive Judgments of Semantic Memory Reports: The Influence of Personality Traits and Cognitive Styles, pp. 79–102; Goldberg (1992). The Development of Markers for the Big Five Structure, pp. 26–42.
[84] Buratti & Allwood, Regulating Metacognitive Processes—Support for a Meta-metacognitive Ability, p. 18.

their clients' interests.[85] This will entail emphasizing the arguments and the evidence that are consistent with the client's interests and downplaying or completely disregarding the information that is inconsistent with the client's interests.

In essence, this means that confirmation bias may occur in practitioners who make every effort to live up to professional standards or even legal demands to be objective, who have an incredibly high level of professionalism, and who might even perceive of themselves as objective. Arguably, it is unfair or even pointless to examine a bias that operates outside of practitioners' conscious awareness, yet it is clear from the practice of the European Court of Human Rights (ECtHR) in, for example, *Hauschildt v. Denmark*,[86] *Saraiva de Carvalho v. Portugal*,[87] and *Padovani v. Italy*[88] as well as from the practice of the International Criminal Court (ICC) Appeals Chamber, in *The Prosecutor v. Katanga and Ngudjolo Chui*,[89] that legal actors have duties to *be* impartial not just *appear to be* so. Supposedly, this means that legal actors should be concerned with and try to mitigate biases that threaten their ability to reason impartially, regardless of whether the influences are conscious or subconscious. It is the *effect* on the behaviour, and more specifically, the decision-making, that is relevant. Hence, the requirements established by these courts seem to presuppose that legal actors can take control over biases and, by doing so, they themselves are capable of ensuring that they do not deviate from what is expected of them. It is clear that these requirements have neuroscientific limitations.[90] In an applied setting it is very unlikely that decision-makers will be able to exercise such control in relation to their own thinking and reasoning, which highlights the need to research and implement debiasing techniques. A first step in this process is understanding why confirmation bias occurs.

2.2.2 Why Does Confirmation Bias Occur?

One essential and necessary aspect of mitigating confirmation bias is understanding why it occurs. This section provides an explanatory framework based on insights from cognitive psychology (Section 2.2.2.1), emotional and motivational psychology (Section 2.2.2.2), and social psychology and organizational psychology (Section 2.2.2.3). While the aim of this section is to promote a general understanding of how confirmation bias is explained by these respective psychological

---

[85] See, for example, The Swedish Code of Judicial Procedure 21 ch. 7 § and 1 § Vägledande Regler om God Advokatsed.
[86] ECtHR Hauschildt v. Denmark, judgment of 24 May 1989, 10486/83.
[87] ECtHR, Saraiva de Carvalho v. Portugal, judgment of 25 July 2017, 17484/15.
[88] ECHR, Padovani v. Italy, judgment of 26 February 1993, 13396/87.
[89] ICC Appeals Chamber, The Prosecutor v. Katanga and Ngudjolo Chui, ICC-01/04-01/07 OA 8, 27 August 2009.
[90] Pessoa (2008). On the Relationship between Emotion and Cognition, Nature Reviews Neuroscience 9 (2), p. 148.

fields, there are also subsections relating to specific investigative settings such as suspect interviews or crime scene investigations in which the explanations have been converted into debiasing techniques. For example, if cognitive psychologists are correct that confirmation bias is a result of high cognitive load, then cognitive load should be reduced through, for example, using standardized models for suspect interviews rather than requiring interviewers constantly to come up with new neutral questions to ask the suspect, which is a cognitively more challenging task. Similarly, if social psychologists are right that confirmation bias is a self-enhancement bias, then changing the decision-maker between, for example, an arrest and the subsequent suspect interview would be an effective debiasing technique. While some techniques show promising results, research so far has focused more on the prevalence than the mitigation of confirmation bias and there are still no foolproof methods for bias mitigation. Hence, to maximize the chances of effectively mitigating bias, the best way forward is to gain a sound understanding of its causes, and on the basis of those causes to formulate and test potential debiasing techniques.

Effective bias mitigation requires taking into consideration the specifics not only of a certain jurisdiction but also the range of practitioners operating within the context of criminal cases. This entails *inter alia* police officers, crime scene investigators (CSIs), forensic analysts, forensic doctors, prosecutors, defence counsels, and judges. For the practitioners who are traditionally expected to be objective, that is, police officers, prosecutors, and judges, this is often reinforced by legal norms while other categories of practitioners would be expected to abide by different codes of conduct or ethical codes. Also, like other humans, all these practitioners do not only have limited cognitive resources but they are also emotional creatures, who work within social groups as well as organizational settings. This means that the explanations of confirmation bias are not mutually exclusive but rather mutually supportive. In other words, there may be cognitive, emotional, social, as well as organizational causes of confirmation bias and the importance of each of these may vary between different contexts as well as between different individuals. Consequently, effective bias mitigation is neither something static or simple nor something that has a single 'one size fits all' solution but rather, it needs to be addressed from multiple angles simultaneously. While this is indeed a challenge, the framework provided below provides a good starting point.

2.2.2.1 Cognitive Explanations
Cognition refers to human's processing of information, that is, how humans acquire, handle, and use information about the world, including perception, memory, thought, and language.[91] Decision-making primarily falls within the subcategory

---

[91] Passer & Smith (2011). Psychology: The Science of Mind and Behavior, p. 16.

of thought but is also closely related to the other subcategories since humans, for instance, have to use information stored in memory in order to make a decision.[92]

Research in the field of cognitive psychology suggests that the average number of digits that adult humans without any cognitive impairments can actively store and process in their working memory[93] is seven.[94] This is fewer digits than many case file numbers have. Given these limitations, and the fact that criminal cases always contain far more information than the case file numbers, there is a risk that properly processing crime relevant information is simply too cognitively demanding and that criminal investigators and other practitioners cannot seriously consider more than one hypothesis at the time.[95] Although highly intelligent individuals often have a better than average working memory capacity[96] and therefore have a potential advantage in processing large volumes of information,[97] intelligence is not necessarily a protective factor in relation to confirmation bias.[98] For example, highly intelligent individuals may be very skilled at arguing and therefore also able to provide both themselves and others with persuasive arguments supporting a certain hypothesis. It is not necessarily the case that individuals will note the bias in their own reasoning (Section 2.2.2.3), as they may be biased for other reasons than cognitive limitations, for example motivational, social, and/or organizational reasons. Highly intelligent individuals may also be very motivated to reach certain career goals by, for example, persuading others of their skills. Also, as indicated by the so-called BADE (Bias Against Disconfirmatory Evidence) experiments, there are some indications that individuals with cognitive impairments are more susceptible to confirmation bias than others,[99] but the findings are mixed.[100] For example,

---

[92] Lundh, Montgomery, & Waern (1992). Kognitiv psykologi.

[93] Baddeley (2002). Is Working Memory Still Working? pp. 851–864.

[94] Miller (1956). The Magical Number Seven, Plus or Minus Two: Some Limits on Our Capacity for Processing Information, pp. 81–97.

[95] Evans (2006). The Heuristic-analytic Theory of Reasoning: Extension and Evaluation, pp. 378–395; De Neys (2006). Dual Processing in Reasoning: Two Systems but One Reasoner, pp. 428–433; Olivers (2009). What Drives Memory-driven Attentional Capture? The Effects of Memory Type, Display Type, and Search type, p. 1275; Soto et al. (2008). Automatic Guidance of Attention from Working Memory, pp. 342–348; Doherty & Mynatt, Inattention to P (H) and to P (D\ ~ H): A Converging Operation, pp. 1–11; Mynatt, Doherty, & Dragan (1990). Information Relevance, Working Memory, and the Consideration of Alternatives, pp. 759–778; Mynatt, Doherty, & Sullivan (1991). Data Selection in a Minimal Hypothesis Testing Task, pp. 293–305.

[96] Swanson (2015). Intelligence, Working Memory, and Learning Disabilities, pp. 175–196.

[97] Fukuda & Vogel (2009). Human Variation in Overriding Attentional Capture, pp. 8276–8733; Griffiths (2020). Understanding Human Intelligence through Human Limitations, pp. 873–883.

[98] Depending on how intelligence is defined, see, for example, Plucker & Shelton (2015). General Intelligence (g): Overview of a Complex Construct and Its Implications for Genetics Research, pp. 21–24; Ashton et al. (2000). Fluid Intelligence, Crystallized Intelligence, and the Openness/Intellect Factor, pp. 198–207; Bates & Shieles (2003). Crystallized Intelligence as a Product of Speed and Drive for Experience: The Relationship of Inspection Time and Openness to G and Gc, pp. 275–287; Melinder et al. (2020). Personality, Confirmation Bias, and Forensic Interviewing Performance, pp. 961–971.

[99] Balzan et al. (2013). Confirmation Bias across the Psychosis Continuum: The Contribution of Hypersalient Evidence-hypothesis Matches, pp. 53–69; Buchy, Woodward, & Liotti (2007). A Cognitive Bias against Disconfirmatory Evidence (BADE) is Associated with Schizotypy, pp. 334–337.

[100] Peters et al. (2008). Specificity of the 'Jump-to-Conclusions' Bias in Deluded Patients, pp. 239–244; Bentall & Young (1996). Sensible Hypothesis Testing in Deluded, Depressed and Normal Subjects,

according to one study, patients with schizophrenia were in fact less susceptible to confirmation bias than healthy controls.[101]

Also, human cognition is *coherence driven* which enables us to make sense of the information around us and perceive it as a unified whole despite complexity, ambiguity, incompleteness, and large volumes of information stemming from multiple sensory inputs.[102] For example, sentence-reading experiments illustrate that *you can porbalby raed this esaliy despite the msispeillgns*.[103] Hence, readers are usually able to understand jumbled sentences relatively accurately, as long as the first and last letters are correct.[104] In criminal investigations and proceedings, there is not only this more general human inclination towards coherence but also a drive for coherence determined by the practitioners' roles. An essential part of a prosecutor's job is to make sense of the information obtained in an investigation through categorizing conduct into potential crimes as well as a more specific narrative to be presented in court. Likewise, a forensic doctor's determination of cause of death stems from an interpretation of sometimes conflicting or at least complex indications on a deceased individual's body. In the process of making sense of the information around them, there is a risk that practitioners in criminal cases, just like other humans, fill in gaps as well as overlook some aspects so that the totality of the evidence will make sense. For example, research into so-called *confirmatory visual search patterns* suggest that humans are blind to, or at least slow to notice, states of the environment that they do not expect to be true,[105] resulting in a visual confirmation bias.[106] Thus, confirmation bias in visual assessments which are common not least in the forensic sciences such as visual comparisons of shoe prints, fingerprints, tools and tool marks, tyres and tyre marks, and so on can have strong explanatory value for the forensic confirmation bias (Chapter 3.5.4).

As indicated by the beginning of this section, humans may be unable to actively consider all relevant information even in relation to tasks that are not necessarily

---

pp. 372–375; Speechley, Whitman, & Woodwards (2010). The Contribution of Hypersalience to the 'Jumping to Conclusions' Bias Associated with Delusions in Schizophrenia, pp. 7–17.

[101] Doll et al. (2014). Reduced Susceptibility to Confirmation bias in Schizophrenia, pp. 715–728.
[102] See, for example, Ogilvie (1999). Cognitive Coherence.
[103] See, for example, Rayner et al. (2006). Raeding Wrods with Jubmled: There's a Cost, pp. 192–193.
[104] See, for example, Tydgat & Grainger (2009). Serial Position Effects in the Identification of Letters, Digits and Symbols, pp. 480–498; Adelman, Marquis, & Sabatos-DeVito (2010). Letters in Words are Read Simultaneously, not in Left-to-Rights Sequence, pp. 1799–1801.
[105] Simons & Chabris (1999). Gorillas in Our Midst: Sustained Inattentional Blindness for Dynamic Events, pp. 1059–1074.
[106] Rajsic, Taylor, & Pratt (2017). Out of Sight, Out of Mind: Matching Bias Underlies Confirmatory Visual Search, pp. 498–507; Rajsic, Wilson & Pratt (2017). The Price of Information: Increased Inspection Costs Reduce the Confirmation Bias in Visual Search, pp. 1–20; Kozlov & Zvereva (2015). Confirmation Bias in Studies of Fluctuating Asymmetry, pp. 293–297; Nakhaeizadeh, Dror, & Morgan (2015). Cognitive bias in Forensic Anthropology: Visual Assessment of Skeletal Remains is Susceptible to Confirmation Bias, pp 208–214; Carrasco (2014). Visual Attention: The Past 25 Years, pp. 1484–1525; Gilbey & Hill (2012). Confirmation Bias in General Aviation Lost Procedures, pp. 785–795.

that cognitively challenging, such as remembering a case file number. Needless to say, criminal investigations in general and particularly those resulting in giant trials are far more cognitively challenging. When it comes to giant investigations and trials this is a reality both in national[107] and international jurisdictions,[108] although in the latter context, giant trials are the rule rather than the exception. This is clear from the often very lengthy investigations into core international crimes. On average, investigations and proceedings into core international crimes lasts 4.9 years,[109] with much longer times spans in individual cases. For example, in the ICC case *The Prosecutor v. Bosco Ntaganda*,[110] approximately 17 years had passed (2002–2019) between the commencement of the crime and the first conviction. The hearings before the Trial Chamber alone lasted 248 days, 2,129 victims had been authorized to participate in the trial, and 1,791 items were admitted into evidence.[111] There are similar cases, although not with quite as lengthy investigations, in national jurisdictions, including the case against the Congolese ex-warlord 'Sheka' who was sentenced to life in prison in November 2020.[112] This trial, which was held at a military court in the Democratic Republic of Congo (DRC) and lasted for about two years, concerned a series of attacks in which the Nduma Defence of Congo (NDC) militia and two other groups allegedly had raped nearly 400 people in 13 villages, had recruited at least 154 children into its ranks, and the soldiers had allegedly razed almost 1,000 homes and businesses and led about 1,000 people off into forced labour. Similarly, the Court proceedings against Anders Behring Breivik, for terrorist crimes directed at the Norwegian government headquarters and a youth politician summer camp at Utøya, in Oslo District Court, lasted for about 10 weeks, with 160 legal representatives for 800 victims directly or otherwise affected by the attacks.[113] However, not only core international crimes (e.g. genocide, war crimes, crimes against humanity) and terrorism produce lengthy and cognitively challenging investigations and proceedings. For example, in more average cases in national jurisdictions it is common that multiple charges against the same defendant are joined in the same trial rather than severed. Sometimes, the defendant is believed to have used a similar *modus operandi* for all the crimes, for example a specific way of committing fraud, and this not only increases cognitive

---

[107] See, for example, Wahlberg, Jätterättegångarna kan strida mot Europakonventionen—'svårt att få en överblick', Veckans Juridik 20150326.

[108] Smeulers, Hola, & van den Berg (2013). Sixty-five Years of International Criminal Justice: The Facts and Figures.

[109] Smeulers, Hola, & van den Berg (2013). Sixty-five Years of International Criminal Justice: The Facts and Figures, p. 18.

[110] ICC, Situation in the Democratic Republic of the Congo, The Prosecutor v. Bosco Ntaganda, Trial Chamber, Transcript, 8 July 2019, ICC-01/04-02/06-T-265-ENG, p. 4.

[111] Judge Robert Fremr giving a procedural overview in the Judgment of Trial Chamber VI in the Ntaganda case, see ICC, Situation in the Democratic Republic of the Congo, The Prosecutor v. Bosco Ntaganda, Trial Chamber, Transcript, 8 July 2019, ICC-01/04-02/06-T-265-ENG, p. 4.

[112] Africa News (2020). Congolese Ex-warlord 'Sheka' sentenced to life in prison.

[113] Oslo District Court, TOSLO-2011-188627-24.

load but also may make the charges, and the evidence pertaining to each charge, difficult to separate from one another.[114]

2.2.2.2 Emotional and Motivational Explanations

Criminal inquiries and proceedings regularly prompt emotional reactions, based on, for example, the alleged *modus operandi* of the perpetrator, emotionally charged photos from the crime scene, and/or the death of individuals, sometimes on a very large scale and/or including child victims. The character and intensity of such emotional reactions will vary depending on case specific circumstances. For example, as police, military, crime scene investigators, and other first responders rush to a public place which has just been subject to a supposed terrorist attack with mass destruction and causalities, they may experience intense stress, fear, or even panic. It is not difficult to think of examples of such cases: to mention a few, the bomb blast in downtown Beirut in 2005 which killed former Lebanese prime minister Rafik Hariri as well as 22 other individuals;[115] the Breivik case in Norway in 2011;[116] the Westgate shopping mall attack in Nairobi in 2013;[117] and the Paris attacks in 2015.[118] Some crimes are by their very nature emotionally charged, and this is indeed the case when it comes to crimes of extreme gravity such as those involving terrorism or crimes against humanity, genocide, war crimes, and so on. Arguably, these crimes lack proportionate punishment, as pointed out by Hannah Arendt in her observations of the Nuremberg trials in 1945: 'we are not equipped to deal, on a human level, with a guilt that is beyond crime'.[119]

Since 1945 there have been several other examples which highlight this point, not least the multiple war crimes dealt with by the Special Court of Sierra Leone (SCSL), and more specifically the conscription, enlistment, and use of child soldiers during the Sierra Leonian civil war (1991–2000).[120] As confirmed by the convictions in these cases, the child soldiers were often drugged and coerced by their commanders to conduct amputations of the hands or arms of civilians, as well as other types of inhumane and violent treatments.[121] These circumstances continue

---

[114] Tanford, Penrod, & Collins (1985). Decision Making in Joined Criminal Trials: The Influence of Charge Similarity, Evidence Similarity, and Limiting Instructions, pp. 319–337.
[115] Special Tribunal for Lebanon (STL), The Prosecutor v. Ayyash et al., STL-11-01.
[116] Oslo District Court, TOSLO-2011-188627-24.
[117] BBC, Kenya Westgate Mall Attack: What We Know, The Milimani Court in Nairobi.
[118] Ben-Ezra et al. (2017). Psychological Reactions Following the November 2015 Paris Attacks: Perceiving the World as Unjust and Unsafe.
[119] Hannah Arendt, cited in Douglas (2016). The Right Wrong Man: John Demjanjuk and the Last Great Nazi War Crimes Trial, p. 6, referring to Arendt & Jasper (1992). Hannah Arendt and Karl Jaspers: Correspondence, 1926–1969, p. 39.
[120] Special Court of Sierra Leone (SCSL), Brima, Kamara, & Kanu, SCSL-2004-16-A; Norman, Fofana, & Kondewa, SCSL-04-14-A; Sesay, Kallon, & Gbao, SCSL-04-15-A; Taylor, Appeals Chamber, SCSL-03-01-A.
[121] SCSL, Taylor case, Appeals Chamber, Judgment 26 September 2013, SCSL-03-01-A and the so-called AFRC case against Brima, Kamara, & Kanu, Appeals Chamber Judgment, 22 February 2008, SCSL-2004-16-A.

to generate public outrage.[122] However, even crimes that are traditionally considered less severe are likely to generate emotional reactions. The examination of a high-volume blood crime scene in an alleged murder case is one example. In fact, a survey study of 225 CSI's operating in the United States suggests that about one in 10 CSI's suffer symptoms similar to post-traumatic stress disorder (PTSD).[123] Similar but not directly comparable results were found in Slovenian[124] and Korean CSIs.[125] These findings are anticipated given that CSIs, as well as other first responders, are repeatedly and frequently exposed to scenes of violent injury, death, and so on, and their work may require them to engage in fairly intricate tasks like examining, smelling, touching, and collecting dead and decomposed bodies and bodily fluids.[126] Other research suggests that exposure to a victim or a victim's family may exasperate symptoms of trauma and may even lead directly to PTSD.[127] Also, although other non-violent or less violent crimes, like burglaries or financial crimes, are not necessarily as strongly emotionally charged per se, they can also generate emotional reactions like disappointment, contempt, or anger, stemming from, for example, an upset plaintiff or the frequency of the crimes.

It is today unknown whether some types of crimes are clearly associated with certain types of emotions more than other emotions as well as whether and how this impacts on practitioners' decision-making processes. Overall, it seems that emotions are neither inherently a threat to the administration of justice nor inherently a promise.[128] This can be more easily grasped when considering in detail what emotions are. Both within and between different scientific disciplines, emotions are understood differently[129] and studied differently,[130] but the definition provided below stems from the field of emotional and motivational psychology, which entails research using a range of methodologies which has been conducted from the

---

[122] See, for example, Human Rights Watch (2008). Coercion and Intimidation of Child Soldiers to Participate in Violence.

[123] Rosansky et al. (2019). PTSD Symptoms Experienced and Coping Tactics Used by Crime Scene Investigators in the United States, pp. 1444–1450.

[124] Mrevlje (2018). Police Trauma and Rorscach Indicators: An Exploratory Study, pp. 1–19.

[125] Yoo et al. (2013). Factors Influencing Post-Traumatic Stress on Korean Forensic Science Investigators, pp. 136–141, Nho & Kim (2017). Factors Influencing Post-Traumatic Stress Disorder in Crime Scene Investigators, pp. 39–48.

[126] Rosansky et al. (2019). PTSD Symptoms Experienced and Coping Tactics Used by Crime Scene Investigators in the United States, pp. 1444–1450.

[127] Slack (2020). Trauma and Coping Mechanisms Exhibited by Forensic Science Practitioners: A Literature Review, pp. 310–316; Sollie, Kop, & Euwema (2017). Mental Resilience of Crime Scene Investigators: How Police Officers Perceive and Cope with the Impact of Demanding Work Situations, pp. 1580–1603.

[128] Lidén (2020). Emotions in International Criminal Justice—A Threat and a Promise?

[129] Richardson (2012). The Heart of William James; Nussbaum (2001). Love's Knowledge: Essays on Philosophy and Literature; Damasio (2018). The Strange Order of Things: Life, Feeling, and the Making of Cultures.

[130] Ask (2006). Criminal Investigation: Motivation, Emotion and Cognition in the Processing of Evidence; Wistrich, Rachlinski, & Guthrie (2015). Heart Versus Head: Do Judges Follow the Law or Follow their Feelings? pp. 856–911; Rossner (2019). Storytelling Rituals in Jury Deliberations; Bergman Blix & Wettergren (2018). Professional Emotions in Court: A Sociological Perspective.

early 1900s, leading up to the suggested definition in the 1970s.[131] Following this definition, emotions are:

(1) *subjective feelings*, that is, the sensations of fear, anger, joy, and so on,
(2) *social phenomena*, through emotion expression we send recognizable facial, postural, and vocal signs that communicate the quality and intensity of our emotionality to others,
(3) *bases for motivation*, emotions motivate us to draw, for example, certain conclusions and/or form motivation desires to act, as well as
(4) *biological reactions*, that is, energy-mobilizing responses that prepare the body for adapting to whatever situation one faces.[132]

When it comes to emotions as an explanation of confirmation bias, this can relate to all four aspects above but most clearly so with emotions as bases for motivation, and biological reactions. These are more subtle subconscious aspects of emotion which can still impact greatly on the decision-making processes of practitioners as well as on their ability to live up to professional standards.

Emotions as bases for motivation have clear connections to what some researchers today refer to as *motivated reasoning* or *motivated cognition*.[133] For example, in a sample of Swedish criminal investigators ($N = 61$) who were asked to assess witness reliability, the investigators in whom anger had been experimentally induced, relied more heavily on stereotypical information, that is, information relating to the witness' individual characteristics than the other investigators, in whom sadness had been experimentally induced, did. Similarly, US judges seem to favour the litigant who generates the more positive affective response. For example, when asked to determine whether the act of pasting a false US entry visa into a genuine foreign passport constituted '*forging an identification card*' under Ohio statutes, the judges' assessments varied significantly depending on the level of sympathy elicited by the description of the defendant.[134] The defendant was either described as a hired killer who had sneaked into the United States to track down and kill someone who had stolen drug proceeds from a cartel (killer condition) or a father trying to earn money for a liver transplant for his critically ill nine-year-old daughter (father condition).[135] This, and other similar research suggests

---

[131] Hull (1951). Essentials of Behavior; Miller (1971). Selected Papers; Berridge (2018). Evolving Concepts of Emotion and Motivation, pp. 1–20.

[132] Izard (1993). Four Systems for Emotion Activation: Cognitive and Noncognitive Processes, pp. 68–90; Reeve (2018). Understanding Motivation and Emotion; Passer & Smith (2008). Psychology, the Science of Mind and Behaviour, p. 502.

[133] Hughes & Zaki (2015). The Neuroscience of Motivated Cognition, pp. 62–63; Kunda (1990). The Case for Motivated Reasoning, pp. 480–493.

[134] Wistrich, Rachlinski, & Guthrie (2015). Heart Versus Head: Do Judges Follow the Law or Follow their Feelings? p. 876.

[135] Wistrich, Rachlinski, & Guthrie (2015). Heart Versus Head: Do Judges Follow the Law or Follow their Feelings? pp. 856–911.

that judges' emotional reactions towards a defendant influence how judges perceive, remember, and process information related to the defendant or plaintiff.[136] Importantly, there is no indication in this research that judges are aware of their motivation to reach a certain conclusion.[137] Furthermore, it is possible that such an influence is also difficult to detect for outside observers, as judges are likely to argue in conventionally relevant terms such as the language of the statute or the legislative history, but affective preferences trigger the operation of cognitive processes that shifts their reasoning to the desired conclusion (Section 2.2.2.2).

In an applied setting, there are many conceivable situations in which decision-makers may subconsciously be motivated to reach one conclusion rather than the other. This includes issues of law such as that exemplified above as well as issues of fact. For example, many crimes require that an individual is legally classified as a child, such as child trafficking, child pornography, conscripting or enlisting child soldiers, and rape or sexual exploitation of a child. Given that there is often a lack of sound evidence regarding such age elements,[138] and so far, no precedence on what evidence can be expected, it is possible that judges' propensities to either be on the side of the (child) victim or the alleged perpetrator, will influence their assessments of whether evidentiary requirements have been fulfilled.

On a related note, it has been argued that confirmation bias is, in fact, an artefact of *primary error detecting and minimization*.[139] In other words, practitioners who, contrary to legal norms, believe that false negatives (not even identifying or acquitting a guilty defendant) are the worst possible mistakes, will be more prone to select and prioritize incriminating evidence than practitioners who, in line with legal norms believe that false positives (convicting an innocent defendant) are the worst possible mistakes.[140] Hence, the *fear* of a false negative will impact differently on decision-making processes than the *fear* of a false positive. Importantly, while the fear of a false positive is indeed entrenched and expected among practitioners, it is also clear from the standard of beyond *reasonable* doubt that not any remote or unreasonable fear of committing such an error should have an impact. This would suggest, for example, that individual judges' preparedness to take risks in either direction could influence their susceptibility to confirmation bias, as well as in which direction this bias will operate (to the advantage or disadvantage of the accused) a topic which will be discussed more in detail in relation to judges' decision-making (Chapter 4.3).

---

[136] Holyoak & Simon (1999). Bidirectional Reasoning in Decision Making by Constraint Satisfaction, pp. 3–31; Simon, Stenstrom & Read (2015). The Coherence Effect: Blending Cold and Hot Cognitions, pp. 369–394.
[137] See, for example, Schultheiss & Pang (2007). Measuring Implicit Motives, pp. 322–344.
[138] Lidén (2020). Child Soldier or Soldier? Estimating Age in Cases of Core International Crimes: Challenges and Opportunities, pp. 323–460.
[139] Friedrich (1993). Primary Error Detection and Minimization (PEDMIN) Strategies in Social Cognition: A Reinterpretation of Confirmation Bias Phenomena, pp. 298–319.
[140] Rassin (2020). Context Effect and Confirmation Bias in Criminal Fact Finding, p. 86.

A question which should be addressed by this stage is why emotions may shift judges' reasoning in a certain direction, and why they may remain unaware of such influences. This is where the aspect of emotions as biological reactions comes in. Evidence from neuroscientific research suggests that emotions, or *'somatic states'*,[141] can have biasing actions on decisions because they influence the patterns of neurotransmitter (dopamine, serotonin, noradrenalin, acetylcholine) release.[142] The neurotransmitter release, in turn, modulates the synaptic activity in the brain, which ultimately impacts on thinking and reasoning.[143] These emotional influences are most likely subconscious.[144] Whether, in a given case, the emotional influence facilitates or complicates rational decision making is, according to Bechara and Damasio, contingent on whether the emotion at hand is integral, that is, relevant, to the decision-making task.[145]

Criminal justice, directly or indirectly, acknowledges some types of emotions as relevant. For example, it can be argued that *fear* is a crucial part of different types of risk assessments pertaining to the accused or already convicted. This is the case when a judge is to decide whether someone should be detained awaiting trial (Chapter 4.3) since such legislation often entails determinations of whether there is a risk that suspects will relapse into crime of a similar nature, will flee, or will manipulate/impact on evidence against them. Similarly, forensic psychiatrists' evaluations of whether patients in closed psychiatric care should be allowed leave or early release usually entail an assessment of whether the patients would constitute a risk to themselves or others. However, legally speaking, the fear of such risks materializing should be based on evidence rather than an overall impression of the individual. In practice, however, this distinction is difficult to maintain. Practitioners are not necessarily aware of where their emotions stem from. A judge who perceives the evidence as strong cannot reasonably distinguish between when that perception is based on the evidence per se and/or an emotion that triggers a certain perception of the evidence. When it comes to fear specifically, as well as anxiety and worry, it should be noted that these have been linked to increased levels of confirmation bias, although so far only tested in contexts that are relatively distinct from the legal context.[146]

---

[141] Bechara & Damasio (2005). The Somatic Marker Hypothesis: A Neural Theory of Economic Decision, pp. 336–372.
[142] Bechara & Damasio (2005). The Somatic Marker Hypothesis: A Neural Theory of Economic Decision, p. 343.
[143] Bechara & Damasio (2005). The Somatic Marker Hypothesis: A Neural Theory of Economic Decision, p. 343; Rolls, Grabenhorst & Deco (2010). Choice, Difficulty, and Confidence in the Brain, pp. 694–706.
[144] Bechara & Damasio (2005). The Somatic Marker Hypothesis: A Neural Theory of Economic Decision, pp. 348–349.
[145] Bechara & Damasio (2005). The Somatic Marker Hypothesis: A Neural Theory of Economic Decision, p. 351.
[146] de Jong, Mayer, & van den Hout (1997). Conditional Reasoning and Phobic Fear: Evidence for a Fear-confirming Reasoning Pattern, pp. 507–516; de Jong et al. (1998). Hypochondriasis: The Role of Fear-confirming Reasoning, pp. 65–74; Smeets, de Jong, & Mayer (2000). 'If You Suffer from

To reconnect to the section on cognitive explanations, it is today fairly widely accepted that emotion and cognition are intertwined entities and that 'complex cognitive-emotional behaviors have their basis in dynamic coalitions of network of brain areas'[147] and these 'conjointly and equally contribute to the control of thought and behavior'.[148] In other words, it is essential to consider that that emotion and cognition in interaction produce confirmation bias.[149] For example, during the investigation of an emotionally charged crime scene following an alleged terrorist attack or similar, not only the emotional content per se is relevant but also the cognitive load associated with such an investigation. For example, it could be that training and preparedness to deal with such scenes reduce cognitive load and that this in turn improves emotion regulation, and thereby also reduces the risk of confirmation bias. While this possibility has not been specifically evaluated, it is essential to think of bias mitigation not only with reference to emotional or only cognitive explanations and so on but also ideally the interaction between such explanations. This approach appears particularly valuable when it comes to emotional components. It is unlikely that emotional reactions to loaded stimuli such as a high-volume blood scene can be prevented or even effectively reduced. Hence, it may seem like a waste of time even to consider these components from a debiasing perspective. However, thinking of emotions and cognition in interaction is a possible way forward in this regard.

2.2.2.3 Social and Organizational Explanations

In criminal investigations and proceedings, group decision-making is not only common but sometimes also a legal requirement, as manifested by, for example, provisions dictating how many judges are required for the court to be competent to make decisions as well as the more specific composition of judges. The more specific number and composition of judges clearly vary between different jurisdictions and cases, often with requirements of mixed compositions (e.g. not two judges from the same country at the ICC, following Article 36(7) Rome Statute of the ICC)[150] in international criminal law that do not exist in national jurisdictions. This social context is relevant and is also the main focus of social psychology,

---

a Headache, then You have a Brain Tumour': Domain-specific Reasoning 'Bias' and Hypochondrias, pp. 763–777; Muris, Debipersad, & Mayer (2013). Searching for Danger: On the Link Between Worry and Threat-Related Confirmation Bias in Children, pp. 604–609;
Jonas, Graupmann, & Frey (2006). The Influence of Mood on the Search for Supporting versus Conflicting Information: Dissonance Reduction as a Means of Mood Regulation, pp. 3–15.

[147] Pessoa (2008). On the Relationship between Emotion and Cognition, p. 148.
[148] Pessoa (2008). On the Relationship between Emotion and Cognition, p. 148.
[149] Lidén (2020). Emotions and Cognition in International Criminal Justice: An Exploration from Cognitive Biases to Emotional Intelligence, pp. 1–15.
[150] Abtahi, Ogwuma, & Young (2013). The Composition of Judicial Benches, Disqualification and Excusal of Judges at the International Criminal Court, pp. 379–398; Hobbs (2016). Towards a Principled Justification for the Mixed Composition of Hybrid International Criminal Tribunals, pp. 177–197.

which attempts to understand and explain how the thought, feelings, and behaviour of individuals are influenced by the actual, imagined, or implied presence of others.[151] This context can be both a protective and a risk factor for confirmation bias, depending on group-specific characteristics. The range of factors that can vary across groups of investigators, judges, and so on, is enormous, including for example the composition of males/females, their ages, years of experience, their formal work titles, internal and external relationships, workplace culture, and so on. Also, when it comes to transnational crimes or core international crimes, these groups often consist of individuals originating from different countries and jurisdictions, in which social norms for how group decision-making is to happen may vary. To illustrate, the election rules for the ICC judges, set out in Article 36 of the Rome Statute of the ICC, requires, *inter alia*, that the selection shall take into account the representation of the principal legal systems of the world, equitable geographical representation, and a fair representation of female and male judges. Furthermore, no two judges may be nationals of the same country.[152] The same rules apply in relation to the staff at the Office of the Prosecutor (OTP) at the ICC, following Articles 44(3) and 36(8) of the Rome Statute of the ICC. Also outside the ICC, practitioners from a range of jurisdictions come together on *ad hoc* basis through the coordination of the International Criminal Police Organization (INTERPOL), which in itself also consists of members from different jurisdictions, following Articles 4 to 7 of the Constitution of INTERPOL.

Social psychology offers quite a few insights relevant to understanding of confirmation bias both in individuals and in groups. It seems confirmation bias is stronger in relation to self-generated hypotheses than hypotheses generated by others, a notion which has been confirmed in both legal contexts such as police interviews with suspects[153] and judges' decision-making,[154] as well as non-legal contexts.[155] Accordingly, confirmation bias is sometimes referred to as a *self-enhancement* or *self-serving bias*.[156] Individuals want to protect their self-esteem and self-image, appear consistent in social interactions,[157] and are sometimes more interested in convincing others that they are right than finding the truth in a given

---

[151] Allport (1958). The Nature of Prejudice, p. 3.

[152] Sienho & Morin (2009). Multiculturalism and International Law: Essays in Honour of Edward McWhinney.

[153] Lidén, Gräns, & Juslin (2018). The Presumption of Guilt in Suspect Interrogations: Apprehension as a Trigger of Confirmation Bias and Debiasing Techniques, pp. 336–354.

[154] Lidén, Gräns, & Juslin (2018). 'Guilty, No Doubt': Detention Provoking Confirmation Bias in Judges' Guilt Assessments and Debiasing Techniques, pp. 219–247.

[155] Dunbar & Klahr (1989). Developmental Differences in Scientific Discovery Processes, pp. 109–143; Klahr (2000). Designing Good Experiments to Test 'Bad' Hypotheses, pp. 355–402; Schunn & Klahr (1993). Other vs. Self-generated Hypotheses in Scientific Discovery, pp. 365–378; Haverkamp (1993). Confirmatory Bias in Hypothesis Testing for Client-identified and Counselor Self-generated Hypotheses, pp. 303–315.

[156] Schunn & Klahr (1993). Other vs. Self-generated Hypotheses in Scientific Discovery; Klahr (1990). Designing Good Experiments to Test 'Bad' Hypotheses, pp. 355–402.

[157] Cialdini (2009). How to Persuade People to Say Yes, pp. 2–7.

situation.[158] Consequently, individuals have a *bias blind spot*, that is, while they are reasonably good at identifying bias in the judgment and decisions of others, they are largely blind in relation to their own biases.[159]

Arguably, given that individuals have a bias blind spot, a reasonable conclusion is that working in a group would be a protective factor, since in the group lots of individuals, as well as potential individual biases, are pitted against one another, and this should create a *'productive conflict'*.[160] Apart from group members' ability to act as devil's advocates in relation to one another,[161] the group's greater cumulative knowledge and potential to deal with more information supports the idea of groups as superior decision-makers than individuals.[162] While this is a possibility in well-functioning groups, group processes can also, in fact, help explain why groups not only maintain hypotheses long after they should have been abandoned, but can also exacerbate bias in individual group members.[163] Importantly, such tendencies can be present even in groups that are formed arbitrarily and with the purpose of carrying out just one specific task,[164] which is often the case with, for instance, investigative teams or the court where the composition of members is quite dynamic and varies from case to case. The more specific mechanisms that can produce or exacerbate confirmation bias in groups are, for instance, the emergence of group norms, conformity, and role-induced bias, mechanisms that were identified in early social psychology studies by pioneers such as Muzafer Sherif (1936),[165] Solomon Asch (1952),[166] and Stanley Milgram

---

[158] Mercier (2016). The Argumentative Theory: Predictions and Empirical Evidence, pp. 689–700; Mercier & Sperber (2011). Why do Humans Reason? Arguments for an Argumentative Theory, pp. 57–111; Sperber et al. (2010). Epistemic Vigilance.

[159] Pronin, Lin, & Ross (2002). The Bias Blind Spot: Perceptions of Bias in Self Versus Others, pp. 369–381.

[160] Nickerson (1998). Confirmation Bias: A Ubiquitous Phenomenon in Many Guises, p. 175; Pronin, Gilovich, & Ross (2004). Objectivity in the Eye of the Beholder: Divergent Perceptions of Bias in Self Versus Others, pp. 781–799; Cooper, Woo, & Dunkelberg (1988). Entrepreneurs' Perceived Chance of Success, pp. 97–108; Feeser & Willard (1990). Founding Strategy and Performance: A Comparison of High and Low Growth High Tech Firms, pp. 87–98; McCarthy, Schoorman, & Cooper (1993). Reinvestment Decisions by Entrepreneurs: Rational Decision-making or Escalation of Commitment, pp. 9–24.

[161] Valacich & Schwenk (1995). Devil's Advocacy and Dialectical Inquiry Effects on Face-to-Face and Computed-mediated Group Decision Making, pp. 158–173; Schwind & Buder (2012). Reducing Confirmation Bias and Evaluation Bias: When are Preference-inconsistent Recommendations Effective—and When Not?, pp. 2280–2290; Schwind et al. (2012). Preference-inconsistent Recommendations: An Effective Approach for Reducing Confirmation Bias and Stimulating Divergent Thinking? pp. 787–796.

[162] Huber (1980). Managerial Decision Making.

[163] Stasser & Stewart (1992). Discovery of Hidden Profiles by Decision-making Groups: Solving a Problem versus Making a Judgment, pp. 426–434.

[164] Taylor, Peplau, & Sears (2003). Social Psychology, p. 345.

Tajfel (1970). Experiments in Intergroup Discrimination, pp. 96–102; Tajfel (1969). Cognitive Aspects of Prejudice, pp. 79–97; Brewer & Brown (1998). Intergroup Relations, pp. 554–594.

[165] Sherif (1936). The Psychology of Social Norms; Taylor, Peplau, & Sears (2003). Social Psychology.

[166] Asch (1955). Opinions and Social Pressure, pp. 31–35; Bond & Smith (1996). Culture and Conformity: A Meta-Analysis of Studies Using Asch's (1952b, 1956) Line Judgment Task, pp. 111–137; Baron, Vandello, & Brunsman (1996). The Forgotten Variable in Conformity Research: Impact of Task Importance on Social Influence, pp. 915–927.

(1963).¹⁶⁷ However, the more specific tendencies that are of primary relevance to confirmation bias in groups were identified later; *group polarization* by Serge Moscovici and Marisa Zavalloni (1969)¹⁶⁸ and *group think* by Irving Janis (1982).¹⁶⁹

Essentially, group polarization means that the group comes to function as one large individual with a very strong confirmation bias. It refers to situations in which a group of like-minded people discuss an issue and the average opinion of group members tend to become more extreme and daring.¹⁷⁰ This is partly because group interaction makes each individual feel less personal responsibility for the consequences of the decisions¹⁷¹ and partly because group members provide each other with persuasive arguments in a bid-like process where group members continuously bid above each other with hypothesis-consistent arguments.¹⁷² Consequently, the advantages of the preferred alternative are emphasized and disadvantages downplayed, increasing the individual members' previous beliefs and simultaneously decreasing the likelihood of anyone presenting opposing ideas, because of the fear of making a fool of oneself in front of the group majority.¹⁷³

The processes described above will, in practice, also interact with documented effects on decision making of having a social role and what one believes is mandated by this role.¹⁷⁴ For example, a prosecutor's office tasked with charging those most responsible for atrocities such as genocide, may have a natural inclination to downplay conflicting evidence.¹⁷⁵ How a prosecutor comes to perceive of his or her role is likely to stem from norms and values communicated in interaction with older colleagues and leaders, or imposed by the organization, and so on. This does not necessarily extinguish individuals' own understanding of their occupational role or completely prevent them from taking actions that deviate from group norms. It does, however, provide a baseline on which one can rely to promote a picture of oneself as a competent police officer, prosecutor, or judge. Therefore, group

---

[167] Milgram (1963). Behavioral Study of Obedience, pp. 371–378; Hogg & Vaughan (2010). Essentials of Social Psychology, pp. 138–141; Smith, Bond, & Kagitçibaşi (2006). Understanding Social Psychology across Cultures: Living and Working in a Changing World; Berkowitz (1999). Evil is More than Banal: Situationism and the Concept of Evil, pp. 246–253; Milgram (1992). The Individual in a Social World: Essays and Experiments; Elias (1983). The Court Society; Meeus & Raaijmakers, Obedience in Modern Society: The Utrecht Studies, pp. 155–175; Mermillod et al. (2015). Destructive Obedience Without Pressure, pp. 345–351.

[168] Moscovici & Zavalloni (1969). The Group as a Polarizer of Attitudes, pp. 124–135.

[169] Janis (1982). Groupthink, Psychological Studies of Policy Decisions and Fiascoes.

[170] Moscovici & Zavalloni (1969). The Group as a Polarizer of Attitudes, pp. 124–135; Lamm & Myers (2008). Group-Induced Polarization of Attitudes and Behavior, pp. 145–187; Myers & Lamm (1976), The Group Polarization Phenomenon, pp. 602–627; Isenberg (1986). Group Polarization: A critical Review and Meta-analysis, pp. 1141–1151.

[171] Moscovici & Zavalloni (1969). The Group as a Polarizer of Attitudes, pp. 124–135; Wallach & Kogan (1965). The Roles of Information, Discussion, and Consensus in Group Risk Taking, pp. 1–19.

[172] Sia, Tan, & Wei (2002). Group Polarization and Computed Mediated Communication: Effects of Communication Cues, Social Presence, and Anonymity, pp. 70–90; McGarthy et al. (1992). Group Polarization as Conformity to the Most Prototypical Group Member, pp. 1–20.

[173] Christianson & Montgomery (2008). Kognition i ett Rättspsykologiskt Perspektiv, pp. 114–115.

[174] Engel & Glöckner (2013). Role-induced Bias in Court: An Experimental Analysis, pp. 272–284.

[175] Engel & Glöckner (2013). Role-induced Bias in Court: An Experimental Analysis, pp. 272–284.

norms are likely to function not only as a type of glue that enables common action but also as an instruction to self-fulfilment in one's career.[176]

Groupthink is different from group polarization in that not all the group members have a preference for a certain alternative at the outset, yet there is a strong drive towards reaching consensus, in fact so strong that the decision-making processes are no longer rational.[177] Consequently, decision alternatives are inadequately considered and the group fails to consult outside expertise.[178] This has important implications for the prevalence of confirmation bias in groups, since the disregard of alternative hypothesis on an individual level is reinforced by the will to reach consensus on a group level.

Hence, groupthink can result in what Hastie and colleagues refer to as *verdict-driven juries*[179] but also that the investigation preceding the verdict has been greatly skewed towards finding hypothesis confirming information. In fact, groupthink was identified in the Swedish Government Official Reports as a contributing factor to the eight wrongful convictions against serial false confessor Mr Bergwall, despite the lack of other substantial evidence.[180] The report described how, 'within the group, a group think seems to have developed and an endeavor to reach consensus, which probably explains why alternative scenarios where insufficiently investigated. Rather, the investigators primarily focused on information which supported the confessions.'[181]

Furthermore, since groups like investigative teams or benches of judges operate within an organization,[182] it is also essential to understand how these groups, as well as the group members and their susceptibility to confirmation bias, may be influenced by organizational values and reinforcement patterns.[183] This is the study of organizational psychology.[184] Quite tellingly, a primary defining characteristic of an organization is *patterned* human behaviour, that is, a structure has been imposed from formal job descriptions as well as organizational polices[185] and the organization attempts to influence the employees' behaviours, for example

---

[176] Reicher & Haslam (2006). Rethinking the Psychology of Tyranny: The BBC Prison Study; Tajfel (1981). Human Groups and Social Categories: Studies in Social Psychology; Tajfel (1978). Interpersonal Behaviour and Intergroup Behaviour, pp. 27–60; Tajfel & Turner (2001). An Integrative Theory of Intergroup Conflict, pp. 33–34; Turner (1985). Social Categorization and the Self-concept: A Social Cognitive Theory of Group Behavior, pp. 77–122; Turner et al. (1994). Self and Collective: Cognition and Social Context, pp. 454–463.

[177] Janis (1982). Groupthink, Psychological Studies of Policy Decisions and Fiascoes.

[178] Janis (1982). Groupthink, Psychological Studies of Policy Decisions and Fiascoes; Tschan et al. (2009). Explicit Reasoning, Confirmation Bias, and Illusory Transactive Memory: A Simulation Study of Group Medical Decision Making, pp. 271–300.

[179] Hastie, Penrod, & Pennington (1983). Inside the Jury.

[180] Swedish Government Official Reports, SOU 2015:52 p. 82.

[181] Swedish Government Official Reports, SOU 2015:52 p. 82.

[182] Jex & Britt (2014). Organizational Psychology: A Scientist-Practitoner Approach, p. 2.

[183] Luthans & Kreitner (1984). Organizational Behavior Modification and Beyond: An Operant and Social Learning Approach.

[184] Jex & Britt (2014). Organizational Psychology: A Scientist-Practiener Approach, p. 2.

[185] Katz & Kahn (1978). The Social Psychology of Organizations.

through *reinforcement*, that is, any stimulus that increases the probability of a given appreciated behaviour.[186] While the word 'results' may seem inappropriate in the context of criminal law, it is no secret that police and prosecution authorities as well as courts around the world are expected to show results, for example in terms of the number of solved cases or prosecuted and/or convicted individuals. Such goals are sometimes more outspoken and specific. For example, in the Preamble of the Rome Statute of the ICC it is outlined, *inter alia*, that the States Parties are '[d]etermined to put an end to impunity for the perpetrators of these crimes and thus to contribute to the prevention of such crimes'. Also, investigations into core international crimes are usually associated with very high costs, according to some even disproportionately high in relation to the number of convictions at the court so far.[187] Similar goals, but less specific ones are found in many national legal systems, which are tasked to ensure private individual's security before the law and the rule of law,[188] usually by solving more crimes, and/or specific crimes being prioritized. Such incentives created by the organization can maintain or even fuel a confirmation bias in individual or groups of legal actors. Notably, this also means that displaying confirmation bias can be at least somewhat rational since it may increase goal-fulfilment, at least superficially.

Trying to understand and correct bias only with reference to the humans will therefore be challenging.[189] This extends the understanding of bias mitigation, as explained by cognitive and emotional/motivation factors. Not only does emotion and cognition interact in creating behaviours[190] but behaviours are also dictated by the social and organizational context in which an individual operates. Hence, a multilevel analysis is required where all the legal system's components, that is, the individuals, the groups, and the organization at large, are included.[191] For example, individuals have different levels of organizational commitment[192] as well as needs for self-actualization,[193] which is related to the extent to which they will be impacted by organizational norms. However, organizational values and goals are

---

[186] Luthans & Kreitner (1984). Organizational Behavior Modification and Beyond: An Operant and Social Learning Approach; Ludwig, Geller, & Clarke (2010). The Additive Impact of Group and Individual Publicly Displayed Feedback: Examining Individual Response Patterns and Response Generalization in a Safe-driving Occupational Intervention, pp. 338–366; Camden, Price & Ludwig (2011). Reducing Absenteeism and Rescheduling among Grocery Store Employees with Point-contingent Rewards, pp. 140–149; Jex & Britt (2014). Organizational Psychology: A Scientist-Practitioner Approach, p. 314.
[187] Mbakwe (2012). ICC Gets First Conviction after 10 Years in Existence; Davenport (2014). International Criminal Court: 12 years, $1 Billion, 2 Convictions.
[188] Pessoa (2008). On the Relationship between Emotion and Cognition, p. 148.
[189] See, for example, Gould, Stapley, & Stein (2006). The Systems Psychodynamics of Organizations—Integrating the Group Relations Approach, Psychoanalytic and Open Systems Perspective, p. 3; Visholm (2004). Organisationspsykologi och Psykodynamisk Systemteori, pp. 40–41.
[190] Pessoa (2008). On the Relationship between Emotion and Cognition, p. 148.
[191] Visholm (2004). Organisationspsykologi och psykodynamisk systemteori, p. 49.
[192] Jex & Britt (2014). Organizational Psychology: A Scientist-Practitioner Approach, p. 247.
[193] Jex & Britt (2014). Organizational Psychology: A Scientist-Practitioner Approach, p. 294.

often the necessary legitimate basis for law enforcement authorities and are unlikely to change. Also, such changes have strong political elements which largely fall outside the scope of this book. Hence, the measures discussed and/or suggested as debiasing techniques acknowledge organizational values and goals as ever present, and are more focused on how bias can be mitigated when accepting rather than changing that context.

3
Confirmation Bias in Criminal Investigations

3.1 Introduction

Contrary to fairly common beliefs, there is no *'judicial exceptionalism'*[1] making legal actors or other actors operating within the legal context generally more resistant to confirmation bias than others.[2] Also, since individuals have a bias blind spot (Chapter 2.2.2.3), they are often unable to detect bias in their own reasoning and decision-making.[3] In fact, confirmation bias and other related biases have been studied and found in several distinct legal fields including civil law,[4] migration law,[5] environmental law,[6] bankruptcy law,[7] damages,[8] and arbitration.[9] This chapter will focus on criminal investigations and proceedings. These involve a range of practitioners such as police officers, crime scene investigators, forensic analysts, forensic doctors, prosecutors, and judges who are involved in distinct, complex, and highly influential decision-making processes. These practitioners are also expected to reason in open-minded and objective ways in order to protect the legitimacy, integrity, and accuracy of the criminal procedure. Since confirmation

---

[1] Edmond & Martire (2019). Just Cognition: Scientific Research on Bias and Some Implications for Legal Procedure and Decision-making, p. 644.

[2] Gleeson (2000). The Rule of Law and the Constitution, p. 129; The High Court of Australia, Vakauta v. Kelly (1989) 167 CLR 568, 5 October 1989; House of Lords, Earsferry in Helow v. Home Secretary (2008) 1 WLR 2416; Jones, Brookman, & Williams (2020). We Need to Talk about Dialogue: Accomplishing Collaborative Sensemaking in Homicide Investigations, pp. 1–18.

[3] Pronin, Lin, & Ross (2016). The Bias Blind Spot: Perceptions of Bias in Self versus Others, pp. 369–381.

[4] Wistrich & Rachlinksi (2017). Implicit Bias in Judicial Decisions Making—How It Affects Judgment and What Judges Can Do About It, pp. 1–44.

[5] Wistrich, Rachlinski, & Guthrie (2015). Heart versus Head: Do Judges Follow the Law or Follow Their Feelings?, pp. 856–911; Veldhuizen et al. (2016). Interviewing Asylum Seekers: A Vignette Study on the Questions Asked to Assess Credibility of Claims about Origin and Persecution, pp. 3–22.

[6] Wistrich, Rachlinski, & Guthrie (2015). Heart versus Head: Do Judges Follow the Law or Follow Their Feelings?, pp. 856–911.

[7] Rachlinski, Guthrie, & Wistrich (2006). Inside the Bankruptcy Judge's Mind, pp. 1227–1265; Rachlinski, Guthrie, & Wistrich (2007). Heuristics and Biases in Bankruptcy Judges, pp. 167–186.

[8] Rachlinski, Wistrich, & Guthrie (2015). Can Judges Make Reliable Numeric Judgments? Distorted Damages and Skewed Sentences, pp. 696–739.

[9] Helm, Wistrich, & Rachlinski (2016). Are Arbitrators Human? pp. 666–692.

bias is a more or less subconscious bias (Chapter 2.2.1), this is indeed a challenging task even for highly motivated and competent practitioners. Thus, the more specific purpose of this chapter is to enable an understanding of how confirmation bias may manifest itself in criminal investigations and proceedings as well as what can be done to mitigate it.

This chapter begins by addressing overall manifestations of confirmation bias in the *search* for crime relevant information (Section 3.2) in so-called suspect-driven investigations (Section 3.2.1) as well as in the *evaluation* of crime relevant information (Section 3.3) which entails the topics '*believing is seeing*' (Section 3.3.1) and asymmetrical scepticism (Section 3.3.2). This division into search and evaluation of information coincides with the different stages of human information processing known to be influenced by confirmation bias, that is, exposure and selection,[10] interpretation,[11] and memory of information.[12] This provides the necessary foundations for understanding possible consequences of confirmation bias in criminal cases, a topic which is addressed in the subsequent section on how confirmation bias relates to both false positives, that is, wrongful convictions, as well as false negatives, that is wrongful acquittals (Section 3.4). Thereafter, manifestations of confirmation bias in more specific investigative settings are discussed and possible debiasing techniques outlined in relation to each of the settings (Section 3.5). This entails understanding and mitigating bias in suspect, witness, and plaintiff interviews (Section 3.5.1), suspect line-ups (Section 3.5.2), crime scene investigations (Section 3.5.3), forensic analysis (Section 3.5.4) entailing forensic science (Section 3.5.4.2), forensic medicine (Section 3.5.4.3), forensic anthropology (Section 3.5.4.4) as well as prosecutorial decision-making (Section 3.4.2) and judges' decision-making (Section 3.4.3). Each of these sections entail the subsections 'understanding bias' and 'mitigating bias'. In the mitigation section, reference will be made to the explanations provided in cognitive, emotion, and motivation as well as social and organizational psychology (Section 3.2.2) and the reader is referred back to these chapters for details. Also, where relevant, these sections outline and discuss relevant legislation, guidelines, and practice in both national and international jurisdictions.

---

[10] Hart et al. (2009). Feeling Validated Versus Being Correct: A Meta-Analysis of Selective Exposure to Information, pp. 559–584.

[11] Confirmation bias when interpreting information has not yet been meta-analysed but the occurrence is supported by multiple individual studies.

[12] Eagly et al. (1999). The Impact of Attitudes on Memory: An Affair to Remember, pp. 64–89.

3.2 Search for Information

3.2.1 Suspect-driven Investigations

The need for the Metropolitan Police Service together with its partners to help London move from chaos to certainty was paramount.[13]

Assistant Commissioner Alan Brown,
Metropolitan Police Strategic Command on 7 July 2006

On the 7 July 2005, four bombs were detonated in central London, three in trains moving between busy Underground stations, and one on a double-decker bus, resulting in the death of 52 civilians and around 700 people with physical injuries.[14] Assistant Commissioner Alan Brown, Metropolitan Police Strategic Command at the relevant time, described the chaos following the bombings and how, in the immediate aftermath, there was much confusion relating to the number of deaths, how the bombs had been initiated, the motive of the bombers, and whether there were more to follow.[15] Just as the Metropolitan Police Service (MPS) had only started investigating these matters, two weeks later, on the 21 July 2005, the London transportation system was again exposed, but this time the attempted and coordinated suicide bombings failed. Thus, unlike the first attacks, these failed attacks left no causalities, but the suspects, now identified as Mr Ibrahim, Mr Omar, Mr Ramzi Mohammed, and Mr Osman,[16] remained at large. Since according to the available intelligence, future attacks were being actively planned,[17] the police launched an extensive operation to find the failed suicide bombers.[18] As part of this operation, 21 Scotia Road in London was placed under surveillance because this was the address where two of the suspects lived, one of whom was Mr Osman. To assist the surveillance, the surveillance team had photos of the suspects. Unsurprisingly, given the context and also the briefings preceding the operation, many of the involved officers, including the Special Firearms Officers (SFOs), described how they believed that they would have to confront and even shoot a suicide bomber.[19]

In the morning on the 22 July 2005, Mr de Menezes, who lived at the same address in Scotia Road as the two suspects, left for work through the apartment building's

---

[13] London Assembly, Report of the 7 July Review Committee, June 2006, citing Transcript of Committee meeting, 3 November 2005, vol. 2, p. 7.
[14] Intelligence and Security Committee (2006). Report into the London Terrorist Attacks on 7 July 2005, p. 2; ECtHR, Grand Chamber, Armani da Silva v. the United Kingdom, Judgment, 5878/08, p. 3.
[15] Intelligence and Security Committee (2006). Report into the London Terrorist Attacks on 7 July 2005, p. 2.
[16] European Court of Human Rights (ECtHR), Grand Chamber, Case of Armani da Silva v. the United Kingdom, Application No. 5878/08, Strasbourg, 30 March 2016.
[17] ECtHR, Grand Chamber, Armani da Silva v. the United Kingdom, Judgment, 5878/08, p. 3.
[18] ECtHR, Press Release issued by the Registrar of the Court, 30 March 2016, p. 2.
[19] ECtHR, Grand Chamber, Armani da Silva v. the United Kingdom, Judgment, 5878/08, p. 12.

common doorway.[20] After an officer in the surveillance van saw Mr de Menezes, the surveillance team initially described him as a 'good possible likeness'[21] to Mr Osman, while according to other reports he was 'not identical'.[22] However, the head of the surveillance team did not communicate to the SFOs, who had still not arrived at Scotia Road, that some members of his team thought that the subject (Mr de Menezes) was in fact *not* Mr Osman and there were also indications later on that the surveillance log had been altered.[23] Because the SFOs were not present, and the surveillance team did not stop Mr de Menezes to identify him, Mr de Menezes got on and off a bus and then, after having entered a train on the Stockwell Underground station, the SFOs entered the train and shot Mr de Menezes dead.[24]

Hence, the context with the previous bombings, the available intelligence, and the pre-operation briefings, created expectations that the surveillance team would spot a suicide bomber leaving the doorway at 21 Scotia Road. Together with other circumstances, it is likely that this hypothesis made at least some members of the surveillance team, and seemingly also the head of the surveillance team, unable to see the limits of the information available to them at the time. Factually speaking, Mr de Menezes only shared two things with Mr Osman: (i) the same doorway, and (ii) partially similar physical appearances, although the level of similarity was clearly disputed.[25] These two clearly doubtful criteria seem to have created a strong enough belief to intervene, fairly drastically, in relation to Mr de Menezes, without ever attempting to search for information that contradicted the belief, such as ensuring that Mr de Menezes identified himself.[26] Furthermore, this belief may also have tainted the SFOs' information processing as they both reported that Mr de Menezes was wearing a 'bulky' jacket when they saw him,[27] but CCTV footage showed he was wearing a thin denim jacket.[28] Combined, these circumstances not only resulted in an entirely innocent member of the public being killed in error[29] but also that the resources were invested in the wrong line of inquiry and Mr Osman fled to Italy, where only later on was he arrested, charged, and convicted for conspiracy to commit murder, together with Mr Ibrahim, Mr Ramzi Mohammed, and Mr Omar.[30] Later also a few other individuals were charged and convicted

---

[20] ECHR, Grand Chamber, Armani da Silva v. the United Kingdom, Judgment, 5878/08, p. 5.
[21] ECtHR, Grand Chamber, Armani da Silva v. the United Kingdom, Judgment, 5878/08, p. 5.
[22] ECtHR, Grand Chamber, Armani da Silva v. the United Kingdom, Judgment, 5878/08, p. 5.
[23] ECtHR, Grand Chamber, Armani da Silva v. the United Kingdom, Judgment, 5878/08, pp. 13–14.
[24] ECtHR, Grand Chamber, Armani da Silva v. the United Kingdom, Judgment, 5878/08, p. 14.
[25] ECtHR, Grand Chamber, Armani da Silva v. the United Kingdom, Judgment, 5878/08, p. 14.
[26] ECtHR, Grand Chamber, Armani da Silva v. the United Kingdom, Judgment, 5878/08, p. 28.
[27] ECtHR, Grand Chamber, Armani da Silva v. the United Kingdom, Judgment, 5878/08, p. 16.
[28] ECtHR, Grand Chamber, Armani da Silva v. the United Kingdom, Judgment, 5878/08, p. 16.
[29] ECtHR, Grand Chamber, Armani da Silva v. the United Kingdom, Judgment, 5878/08, p. 14.
[30] Intelligence and Security Committee (2006). Report into the London Terrorist Attacks on 7 July 2005 and The Guardian (2008). The July 21 failed bombings, Timeline of events before and after the attempted bomb attacks in London on July 20 2005. <https://www.theguardian.com/uk/2008/feb/04/terrorism.world1>.

for assisting the bombings.[31] As regards the 7th July bombings, while there were intelligence suggesting links between this and the 21 July bombings,[32] the 7th July bombings were conducted by different individuals who all perished during the attack, and these were later identified as Mr Siddeque Khan, Mr Hussein, Mr Tanweer, and Mr Lindsay.[33]

The tendency to identify a suspect quickly and then let a hypothesis that the suspect is guilty dominate how information is sought is fairly common, not least in high-profile cases where law-enforcement personnel are under tremendous pressure to arrest someone and/or convict them. This is evident in another case from the same year, this time from Lebanon and within the jurisdiction of the later established Special Tribunal for Lebanon (STL), namely the Ayyash et al. case.[34] In downtown Beirut, on 14 February 2005, a major explosion killed former Lebanese Prime Minister Rafik Hariri and 22 other individuals.[35] Shortly after the assassination the United Nations International Independent Investigation Commission (UNIIIC) was established, initially led by senior German prosecutor Detlev Mehlis.[36] In the so-called Mehlis Report, Syrian and Lebanese officials were implicated[37] and Mr Mehlis also publicly told an Arab newspaper that he believed Syria was directly responsible for Hariri's assassination.[38] The report resulted in four allegedly pro-Syrian Lebanese generals, including Mr El-Sayyed, the director of the Lebanese *Sûreté Générale*,[39] being arrested and detained in August/September 2005.[40] In November 2005, a key witness in the report publicly recanted his testimony, saying he had been coerced,[41] only days after another witness allegedly was paid to testify.[42] However, the four generals were held in a Lebanese prison for almost four years.[43] It was not until 2009, after the Hariri file had been

---

[31] ECtHR, Grand Chamber, Armani da Silva v. the United Kingdom, Judgment, 5878/08, p. 54.
[32] ECtHR, Grand Chamber, Armani da Silva v. the United Kingdom, Judgment, 5878/08, p. 54.
[33] Intelligence and Security Committee (2006). Report into the London Terrorist Attacks on 7 July 2005, p. 2.
[34] STL, The Prosecutor v. Ayyash et al., STL-11-01.
[35] Bosco, The Assassination of Rafik Hariri: Foreign Policy Perspectives, p. 354.
[36] Security Council Resolution 1595, UN Doc.S/RES//1595 (2005), 7 April 2005, para. 1; Alamudding & Bonini (2014). The UN Investigation of the Hariri Assassination. In Alamuddin, Nabil Jurdi, & Tolbert (Eds), The Special Tribunal for Lebanon: Law and Practice, p. 52.
[37] Harris (2013). Investigating Lebanon's Political Murders: International Idealism in the Realist Middle East, pp. 9–27.
[38] Bosco (2009). The Assassination of Rafik Hariri: Foreign Policy Perspectives, p. 354.
[39] Separate Opinion of Judge David Re, STL Trial Chamber's Judgment in The Prosecutor v. Salim Jamil Ayyash, Hassan Habib Merhi, Husseing Hassan Oneissi, Assad Hassan Sabra, pp. 2232–2233.
[40] Alamuddin & Bonini (2014). The UN Investigation of the Hariri Assassination, in Alamudding, Nabil Jurdi, & Tolbert (Eds), The Special Tribunal for Lebanon: Law and Practice, p. 52.
[41] Alamuddin & Bonini (2014). The UN Investigation of the Hariri Assassination. In Alamudding, Nabil Jurdi, & Tolbert (Eds), The Special Tribunal for Lebanon: Law and Practice, pp. 60–61.
[42] Blanford (2006). Killing Mr Lebanon: The Assassination of Rafik Hariri and its Impact of the Middle East, pp. 178–179.
[43] Alamuddin & Bonini (2014). The UN Investigation of the Hariri Assassination, in Alamudding, Nabil Jurdi, & Tolbert (Eds). The Special Tribunal for Lebanon: Law and Practice, pp. 60–61.

transferred to the STL, that the STL Prosecutor requested that the generals be released based, *inter alia*, on the 'inconsistencies in the statements of key witnesses and a lack of corroborative evidence to support these statements'.[44] As a result, the pre-trial judge ordered the generals' immediate release.[45] Later, based on, for example, forensic expert statements of how the bombings happened[46] as well as analysis of telephone communications believed to be instrumental for the planning of the assassination,[47] four other suspects were identified and their guilt tried *in absentia* by the STL.[48] On the 18 August 2020,[49] the Trial Chamber's judgment in the so-called Ayyash et al. case[50] was pronounced, acquitting three of the four suspects while convicting Mr Ayyash on all charges and sentencing him to lifetime imprisonment.[51] This entailed participation in a conspiracy to commit a terrorist act to assassinate Mr Hariri, having committed a terrorist act as a co-perpetrator by means of an explosive device, having committed the intentional homicide of Mr Hariri also as a co-perpetrator, with premeditation, by using explosive materials, equivalent to approximately 2,500 kilograms of TNT, as well as seven other counts.[52] Hence, the early suspect identification contributed to the fact that four generals were wrongfully detained for almost four years. The detention of the four generals was criticized by the UN Human Rights Council's Working Group on Arbitrary Detention (WGAD) as being in contravention of Articles 9 and 14 of the International Covenant on Civil and Political Rights (ICCPR).[53] It also contributed to the length of time of more than 15 years from the assassination to the verdict in the Trial Chamber. Following appeals, the Appeals Chamber ruled that the Ayyash defence had no standing to appeal his conviction in his absence.[54] Furthermore, in June 2021, the Trial Chamber issued an order cancelling the commencement of trial.[55] Hence, the total time span from the original event to the verdict was even longer.[56]

---

[44] STL, Pre-Trial Judge, Order Regarding the Detention of Persons Detained in Lebanon in Connection with the Case of the Attack Against Prime Minister Rafiq Hariri and Others, 29 April 2009, CH/PTJ/2009/06, para. 34.
[45] STL, Pre-Trial Judge, Order Regarding the Detention of Persons Detained in Lebanon in Connection with the Case of the Attack Against Prime Minister Rafiq Hariri and Others, 29 April 2009, CH/PTJ/2009/06, para. 34 (vi)
[46] Blanford (2006). Killing Mr Lebanon: The Assassination of Rafik Hariri and its Impact of the Middle East, pp. 150–151.
[47] Iskandar (2006). Rafiq Hariri and the Fate of Lebanon, pp. 207–208, MacDonald (2010). CBC Investigation: Who Killed Lebanon's Rafik Hariri?
[48] STL, The Prosecutor v. Ayyash et al., STL-11-01.
[49] STL webpage, Judgment in the Ayyash et al. case postponed to 18 August 2020.
[50] STL, The Prosecutor v. Ayyash et al., STL-11-01.
[51] Trial Chamber, STL-11-01/T7TC, p. 7 § 34.
[52] STL-11-01/T/TC, pp. 14–16 §§ 58–65.
[53] WGAD report § 47, STL Trial Chamber, David Re, Separate Opinion, pp. 2246–2247.
[54] STL webpage <https://www.stl-tsl.org/en>.
[55] STL webpage <https://www.stl-tsl.org/en>.
[56] STL webpage <https://www.stl-tsl.org/en>.

In 1994, approximately 11 years before the London bombings and the Beirut explosion, Dutch researchers Wagenaar, van Koppen, and Crombag published their research on so-called *suspect-driven investigations*.[57] While this research stems from analysis of Dutch criminal cases,[58] its focus on human, rather than legal, sources of errors makes it relevant for other national jurisdictions,[59] international jurisdictions,[60] as well as the jurisdictions of so-called hybrid Courts like the STL.[61] This research suggested that investigations may become narrow and one-sided in cases that, unlike the London bombings and Ayyash et al. case, are not high profile, politically sensitive, and which do not generate enormous media attention and associated pressures to get someone arrested and convicted.[62] More specifically, the Dutch researchers analysed 35 criminal cases that were dubious in the sense that they contained legal or logical problems and that were later reversed by the Court of Appeals because of a different evaluation of the evidence or that the defence attorney who had worked on the case remained strongly convinced of his or her client's innocence.[63] Some of the cases were acknowledged wrongful convictions.[64] The Dutch researchers looked for a common denominator in the cases and found one: in all the cases a suspect had been identified at an early stage of the investigation. From that time on the police's working hypothesis, that the suspect was guilty, dictated the investigation so that its only aim was to find hypothesis confirming information; that is, a suspect-driven investigation.[65] This is the opposite of what the researchers refer to as an *offence-driven investigation* in which it is the available information, not a predetermined conclusion about who is the perpetrator, that guides the gradual formation of the case's narrative.[66] Clearly, a suspect-driven investigation carries with it a significant risk that alternative crime hypotheses such as there was another perpetrator or that no crime has been committed at all, are

---

[57] Wagenaar, van Koppen, & Crombag (1995). Anchored Narratives, The Psychology of Criminal Evidence.

[58] Wagenaar, van Koppen, & Crombag (1995). Anchored Narratives, The Psychology of Criminal evidence, p. 11.

[59] Fahsing (2016). The Making of An Expert Detective: Thinking and Deciding in Criminal Investigations, pp. 1–75.

[60] Agirre Aranburu (2010). Gravity of Crimes and Responsibility of the Suspect, p. 234; Lidén (2020). Confirmation Bias in Investigations of Core International Crime: Risk Factors and Quality Control Techniques, pp. 461–528.

[61] Cryer, Robinson, & Vasiliev (2019). An Introduction to International Criminal Law and Procedure, pp. 173–201.

[62] Lidén (2020). Confirmation Bias in Investigations of Core International Crimes: Risk Factors and Quality Control Techniques, pp. 473–482.

[63] Wagenaar, van Koppen, & Crombag (2015). Anchored Narratives, The Psychology of Criminal Evidence, p. 11.

[64] Wagenaar, van Koppen, & Crombag (2015). Anchored Narratives, The Psychology of Criminal Evidence, p. 11.

[65] Wagenaar, van Koppen, & Crombag (2015). Anchored Narratives, The Psychology of Criminal Evidence, pp. 84–88.

[66] Wagenaar, van Koppen, & Crombag (2015). Anchored Narratives, The Psychology of Criminal Evidence, pp. 84–88.

insufficiently investigated.[67] This also means that the accuracy of the investigation is more or less haphazard as it depends on the quality of the original suspicions.

From their findings, Wagenaar and colleagues concluded that Dutch legal actors do not always follow the sort of logic dictated by legal standards but are instead guided by premature hypotheses about a suspect's guilt. While no jurisdiction prohibits that criminal investigators work on the basis of a hypothesis, and this is often fully necessary due to, for example, limited resources and time,[68] investigators and prosecutors in many jurisdictions across the globe are required by law to search for and seriously consider both incriminating and exonerating information. Such regulations can be found in common law countries like the United Kingdom,[69] civil law countries like Sweden,[70] as well as in international jurisdictions, for example in the Rome Statute of the International Criminal Court (ICC).[71] For example, there are legal expectations on investigators expressed in the UK Criminal Procedure and Investigations Act 1996 § 23 combined with Code of Practice section 23(1) under Part II section 3.5.[72] According to these paragraphs, when conducting an investigation: 'the investigator should pursue all reasonable lines of inquiry, whether these point towards or away from the suspect'.

This is similar to the Swedish Code of Judicial Procedure 23 ch. 2 and 4 §§, according to which, during the preliminary investigation, inquiry shall be made concerning who may be reasonably suspected of the offence and whether there are sufficient reasons for prosecution. Furthermore, in this process, the inquiry leader as well as anyone assisting him or her 'shall search for, secure and consider circumstances and evidence both to the suspects advantage and disadvantage'.

Furthermore, according to the Rome Statute of the International Criminal Court, Article 54(1)(a), the Prosecutor 'shall: (a) In order to establish the truth, extend the investigation to cover all facts and evidence relevant to an assessment of whether there is criminal responsibility under this Statute, and, in doing so, investigate incriminating and exonerating circumstances equally'.

Thus, the notion that investigations need to be balanced, comprehensive, and wide in their focus to promote the accuracy and legitimacy of the criminal procedure in the best possible way is shared across jurisdictions. However, since suspect-driven investigations focus more on finding the evidence that supports a

---

[67] Wagenaar, van Koppen, & Crombag (2015). Anchored Narratives, The Psychology of Criminal Evidence, pp. 84–88.
[68] Lidén (2020). Confirmation Bias in Investigations of Core International Crimes: Risk Factors and Quality Control Techniques, pp. 9–21.
[69] Code for Crown Prosecutors, Criminal Procedure and Investigations Act 1996 Part I.
[70] The Swedish Code of Judicial Procedure 23 chs 2–4 §§.
[71] Rome Statute of the IC, Article 54 (1)(a).
[72] Ministry of Justice, Criminal Procedure and Investigations Act 1996, section 23(1), Code of practice, revised in accordance with section 25(4) of the Criminal Procedure and Investigations Act 1996.

certain hypothesis[73] and less on critically evaluating that hypothesis, on its own or in juxtaposition with other hypotheses, they will prevent effective regulation adherence. Consequently, they also become an obstacle to the robust application of the standard of proof 'beyond all reasonable doubt',[74] both nationally[75] and internationally.[76]

Evidently, the soundness of the hypothesis that someone is guilty depends on the quality of the prior investigation leading up to the identification of the suspect(s). Research suggests that suspect identification, and the subsequent risk of a suspect-driven investigation, occur on the basis of a variety of circumstances, often at very early stages and not necessarily preceded by any significant prior investigation. Instead, more superficial circumstances may, in practice, become decisive; for example, a prosecutor's decision to investigate a certain individual using specific tactics[77] or the mere naming of a suspect in an investigation plan based on, for example, uncorroborated testimony.[78] Also decisions to apprehend[79] or arrest[80] an individual based on limited and ambiguous preliminary information can have such effects. Clearly, suspect identification cannot be postponed for too long and there are limitations as to the amount of case-relevant information that can be processed effectively, particularly in fact-rich cases concerning, for example, organized crime or core international crimes.[81] However, relying heavily on such circumstances makes the outcome more dependent on chance than anything else. Arguably this is less of a problem if the case hypothesis turns out to be correct, for example in the sense that the right perpetrator was identified correctly from the outset. However, this disregards the fact that the duty to investigate both incriminating and exonerating circumstances applies equally in all situations, regardless of whether the case hypothesis turns out to be correct or incorrect. The importance of doing so becomes even clearer when considering that, in addition, the evaluation of the collected information/evidence may be one-sided, an issue addressed in the following.

---

[73] Rassin, Eerland, & Kuijpers (2010). Let's Find the Evidence: An Analogue Study of Confirmation Bias in Criminal Investigations, pp. 231–246; Verini (2016). The Prosecutor and the President.

[74] Bring & Diesen (2009). Förundersökning, pp. 197–198.

[75] Supreme Court of Canada, R. v. Lifchus, 1997 3 SCR 320; Court of Appeal of New Zealand, R v. Wanhalla 2007 2 NZLR 573; US Supreme Court Miles v. United States, 1880 103 US 304.

[76] The Rome Statute of the ICC, Article 66(3), Rule 87(A) of the Rules of Procedure and Evidence for the ICTR; Rule 87(A) of the Rules of Procedure and Evidence for the ICTY.

[77] Griffin (2001). The Prudent Prosecutor. Scholarly works, Paper 728 <http://scholars.law.unlv.edu/facpub/728>.

[78] Lidén (2020). Confirmation Bias in Investigations into Core International Crimes: Risk Factors and Quality Control Techniques, pp. 470–471.

[79] Lidén, Gräns, & Juslin (2018). The Presumption of Guilt in Suspect Interrogations: Apprehension as a Trigger of Confirmation Bias and Debiasing Techniques, pp. 336–354.

[80] Fahsing & Ask (2013). Decision Making and Decisional Tipping Points in Homicide Investigations: An Interview Study of British and Norwegian Detectives, pp. 155–165.

[81] Agirre Aranburu & Bergsmo (2020). Investigative Bottlenecks and the Mindset of Quality Control, pp. 1–24.

3.3 Evaluation of Information

3.3.1 Believing is Seeing

In conclusion, all the documents examined admit ... a divergent interpretation that makes the conclusion they [the prosecution; own addition] reach is equivocal, and this should favor the defendants. And if we analyse them from the point of view of the defense, they all admit exculpatory interpretations. Therefore, this evidence is insufficient to support the accusation ....

The First Section of the Criminal Chamber of the Spanish National
High Court in the Egunkaria case[82]

On 20 February 2003, the Spanish Guardia Civil raided the offices of *Euskaldunon Egunkaria*, Spain's leading Basque-language newspaper, and arrested 10 members of staff.[83] Among those accused of helping the violent separatist group Euskadi Ta Askatasuna (ETA) in its campaign for an independent Basque country,[84] was Mr Otamendi Egiguren, a Spanish journalist and publication director of *Euskaldunon Egunkaria* at the material time.[85] Mr Otamendi Egiguren was being held *in communicado* in police custody and was also subjected to inhumane degrading treatment, as confirmed by the later verdict from the European Court of Human Rights (ECtHR) in *Otamendi Egiguren v. Spain*.[86] The raiding and subsequent closure of the newspaper's offices by Spanish authorities, as well as the arrests, were a manifestation of a narrative of ETA's 'entorno' (environment).[87] More specifically, this constituted a notable change in the anti-terrorism response where punishments were extended not only to persons who belonged to or collaborated with ETA but also to individuals involved in other activities that until that time had been legal and public.[88] This was manifested in, for example, business closures and arrests of publication directors based on the suspicion of their manipulation by

---

[82] La Secci Sección Primera de la Sala de lo Penal de la Audiencia Nacional, Juzgado Central de Instrucción núm. 6, Rollo de Sala núm. 21/05, Sentencia Núm. 27/2010, p. 30. Own translation (shortened in parts) of: 'En conclusion, todos los documentos examinados admiten, desde la perspectiva más favorable a las acusaciones, una interpretación divergente que hace que la conclusion a la que estas llegan sea equívoca, debiendo favorecer a los procesados. Y si los analizamos desde el punto de vista de las defensas todos ellos admiten interpretatciones exculpatorias. Por lo tanto, por una u otra vía esta prueba es insuficiente para sostener la imputación, cuando no excluyente.'

[83] Bulent Yusuf, The Persecution of a Newspaper, New Statesman, 26, 17 March 2003.

[84] Gemma Ubasart-Gonzáles, ETA and State Action; The Development of Spanish Antiterrorism, 2011.

[85] ECtHR, Otamendi Egiguren v. Spain, Application No. 47303/08.

[86] ECtHR, Otamendi Egiguren v. Spain, Application No. 47303/08.

[87] Ubasart-Gonzáles, ETA and State Action; The Development of Spanish Antiterrorism, p. 579.

[88] Ubasart-Gonzáles, ETA and State Action; The Development of Spanish Antiterrorism, p. 579, 2011.

ETA,[89] some of which were indeed justified, for example in relation to the *Egin* newspaper and the associated radio station *Egin Irratia*.[90] However, when it came to *Euskaldunon Egunkaria*, the connection to ETA and terrorism had been presumed rather than documented. In fact, it has been claimed that the Egunkaria case was only 'the latest example of Spain's unique interpretation of the war on terror, where Basque newspapers, cultural magazines, radio stations, language schools for adults and even children's language schools are accused of harboring terrorist activity'.[91]

Hence, terrorism was perceived as omnipresent. There were 'confirming instances everywhere'[92] and the Basque community 'was full of verifications of the theory'.[93] These hypothesis consistent evaluations of information are manifestations of confirmation bias, documented in legal[94] as well as other contexts.[95] For example, this was evident in participants who were asked to watch a recording from a body-worn camera (BWC) and were then asked whether or not the arrested individual depicted in the recording had any weapons.[96] Some of the participants had been exposed to misinformation from the involved police officer suggesting that the citizen had a knife in his hand. Some reported seeing the knife even if there was indeed none.[97] In the *Egunkaria* case specifically, it was alleged that documents published by *Egunkaria*, some of which had been seized from ETA members,[98] showed that the newspaper was controlled by ETA.[99] This link to ETA had been established by members of the Spanish Guardia Civil who were consulted as experts.[100] When faced with these alleged expert statements, the Spanish National High Court reacted, not only because it believed that the question of a potential link to ETA was under its discretion exclusively[101] but also

---

[89] Ubasart-Gonzáles, ETA and State Action; The Development of Spanish Antiterrorism, p. 579, 2011.
[90] Caminos-Marcet, Terrorism in the Basque Press (1900, 2000, 2008–2009). Analysis of News Paper Editorials about ETA's Fatal Attacks, pp. 1–26.
[91] Bulent Yusuf, The Persecution of a Newspaper, New Statesman, 26, 17 March 2003.
[92] Popper (1963). Conjectures and Refutations, pp. 34–35; Proctor & Capaldi (2005). Why Science Matters: Understanding the Methods of Psychological Research, pp. 28–29.
[93] Popper (1963). Conjectures and Refutations, pp. 34–35.
[94] Jones, Crozier, & Strange (2017). Believing is Seeing: Biased Viewing of Body-worn Camera Footage, pp. 460–74; Ask, Rebelius, & Granhag (2008). The 'Elasticity' of Criminal Evidence: A Moderator of Investigator Bias, pp. 1245–1249; Ask & Granhag (2007). Motivational Bias in Criminal Investigators' Judgments of Witness Reliability, pp. 561–591.
[95] Gallimore (1996). Confirmation Bias in the Valuation Process: A Test for Corroborating Evidence, pp. 261–273; Hergovich, Schott, & Burger (2010). Biased Evaluation of Abstracts Depending on Topic and Conclusion: Further Evidence of a Confirmation Bias within Scientific Psychology, pp. 188–209.
[96] Jones, Crozier, & Strange (2017). Believing is Seeing: Biased Viewing of Body-worn Camera Footage, pp. 460–474.
[97] Jones, Crozier, & Strange (2017). Believing is Seeing: Biased Viewing of Body-worn Camera Footage, pp. 460–474.
[98] Juzgado Central de Instrucción núm. 6, 21/05, Sentencia Núm. 27/2010, p. 24.
[99] Juzgado Central de Instrucción núm. 6, 21/05, Sentencia Núm. 27/2010.
[100] Juzgado Central de Instrucción núm. 6, 21/05, Sentencia Núm. 27/2010, p. 24.
[101] Juzgado Central de Instrucción núm. 6, 21/05, Sentencia Núm. 27/2010, pp. 24–25.

because it strongly disagreed with the offered interpretations. More specifically, the Court noted that 'the narrow and erroneous view according to which everything that has to do with the Basque language and with culture in that language is promoted and/or controlled by ETA leads to an incorrect assessment of facts and figures'.[102]

Subsequently, in relation to the accusations in the *Egunkaria* case, the Court concluded that the prosecution had 'not proven that the defendants had even the slightest relationship with ETA'.[103] Hence, this case illustrates how evaluations, in this case of newspaper articles, can be biased by a hypothesis, and how individuals are prone to 'see what they expect to see'.[104] Yet for more critical and detached outside observers, it becomes apparent that the evaluations are clearly one-sided, exaggerated, or even bordering on the paranoid.

While hypothesis-driven evaluations are not surprising in the context of a potential terrorism threat (Chapter 2.2.2.2), the cited research illustrates that such biased evaluations can occur also in very low-stakes controlled experimental settings.[105] Hence, it doesn't take a terrorist threat to trigger such behaviours. In fact, as outlined in the following, factors such as whether a suspect has been apprehended[106] (Chapter 3.5.1.2) or whether a fingerprint analyst is aware of witness testimony confirming the guilt hypothesis[107] (Chapter 3.5.4.2) can suffice. Since both criminal investigations and proceedings are largely dependent on different individuals' (police officers, prosecutors, forensic doctors, witnesses, and so on) evaluations and their memory of information, whether it be an examined document, a crime scene, or a deceased body, this bias is potentially very problematic for the proper administration of justice. This is even more so given that confirmation bias not only manifests in hypothesis-consistent evaluations/interpretations of information but also in the disregard or downplaying of hypothesis-inconsistent information. The next chapter addresses this tendency.

---

[102] Juzgado Central de Instrucción núm. 6, 21/05, Sentencia Núm. 27/2010, p. 16. Translated from Spanish: 'La estrecha y errónea vision según la cual todo lo que tenga que ver con el euskera y la cultura en esa lengua tiene que estar fomentado y/o controlado por E.T.A. conduce, en el proceso penal, a una errónea valoración de datos y hechos y a la inconsistencia de la imputación.'

[103] Juzgado Central de Instrucción núm. 6, 21/05, Sentencia Núm. 27/2010, p. 32. Translated from Spanish: 'En definitive las acusaciones no han probado que los procesados tengan la más minima relación con E.T.A....'

[104] Rajsic, Wilson, & Pratt (2015). Confirmation Bias in Visual Search, pp. 1353–1364.

[105] Jones, Crozier, & Strange (2017). Believing is Seeing: Biased Viewing of Body-worn Camera Footage, pp. 460–474.

[106] Lidén, Gräns, & Juslin (2018). The Presumption of Guilt in Suspect Interrrogations: Apprehension as a Trigger of Confirmation Bias and Debiasing Techniques, pp. 336–354.

[107] Osborne & Zajac (2016). An Imperfect Match? Crime-related Context Influences Fingerprint Decisions, pp. 126–134.

3.3.2 Asymmetrical Scepticism

The investigative measures that were carried out after Mr Bergwall's confessions were to a large extent focused on searching for evidence that Mr Bergwall was the perpetrator ... Although there were several circumstances in the inquiry that by themselves should have made the investigators doubt that his confessions were true, they did not result in a widened perspective. Instead, those circumstances often resulted in more investigative measures aimed at strengthening the notion that Mr Bergwall had committed the crimes.[108]

An effective mechanism that enables criminal investigators to maintain their hypotheses, even in the face of hypothesis-inconsistent information, is so-called *asymmetrical scepticism*.[109] As implied by the terminology, this refers to how decision-makers tend to approve of hypothesis-consistent information uncritically, whereas they critically scrutinize hypothesis-inconsistent information.[110] Importantly, this asymmetry is not triggered by factors actually impacting on whether the information should be trusted such as, whether a witness has a motive to lie. Instead, the asymmetry is triggered by the implications of the information; that is, whether the information is consistent or inconsistent with a preferred hypothesis. In investigations where asymmetrical scepticism is at play, the result can be one-sided narratives formed on the basis of insufficient evidence, as in the Bergwall cases mentioned above. Mr Bergwall had confessed more than 30 murders, was convicted for eight of them which he most likely did not commit, but then retracted his confessions, resulting in all the cases being reopened and Mr Bergwall ultimately being acquitted of all murders. This resulted in an in-depth official investigation by a Parliamentary Committee in Sweden which noted that, among other things, the investigators and prosecutors had displayed an asymmetry in their processing of crime-relevant information. In this specific case, this behaviour contributed not only to repeated false positives (eight wrongful convictions of Mr Bergwall) but also repeated false negatives, since multiple real perpetrators were never identified in the investigations or dismissed as suspects.

The research on asymmetrical scepticism in the context of criminal cases has been conducted using scenario-based experimental studies. For example, in one study Swedish police officers were presented with a case vignette regarding a

---

[108] Swedish Government Official Reports, Bergwallkommissionen, SOU 2015:52 pp. 591–592.
[109] Ask & Granhag (2007). Motivational Bias in Criminal Investigators Judgments of Witness Reliability, pp. 561–91; Marksteiner et al. (2011). Asymmetrical Scepticism Towards Criminal Evidence: The Role of Goal- and Belief-Consistency, pp. 541–47; Ask & Alison (2010). Investigators' Decision Making. In Pär-Anders Granhag (Ed.), Forensic Psychology in Context: Nordic and International Perspectives, pp. 35–55.
[110] Ask & Granhag (2005). Motivational Sources of Confirmation Bias, pp. 561–591.

homicide, in which a female psychiatrist was found dead in an apartment where she had her office, and another woman, Eva, was encountered injured in the same apartment.[111] Eva's husband was a client of the victim and according to the victim's assistant, Eva had expressed suspicion about a sexual relationship between the victim and the husband. Overall, the case vignette strongly indicated that Eva was the perpetrator. Police officers were then asked to rate the reliability and credibility as well as the witnessing and recall conditions for a witness who stated she heard loud, upset voices from the apartment. Without the police officers being aware of it, there were two versions of the witness testimony that were identical only with one exception. In the incriminating version, the witness stated that the voices belonged to *two women*, whereas in the exonerating version, the witness instead stated that the voices belonged to *a woman and a man*. Half the police officers received the incriminating version whereas the other half received the exonerating version. They were also either placed in low time pressure or high time pressure conditions.

The police officers who received the exonerating version perceived the witness as significantly less reliable and credible, and also thought the witnessing and recall conditions were less favourable, although the background and witnessing conditions were identical in both conditions. This is referred to as *asymmetrical scepticism*, that is, where a decision-maker uncritically approves of hypothesis-consistent information, he or she critically scrutinizes hypothesis-inconsistent information.[112] Furthermore, police officers in high time pressure conditions were more confident that Eva was guilty.

Undoubtedly, asymmetrical scepticism has a functional value for a decision-maker who (subconsciously) wants to reach a certain conclusion.[113] Although Ask and Granhag's studies only use one brief case vignette regarding one type of crime and one suspect, the results have been replicated in the Dutch setting[114] and also specifically when it comes to ambiguous evidence.[115] In real criminal

---

[111] Ask & Granhag (2007): Motivational Bias in Criminal Investigators Judgemnts of Witness Reliability, pp. 561–591.

[112] Klein & Kunda (1992). Motivated Person Perception: Constructing Justifications for Desired Beliefs, pp. 145–168; Stevens & Fiske (2000). Motivated Impressions of a Power Holder: Accuracy under Task Dependency and Misperception under Evaluation Dependency, pp. 907–922; Ditto & Lopez (1992). Motivated Skepticism: Use of Differential Decision Criteria for Preferred and Nonpreferred Conclusions, pp. 568–584; Taber & Lodge (2012). Motivated Skepticism in the Evaluation of Political Beliefs, pp. 157–184; Ditto et al. (2003). Spontaneous Skepticism: The Interplay of Motivation and Expectation in Responses to Favorable and Unfavorable Medical Diagnoses, pp. 1120–1132; Edwards & Smith (1996). A Disconfirmation Bias in the Evaluation of Arguments, pp. 5–24; Lord, Ross, & Lepper (1979). Biased Assimilation and Attitude Polarization: The Effects of Prior Theories on Subsequently Considered Evidence, pp. 2098–2109.

[113] Kruglanski (2016). A Motivated Gatekeeper of Our Minds: Need-for-closure Effects on Interpersonal and Group Processes, pp. 465–496; Kruglanski (1996). Motivated Social Cognition: Principles of the Interface, pp. 493–520; Kunda (1990). The Case for Motivated Reasoning, pp. 480–498; Pyszczynski & Greenberg (1987). Toward an Integration of Cognitive and Motivational Perspectives on Social Inference: A Biased Hypothesis-testing Model, pp. 297–340.

[114] Rassin, Eerland, & Kuijpers (2010). Let's Find the Evidence: An Analogue Study of Confirmation Bias in Criminal Investigations, pp. 231–246.

[115] Alison, Smith, & Morgan (2003). Interpreting the Accuracy of Offender Profiles, pp. 185–195.

investigations, it is easy to see how asymmetrical scepticism can have far-reaching consequences as it implies that investigators or other practitioners will systematically disregard or downplay information that potentially could falsify, or at least cast serious doubts on, a guilty hypothesis, even if such evidence appears right before their eyes.[116] This may also influence the distribution of investigative resources, where a good deal of resources are spent looking for more preferred information and none or very little are spent on other information, as in the Bergwall case mentioned at the beginning of this section. Thus, asymmetrical scepticism and suspect-driven investigations are closely intertwined.

So far, the cited cases and research have illustrated that confirmation bias may result in decision-makers preferring and evaluating information supporting a hypothesis that a certain individual is the perpetrator. However, the research on confirmation bias pertains to virtually any hypothesis, thus including both hypotheses of guilt and innocence. In line with this research, there are several case studies illustrating the fact that confirmation bias can occur in relation to a hypothesis that someone is *not* the perpetrator. In other words, asymmetrical scepticism constitutes a risk both of false positives (wrongful suspicions or convictions) as well as false negative (wrongful dismissals or acquittals). For more on these terms, see Section 3.4.

The evaluations leading up to a dismissal of someone as a perpetrator can often be very one-sided; that is, full of scepticism in relation to information suggesting that someone is potentially a perpetrator and uncritical approval of information suggesting that someone is not the perpetrator. Such dismissals often happen at fairly early stages of an investigation and on seemingly arbitrary criteria. For example, in the 34 years long investigation into the murder of Swedish prime minister Olof Palme in February 1986, Mr Engström was considered a fairly unreliable witness since he behaved in an odd way, was attention seeking, consistently changed his statement about the shooting, and also provided information no other witnesses provided.[117] In 2020, after extensive investigation into far more complex theories of what happened, the final conclusion of the then lead prosecutor was that Mr Engström was the most likely perpetrator.[118] However, since Mr Engström was now deceased, or no charges could be brought before a court and the case was closed.[119] Throughout the course of the years, Mr Engström had contacted the police on multiple occasions, to inform them, for example, that some of the witnesses

---

[116] Ask, Rebelius, & Granhag (2008). The 'Elasticity' of Criminal Evidence: A Moderator of Investigator Bias, p. 1254.

[117] Pettersson (2018). Den Osannolika Mördaren—Skandiamannen och Mordet på Olof Palme.

[118] The Swedish Prosecution Authority (2020). Beslut i Förundersökningen om Mordet på Sveriges Statsminister Olof Palme, The Parliamentary Ombudsman (2021). The Parliamentary Ombudsman's Review of the Prosecutor's Report at the Press Conference on the Palme Investigation.

[119] The Swedish Prosecution Authority (2020). Beslut i Förundersökningen om Mordet på Sveriges Statsminister Olof Palme; The Parliamentary Ombudsman (2021). The Parliamentary Ombudsman's review of the Prosecutor's Report at the Press Conference on the Palme Investigation.

had confused him with the perpetrator,[120] to express discontent that he, being a key witness, was not included in the reconstruction of the shooting.[121] Also, his work colleagues described how Mr Engström had personal reflections about the weapon used to shoot Palme and 'would not stop talking about the Palme case'.[122] Furthermore, it was known to the police that Mr Engström had left his place of work just a few minutes before the shooting, that he was familiar with weapons, and, like many others in Sweden at the relevant time, disliked Prime Minister Palme both personally and politically.[123] This was very much consistent with a profile of the perpetrator which was created with help from the US Federal Bureau of Investigation (FBI), that based the profile on similar US cases. More specifically, the profile suggested that the perpetrator would behave like Mr Engström had, because, even if he did not want to expose himself as a perpetrator, he would be unable to keep quiet about the crime.[124] Over the years, many journalists as well as single private investigators tried to make prosecutors and criminal investigators focus more on Mr Engström as a perpetrator but repeatedly failed.[125]

Of course, with hindsight regarding the investigation's final conclusion, all this information can be seen in a new light. In this new light, Mr Engström comes across as less of a confused attention-seeking witness and more as a calculating perpetrator who mocked the police and intentionally exposed himself in the media in order to ruin any witness testimony against him.[126] Seemingly, since the investigators had already dismissed Mr Engström as a suspect, they were not sceptical enough about his behaviour and interpreted it as signs of his personality rather than having anything to do with his involvement in the crime. It should be noted, however, that even today there is considerable uncertainty regarding whether Mr Engström was involved in the murder at all, even to the extent that the lead prosecutor was criticized for publicly naming him as a suspect.[127]

Yet, most cases in which a perpetrator has not been identified within a couple of years will not be allocated more resources to maintain the investigation but instead become cold cases. Although, in different jurisdictions, it varies exactly when a case goes 'cold', most national jurisdictions have an abundance of this type of case.[128] While cold cases can be greatly informative of confirmation bias in the

---

[120] Pettersson, Den Osannolika Mördaren—Skandiamannen och Mordet på Olof Palme.
[121] Pettersson, Den Osannolika Mördaren—Skandiamannen och Mordet på Olof Palme.
[122] Pettersson, Den Osannolika Mördaren—Skandiamannen och Mordet på Olof Palme.
[123] Pettersson, Den Osannolika Mördaren—Skandiamannen och Mordet på Olof Palme.
[124] Pettersson, Den Osannolika Mördaren—Skandiamannen och Mordet på Olof Palme.
[125] Pettersson, Den Osannolika Mördaren—Skandiamannen och Mordet på Olof Palme.
[126] Pettersson, Den Osannolika Mördaren—Skandiamannen och Mordet på Olof Palme.
[127] The Swedish Parliamentary Ombudsman (2021). The Parliamentary Ombudsman's Review of the Prosecutor's Report at the Press Conference on the Palme Investigation; Dahlman (2020). Öppet Fall—Palmemordet.
[128] Allsop (2018). Cold Case Reviews: DNA, Detective Work, and Unsolved Major Crimes; Davis et al. (2014). Working Smarter on Cold Cases: Identifying Factors Associated with Successful Cold Case Investigations, pp. 375–382.

original investigation, cold case investigations themselves can also entail specific kinds of confirmation bias. For example, the early research available today suggests that the knowledge that the case is, evidently, difficult to solve not only impacts negatively on investigator confidence.[129] It also makes investigators much more pessimistic and less capable of generating alternative hypotheses or lines of inquiry that have not yet been examined, in comparison with live cases.[130] Furthermore, Roach and Pease emphasize that also in cold cases, 'the only way to achieve an objective approach to cold case reviews is to bring in officers with no prior knowledge of it, either from another force or even better, from another country'.[131]

This ties back to the social explanations of confirmation bias (Chapter 2.2.2.3) and a change of decision-maker as a potential debiasing technique (e.g. Section 3.5.1.5.2 and Chapter 4.3.3.1), not only in ongoing live cases but also in cold case investigations.

3.4 Confirmation Bias, False Positives, and False Negatives

Since confirmation bias connotes a one-sidedness in relation to any hypothesis, regardless of the content of the hypothesis, it is associated with a range of different kinds of errors. While a confirmation bias in relation to a guilt hypothesis can result in wrongful suspicions or, in the worst case scenario, wrongful convictions, these are not the only perceivable consequences. Likewise, a confirmation bias can occur in relation to an innocence hypothesis and consequently, guilty individuals may be wrongfully dismissed as suspects or wrongfully acquitted as defendants. Such cases will usually go cold unless some innocent individual is convicted in place of the guilty. While confirmation bias is most commonly spoken of as a factor contributing to wrongful convictions, this greatly underrepresents the problem. Even if, from a legal normative perspective, a wrongful conviction is the worst type of error possible, confirmation bias is also related to the accuracy of the criminal investigations and proceedings in a wider sense. Hence, confirmation bias may result in both false positives (wrongful suspicions/convictions) and false negatives (wrongful dismissals/acquittals). Furthermore, it can pertain to both issues of fact, such as whether a certain individual acted in a certain way, and issues of law, such as what is the proper legal classification of that act.

The concepts of false positives and false negatives both relate to *diagnostic accuracy*, a term commonly used in the medical field as an expression of the extent to which the result of a medical test can be trusted. More specifically, diagnostic

---

[129] Roach (2017). The Retrospective Detective: Cognitive Bias and the Cold Case Investigation.
[130] Roach (2017). The Retrospective Detective: Cognitive Bias and the Cold Case Investigation.
[131] Roach & Pease (2006). Necropsies and the Cold Case. In Rossmo (Ed.). Criminal investigative Failures, pp. 327–348.

accuracy refers to whether a test accurately and fully identifies all those carrying a disease as carrying the disease, while simultaneously excluding accurately and fully all those who are tested for the disease but do not carry the disease.[132] Hence, diagnostic accuracy is divided into two components: *sensitivity* and *specificity*. The sensitivity of a measurement instrument is the probability that a diagnostic test or instrument will be positive in persons who have a disease or condition.[133] Sensitivity is also referred to as true positive rate. Tests or instruments that have high sensitivity *are more likely to rule in, or accurately confirm, the disease or condition* when the disease or condition exists.[134] By contrast, specificity is the ability of a measurement instrument to identify persons without a disease or condition correctly. In statistical terms, this is the probability that diagnostic tests or instruments will give negative results in individuals who do not have the disease or condition.[135] Tests or instruments that have high specificity are able to *rule out a disease or condition more accurately.* Specificity is often referred to as the 'true negative rate', meaning that a test offers an accurate negative result when applied to persons who are genuinely without the disease or condition.[136]

In the medical field, the importance of diagnostic accuracy is fairly straightforward since diagnostic errors (false positives and false negatives) can lead to inaccurate treatment, patient harm, as well as financial costs due to law suits. Empirical research indicates that physicians' overconfidence in their ability to reach accurate diagnosis is a contributing factor to diagnostic errors.[137] Thus, there is a potential issue with *diagnostic calibration*, that is, the relationship between the diagnostic accuracy and confidence in that accuracy.[138] Diagnostic errors may occur when the relationship between accuracy and confidence is miscalibrated or misaligned so that confidence is higher than it should be.[139] It is unknown exactly how physicians' confidence relate to the accuracy of their diagnosis, and how common this problem is,[140] but there are indications that physicians, fairly regularly, are overconfident, that is, they are more confident than they are accurate.[141]

---

[132] Hulley (2007). Designing Clinical Research.
[133] Hulley (2007). Designing Clinical Research.
[134] Plichta et al. (2005). Munro's Statistical Methods for Health Care Research; Ma et al. (2014). Statistical Methods for Multivariate Meta-analysis of Diagnostic Tests: An Overview and Tutorial, pp. 1596–1619.
[135] Plichta et al. (2005). Munro's Statistical Methods for Health Care Research; Ma et al. (2014). Statistical Methods for Multivariate Meta-analysis of Diagnostic Tests: An Overview and Tutorial, pp. 1596–1619.
[136] Hulley (2007). Designing Clinical Research.
[137] Berner & Graber, Overconfidence as a Cause of Diagnostic Error in Medicine, pp. 22–23.
[138] Berner & Graber, Overconfidence as a Cause of Diagnostic Error in Medicine, pp. 22–23.
[139] Berner & Graber, Overconfidence as a Cause of Diagnostic Error in Medicine, pp. 22–23.
[140] Berner & Graber, Overconfidence as a Cause of Diagnostic Error in Medicine, pp. 22–23.
[141] Davis et al. (2005). The Association between Operator Confidence and Accuracy of Ultrasonography Performed by Novice Emergency Physicians, pp. 259–64; Friedman et al. (2001). Are Clinicians Correct When They Believe they are Correct? Implications for Medical Decision Support, pp. 454–58; Friedman et al. (2005). Do Physicians Know When Their Diagnoses are Correct? Implications for Decision Support and Error Reduction?, pp. 334–39; Podbregar et al. (2001), Should

Table 3.1 Four possible outcomes of criminal investigations and proceedings.

Legal classification	Actual status	
	Innocent	*Guilty*
Innocent	True negative	False negative
Guilty	False positive	True positive

Just like physicians, legal actors would benefit from reasoning in terms of diagnostic accuracy. More specifically, the diagnostic accuracy in relation to criminal investigations and proceedings would be the extent to which the investigations and proceedings (the equivalent to a medical test in criminal cases) *accurately and fully identify all those who are innocent as innocent* as well as the extent to which they *accurately and fully identify all those who are guilty as guilty*. A perfect diagnostic accuracy would require that the process is fully *sensitive* (all those guilty are identified as guilty), while the process is also fully *specific* (all those innocent are identified as innocent). Thus, on a general level, there are four possible outcomes of criminal investigations and proceedings and this entails two correct outcomes and two incorrect outcomes (see Table 3.1).

The two correct outcomes are:

- A true negative: an innocent individual is identified as innocent; and
- A true positive: a guilty individual is identified as guilty.

The two incorrect outcomes are:

- A false positive: an innocent individual is identified as guilty; and
- A false negative: a guilty individual is identified as innocent.

While *false positives* in a strict sense would only refer to the final product (i.e. a wrongful conviction), it will here also be taken to entail wrongful suspicions against an individual, even though they never materialize and result in a conviction. *False negatives*, strictly speaking, would entail only wrongful acquittals. If investigators have investigated the real perpetrator but their one-sided mindsets have resulted in their failure to see deficiencies in the evidence presented in court, this may very well result in a wrongful acquittal because it becomes apparent to judges that the

We Confirm Our Clinical Diagnosis Certainty by Autopsies?, pp. 1750–55; Yazbek et al. (2010), Confidence of Expert Ultrasound Operators in Making a Diagnosis of Adnexal Tumor: Effect on Diagnostic Accuracy and Interobserver Agreement, pp. 89–93; Weiner & Schwartz (2016). Contextual Errors in Medical Decision Making: Overlooked and Understudied, pp. 657–62.

narrative has not been proven beyond reasonable doubt. In this book, false negatives will also be used for situations in which true perpetrators are dismissed at an early stage, resulting in that either an innocent individual is suspected and convicted (thus, the false negative may come with a false positive) as well as when the case turns into a cold case because despite efforts, investigators have been unable to identify a perpetrator, even if the perpetrator may very well have been part of the investigation.

While false positives and false negatives are more commonly associated with issues of fact and categorical errors, there is also the possibility of errors relating to issues of law and errors in terms of degree. This is because criminal investigations and proceedings are not only about distinguishing those who are innocent from those who are guilty but also about determining what more specific course of events has taken place, how to legally classify those events, and what the more specific role of an individual is. For example, if investigators hypothesize that a certain individual has committed a crime, this may very well be true, but they may make a mistake as regards which crime has been committed and/or what role the accused had in the criminal act. If a guilty person is convicted for the wrong crime or involvement in the crime, then this can of course entail both a false positive and a false negative. While it is accurate that the individual did commit a crime, the individual did not commit the crime in question since that was committed by someone else who then escapes the legal system's attention.

Determining the role of an accused individual is clearly essential to all crimes but likely to be particularly difficult when it comes to crimes that are believed to have been committed through hierarchies and command structures, or in complicity, that is, questions that arise in all jurisdictions. This is illustrated in, for example, the New York Mafia case.[142] In the quest to bring down New York's mob of organized criminals in the 1980s, law enforcement started pursuing previously untouchable mafia leaders using the Racketeer Influenced and Corrupt Organizations (RICO) Act.[143] The RICO Act allowed leaders to be prosecuted for crimes they ordered others to do rather than committed themselves.[144] Similarly, in international criminal law, there is a long tradition[145] of focusing on those most responsible for core international crimes, that is, those who bear the greatest responsibility because they, as political or military leaders, for example, ordered attacks against civilians,

---

[142] Schneider (2020). Racketeer Influenced and Corrupt Organizations Act (RICO); Baldwin (2010). Racketeer Influenced and Corrupt Organizations Act (RICO) and the Mafia Must Now Welcome Organizational Crime.
[143] Schneider (2020). Racketeer Influenced and Corrupt Organizations Act (RICO); Baldwin (2010). Racketeer Influenced and Corrupt Organizations Act (RICO) and the Mafia Must Now Welcome Organizational Crime; Lloyd (2007). Making Civil RICO 'Suave': Congress Must Act to Ensure Consistent Judicial Interpretations of the Racketeer influenced and Corrupt Organizations Act.
[144] Blakey (2006). RICO: The Genesis of an Idea.
[145] Agirre Aranburu (2010). Prosecuting the Most Responsible for International Crimes: Dilemmas of Definition and Prosecutorial Discretion, p. 2; Dittrich, Lingen, & Osten (2020). The Tokyo Tribunal: Perspectives on Law, History and Memory.

as in the ICC case *The Prosecutor v. Joseph Kony and Vincent Otti*[146] or attacks against historic and religious buildings as in *The Prosecutor v. Ahmad Al Faqi*[147] or provided financial support for armed groups who committed a genocide, as with Félicien Kabuga, the man accused of being the main financier of the Rwandan genocide.[148] However, there is still uncertainty in the determination of who is to be considered the most responsible,[149] as well as great evidentiary difficulties with establishing such responsibility, for example due to heavy reliance on insider witnesses that change their testimony repeatedly.[150] Hence, an early hypothesis of who is/are the most responsible perpetrator(s) entails a risk of a confirmation bias in relation to this hypothesis. While this hypothesis is not wrong in the sense that the accused did commit a crime, they did not necessarily commit the crime for which they are investigated, indicted, or convicted. This constitutes a special kind of false positive as it is the more specific legal classification of an accused's actions that is wrongful, not whether a crime has been committed. This kind of false positive also comes with a false negative as the person truly most responsible goes free. Hence, expanding on the concept of suspect-driven investigations (Section 3.2.1), an investigation can also be *hypothesis driven* in a wider sense, which may also be detrimental to the diagnostic accuracy of the proceedings.

In applied settings, there is often a trade-off between sensitivity and specificity since tests are usually not capable of guaranteeing them both simultaneously. Whether sensitivity or specificity is prioritized is strongly context-dependent and in the context of criminal justice it is clear that specificity should be prioritized over sensitivity, since doubts should be to the advantage of the accused. However, the exact balancing between these two has not been further specified than the standard of beyond reasonable doubt.

3.5 Confirmation Bias in Specific Investigative Settings

3.5.1 Interviews

3.5.1.1 Introduction

Interviews with suspects, witnesses, and plaintiffs regularly occur in both national and international jurisdictions and influence decisions about, for example,

---

[146] The Prosecutor v. Joseph Kony and Vincent Otti, Situation in Uganda, ICC-02/04-01/05.
[147] The Prosecutor v. Ahmad Al Faqi Al Mahdi, Situation in the Republic of Mali, ICC-01/12-01/15. On 27 September 2016.
[148] Mutahi (2020). Rwanda Genocide: How Félicien Kabuga evaded capture for 26 years. <https://www.bbc.co.uk/news/world-africa-52758693>.
[149] Agirre Aranburu (2010). Prosecuting the Most Responsible for International Crimes: Dilemmas of Definition and Prosecutorial Discretion.
[150] Chlevickaite, Hola, & Bijleveld (2020). Thousands on the Stand: Exploring Trends and Patterns of International Witnesses, pp. 819–836.

whether to arrest, press charges, and convict or acquit. This happens in a wide range of cases, from so-called word against word situations in alleged raped cases[151] to cases in which insider witnesses testify about who gave orders to commit a crime against humanity.[152] As such, it is essential to understand the process behind the statements provided by suspects, witnesses, and plaintiffs. Specifically, an interviewer who has a firm belief that, for example, a suspect is guilty or that a plaintiff is lying may, subconsciously, influence the statement. When it comes to suspects, the phenomenon of false confessions is today fairly well-known, probably much due to dramatized depictions or documentaries such as 'Making a Murderer' or 'Central Park Five'. Undoubtedly, false confessions can have a great distorting power not only in the sense that they misrepresent the suspect's involvement but also in that they can bias other lines of evidence, including witness testimony or forensic evidence. When it comes to witnesses, confirmation bias can manifest in interviewers, more or less subtly, pushing their hypotheses and thereby making the witness provide a story consistent with their hypotheses. Such witness testimony can provide the evidence needed to press charges but is in fact generated by the interviewer and not an accurate representation of the witness' memory. Furthermore, if an interviewer early on gets the impression that a plaintiff is lying, this may impact how the interviewer conducts the interview. The interviewer could begin sending more or less subtle signals to the plaintiff and this, in turn, could affect the plaintiff's tendency to disclose more or less information, or even retract the testimony. Needless to say, all such tendencies are associated with serious risks of false negative as well as false positives. In the following, suspect, witness, and plaintiff interviews are addressed separately (Sections 3.5.1.2, 3.5.1.3, 3.5.1.4) while criminal investigations often entail at least one of each interview type. Thereafter, possible ways to mitigate the bias will be addressed for all types of interviews jointly, while pointing out relevant differences. Specifically, this entails investigative interviewing, training and adherence (Section 3.5.1.5.1) as well as changing decision-maker (Section 3.5.1.5.2).

3.5.1.2 Understanding Bias—Suspect Interviews

A heavily criticized aspect of the investigation into the assassination of former Lebanese Prime Minister Rafik Hariri in February 2005 was the way in which those initially suspected of the crime, 'the four generals' were treated, including how

---

[151] Crown Prosecution Service (2011). Guidance for Charging Perverting the Court of Justice and Wasting Police Time in Cases Involving Allegedly False Allegations of Rape and/or Domestic Abuse; Saunders (2018). Rape as 'One Person's Word against Another's': Challenging the Conventional Wisdom, pp. 161–181.

[152] Office of the Prosecutor (OTP), International Criminal Court (ICC) (2019). Full Statement of the Prosecutor, Fatou Bensouda, on External Expert Review and Lessons Drawn from the Kenya Situation; Lidén (2021). The Time Variable in Relation to Insider Witnesses: Quantitative and Qualitative Analysis of ICC Cases, pp. 1–43; Chlevickaite & Holá (2016). Empirical Study of Insider Witnesses' Assessments at the International Criminal Court, 673–702.

one of them, Mr El-Sayyed, was interviewed. The suspicions against Mr El-Sayyed were based primarily on the declarations of two individuals identified as witnesses. The first witness, Mr Hussam Hussam, withdrew his testimony at a press conference on the 27 November 2005[153] and the other witness, Zuahir Ibn Mohammed Said Saddik, was allegedly paid to testify against Mr El-Sayyed.[154] However, before that, on the 2 September 2005, Mr El-Sayyed was interviewed by a police officer working for the United Nations, who used a rather confrontative interviewing style accusing Mr El-Sayyed of 'bullshitting'[155] and who also ascertained his authority through statements like 'I hit the table when I want. Is it clear?'[156] As Mr El-Sayyed testified before the STL, Presiding Judge David Re explicitly acknowledged the inappropriateness of the interviewing style, describing it as 'disgraceful'[157] and 'far below international standards'.[158]

The research available today has identified several possible manifestations of confirmation bias in suspect interviews. The bias seems to stem from the interviewer's explicit or implicit expectation that the suspect is guilty. Expectations of guilt can arise for a number of reasons including high probability of guilt[159] and/or decisions to apprehend a suspect,[160] and they can be more or less well founded on the available evidence. In fact, since at least some level of suspicion is required to deprive suspects of their liberty and/or keep them for questioning, the very interview in itself is a manifestation of an expectation of guilt. Such expectations seem to carry with them a significant biasing potential even if only low evidentiary standards such as reasonable suspicion have been met.[161] Since it is common in many jurisdictions that the police or prosecutor can apprehend or arrest a suspect on the basis of reasonable suspicion or similar, it is possible that a bias against the suspect is often introduced at a very early stage.[162] It deserves to be emphasized

---

[153] Separate Opinion of Judge David Re, STL Trial Chamber's Judgment in The Prosecutor v. Salim Jamil Ayyash, Hassan Habib Merhi, Hussein Hassan Oneissi, Assad Hassan Sabra, p. 2234 and WGAD report § 18.
[154] Blanford (2006). Killing Mr Lebanon: The Assassination of Rafik Hariri and its Impact of the Middle East, pp. 178–179.
[155] Separate Opinion of Judge David Re, STL Trial Chamber's Judgment in The Prosecutor v. Salim Jamil Ayyash, Hassan Habib Merhi, Hussein Hassan Oneissi, Assad Hassan Sabra, 2238 § 23.
[156] Separate Opinion of Judge David Re, STL Trial Chamber's Judgment in The Prosecutor v. Salim Jamil Ayyash, Hassan Habib Merhi, Hussein Hassan Oneissi, Assad Hassan Sabra, 2238 § 23.
[157] Separate Opinion of Judge David Re, STL Trial Chamber's Judgment in The Prosecutor v. Salim Jamil Ayyash, Hassan Habib Merhi, Hussein Hassan Oneissi, Assad Hassan Sabra, p. 2238 § 24.
[158] Separate Opinion of Judge David Re, STL Trial Chamber's Judgment in The Prosecutor v. Salim Jamil Ayyash, Hassan Habib Merhi, Hussein Hassan Oneissi, Assad Hassan Sabra, p. 2239 § 24.
[159] Kassin, Goldstein, & Savitsky (2003). Behavioral Confirmation in the Interrogation Room: On the Dangers of Presuming Guilt, pp. 187–203; Hill, Memon, & McGeorge (2008). The Role of Confirmation in Suspect Interviews: A Systematic Evaluation, pp. 357–37.
[160] Lidén, Gräns, & Juslin (2018). The Presumption of Guilt in Suspect Interrogations: Apprehension as a Trigger of Confirmation Bias and Debiasing Techniques, pp. 336–354.
[161] Lidén, Gräns, & Juslin (2018). The Presumption of Guilt in Suspect Interrogations: Apprehension as a Trigger of Confirmation Bias and Debiasing Techniques, pp. 336–354.
[162] Lidén, Gräns, & Juslin (2018). The Presumption of Guilt in Suspect Interrogations: Apprehension as a Trigger of Confirmation Bias and Debiasing Techniques, pp. 336–354.

that the law itself often requires legal actors to hypothesize about a suspect's guilt at an early stage, that is, 'before one has data'.[163]

In fact, even without any legal incentive to hypothesize about the suspect's guilt, research suggests that stereotypes, for example negative stereotypes pertaining to certain ethnic groups, can create expectations about suspects from such groups.[164] Such tendencies have been noted, for example, in interview studies with criminal defence lawyers who had represented suspects from various ethnicities within England and Wales, many of whom had represented more than 1,000 suspects. This was illustrated in how the defence lawyers described different police interviewing practices in affluent versus deprived areas. Specifically, one of the defence lawyers described that:

> [t]here are police stations, they do have stereotypical branding, and attitudes are different in different areas, particularly in London. These attitudes are different in south London deprived areas where the predominantly black community lives, for example, Brixton and that area. If you are in Brixton police station, Brixton has a reputation and the officers there are convinced that they are dealing with the most hardened criminals. Whereas, if you go further south, a slightly more affluent area, attitudes are very different. Interview techniques are different.[165]

Another defence lawyer described how:

> 80 % plus of the people that I represent are from the Asian Muslim ethnic origin. Unfortunately … the way some police officers view Asian Muslim suspects is that they are guilty before they have even been tried, because they are Asian. It's quite clear sometimes that they are not information gathering. They are trying to prove a case against them.[166]

This view is in line with official statistics suggesting that in the United Kingdom, Black, Asian, and Minority Ethnic (BAME) communities are more likely to live in deprived neighbourhoods as compared to White groups.[167] Police officers may believe that people from deprived areas are more likely to be involved in criminal activity[168] and those beliefs can affect their approaches towards suspects from

---

[163] Doyle (2001). The Adventures of Sherlock Holmes, p. 14.
[164] Minhas & Walsh (2020). Prejudicial Stereotyping and Police Interviewing Practices in England: An Exploration of Legal Representatives' Perceptions, pp. 1–16.
[165] Minhas & Walsh (2020). Prejudicial Stereotyping and Police Interviewing Practices in England: An Exploration of Legal Representatives' Perceptions, p. 8.
[166] Minhas & Walsh (2020). Prejudicial Stereotyping and Police Interviewing Practices in England: An Exploration of Legal Representatives' Perceptions, pp. 9–10.
[167] Office for National Statistics (2020). Coronavirus (COVID-19) Related Deaths by Ethnic Group, England and Wales: 2 March 2020 to 10 April 2020.
[168] Bowling (2018). How Police Stop Define Race and Citizenship, pp. 1–4.

deprived neighbourhoods.[169] The use of such negative stereotypes can potentially lead police officers to believe that people from an area/ethnicity are engaged in a particular crime.[170]

Whilst statements from experienced defence lawyers are informative of their perceptions of real-world practices, interview data do not necessarily meet established scientific standards on how to study confirmation bias. However, in fact, the available experimental data are consistent with the views expressed by the cited defence lawyers. This experimental data also extends outside the United Kingdom to include other jurisdictions. Specifically, experimental research suggests that presence of guilt expectations, whether based on previous decisions made and/or stereotypes about the groups the suspect belongs to, can manifest in three primary ways.

First, the research suggests that a guilt hypothesis may result in the interviewer asking the suspect more guilt-presumptive questions.[171] To illustrate, Swedish police officers holding a guilt hypothesis asked questions more often that were indicative of a guilt presumption (e.g. 'Why did you point a gun at the plaintiff?') in a case regarding unlawful threat where the pointing of a gun was disputed by the suspect. Vice versa, for police officers not holding such guilt hypothesis, it was more common to ask neutral questions like 'Can you please tell me what happened before the police arrived?', in a case concerning assault against a partner in the common home. Even innocence-presumptive questions were asked by these police officers (e.g. 'Are you only confessing to protect your friends?') in a case concerning inflicting damage where the suspect was the only one left at the crime scene from which his friends had fled. Similar trends were found in two other studies pertaining to US and UK jurisdictions but using students rather than police officers as participants.[172] In the research conducted with the Swedish police officers, the bias was reduced when the interviewers were asked to choose interview questions from a list rather than generate the questions themselves, probably because choosing questions is a cognitively less challenging task than producing questions oneself (Chapter 2.2.2.1).[173]

---

[169] Smith & Alpert (2007). Explaining Police Bias: A Theory of Social Conditioning and Illusory Correlation, pp. 1262–1283.

[170] Weisburd et al. (2011). The Possible 'Backfire' Effects of Hot Spots Policing: An Experimental Assessment of Impacts on Legitimacy, Fear and Collective Efficacy, pp. 297–320.

[171] Kassin, Goldstein, & Savitsky (2003). Behavioral Confirmation in the Interrogation Room: On the Dangers of Presuming Guilt, pp. 187–203; Hill, Memon, & McGeorge (2008). The Role of Confirmation in Suspect Interviews: A Systematic Evaluation, pp. 357–37; Lidén, Gräns, & Juslin (2018). The Presumption of Guilt in Suspect Interrogations: Apprehension as a Trigger of Confirmation Bias and Debiasing Techniques, pp. 336–354.

[172] Kassin, Goldstein, & Savitsky (2003). Behavioral Confirmation in the Interrogation Room: On the Dangers of Presuming Guilt, pp. 187–203; Hill, Memon, & McGeorge (2008). The Role of Confirmation in Suspect Interviews: A Systematic Evaluation, pp. 357–371.

[173] Lidén, Gräns, & Juslin (2018). The Presumption of Guilt in Suspect Interrogations: Apprehension as a Trigger of Confirmation Bias and Debiasing Techniques, pp. 336–354.

Secondly, a guilt hypothesis may also result in the suspect's statement being perceived as less credible even if the content of the statement is kept constant.[174] For instance, when police officers interviewed suspects who had previously been apprehended, they rated the suspect's statement as less credible than police officers who rated the exact same statement for a suspect who had not been apprehended.[175] However, this effect was qualified by an interaction meaning that the effect was larger when police officers themselves, rather than their colleague, had decided to apprehend, which relates back to the social explanation of confirmation bias (Chapter 2.2.2.3)[176]

Thirdly, a guilt hypothesis may set in motion a process of behavioural confirmation.[177] Not only does a guilt hypothesis influence the interviewer's behaviour but also that of the suspect. Guilt-presumptive questioning styles seemed to influence the suspect's verbal behaviour. Independent observers rated the behaviours of these suspects as significantly more nervous, more defensive, and less plausible, and therefore more likely to be guilty.[178] The effects were more pronounced for innocent than for guilty suspects.[179] This is particularly concerning given the connection between confrontational/manipulative interviews and false confessions[180] as well as non-strategic use of evidence,[181] all of which make it even more difficult to decide whether a suspect is lying or telling the truth.

3.5.1.3 Understanding Bias—Witness Interviews

> *I believe you were in the storage room when Adriano shot Adam. I am not saying you pulled the trigger but I am claiming you were there.*[182]
> Police interviewing a witness in the Adriano Cadiz case

There is a clear difference between a witness interview which aims to obtain correct and reliable information, and a witness interview which aims to confirm a

---

[174] Lidén, Gräns, & Juslin (2018). The Presumption of Guilt in Suspect Interrogations: Apprehension as a Trigger of Confirmation Bias and Debiasing Techniques, pp. 336–354.

[175] Lidén, Gräns, & Juslin (2018). The Presumption of Guilt in Suspect Interrogations: Apprehension as a Trigger of Confirmation Bias and Debiasing Techniques, pp. 336–354.

[176] Lidén, Gräns, & Juslin (2018). The Presumption of Guilt in Suspect Interrogations: Apprehension as a Trigger of Confirmation Bias and Debiasing Techniques, pp. 336–354.

[177] Hill, Memon, & McGeorge (2008). The Role of Confirmation Bias in Suspect Interviews: A Systematic Evaluation, pp. 357–371.

[178] Vrij (2008). Detecting Lies and Deceit: Pitfall and Opportunities.

[179] Hill, Memon, & McGeorge (2008). The Role of Confirmation Bias in Suspect Interviews: A Systematic Evaluation, pp. 357–371.

[180] Davis & Leo (2006). Strategies for Preventing False Confessions and their Consequences, pp. 121–149; Leo & Drizin (2010). The Three Errors: Pathways to False Confession and Wrongful Conviction, pp. 9–30.

[181] Hartwig et al. (2005). Detecting Deception via Strategic Disclosure of Evidence, pp. 469–484; Kassin (2005). On the Psychology of Confessions: Does Innocence put Innocence at Risk?, pp. 215–228; Leo & Drizin (2010). The Three Errors: Pathways to False Confession and Wrongful Conviction, pp. 9–30.

[182] Swedish Police Reference No. K1427657-17. Police interview with Trajan Popov, 22 November 2017, starting 11:47, ending 15:48. Attunda District Court, Case No. B 9865-17, convicted the defendant and the conviction was affirmed by the Appellate Court, see Svea Court of Appeal, B 7958-18.

predetermined conclusion.[183] In the former type of interview, interviewers ask open-ended questions and, on the basis of the information provided by the witness, and ideally also other evidence, a hypothesis is eventually formed. In the latter type of interview, there is a hypothesis about what has happened already before the interview and this hypothesis dictates which questions are asked, how the witness' answers are evaluated, as well as the conclusions drawn from the interview. Hence, the latter type of interview can generate a witness testimony which, seemingly, corroborates a certain course of events but which is, in fact, only a product of how the witness has been interviewed. This is sometimes referred to as *police-generated witness testimony*[184] and is a manifestation of confirmation bias in the interviewer and/or the investigative team behind the interview.

In the Adriano Cadiz case, the Swedish murder case cited at the top of this section, the witness, Mr Popov, consistently claimed throughout the four first interviews that he had not been in the storage room where the murder allegedly had taken place at the relevant time.[185] However, by the end of the fourth interview, the police officer explicitly told Mr Popov about his own hypothesis, namely that Mr Popov had indeed been in the storage room at the relevant time and had also witnessed when Adriano had fired the gunshots that killed Adam.[186] According to the police's own notes from the interview, Mr Popov was crying and was also 'notably relieved when he realized that the interview was over'.[187] Seemingly, the fourth interview constituted a breaking point as in the fifth interview conducted with him later the same day, Mr Popov mentioned for the first time that he had been in the storage room at the relevant time and had also witnessed the shooting.[188] In a subsequent interview, the police pointed out that Mr Popov's account of the shooting was inconsistent with the autopsy report which stated how the shooting must have happened.[189] The police also asked Mr Popov repeated questions regarding from which angle the shot was fired.[190] This resulted in Mr Popov modifying his account so as to fit in with the autopsy report.[191] While these circumstances were pointed out by the defence during both the investigation and the court proceedings, Adriano was convicted in two instances.[192] During cross-examination in the first instance when asked why he changed his testimony, Mr Popov answered: 'because

---

[183] Nickerson (1998). Confirmation Bias: A Ubiquitous Phenomenon in Many Guises, pp. 174–175.
[184] Thompson (2012). Judicial Gatekeeping of Police-Generated Witness Testimony, pp. 329–395.
[185] Swedish Police Reference No. K1427657-17. Interview 1: 2017-11-14, starting 01:26, ending 01:40; Interview 2: 2017-11-14, starting 03:20, ending 06:08; Interview 3: 2017-11-15, starting 11:49, ending 13:22; Interview 4: 2017-11-22, starting 11:47, ending 15:48.
[186] Police interview with Mr Popov, 22 November 2017, starting 11:47, ending 15:48.
[187] Interview 20171122, starting 11:47, ending 15:48, p. 118.
[188] Interview 20171122, starting 23:12, ending 00:23.
[189] Interview 20180117, starting 10:52, ending 14:03, p. 130.
[190] Interview 20180117, starting 10:52, ending 14:03, p. 132.
[191] Interview 20180117, starting 10:52, ending 14:03, p. 132.
[192] Attunda District Court, Case No. B 9865-17, convicted the defendant and the conviction was affirmed by the Appellate Court, see Svea Court of Appeal, B 7958-18.

they promised that he [referring to the suspect] would not get out'.[193] That such promises were made by the police is confirmed by the audio recordings of the interviews.[194]

In many jurisdictions, including the Swedish, there are explicit prohibitions against promises aimed at eliciting statements with a certain content,[195] although with some variations in, for example, the United States.[196] The fact that the police would make hollow and legally questionable promises to Mr Popov is clearly illustrative of their hypothesis that Mr Popov had witnessed the shooting. This hypothesis came to dominate the interview. By clearly expressing his own belief, confronting Mr Popov with the conflicting autopsy report, and asking repeated questions, the interviewer fairly bluntly communicated to Mr Popov that Mr Popov's own account was not accepted. This constitutes a pronounced risk of *witness contamination*,[197] which is known to be pronounced especially if witnesses perceive that, unless they provide an account that is line with the interviewer's hypothesis, there is a risk that they themselves will (formally or informally), become suspects.[198]

Witness interviews are often, on their own, or in combination with a suspect line-up (Section 3.5.2), important pieces of the puzzle laid by criminal investigators and prosecutors. Simultaneously, witness testimony is widely cited as a leading factor in wrongful convictions across the world.[199] There is plenty of research suggesting that when police officers believe that the suspect is guilty, this belief is more or less subtly transferred to witnesses, for instance because the interviewer communicates suggestive information or poses leading questions which makes the witness adjust his or her account so that it is consistent with the police's belief.[200]

To illustrate, Marion and colleagues have studied how alibi witnesses react when informed about an innocent suspect's confession.[201] A naïve participant and a confederate (a researcher acting as participant for the purposes of the study)

---

[193] Audio recording 2 of interview with Mr Popov from Attunda District Court, B9865-17, time: 00:35:14–00:35:41.
[194] Interview 20180117, starting 10:52, ending 14:03, p. 132.
[195] The Swedish Code of Judicial Procedure, 23 ch. 12 §.
[196] Hon & King (1999). Why Prosecutors are Permitted to Offer Witness Inducements: A Matter of Constitutional Authority, pp. 155–181; Joselow (2019). Promise-Induced False Confessions: Lessons from Promises in Another Context, pp. 1641–1687.
[197] Smalarz & Wells (2015). Contamination of Eyewitness Self-Reports and the Mistaken-Identification Problem, pp. 120–124; Sporer et al. (1995). Choosing, Confidence, and Accuracy: A Meta-Analysis of the Confidence-Accuracy Relation in Eyewitness Identification Studies, pp. 315–327.
[198] Williamson (2006). Investigative Interviewing: Rights, Research, Regulation. In Sherman et al. (2003). Bearing False Witness under Pressure: Implicit and Explicit Components of Stereotype-Driven Memory Distortions, pp. 213–246.
[199] <https://www.innocenceproject.org/eyewitness-identification-reform/>.
[200] Hasel & Kasin (2009). On the Presumption of Evidentiary Independence: Can Confessions Corrupt Eyewitness Identifications?, pp. 122–126; Kassin, Bogart, & Kerner (2012). Confessions that Corrupt: Evidence from the DNA Exoneration Case files, pp. 41–45; Pettit, Fegan, & Howie (1990). Interviewer Effects on Children's Testimony.
[201] Marion et al. (2016). Lost Proof of Innocence: The Impact of Confessions Alibi Witnesses, pp. 65–71.

completed a series of problem-solving tasks when the experimenter informed them that a sum of cash had just been stolen from an adjacent office and, subsequently, the confederate was accused of the theft. The confederate stated they had both been in the room carrying out tests when the cash was stolen. Participants were then asked to corroborate this as alibi witnesses, both before and after being informed that the confederate had either denied (denial condition) or confessed (confession condition) to stealing the cash. In a third condition, participants were told that the confederate had confessed and that their continued corroboration of the alibi would imply their complicity in the theft (implied guilt condition). Of alibi witnesses who initially corroborated the suspect's statement, only 45 per cent maintained that corroboration when informed that the suspect had confessed compared to 95 per cent of the participants who believed that the suspect was still denying.[202] Even fewer (20 per cent) maintained their corroboration when the experimenter insinuated that their support of the alibi might imply their complicity. The confession also decreased alibi witnesses' confidence in the accuracy of their alibi and their belief in the confederate's innocence. This suggests that in cases with false confessions (e.g. police-induced confessions),[203] an innocent confessor can be stripped of a vital source of exculpatory evidence if the alibi witness is informed about the confession. This is clearly problematic, especially together with research suggesting that confessions can augment or even produce incriminating evidence such as eyewitness identifications.[204] Confessions can also make witnesses perceive that there is greater similarity between a facial composite and a suspect,[205] thereby potentially creating an illusion of corroboration. This not only poses a threat to the presumption of evidentiary independence, it can also help explain why, in cases of wrongful convictions, it sometimes seems as though there was a complete absence of exculpatory evidence in the original proceedings.[206]

Confirmation bias can also be displayed in interrogators asking questions that include or presume details that were not already mentioned by the witness.[207] As a result, the risk of conscious or subconscious false testimony is heightened, particularly with vulnerable and/or child witnesses.[208] This is related to what prior

---

[202] Marion et al. (2016). Lost Proof of Innocence: The Impact of Confessions Alibi Witnesses, pp. 65–71.
[203] Kassin et al. (2010). Police-induced Confessions: Risk Factors and Recommendations, pp. 3–38; Kassin (2005). On the Psychology of Confessions: Does Innocence put Innocence at Risk? pp. 215–218.
[204] Hasel & Kasin (2009). On the Presumption of Evidentiary Independence: Can Confessions Corrupt Eyewitness Identification?, pp. 122–126; Kassin, Bogart, & Kerner (2012). Confessions that Corrupt: Evidence from the DNA Exoneration Case files, pp. 41–45.
[205] Charman, Gregory, & Carlucci (2009). Exploring the Diagnostic Utility of Facial Composites: Beliefs of Guilt Can Bias Perceived Similarity between Composite and Suspect, pp. 76–90.
[206] Marion et al. (2016). Lost Proof of Innocence: The Impact of Confessions Alibi Witnesses, pp. 65–71.
[207] Ceci & Bruck (1995). The Role of Interviewer Bias, pp. 87–108; Powell, Garry, & Brewer (2009). Eyewitness Testimony, pp. 1–42.
[208] Powell, Garry, & Brewer (2009). Eyewitness Testimony, pp. 1–42; Ernberg, Tidefors, & Landström (2016). Prosecutors' Reflections on Sexually Abused Preschoolers and their Ability to Stand Trial,

information interviewers have when conducting the interview, since that prior information seems to bias their search for information during the interview.[209]

The influence of prior information on subsequent questioning has been studied empirically by, for instance, Powell and colleagues. Their participants were 100 Australian police officers, all authorized to conduct investigative interviews with children after having completed specialized training in this area. The police officers were asked to conduct interviews regarding activities the children participated in as part of the experiment.[210] However, false activities were also made up, that is, activities that the children did not take part in. The police officers were divided into two conditions: (i) the non-biased condition, in which they were told that a lady went to the children's school to conduct an event called the 'Deakin Activities' which involved several unspecified activities, and (ii) the biased condition, where detailed background information (specific for each activity) that 'may or may not have occurred' was provided. For the true activities, both correct and incorrect details were provided, and for the false activities the details were all incorrect. The police officers were then asked to elicit an accurate and detailed account of the event, using the techniques they would normally use to interview a child in their line of work. Consistent with previous findings, the results demonstrated that knowledge of prior information biases interviewers as it increases their usage of leading questions[211] in the direction implicated by the provided details.[212] However, it seemed this effect was moderated by interviewer skills. Poorer interviewers asked fewer open questions and more leading questions when they were biased towards particular details than when they were not biased, whereas good interviewers asked the same proportion of open and leading questions regardless of whether they had received biasing information. Thus, even if confirmation bias seems to occur automatically when interviewers receive knowledge about a case, they might be able to counter or even mask the bias if they are skilled interviewers.[213]

Since prior information seems to bias interviewers' search for and evaluation of information, it is clearly relevant what information is available to them prior to

---

pp. 21–29; Magnusson et al. (2018). Taking the Stand: Defendant Statements in Court Cases of Alleged Sexual Abuse against Infants, Toddlers and Preschoolers, pp. 1–16; Pope (1998). Pseudoscience, Crossexamination, and Scientific Evidence in the Recovered Memory Controversy, pp. 1160–1181.

[209] Pettit, Fegan, & Howie (1990). Interviewer Effects on Children's Testimony; Powell, Hughes-Scholes, & Sharman (2012). Skill in Interviewing Reduces Confirmation Bias, pp. 126–134.

[210] Powell, Hughes-Scholes, & Sharman (2012). Skill in Interviewing Reduces Confirmation Bias, pp. 126–134.

[211] Powell & Snow (2007). Guide to Questioning Children during the Free-narrative Phase of an Investigative Interview, pp. 57–65.

[212] Ceci & Bruck (1995). The Role of Interviewer Bias, pp. 87–108; Pettit, Fegan, & Howie (1990). Interviewer Effects on Children's Testimony; Thompson et al. (1997). What Did the Janitor Do? Suggestive Interviewing and the Accuracy of Children's Accounts, pp. 405–426.

[213] Williamson (2006). Investigative Interviewing: Rights, Research, Regulation. In Bull (2014). Investigative Interviewing.

the interview. A trigger of confirmation bias which is likely to be common in child interviews is information that parents convey to the police. This information may come to function as a hypothesis which the interviewer subconsciously aims to confirm through how the child is interviewed. Hence, in an applied setting it will often be difficult to know whether the child is providing a certain account based on their own memory and perception or whether it stems from the parents and/or how the interview was conducted. This is exemplified in the B case, concerning rape or sexual assault: the six-year-old plaintiff, when confronted with what allegedly happened, first said, on multiple occasions, that she had to think, but then confirmed that: 'Yes, that happened'.[214] When the interrogator then asked: 'What happened, so that I can understand?', B responded: 'What my mum said'.[215] Confronting B with what she, allegedly, told her mother and thereafter trying to make B agree with the suggestions, is not only contrary to recommendations for child interviews[216] but also displays a confirmatory search for information. That B in the end answered 'What my mum said' could be an indication that she had no idea whatsoever what her mother said, even if this could also be a result of, for example, lacking vocabulary or feelings of shame. In child interviews, the question of what prior information the interviewer should have is particularly difficult since children on the one hand might be susceptible to suggestions[217] but on the other hand might also need more support in disclosing, due to, for example, limited vocabulary or perceived negative consequences of disclosure.[218]

In a similar vein, in both national and international investigations, there may be cultural differences[219] which may exacerbate the risk that an interviewer's hypothesis comes to dominate the interview. One example of this which is relevant in all jurisdictions across the world is age estimation based on statements provided by witnesses as well as plaintiffs. Since age is constructed, understood, and used differently across different cultures, the legal culture's understanding of age as something entirely chronological can deviate from the understandings of age held by interviewees. Therefore, in practice, the interviewees may have no other real options than to agree with a suggestion about their ages, more or less subtly implied by the interviewer. This has been relevant not least in cases before the SCSL

---

[214] Svea Court of Appeal, B 2450-16.
[215] Svea Court of Appeal, B 2450-16, pp. 7–8.
[216] Brainerd & Reyna (1996). Mere Memory Testing Creates False Memories in Children, pp. 467–478; Ceci & Bruck (1993). Suggestibility of the Child Witness: A Historical Review and Synthesis, pp. 403–439; Portwood & Reppucci (1996). Adults' Impact on the Suggestibility of Preschooler's Recollections, pp. 175–198.
[217] Muir-Broaddus et al. (1998). Conservation as a Predictor of Individual Differences in Children's Susceptibility to Leading Questions, pp. 454–458.
[218] Magnusson, Ernberg, & Landström (2017). Preschoolers' Disclosures of Child Sexual Abuse: Examining Corroborated Cases from Swedish Courts, pp. 199–209; Lemaigre, Taylor, & Gittoes (2017). Barriers and Facilitators to Disclosing Sexual Abuse in Childhood and Adolescence: A Systematic Review, pp. 39–52.
[219] Vredeveldt (2020). Beyond WEIRD Witnesses: Eyewitness Memory in Cross-Cultural Contexts.

and the ICC concerning the war crime of conscripting, enlisting, or using child soldiers, that is, individuals under the age of 15 years, in armed battle.[220] In these cases, birth certificates and other documentation of chronological age have regularly been missing. Considering that many of the interviewed individuals grew up in communities where age is a social construct, related more strongly to, for example, significant life events[221] or functional and physiological attributes[222] than to the time that has passed since birth, it is doubtful whether they were at all aware of their chronological ages. For example, in the Taylor case before the SCSL, Sumana told the Court that his father 'used to tell him'[223] that he was 14 years old at the relevant time and that he was abducted during the 'mango season'.[224] In the same case, Tholley testified that she had not yet had her menses when she was raped.[225] Lacking other more reliable sources of information, it is likely that the interviewer, consciously or subconsciously, forms perceptions of the interviewee's age based on, for example, the interviewee's physical appearance or demeanour, assessments which are known to be difficult and often erroneous.[226] In fact, when a social worker who had interviewed alleged child soldiers in Ituri, the Democratic Republic of the Congo (DRC) as part of an investigation into war crimes allegedly committed by Mr Lubanga, the social worker stated that 'the children were smaller than the Kalashnikovs they were carrying'.[227] This statement was not only heavily criticized by the defence as a bias in favour of the prosecution but is also indicative of how such impressions can be formed, on more or less good grounds. Lacking proper documentation, it is unknown whether and to what extent this specific interviewer or other interviewers, consciously or subconsciously, push their age hypotheses. As illustrated by the research conducted by Powell and colleagues, the skill of the interviewer is an important factor in the careful balancing between on the one hand supporting the interviewee and on the other hand not influencing the interviewee.[228]

---

[220] Lidén (2020). Child Soldier or Soldier? Estimating Age in Cases of Core International Crimes, pp. 323–460.
[221] Vaska et al. (2016). Age Determination in Refugee Children: A Narrative History Tool for Use in Holistics Age Assessment, p. 527.
[222] Smith & Brownless (2011). Age Assessment Practices: A Literature Review and Annotated Bibliography; Durham (2000). Youth and the Social Imagination in Africa, pp. 113–120; Jelliffe (1966). Age Assessment in Field Surveys of Children of the Tropics, pp. 826–828.
[223] SCSL Taylor Trial Chamber Judgment, § 1378.
[224] SCSL Taylor Trial Chamber Judgment, § 1378.
[225] SCSL, Taylor Trial Chamber Judgment, § 1454.
[226] Clifford, Watson, & White (2018). Two Sources of Bias Explain Errors in Facial Age Estimation, pp. 1–10.
[227] ICC, Situation in the Democratic Republic of the Congo, The Prosecutor v. Thomas Lubanga Dyilo, Testimony of P-0046 before Pre-Trial Chamber 1, video excerpt EVD-OTP-00479, and the respective Transcript of Testimony, T-37-FR, p. 23, lines 8–12.
[228] Powell, Hughes-Scholes, & Sharman (2012). Skill in Interviewing Reduces Confirmation Bias, pp. 126–134; Myklebust, Oxburg, & Webster (2020). Interviewing Victims and Witnesses of Crime. In Agirre et al. (Eds). Quality Control in Criminal Investigations (pp. 297–321).

3.5.1.4 Understanding Bias—Plaintiff Interviews

When it comes to plaintiffs, the available research indicates that confirmation bias may be present, for example, in the evaluation of alleged rape victims' accounts.[229] Specifically, it seems that delayed reporting frequently triggers notions that the evidence will be insufficient for a conviction or even for pressing charges,[230] that is, an 'insufficient evidence hypothesis', and indeed, rape cases are often dropped due to a perceived lack of evidence.[231] Also, delayed reporting can trigger suspicions that the report is false,[232] that is, a 'false report hypothesis'. Such hypotheses, in turn, can trigger confirmation bias, especially combined with other factors after, during, and before the rape, that may raise investigators' and prosecutors' suspicions. This includes, for example, if the plaintiff provides inconsistent testimony[233] (after the event), did not resist[234] (during the event), or was intoxicated,[235] wearing certain attire,[236] as well as the plaintiff's background characteristics[237] (before the event). Yet, it should be noted that the findings are mixed regarding the prevalence of such beliefs or 'rape myths' among police officers.[238] This should be seen in the light of research suggesting that among police officers there is a belief that the incidence of false reports is high.[239]

---

[229] Koppelaar, Lange, & van de Velde (1997). The Influence of Positive and Negative Victim Credibility on the Assessment of Rape Victims: An Experimental Study of Expectancy—Confirmation Bias, pp. 61–85.

[230] Koppelaar, Lange, & van de Velde (1997). The Influence of Positive and Negative Victim Credibility on the Assessment of Rape Victims: An Experimental Study of Expectancy—Confirmation Bias, pp. 61–85.

[231] Lovett & Kelly (2009). Different Systems, Similar Outcomes? Tracking Attrition in Reported Rape Cases across Europe, in Final Research Report, Child and Women Abuse Studies Unit London Metropolitan University, London; Russo (2000). Date Rape: A Hidden Crime.

[232] Koppelaar, Lange, & van de Velde (1997). The Influence of Positive and Negative Victim Credibility on the Assessment of Rape Victims: An Experimental Study of Expectancy—Confirmation Bias, pp. 61–85.

[233] Dhami, Lundrigan, & Thomas (2018). Police Discretion in Rape Cases, pp. 157–169.

[234] Dhami, Lundrigan, & Thomas (2018). Police Discretion in Rape Cases, pp. 157–169.

[235] Schuller & Wall (1998). The Effects of Defendant and Complainant Intoxication on Mock Jurors' Judgments of Sexual Assault, pp. 555–573; Goodman-Delahunty & Graham (2010). The Influence of Victim Intoxication and Victim Attire on Police Responses to Sexual Assault, pp. 22–40,

[236] Goodman-Delahunty & Graham (2010). The Influence of Victim Intoxication and Victim Attire on Police Responses to Sexual Assault, pp. 22–40,

[237] Page (2008). Gateway to Reform: Policy Implications of Police Officers' Attitudes towards Rape, pp. 44–58; Page (2008). Judging Women and Defining Crime: Police Officers' Attitudes Towards Women and Rape, pp. 389–411; Page (2010). True Colours: Police Officers and Rape Myth Acceptance, pp. 315–334.

[238] Goodman-Delahunty & Graham (2010). The Influence of Victim Intoxication and Victim Attire on Police Responses to Sexual Assault, pp. 22–40; Schuller & Stewart (2000). Police Responses to Sexual Assault Complaints: The Role of Perpetrator/Complainant Intoxication, pp. 535–551; Schuller & Wall (1998). The Effects of Defendant and Complainant Intoxication on Mock Jurors' Judgments of Sexual Assault, pp. 555–573. See also Ask & Landström (2010). Why Emotions Matter: Expectancy Violation and Affective Response Mediate the Emotional Victim Effect, pp. 392–401; Campbell, Menaker, & King (2015). The Determination of Victim Credibility by Adult and Juvenile Sexual Assault Investigators, pp. 29–39; Lovett & Kelly (2009). Different Systems, Similar Outcomes? Tracking Attrition in Reported Rape Cases across Europe, in Final Research Report, Child and Women Abuse Studies Unit London Metropolitan University, London.

[239] McMillan (2015). Police Officers' Perceptions of False Allegations of Rape, pp. 9–21.

To illustrate, a 'false report hypothesis' can cause investigators and/or prosecutors, however unintentionally, to look only or primarily for evidence that supports the 'false report hypothesis' and/or to systematically downgrade information suggesting that the report may in fact be true. Furthermore, a 'false report hypothesis' may very well become apparent in the plaintiff interview, for example in a critical tone towards the plaintiff, causing the plaintiff to become withdrawn and not disclose important pieces of information about what occurred.[240] Furthermore, the evaluation of the plaintiff's statement may shift to focusing selectively on those features of the testimony that are compatible with a preferred hypothesis.[241] If the plaintiff is reserved this can, in turn, serve to create further suspicions in the mind of an investigator that the report is false. Should the plaintiff pick up on this suspicion, they might decide not to participate further in the investigation or back out altogether. This completes the circle by seeming to confirm the investigator's belief that the plaintiff was lying from the outset, and this explains why the plaintiff stopped collaborating. This process of behavioural confirmation is similar but different in effect to that noted in relation to suspects (Section 3.5.1.2). Not only does a 'false report hypothesis' influence the interviewer's behaviour but also that of the plaintiff, in a mutually reinforcing circle, ultimately confirming, superficially, the interviewer's suspicions.

Hence, just as a hypothesis about guilt can result in that a suspect is asked guilt-presumptive questions and is not believed when denying, confirmation bias can also manifest as a hypothesis of innocence, expressed through, for example, disbelief against a rape victim. This highlights the fact that confirmation bias, while more commonly associated with false positives (wrongful convictions) can also be an important contributing factor in false negatives (wrongful acquittals or decisions to not investigate/prosecute).

3.5.1.5 Mitigating Bias
3.5.1.5.1 Investigative interviewing, training, and adherence
Today, investigative interviewing is a widely acknowledged and relatively well-established framework for how to conduct proper suspect, witness, and plaintiff interviews, including countering of biased questioning.[242] A crucial aspect of this framework is that the interviewee, that is, the suspect, witness, or plaintiff, shall be the one who is the most active while the role of the interviewer is merely to facilitate

---

[240] This possibility has been pointed out by practitioners but not systematically and empirically evaluated; see Monahan & Polk, The Effect of Cultural Bias on the Investigation and Prosecution of Sexual Assault.
[241] Shafir (1995). Compatibility in Cognition and Decision, p. 257; Bogaard et al. (2014). Contextual Bias in Verbal Credibility Assessment: Criteria-Based Content Analysis, Reality Monitoring and Scientific Content Analysis, Applied Cognitive Psychology, 28, pp. 79–90.
[242] Williamson (2006). Investigative Interviewing: Rights, Research, Regulation. In Bull (2014). Investigative Interviewing.

the interviewee's free recall, not in any way to direct or influence the interviewee's account.[243] As a debiasing technique, investigative interviewing is linked to the cognitive explanations of confirmation bias (Chapter 2.2.2.1). By being less active/directing and using a standardized framework for interviews, cognitive load is reduced. As such, conducting the interview becomes a cognitively less demanding task for the interviewer,[244] and because of this, interviewers are less likely to fall into the trap of pushing their hypotheses.[245]

The investigative interviewing framework has been incorporated by several national and international bodies such as the Norwegian Police Academy (Politihøgskolen), the National Police Academy in Quebec (École Nationale de Police), and the ICC.[246] Some of these organizations also have continuous training for their staff on investigative interviewing. In other contexts, the framework is part of police academy curriculum, but with no mandatory follow-ups or other types of adherence controls among practitioners.[247]

While incorporation of the investigative interviewing framework and associated training sessions are clearly steps in the right direction, some research suggests that investigators do not, in applied settings, adhere to the framework.[248] As a response, researchers have examined police interview training programmes[249] and procedures[250] to improve interview performance and safeguard interviewees' legal rights, not the least those of suspects. While such endeavours have resulted in valuable insights for improvements,[251] the underlying problem may be less structural and more individual. As pointed out by Adams-Quackenbush and colleagues, for training to be effective, some barriers in cognition must be overcome.[252] For instance, there must be a desire to learn and a positive attitude towards the new

---

[243] Waterhouse et al. (2016). Investigative Interviewing in England and Wales: Adults, Children and the Provision of Support for Child Witnesses, pp. 112–129; Bull (2013). Investigative Interviewing.

[244] Vrij & Granhag (2014). Eliciting Information and Detecting Lies in Intelligence Interviewing: An Overview of Recent Research, pp. 936–944.

[245] Lidén, Gräns, & Juslin (2018). The Presumption of Guilt in Suspect Interrogations: Apprehension as a Trigger of Confirmation Bias and Debiasing Techniques, pp. 336–354.

[246] These bodies collaborate with the International Investigative Interviewing Research Group (iIIRG), see <https://iirg.org/> (accessed 16 February 2023).

[247] Rikspolisstyrelsens utvärderingsfunktion (2013). Rapport 2013:7, Polisens Förhör med Misstänkta, Svensk utbildning i internationell belysning, Granhag, Strömwall & Cancino Montecinos.

[248] Powell (2002). Specialist Training in Investigative and Evidential Interviewing: Is It Having any Effect on the Behavior of Professionals in the Field, pp. 44–55.

[249] Clarke & Milne (2014). National Evaluation of the PEACE Investigative Interviewing Course, Report No. PRAS/149; McGurk, Carr, & McGurk (1993). Investigative Interviewing Courses for Police Officers: An Evaluation, Paper No. 4.

[250] Blackstock et al. (2014). Inside Police Custody: Training Framework on the Provisions of Suspects' Rights.

[251] Milne & Bull (1999). Investigative Interviewing: Psychology and Practice.

[252] Adams-Quackenbush, Horselenberg, & van Koppen (2018). Where Bias Begins: A Snapshot of Police Officers' Beliefs About Factors that Influence the Investigative Interview with Suspects, pp. 1–8.

information.[253] There must also be an acceptance that current knowledge is no longer sufficient or is actually wrongful, the new knowledge must appear plausible, and above all, the new knowledge cannot conflict with pre-existing beliefs or personally held conceptions about the topic.[254] In fact, if recipients are not ready to accept the new information as valid, presenting contradictory information can even strengthen the intensity of individually held beliefs about how interviews should be conducted.[255]

Hence, understanding to what extent the investigative interviewing framework is an effective debiasing technique requires an understanding of to what extent police officers rely on personal or pseudoscientific beliefs instead of their education and training. The prevalence of pseudoscientific beliefs relating to suspect interviews has been demonstrated in a few studies.[256] For instance, one study included 101 police officers from the Netherlands, the United Kingdom, and North America, with working experience ranging from four to 45 years, and most of which had received specialized interview training (72.3 per cent) at least once during their career.[257] The police officers were asked to indicate their agreement/disagreement with statements either consistent or contradictory with the literature on investigative interviewing.[258] This entailed statements on the three more specific themes: (i) *best practices for interviewing*, for example 'Trained officers can distinguish between truth and lies with high accuracy'; (ii) *confessions*, for example, 'Innocent people do not confess to crimes'; and)iii) *interviewee vulnerabilities*, for example, 'Hunger and poor sleep can impair judgment and decision-making in suspects'.[259] Although, overall, the survey responses were positively skewed towards agreement with literature-consistent statements, some differences appeared when the responses were analysed by theme. The majority of the sample somewhat agreed or strongly agreed with statements on confessions (62 per cent), while agreement was

---

[253] Posner et al. (1982). Accommodation of a Scientific Conception: Toward a Theory of Conceptual Change, pp. 211–227; Richardson (2016).The Role of Attitudes and Beliefs in Learning to Teach, pp. 102–119.

[254] Posner et al. (1982). Accommodation of a Scientific Conception: Toward a Theory of Conceptual Change, pp. 211–227; Richardson (2016).The Role of Attitudes and Beliefs in Learning to Teach, pp. 102–119.

[255] Batson, Rational Processing or Rationalization? (1975). The Effect of Disconfirming Information on a Stated Religious Belief, pp. 176–184; Nickerson (1998). Confirmation Bias: A Ubiquitous Phenomenon in Many Guises, pp. 175–220.

[256] Lilienfeld & Landfield (2008). Science and Pseudoscience in Law Enforcement: A User-friendly Primer, pp. 1215–1230; Adams-Quackenbush, Horselenberg, & van Koppen (2018). Where Bias Begins: A Snapshot of Police Officers' Beliefs About Factors that Influence the Investigative Interview with Suspects, pp. 1–8.

[257] Adams-Quackenbush, Horselenberg, & van Koppen (2018). Where Bias Begins: A Snapshot of Police Officers' Beliefs About Factors that Influence the Investigative Interview with Suspects, pp. 1–8.

[258] Adams-Quackenbush, Horselenbergn & van Koppen (2018). Where Bias Begins: A Snapshot of Police Officers' Beliefs About Factors that Influence the Investigative Interview with Suspects, pp. 1–8.

[259] Adams-Quackenbush, Horselenberg, & van Koppen (2018). Where Bias Begins: A Snapshot of Police Officers' Beliefs About Factors that Influence the Investigative Interview with Suspects, pp. 1–8.

a bit lower for best practices (49.5 per cent) and interviewee vulnerabilities (47.4 per cent).[260]

Although the example study outlined above demonstrates a fairly high level of agreement with literature-consistent statements, it should be noted that this was found in a sample of presumably knowledgeable officers,[261] and that lower levels of agreement have been found in other studies.[262] To the extent that pseudo-scientific beliefs are present and maintained, this is likely to disrupt the process of implementing training in investigative interviewing. Moreover, the longer a belief is held, the stronger the belief becomes.[263] Thus, implementing effective debiasing techniques can itself be hindered by a confirmation bias. This confirmation bias consists in police officers maintaining their beliefs about how an interview should be conducted, even when faced with empirical evidence to the contrary.

The beliefs in question can have many sources such as personal experience, notions that are 'inherited' from colleagues in the organization, and/or pseudoscientific or even unscientific depictions (in the media or other sources) of allegedly effective interviewing techniques.[264] For instance, according to a study conducted in 2007, some police officers believe that isolating a suspect in a small interrogation room and interrupting the suspect's denial are good interview practices for eliciting a confession, despite the numerous research studies suggesting the opposite.[265] There are also multiple possible reasons as to why these beliefs are maintained, for example because the mechanisms used to evaluate whether the beliefs are true are ineffective or misguided. This can be related to inappropriate definitions of success. To illustrate, police officers may think of (inappropriate) interviewing techniques as solid, because the techniques 'made the suspect talk', or even confess, which are not necessarily indicators of truthful suspect statements. Even if beliefs hold little or no credence outside individuals' perceptions, individuals still tend to make decisions based on their beliefs, particularly in high stress and high cognitive

---

[260] Crime Academy and Review Group, Investigative Interviewing Policy; Adams-Quackenbush, Horselenberg, & van Koppen (2018). Where Bias Begins: A Snapshot of Police Officers' Beliefs About Factors that Influence the Investigative Interview with Suspects, pp. 1–8.

[261] Adams-Quackenbush, Horselenberg, & van Koppen (2018). Where Bias Begins: A Snapshot of Police Officers' Beliefs About Factors that Influence the Investigative Interview with Suspects, p. 7.

[262] Chaplin & Shaw (2016). Confidently Wrong: Police Endorsement of Psych-Legal Misconceptions, pp. 208–216.

[263] Burns (2004). Heuristics as Beliefs and as Behaviors: The Adaptiveness of the 'Hot Hand', pp. 208–216; Marietta & Barker (2007). Values as Heuristics: Core Beliefs and Voter Sophistication in the 2000 Republican Nomination Contest, pp. 49–78.

[264] Lilienfeld & Landfield (2008). Science and Pseudoscience in Law Enforcement: A User-Friendly Primer, pp. 1215–1230; Jordan et al. (2019). A Test of the Micro-Expressions Training Tool: Does it Improve Lie Detection? Pp. 222–235; Jupe & Keatley (2020). Airport Artificial Intelligence Can Detect Deception—Or am I Lying? Pp. 1–14.

[265] Kassin et al. (2007). Police Interviewing and Interrogation: A Self-Report Survey of Police Practices and Beliefs, pp. 381–400.

load situations.[266] Under these circumstances, individuals are likely to come to their conclusions quickly and use very little of the information available to them.[267] Thus, when rapid decision-making is required, low-effort belief heuristics can override knowledge and expertise.[268] Some research has acknowledged that previous experience and heuristics can be beneficial in police investigations[269] since police officers develop a type of cognition specific to their work which facilitates fast and efficient decision-making and execution.[270] Yet, those types of cognitions can also act as a barrier to objective and logical thinking, which can lead to biased behaviour.[271] For instance, interviewers who believe that only guilty individuals confess, and who simultaneously believe that the suspect who is currently with them in the interrogation room is guilty, are more likely to push for a confession.[272] Also, police officers who rely on stereotypical, non-validated deception cues may act in accordance with these beliefs.[273] This can entail risks such as guilt-presumptive or even confrontational questioning (also in relation to innocent suspects) and/or a trusting attitude in relation to lying suspects who do not communicate any stereotypical deception cues. Hence, while investigative interviewing is known to be effective in mitigating bias, including confirmation bias, there are some attitude and adherence issues that need to be properly addressed for investigative interviewing to reach its full potential as a debiasing technique.

---

[266] Evans (2006). The Heuristic-Analytic Theory of Reasoning: Extension and Evaluation, pp. 378–395; De Neys & Glumicic (2008). Conflict Monitoring in Dual Process Theories of Thinking, pp. 1248–1299.

[267] Keinan (1987). Decision Making under Stress: Scanning of Alternatives under Controllable and Uncontrollable Threats, pp. 639–644; Trippas, Handley, & Verde (2013). The SDT Model of Belief Bias: Complexity, Time and Cognitive Ability Mediate the Effects of Believability, pp. 1393–1402; Wastell et al. (2012). Identifying Hypothesis Confirmation Behaviours in a Simulated Murder Investigation: Implications for Practice, pp. 184–198.

[268] De Neys (2011). Bias and Conflict: A Case for Logical Intuitions, pp. 23–38; Kozhevnikov & Hegarty, Impetus Beliefs as Default Heuristics: Dissociation Between Explicit and Implicit Knowledge about Motion, pp. 439–453; Shah & Oppenheimer (2008). Heuristics made Easy: An Effort-Reduction Framework, pp. 207–222.

[269] Snook & Cullen (2016). Bounded Rationality and Criminal Investigations: Has Tunnel Vision been Wrongfully Convicted? Pp. 71–89.

[270] Kahneman (2003). A Perspective on Judgment and Choice: Mapping Bounded Rationality, pp. 697–720.

[271] Kahneman (2003). A Perspective on Judgment and Choice: Mapping Bounded Rationality, pp. 697–720.

[272] Kassin (2008). False Confessions: Causes, Consequences, and Implications for Reform, pp. 112–121; Kassin, Goldstein, & Savitsky (2003). Behavioral Confirmation in the Interrogation Room: On the Dangers of Presuming Guilt, pp. 187–203; Narchet, Meissner & Russano (2011). Modeling the Influence of Investigator Bias on the Elicitation of True and False Confessions, pp. 452–465; Lidén, Gräns, & Juslin (2018). The Presumption of Guilt in Suspect Interrogations: Apprehension as a Trigger of Confirmation Bias and Debiasing Techniques, pp. 336–354.

[273] Meissner & Kassin (2002). 'He's Guilty!': Investigator Bias in Judgments of Truth and Deception, pp. 469–480; Meissner & Kassin (2015). You're Guilty, So Just Confess! Pp. 85–106; Olson (2013). 'You Don't Expect Me to Believe that, Do You?': Expectations Influence Recall and Belief of Alibi Information, pp. 1238–1247.

3.5.1.5.2 Changing decision-maker

The notion that changing the decision-maker between, for example, apprehension and interview may help reduce bias is in line with the idea that confirmation bias is a self-enhancement bias, as suggested by social psychological findings (Chapter 2.2.2.3). So far, the change of decision-maker as a debiasing technique has only been evaluated in one study addressing police interviews specifically[274] but a few more studies pertaining to other contexts.[275] In the study regarding police interviews, Swedish police officers demonstrated a somewhat stronger guilt presumption in their interview questions in relation to suspects they themselves had apprehended, compared to suspects apprehended by a police colleague or a prosecutor. Also, for police officers' ratings of how credible the suspect statement was, the decision-maker variable had significant influences as police officers perceived of the suspects they themselves had apprehended as less trustworthy than non-apprehended suspects, while such differences did not appear in relation to the prosecutor's or police colleague's decisions. Hence, while a change of decision-maker seems to hold some potential as a debiasing technique, it still needs further evaluation.

3.5.1.6 Conclusion

Statements from suspects, witnesses, and/or plaintiffs are a continuous and common element in practically all criminal cases. For some crimes, for example alleged rapes or domestic violence, they are also often the only or primary evidence available. This makes it all the more important to understand the mechanisms behind the statement, that is, how the interview was conducted. If interviewers have pushed their hypothesis about who the perpetrator is or what the more specific course of event is, there is a risk that this has significantly impacted on the statement. For example, suspects may falsely confess, witnesses may provide false testimony, and plaintiffs may decide to not collaborate as they do not feel they are well-received by the police. This poses obvious risks of both false positives and false negatives.

Investigative interviewing is the best available framework for countering biased questioning. This, however, requires not only implementation and training but also adherence in individual cases. Investigators may have own beliefs about how to best interview suspects, witnesses, and plaintiffs and be reluctant to use the investigative interviewing framework. Tackling faulty beliefs in investigators is

---

[274] Lidén, Gräns, & Juslin (2018). The Presumption of Guilt in Suspect Interrogations: Apprehension as a Trigger of Confirmation Bias and Debiasing Techniques, pp. 336–354.
[275] Lidén, Gräns, & Juslin (2018). From Devil's Advocate to Crime Fighter: Confirmation Bias and Debiasing Techniques in Prosecutorial Decision Making, pp. 494–526; Lidén, Gräns, & Juslin (2018). 'Guilty, No Doubt': Detention Provoking Confirmation Bias in Judges' Guilt Assessments and Debiasing Techniques, pp. 219–247.

thus essential for investigative interviewing to reach its full potential as a debiasing technique. This is likely to be more successful if combined with a change of decision-maker, for example between apprehending and questioning a suspect. With a decision to apprehend someone, police officers may subconsciously tend to want to defend themselves ,and/or their decision, and this can manifest in guilt-presumptive questioning. When it comes to, for example, child witnesses, there is often reason to prioritize factors such as building rapport and trust, which may require that the same individual sees the child across multiple interviews. Unlike the example with a previous arrest of a suspect, such an interviewer does not necessarily have a hypothesis about what has happened, even if such a hypothesis can of course arise for other reasons as well, for example the information provided by a parent. In this regard, it should be noted that the change of decision-maker as a debiasing technique has, so far, only been evaluated empirically with regard to suspect interviews.

3.5.2 Suspect Line-ups

3.5.2.1 Introduction
Suspect line-ups, whether they are live or based on photos, usually have the purpose of evaluating whether a guilt hypothesis can be corroborated through a witness identification of the suspect as the perpetrator. Just like in other decision-making contexts, hypothesis testing within the frames of a suspect line-up can be tainted by a hypothesis at hand. Specifically, the administrators of the line-up may, subconsciously, have created a test that can only confirm their hypothesis. This can be the case, for example, because in practice there is only one individual, the suspect, who fits the description provided by the witness, and/or because the administrator of the line-up subconsciously, through verbal or non-verbal behaviour, directs the witness to identify the individual the police believe is the suspect. Even for witnesses who have fairly good recollection of a perpetrator's physical appearance, suspect line-ups can become quite suggestive. There is a number of reasons why a line-up can become suggestive including subtle cues like going for another round if the witness fails to identify the 'right' person in the first round, or well-intended questions or comments from the line-up administrator like 'how about person number 2?' or 'are you sure?'. In such circumstances, even for witnesses who do indeed recognize an individual as the perpetrator, it will be difficult to determine whether the identification is based on the witness memory from a crime scene or if the witness simply inferred who the suspect was based on how the line-up was conducted. Not even witnesses themselves are necessarily consciously aware of this distinction; very confident witnesses are sometimes wrong. The following sections address how confirmation bias can manifest in a suspect line-up in more detail (Section 3.5.2.2) as

well as a possible bias mitigation measure, that is, to pre-test the line-up (Section 3.5.3.2.1).

3.5.2.2 Understanding Bias

> *When the resemblance was the very reason why the suspect was included in the parade, the parade could as well be omitted, since it confirms only a matter that was known from the beginning.*[276]
>
> Wagenaar, 1989

In 1976, John Demjanjuk, a factory worker from Cleveland, Ohio, was identified for the first time as 'Ivan Grozny' (Ivan the Terrible), a man who not only operated the gas chambers in the Nazi death camp near Treblinka[277] but who had also distinguished himself by his cruelty to victims.[278] From the outset, Mr Demjanjuk denied he had worked in any concentration camp. As a result, the legal procedure became to a large extent dependent upon proof of his identity. To this end, the prosecutors referred to identifications by multiple witnesses,[279] made from photo line-ups, one which can be seen in Figure 3.1.

Before being exposed to the photo line-up, some of the witnesses had stated that 'Ivan the Terrible' had a round face, a short neck and was starting to go bald.[280] Willem Albert Wagenaar, a Dutch psychologist, who was the expert witness hired by the defence in the case,[281] argued that Mr Demjanjuk was the only plausible candidate in the line-up since he was the only one who fulfilled the description provided by the witnesses. Hence, the photo line-up, rather than being an actual critical test, could only confirm the investigative hypothesis, namely that Mr Demjanjuk was 'Ivan the Terrible'.

Wagenaar based his claim on an empirical evaluation of the photo line-up conducted with mock witnesses.[282] In this evaluation, Wagenaar showed the photo line-up to mock witnesses who were instructed that '[w]e are looking for a man with a full round face, a short wide neck, a bald pate starting. We will give you a set of eight photographs: please point to the person who is most likely to be the wanted person.'

Under these conditions, all the witnesses selected Mr Demjanjuk. Thereafter, when mock witnesses were given a different photo line-up in which Mr Demjanjuk's

---

[276] Wagenaar (1988). Identifying Ivan—A Case Study in Legal Psychology, pp. 10–11.
[277] Douglas (2016). The Right Wrong Man: John Demjanjuk and the Last Great Nazi War Crimes Trial, pp. 36–38.
[278] Wagenaar (1988). Identifying Ivan—A Case Study in Legal Psychology, p. 1.
[279] Wagenaar (1988). Identifying Ivan—A Case Study in Legal Psychology, p. 4.
[280] Wagenaar (1988). Identifying Ivan—A Case Study in Legal Psychology, pp. 102–104.
[281] Ewing (2009). Minds on Trial: Great Cases in Law and Psychology, pp. 122–125.
[282] Wagenaar (1988). Identifying Ivan—A Case Study in Legal Psychology, p. 4.

Figure 4.1: Page 3 of the album. No. 16 is Demjanjuk, No. 17 is Fedorenko.

Figure 3.1 Photo line-up used for identification of 'Ivan the Terrible' with Photo No. 16 at the bottom left corner showing John Demjanjuk (1951). No copyright holder identified.

picture was interspersed with pictures of individuals who all shared the same physical characteristics as him (round face, short neck, and so on), only 8 per cent of them identified Mr Demjanjuk as 'Ivan the Terrible'. Wagenaar concluded that 'it is 100 per cent possible to guess that Demjanjuk is the target. This does not mean that the real witnesses did not recognize Demjanjuk, it only means that the photospread was not a fair lineup.'[283]

In other words, the investigators had, knowingly or unknowingly, created a test which could only confirm their hypothesis, rather than objectively evaluate it.[284] As pointed out by Wagenaar, the result of this test could neither prove that Mr Demjanjuk was nor that he was not 'Ivan the Terrible'. However, the test did demonstrate that the line-up was biased against Mr Demjanjuk and therefore entailed risks of both a false positive and a false negative. As such, a line-up in which only one individual, the suspect, fulfils the description provided by the witness, can only confirm a matter that was known from the beginning, namely that the suspect to some extent resembled the perpetrator, which clearly does not equate with guilt.

Wagenaar's empirical evaluation of the photo line-up in the Ivan the Terrible case was neither the first nor the last of its kind. In fact, Wagenaar employed a paradigm to measure the fairness of a line-up based upon mock witnesses' assessments, which had been proposed by Doob and Kirschenbaum in 1973.[285] In this paradigm, mock witnesses are provided with a verbal description of the suspect and then asked whether they can identify the suspect in the line-up. This paradigm has been an important foundation in research examining subjective influences in suspect line-ups.[286] It has also been essential for several other expert testimonies and opinions in real cases from a range of jurisdictions. This includes several high-profile cases like the identification of Abdel Basset al-Megrahi as the Lockerbie bomber by a single witness.[287] In the Lockerbie case, a Maltese shop owner, Mr Gauci, had identified Mr al-Megrahi as the person who purchased clothing allegedly packed in the suitcase that contained the explosives that blew up Pan Am Flight 103 over the residential village of Lockerbie in Scotland on 21 December 1988.[288] Mr Gauci made his first tentative identification of Mr al-Megrahi in February 1991, over two years after the clothing purchase, and later, in 1999, he also identified Mr al-Megrahi in a line-up.[289] A few months prior to the line-up, Mr Gauci had been exposed to at least one photo of Mr al-Megrahi. At this time,

---

[283] Wagenaar (1988). Identifying Ivan—A Case Study in Legal Psychology, pp. 132–133, 171–172.

[284] Technical Working Group for Eyewitness Evidence (1999). Eyewitness Evidence: A Guide for Law Enforcement, for the US context, and the Swedish National Police Board's recommendations for line-ups, Vittneskonfrontation, RPS Rapport 2005:2, p. 1.

[285] Wagenaar (1988). Identifying Ivan—A Case Study in Legal Psychology, p. 132; Wells, Leippe, & Ostrom, Guidelines for Empirically Assessing the Fairness of a Lineup, pp. 285–293.

[286] Steblay, Dysart, & Wells (2011). Seventy-two Tests of the Sequential Lineup Superiority Effect: A Meta-Analysis; Dysart & Fulero (2001). Eyewitness Accuracy Rates in Sequential and Simultaneous Lineup Presentations: A Meta-Analytic Comparison, pp. 459–473.

[287] Killgore (2009). Convicted Lockerbie Bomber Probably Not Guilty—So Who Is the Real Criminal?; Carrell (2009). Police Coached Lockerbie Witness to Identify Libyan as Bomber, Appeal Lawyers Claim.

[288] Loftus (2013). Eyewitness Testimony in the Lockerbie Bombing Case, pp. 584–590; Brown, Deffenbacher, & Sturgill (1977). Memory for Faces and the Circumstances of Encounter, pp. 311–318.

[289] Loftus (2013). Eyewitness Testimony in the Lockerbie Bombing Case, pp. 584–590.

there were also numerous 'Wanted' posters available in Libya and its neighbouring countries.[290] It is well-known that such post-event information can become incorporated into the witness's memory and cause an alteration to, distortion of, or even supplementation to the memory,[291] due to issues with source monitoring.[292] Thus, as manifested by the 'Wanted' posters, there was already a belief that Mr al-Megrahi was guilty. Due to the circumstances under which the identification was conducted, this belief was very likely to be confirmed, yet, as noted also in relation to the identification of 'Ivan the Terrible', the identification would not necessarily be correct. After Mr al-Megrahi's conviction in 2001,[293] he was released from prison in 2009 on compassionate grounds because of advancing cancer.[294] Before that, in 2007, the Scottish Criminal Cases Review Commission expressed deep reservations about the conviction and concluded that there might have been a miscarriage of justice.[295] In November 2020, approximately eight years after Mr al-Megrahi's death, Scotland's Highest Court began hearing a posthumous appeal in this case.[296] The proceedings against Mr al-Megrahi have subsequently been heavily challenged regarding their lack of fairness and impartiality.[297]

Another example of a high-profile case in which the paradigm was used to assess the fairness of a suspect line-up is the murder of Swedish prime minister Olof Palme in 1986.[298] The main suspect in this case, Christer Pettersson, was convicted[299] but then acquitted on appeal,[300] largely because the identification of Mr Pettersson, by the prime minister's wife Lisbeth Palme, was considered to have very low evidentiary value.[301] Prior to the identification, Mrs Palme had been informed that the suspect had problems with alcohol and a facial composite had circulated in the media.[302] During the line-up, the suspect stood out among the foils, due to his

---

[290] Loftus (2013). Eyewitness Testimony in the Lockerbie Bombing Case, p. 587.
[291] Loftus (2013). Eyewitness Testimony in the Lockerbie Bombing Case, p. 587.
[292] Source monitoring involves judgments regarding the origin of information, see Johnson, Hastroudi, & Lindsay (1993). Source Monitoring, pp. 3–28; Bayen (2000). The Use of Schematic Knowledge about Sources in Source Monitoring, pp. 480–500; Mastroberardino & Marucci (2013). Interrogative Suggestibility: Was it Just Compliance or a Genuine False Memory?: Interrrogative Suggestibility and Source Monitoring, pp. 274–286.
[293] Her Majesty's Advocate v. Al Megrahi, 2002.
[294] Loftus (2013). Eyewitness Testimony in the Lockerbie Bombing Case, p. 589.
[295] Oliver (2007). Libyan Granted New Appeal over Lockerbie Conviction; Adams, How the Trial of the Century Ended as our Worst Embarrassment.
[296] The New York Times (2020). Appeal in Lockerbie Bombing Reaches Scotland's Highest Court. <https://www.nytimes.com/2020/11/24/world/europe/lockerbie-bombing-megrahi-appeal-scotland.html> (accessed 17 February 2023).
[297] See, for example, Köchler (1998). Lockerbie Trial Observer Mission.
[298] The Swedish Government Official Report, SOU 1999:98 Granskningskommissionens Betänkande, Brottsutredningen efter Mordet på Statsminister Olof Palme.
[299] Stockholm District Court, Case No. B 847/88.
[300] Svea Court of Appeal, Case No. 1952/89.
[301] The Swedish Government Official Report, SOU 1999:98 Granskningskommissionens Betänkande, Brottsutredningen efter Mordet på Statsminister Olof Palme, pp. 727–737.
[302] Granskningskommissionens betänkande, Brottsutredningen efter Mordet på Statsminister Olof Palme, SOU 1999:88, pp. 736–738.

physical appearance and outfit.[303] This became evident in Mrs Palme's comment while observing the line-up, namely that the identity of the perpetrator was 'plain as day' to her.[304] Mrs Palme also maintained that she was certain about her identification over the course of time.[305] In its acquittal, the Court of Appeal referred to a report from the so-called Devlin Committee, which was based on observations from two wrongful convictions following false identifications in the 1970s in the United Kingdom.[306] According to this report, as well as sound and replicated research on the topic, even witnesses who themselves are convinced they have identified the perpetrator are often wrong.[307] After 34 years of investigation into the murder of Mr Palme, and the passing away of both the defendant and Mrs Palme, the Chief Prosecutor concluded that the real perpetrator was probably someone else, Mr Engström, and since also Mr Engström was now deceased, the investigation was closed.[308]

The examples of high-profile cases in which dubious and biased line-ups were used are numerous and while not dealt with in detail here, will only be mentioned for the interested reader. These include the cases of Barry George, convicted but then acquitted of the murder of British TV presenter Jill Dando who was shot on the doorstep of her home,[309] and Omar Deghayes, a British resident detained in Guantanamo Bay.[310] These examples highlight the fact that bias in identification procedures has close ties to false positives but also to false negatives, and there is no reliable way of distinguishing between the two.

In line with recommendations on how to conduct such line-ups, all individuals included should, in terms of physical appearance, meet the description provided by a witness prior to the line-up.[311] This is to avoid witnesses making relative judgments ('who looks most like the perpetrator?') and instead involve themselves in absolute judgments ('do I recognize this person as the perpetrator?'). Clearly, in line-ups where the perpetrator is absent, relative judgments can result in suspects

---

[303] Granskningskommissionens betänkande, Brottsutredningen efter Mordet på Statsminister Olof Palme, SOU 1999:88, pp. 736–738.

[304] Granskningskommissionens betänkande, Brottsutredningen efter Mordet på Statsminister Olof Palme, SOU 1999:88, p. 730. Translation from Swedish ('helt klar') to English ('plain as day').

[305] Lindström (2018). Lisbet Palme var Säker på vem Mördaren var, Granskningskommissionens betänkande, Brottsutredningen efter Mordet på Statsminister Olof Palme, SOU 1999:88, pp. 727–736.

[306] Lord Devlin, Report to the Secretary of State for the Home Department of the Departmental Committee on Evidence of Identification in Criminal Cases, Home Office 1976.

[307] Lord Devlin, Report to the Secretary of State for the Home Department of the Departmental Committee on Evidence of Identification in Criminal Cases, Home Office 1976.

[308] See for example the Swedish Police Authority's webpage, <https://polisen.se/om-polisen/polisens-arbete/palmeutredningen/> (accessed 17 February 2023). The Swedish Parliamentary Ombudsmen (2021). The Parliamentary Ombudsman's Review of the Prosecutor's Report at the Press Conference on the Palme Investigation.

[309] Roberts (2003). The Perils and Possibilities of Qualified Identification: R v George, pp. 130–136.

[310] Stafford Smith (2005). From Brighton to Camp Delta, pp. 19–24.

[311] Technical Working Group for Eyewitness Evidence (1999). Eyewitness Evidence: A Guide for Law Enforcement, for the US context, and the Swedish National Police Board's recommendations for line-ups, Vittneskonfrontation, RPS Rapport 2005:2.

who resemble the perpetrator, and who were included in the line-up on that basis (alone or together with other evidence), are wrongfully identified as perpetrators. While such identifications can easily be confused with confirmation of a guilt hypothesis, it is in fact just confirmation of what was already known, that is, that the suspect resembles the perpetrator, reiterating again Wagenaar's conclusion in the 'Ivan the Terrible' case. This distinction is crucial as in such situations, police officers may feel validated that they have designed and conducted a line-up that critically evaluates, and confirms, their guilt hypothesis, while in fact they have designed a line-up that is only capable of confirming their guilt hypothesis without any critical evaluation. As previously acknowledged, designing tests that can only confirm a guilt hypothesis is a manifestation of confirmation bias, and a dangerous one as it is likely to make investigators 'feel validated' while not necessarily 'being correct'.[312]

Research on suspect line-ups illustrate that when line-up administrators, for example police officers, are aware of the suspect's identity, they will, unknowingly, construct and conduct a line-up which is more likely to result in a positive identification of the suspect than if the administrator had been blind to the suspect's identity.[313] Studies also confirm that an administrator's knowledge can result in that witnesses are more likely to identify the suspect.[314] Importantly, this is true also for target-absent line-ups, that is, when the suspect is innocent and the real perpetrator is not in the line-up at all.[315] The reason for this is likely to be *hypothesis leakage*, that is, that the administrator, subconsciously, leaks the hypothesis to the witness, who is then more likely to identify the suspect as the perpetrator.[316] This was apparent in a study in which participants acting as criminal investigators administered a line-up with ignorant witnesses.[317] Half of the participants administering the line-up were told who the suspect was and the other half was not. All administrators used the same scripted instructions and none of them explicitly and consciously told the witnesses who the suspect was. However, the suspect was more than twice as likely to be identified when the administrator was aware of the suspect's identity (25 per cent) compared to when the administrator did not know

---

[312] Hart et al. (2009). Feeling Validated Versus Being Correct: A Meta-Analysis of Selective Exposure to Information, pp. 555–588.

[313] Greathouse & Kovera (2009). Instruction Bias and Lineup Presentation Moderate the Effects of Administrator Knowledge on Eyewitness Identification, pp. 70–82; Rodriguez (2014). The Effect of Line-up Administrator Blindness on the Recording of Eyewitness Identification Decisions, pp. 69–79.

[314] Philips et al. (1999). Double-blind Photoarray Administration as a Safeguard against Investigator Bias, pp. 940–951; Haw & Fisher (2004). Effects of Administrator-witness Contact on Eyewitness Identification Accuracy, pp. 1106–1112.

[315] Philips et al. (1999). Double-blind Photoarray Administration as a Safeguard against Investigator Bias, pp. 940–951; Haw & Fisher (2004). Effects of Administrator-witness Contact on Eyewitness Identification Accuracy, pp. 1106–1112.

[316] Greathouse & Kovera (2009). Instruction Bias and Lineup Presentation Moderate the Effects of Administrator Knowledge on Eyewitness Identification, pp. 70–82.

[317] Canter, Hammond, & Youngs (2013). Cognitive Bias in Line-up Identifications: The Impact of Administrator Knowledge, pp. 83–88.

(10.83 per cent). This was probably because the administrators subconsciously conveyed information about the suspect's identity through their behaviour, which enabled witnesses to draw conclusions about who the suspect was.

The effect of such hypothesis leakage is likely to vary with the witness' susceptibility to leading information.[318] On a general level, there is no doubt that witness identifications are sensitive to external influences.[319] Also, the manifestations of an administrator's knowledge can be more or less subtle, such as verbal cues like 'what about this picture over here?' or 'have a careful look at number', which direct the focus towards a particular person in the line-up, or, 'take another look and make sure he's the one', encouraging a witness to reconsider or even reject their previous identification decision.[320] Thus, knowledgeable administrators may ask the witness questions about the line-up members that will confirm the administrators' hypothesis that the suspect is the perpetrator but not questions that will (or potentially could) disprove this hypothesis.[321] Non-verbal cues like various facial gestures (frowning, rolling the eyes, smiling, etc.) or body movements (folding the arms, nodding the head, leaning toward or away from the witness etc.) may also be influential.[322] Yet another cue that seems to increase the likelihood of errors is if the administrator decides to 'try again', that is, to initiate a second lap if the witness could not identify the suspect in the first lap.[323] Hence, a line-up administrator's verbal and non-verbal behaviour, which on the surface may seem harmless or even helpful and encouraging to the witness, may impact upon whether and who the witness chooses to identify.[324] Thus, a test aiming objectively to evaluate whether a guilt hypothesis is true may in fact bias the witness due to the police's subconscious information transfer. As Krane and colleagues point out, this may occur regardless of the best intentions of the criminal investigator.[325] This is also the reason why it is often recommended that the investigator

---

[318] Murphy & Greene (2016). Perceptual Load Affects Eyewitness Accuracy and Susceptibility to Leading Questions, pp. 1–10.
[319] Wells (1988). Eyewitness Identification Procedures: Recommendations for Line-ups and Photospreads, pp. 1–39; Wells et al. (2000). From the Lab to a Police station: a Successful Application of Eyewitness Research, pp. 581–598.
[320] Philips et al. Double-blind Photoarray Administration as a Safeguard against Investigator Bias, pp. 940–951.
[321] Greathouse & Kovera (2009). Instruction Bias and Lineup Presentation Moderate the Effects of Administrator Knowledge on Eyewitness Identification, pp. 70–82.
[322] Philips et al. Double-blind Photoarray Administration as a Safeguard against Investigator Bias, pp. 940–951.
[323] Lidén (2023). 'That's Him!' Evaluating a Guilt Hypothesis in the Context of a Suspect Lineup. In Bystranowski, Janik & Próchnicki (Eds) Judicial Decision-Making: Integrating Empirical and Theoretical Persepctives (pp. 49–78).
[324] Clark, Marshall, & Rosenthal (2009). Line-up Administrator Influences on Eyewitness Identification Decisions, pp. 63–75.
[325] Krane (2008). Sequential Unmasking: A Means of Minimizing Observer Effects in Forensic DNA Interpretation, pp. 1006–1007.

who administers the line-up should be blind to the suspect's identity.[326] However, in practice this might be difficult, at least in small communities where most police officers are involved in the case in one sense or the other. Also, there are still several unanswered questions as regards how confirmation bias may manifest itself in suspect line-ups. For example, it is unknown whether confirmation bias may influence choices regarding presentation method (e.g. simultaneous versus sequential)[327] and line-up composition.[328]

3.5.2.3 Mitigating Bias
3.5.2.3.1 Pre-testing the line-up

While today there are recommendations for line-ups based on psychological research in several jurisdictions, compliance rates are largely unknown. In fact, figures from, for example, the different US-based Innocence Projects indicate that compliance may still be relatively low, since wrongful witness identifications seem to have played a role in over 70 per cent of wrongful convictions which were later overturned through DNA testing.[329] A likely contributing factor to this is that law enforcement agencies, despite available recommendations, have limited knowledge of factors that can influence eyewitness memory and identifications, and such tendencies have been found in a range of jurisdictions including, for example, the United States,[330] the United Kingdom,[331] Canada,[332] Sweden,[333] and

---

[326] The Swedish National Police Board's recommendations for line-ups, Vittneskonfrontation, RPS Rapport 2005:2, p. 20.

[327] Steblay et al. (2001). Eyewitness Accuracy Rates in Sequential and Simultaneous Lineup Presentations: A Meta-anaytic Comparison, pp. 459–447; Steblay, Dysart, & Wells (2011). Seventy-two Tests of the Sequential Lineup Superiority Effect: A Meta-analysis and Policy Discussion, pp. 99–139; Sporer (1995). Choosing, Confidence, and Accuracy: A Meta-analysis of the Confidence-accuracy Relation in Eyewitness Identification Studies, pp. 315–327; Willmott & Sherretts (2016). Individual Differences in Eyewitness Identification Accuracy between Sequential and Simultaneous Line-ups: Consequences for Police Practice and Jury Decision, pp. 228–239.

[328] Behrman & Richards (2005). Suspect/foil Identification in Actual Crimes and in the Laboratory: A Reality Monitoring Analysis, pp. 279–301; Horry et al. (2012). Predictors of Eyewitness Identification Decisions from Video Lineups in England: A Field Study, pp. 257–265; Meissner & Brighman (2001). Thirty Years of Investigating the Own-race Bias in Memory for Faces: A Meta-analytic Review, pp. 3–35; Porter, Moss, & Reisberg (2014). The Appearance-Change Instruction Does Not Improve Line-up Identification Accuracy, pp. 151–160.

[329] The Innocence Project, <https://www.innocenceproject.org/causes/eyewitness-misidentification/2023> (accessed 17 February 2023); Valentine & Heaton (1999). An Evaluation of the Fairness of Police Line-Ups And Video Identifications, pp. 59–72.

[330] Benton et al. (2006). Eyewitness Memory is Still Not Common Sense: Comparing Jurors, Judges and Law Enforcement to Eyewitness Experts, pp. 115–129; Wogalter, Malpass, & McQuiston (2004). A National Survey of US Police on Preparation and Conduct of Identification Lineups, pp. 69–82.

[331] Kebbell & Milne (1998). Police Officers' Perception of Eyewitness Performance in Forensic Investigations, pp. 323–330.

[332] Winterdyk (1988). Canadian Police Officers and Eyewitness Evidence: A Time for Reform, pp. 175–191.

[333] Granhag, Strömwall, & Hartwig (2005). Eyewitness Testimony: Tracing the Beliefs of Swedish Legal Professionals, pp. 709–727.

Taiwan.[334] The reasons for this may be several. It could be that the recommendations have not been implemented, and several studies point to this risk.[335] Yet, it could also be that, despite implementation and sometimes substantial judicial reform, police officers still have limited knowledge and understanding of factors that may bias line-ups and/or do not incorporate such knowledge in their work. Some studies confirm this risk.[336] In fact, the risk has been illustrated not only in the United States but also in Canada,[337] China,[338] and Taiwan.[339] For example, in Canada, police officers showed limited understanding of eyewitness factors, with average scores of 61 per cent, with lower percentages noted in other jurisdictions. For yet other jurisdictions, information is lacking.[340] Hence, in this chapter, a step-by-step guide is provided on how to screen the line-up for bias. If this guide is followed, it functions as a debiasing technique as it allows investigators to adjust the line-up before witness are exposed to it. Importantly, this provides protection both against false positives and false negatives. For example, if it is ensured that foils also meet the standard description, an identification of the suspect is more likely to be based on recognition from the actual crime scene or other places of interest rather than a relative judgment of resemblance, decreasing the risk of a false positive. Likewise, a witness identification made under such circumstances is less likely to be disapproved in court due to bias in the line-up. Clearly, this is essential when the witness has in fact identified the right person as the perpetrator, in order to avoid false negatives. Thus, to allow for bias mitigation in line-ups, Steps 1 to 3 should be undertaken before the line-up is shown to witnesses.

Step 1: Establishing the baseline for a balanced line-up To assess whether a line-up is biased, the line-up needs to be related to a baseline. This baseline is an effective comparison since it outlines what the outcome would have been in a fair and unbiased line-up. Thus, comparing the line-up to the baseline will enable detection and removal of any potential bias.

---

[334] Huang & Shih (2020). The Good, the Bad and the Ugly of Eyewitness Identification Practice in Police Officers—A Self-Report Survey Study, pp. 1–22.

[335] Police Executive Research Forum (2013). A National Survey of Eyewitness Identification Procedures in Law Enforcement Agencies.

[336] Wise, Safer, & Maro (2011). What US Law Enforcement Officers Know and Believe about Eyewitness Factors, Eyewitness Interviews and Identification Procedures, pp. 488–500; Technical Working Group for Eyewitness Evidence (1999). Eyewitness Evidence: A Guide for Law Enforcement; Wogalter, Malpass, & McQuiston (2004). A National Survey of US Police on Preparation and Conduct of Identification Lineups, pp. 69–82.

[337] Fraser et al. (2013). Is the Accuracy of Eyewitness Testimony Common Knowledge?, pp. 498–510.

[338] Jiang & Luo (2016). Legal Professionals' Knowledge of Eyewitness Testimony in China: A Cross-Sectional Survey.

[339] Huang & Shih (2020). The Good, the Bad and the Ugly of Eyewitness Identification Practice in Police Officers—A Self-Report Survey Study, pp. 1–22.

[340] Clarke et al. (2011). Interviewing Suspects of Crime: The Impact of PEACE Training, Supervision and the Presence of a Legal Advisor.

How the baseline is established depends on the number of individuals included in the line-up, counting the suspect as well as the fillers. This number is used to determine the distribution of identifications (in percentage terms) that would be expected among naïve observers, if the line-up was perfectly balanced. For example, in a line-up with eight individuals who all meet the description provided by the witness the expected distribution of identifications should be:

100 ÷ 8 individuals
= 12.50 % for each individual

Thus, in a perfectly balanced line-up, in which all individuals fulfil the description provided by the witness, naïve observers should not have any reason to identify one of the individuals more than any other. This means that, if the line-up is perfectly balanced, 12.5 per cent of the naïve observers will identify each individual, including the suspect.

However, a *perfectly* balanced line-up may be difficult to accomplish in practice. This is because there might be characteristics of the individuals, other than those described by the witness, which make them more likely to be identified as a perpetrator than someone else. This can be due to, for example, stereotypical ideas about what a person with a criminal lifestyle looks like. In fact, if a line-up is perfectly balanced, with identical numbers of identifications for each individual, one could argue that the task has been made too difficult for the witness. All the individuals included in the line-up are so similar to the perpetrator that the witness will have great difficulty distinguishing them from one another. It is therefore reasonable to accept deviations from perfect balance, but the question is: how much deviation can be accepted? This question will be dealt with in the next step.

Step 2: Evaluation with naïve observers Table 3.2 exemplifies three different outcomes using the same example of a line-up including eight individuals, as in Step 1. Here it is assumed that 100 naïve observers are recruited and asked whether they can identify the person who is most likely to be the suspect. For example, in his test in the Ivan the Terrible case (Section 3.5.2), Wagenaar instructed his participants in the following way: 'We are looking for a man with a full round face, a short wide neck, a bald pate starting. We will give you a set of eight photographs: please point to the person who is most likely to be the wanted person.'

Depending on how many of the naïve observers identify the suspect, as opposed to fillers, it is possible to get an idea of whether the line-up is biased towards identifying the suspect.

For example, with Outcome 1 illustrated in Table 3.2, 60 per cent of the observers identified the suspect (No. 3). This is 47.50 per cent more than what would be

Table 3.2 Examples of possible outcomes with distribution of identifications by naïve observers (%) and deviations from perfect balance (%) in a line-up with eight individuals.

Outcome		Individual (No. in the Line-up)							
		1	2	3	4	5	6	7	8
1	Identifications by naïve observers (%)	1	10	60	15	2	3	8	1
	Deviation from 12.50	−11.5	−2.5	+47.5	+2.5	−10.5	9.5	−4.5	−11.5
2	Identifications by naïve observers (%)	5	20	25	20	2	25	2	1
	Deviation from 12.50	−7.5	+7.5	+12.5	+7.5	−10.5	+12.5	−10.5	−11.5
3	Identifications by naïve observers (%)	13	14	18	15	18	11	9	2
	Deviation from 12.50	+0.5	+1.5	+5.5	+2.5	+5.5	−1.5	−.3.5	−10

Note: Individual no. 3 is here presumed to be the suspect and the remaining individuals are foils.

expected had the line-up been perfectly balanced. Hence, this outcome demonstrates quite a clear bias against the suspect. There has not really been any other plausible candidate. The suspect stands out. An outcome like this would require a change of foils, inclusion of foils that match the description of the perpetrator better, and then a retest with the new foils.

With Outcome 2 it seems that this line-up, as it is constructed now, has really only been about four individuals, Nos 2, 3, 4, and 6, who were all identified by 20 per cent or 25 per cent of the naïve observers. This is clearly better than Outcome 1 but with four individuals, the chances of 'getting it right' (identifying the suspect) by just guessing, that is, without any recollection from the crime scene whatsoever, is 25 per cent (100/4). The diagnosticity of this test can therefore be challenged on good grounds. Hence, also in a situation like this the foils should be replaced with individuals who are more similar in appearance to the suspect.

Outcome 3 is clearly the best outcome out of the three. Even though there are more (5.5 per cent) identifications of the suspect than with a perfect balance, this is unlikely to be a problem as several of the other individuals (Nos 1, 2, 4, and 5) were identified more often than expected. Some of the individuals (Nos 6, 7, and 8) were identified less frequently than expected but, with exception of No. 8, but these deviations were small (−1.5 per cent and 3.5 per cent). It therefore seems that out of eight individuals, seven were considered plausible alternatives by the naïve observers. With an outcome like this, the line-up is so close to being perfectly balanced that it should be considered ready to be tested with witnesses. Ultimately, exactly how balanced a suspect line-up should be for it to be used with the real witness is a decision for investigators to make. There is no general consensus among researchers on this topic but in the opinion of this author, outcomes that are the same or similar to Outcome 3 can be accepted, whereas Outcomes 1 and 2 cannot. However, should any suspicion of bias still be present after the line-up has been conducted with witnesses, this possibility can be effectively discussed in relation to the collected data and also included in the case material and presented in court. This is a transparent approach which enables the best possible preconditions for the court's evaluation of the evidence.

Step 3: Replacing foils and retesting the line-up if necessary If outcomes such as Outcome 1 or 2, or worse, are obtained, foils should be replaced and the line-up evaluated anew until an acceptable balance is obtained. Also, to provide courts with the best available information, the result of such evaluations should be included in the case file and presented in court to illustrate the fact that measures have been undertaken to counter bias in the line-up.

Only after completing Steps 1 to 3 should the real witness take part in the line-up. The benefits of following this procedure, prior to exposing a witness to a line-up, are both that the risks of false positive and negatives can be empirically evaluated and the line-up adjusted accordingly, and that any claims of bias arising, for example, during court proceedings can be evaluated and discussed in a more informed and detailed way, thus ensuring a sound basis for evaluation of the line-up evidence by the court.

3.5.2.4 Conclusion

Suspect line-ups can be fairly persuasive evidence, especially with witnesses stating a high level of confidence in their identifications, yet there are also multiple cases, including high-profile cases, in which witnesses have identified individuals as perpetrators but it later turns out that the witnesses, most probably, were wrong. Confirmation bias in the process of conducting the line-up is a contributing factor to errors. More research is still needed into how a hypothesis at hand may impact on, for example, the choice of foils and type of line-up. Yet hypothesis leakage from an administrator who is aware of the suspect's identity seems to suggest that the administrator can, even subtly, affect a witness' decision in important ways. Specifically, with an administrator who is aware of the suspect's identity, the odds (or risk from the suspect's point of view) that the suspect will be identified as the perpetrator increase significantly, compared to when the administrator is unaware of the suspect's identity. Apart from following available guidelines based on memory and witness psychology, including only to use naïve administrators, an effective debiasing technique is to pre-test the line-up. This will enable detection of even subtle aspects of the line-up, not least the choice of foils, that can cause the line-up to be biased towards the suspect. To conduct such a pre-test enables adjustments and measures to prevent a witness identification being dismissed as unreliable in court due to how the line-up was conducted.

3.5.3 Crime Scene Investigations

3.5.3.1 Introduction

Crime scenes can entail vastly different types of environments ranging from a residential home subjected to domestic burglary to a public place left in chaos following a bomb blast as part of a terrorist attack. Resulting from this large variation there is corresponding variation regarding who will attend the scene, when, with what resources, what primary objectives, and under which more specific circumstances the work is being conducted. Furthermore, crime scene investigators (CSIs) and other first responders will react differently depending on the context. Their reactions may include, for example, different levels of arousal (a state of alertness and of responsiveness to stimuli).[341] Also, different contexts will put different time pressures on the CSIs,[342] depending on whether, for example, there are any remaining external threats present. CSIs susceptibility to confirmation bias will vary with such physiological and emotional components since. Overall feelings of fear[343] and anxiety[344] seem to exacerbate confirmation bias. There is also individual variation in emotion awareness and regulation,[345] but this is not necessarily related to bias susceptibility.[346] However, overall, different scenes are likely to be associated with different emotional reactions, both in terms of quality and intensity. Therefore, different scenes also constitute different starting points when it comes to the risk of confirmation bias.[347]

---

[341] Law & Martin (2020). Concise Medical Dictionary.

[342] Ask & Granhag (2007). Motivational Bias in Criminal Investigators' Judgments of Witness Reliability, pp. 561–591; Hernandez and Preston (2013). Disfluency Disrupts the Confirmation Bias, pp. 178–182; Salman, Turhan, & Vegas (2019). A Controlled Experiment on Time Pressure and Confirmation Bias in Functional Software Testing, pp. 1727–1761.

[343] Almazrouei, Dror, & Morgan (2020). Organizational and Human Factos Affecting Forensic Decision Making: Workplace Stress and Feedback, pp. 1968–1977; Ask & Granhag (2006). Hot Cognition in Investigative Judgments: The Differential Influence of Sadness and Anger; Ask & Granhag (2005). Motivational Sources of Confirmation Bias in Criminal Investigations: The need for Cognitive Closure, pp. 43–63.

[344] Ask & Granhag (2006). Hot Cognition in Investigative Judgments: The Differential Influence of Anger and Sadness, p. 548; Rosansky et al. (2019). PTSD Symptoms Experiences and Coping Tactics Used by Investigators in the United States, pp. 1444–1450.

[345] See, for example, Goldberg et al. (2016). Inter-individual Variability in Emotion Regulation: Pathways to Obsessive-compulsive Symptoms, pp. 105–112.

[346] Subic-Wrana et al. (2014). Levels of Emotional Awareness Scale, pp. 176–181; Lidén, Gräns, & Juslin (2018). 'Guilty, No Doubt': Detention Provoking Confirmation Bias in Judges' Guilt Assessments.

[347] Dror (2017). Human Expert Performance in Forensic Decision Making: Seven Different Sources of Bias, p. 544.

For example, when it comes to high volume crimes such as burglary, attending the crime scene is not necessarily a top priority as it is usually one among other more pressing matters, and if and when the scene is attended, it will usually not expose CSIs to any immediate dangers. In these situations, CSIs will probably be able to remain relatively calm most of the time, although they may of course experience some stress due, for example, to expectations from plaintiffs who are present at the scene, looking over the CSIs' shoulders as they collect traces.[348] It can also be due to more general unrealistic beliefs about what can be accomplished through forensic analysis of the collected traces, often referred to as the 'CSI-effect'.[349] It is also likely that the selection of traces following a domestic burglary is relatively restricted by applicable guidelines, for example that only a very limited number of DNA swabs or fingerprints can be forensically analysed. Due to such resource limitations as well as notions about what type of traces typically have the potential of carrying the investigation forward, the frame for trace collection on domestic burglary scenes is fairly narrow. This is all rather different from, for example, scenes of suspected terrorist attacks. For this latter type of scene, the practitioners who attend, apart from the CSIs, are often first responders such as the military, the fire department, and police, and attending this scene will, most probably, be an immediate priority for them. Even if practitioners attending such scenes are professional, well trained, and experienced, they may still, like all other humans, experience fear and panic. CSIs in a range of jurisdictions have had to deal with scenes after terrorist attacks. Apart from the Ayyash et al. case in Lebanon in 2005, this also includes cases like the London bombings in 2005 (Section 3.2.1), the Breivik case in Norway in 2011,[350] the attack on the Westgate shopping mall in Nairobi in 2013,[351] and the Paris attacks in 2015.[352] In such situations, the top priorities may not be to collect traces but rather to rescue victims in immediate danger and secure the scene to curb the risk of further attacks, fires, and so on. Under these conditions, it is unsurprising that even usually relatively simple standard procedures may fail. This includes, for example, failure to put up crime scene tape[353] or to use appropriate protective clothing.[354] Blunders can also be made; for example essential evidence might be removed from the scene, due to thoughtlessness, insufficient training, and/or stress.[355] Regardless of whether there are any such major sources

---

[348] Kruse (2015). The Social Life of Forensic Evidence, p. 97.
[349] Cole (2015). A Surfeit of Science: The 'CSI Effect' and the Media Appropriation of the Public Understanding of Science, pp. 130–146; Cole & Dioso-Villa (2007). CSI and Its Effects: Media, Juries and the Burden of Proof, pp. 435–469.
[350] Oslo District Court, TOSLO-2011-188627-24.
[351] BBC, Kenya Westgate Mall Attack: What We Know, The Milimani Court in Nairobi.
[352] Ben-Ezra et al. (2017). Psychological Reactions Following the November 2015 Paris Attacks: Perceiving the World as Unjust and Unsafe.
[353] Ayyash et al. Case, Trial Chamber, STL-11-01/T/TC, § 1075.
[354] Ayyash et al. Case, Trial Chamber, STL-11-01/T/TC, § 1075.
[355] Ayyash et al. Case, Trial Chamber, STL-11-01/T/TC, § 1101.

of contamination or not, the outcome is also strongly dependent on whether and to what extent CSIs are able to investigate the scene independently of already formed hypotheses about what might have happened. Hence, the following sections address specifically how confirmation bias can impact the result of a crime scene investigation (Section 3.5.3) as well as possible mitigation strategies like contextual information management (Section 3.5.3.3.1), including multiple CSIs (Section 3.5.3.3.2), using structured strategies for trace collection (Section 3.5.3.3.3) and advanced technology (Section 3.5.3.3.4).

3.5.3.2 Understanding Bias

It is crucial to think of crime scene investigations not only as the actual collection of traces on the scene but also what happens before and after evidence collection. Notably, of these three stages, the evidence collection at the scene is the one that has received most scientific attention and evaluation in relation to the risk of confirmation bias. However, evidence collection is necessarily intertangled with the stages before and after the investigation. All three stages entail complex human judgments, sometimes under time pressure and/or with knowledge of limited investigative resources, and so on. Hence, in the following, confirmation bias will be discussed in relation to all three stages. The stages have been labelled somewhat differently by different researchers but all essentially refer to what happens in:

Stage (1) *Before the crime scene investigation*; involving decisions such as whether a crime is believed to have been committed at all, what crime, whether and when to attend the crime scene, using which resources, etc.,

Stage (2) *During the crime scene investigation*; examination and collection of traces at the crime scene, involving selection based on applicable guidelines as well as the perceived relevance and usefulness of traces; that is, the capacity of the trace to become useful evidence.

Stage (3) *After the crime scene investigation*; this stage is often referred to as *triage*, a process usually taking place away from the crime scene, for example at a police station. This involves assessments of which of the collected traces should be prioritized and sent for forensic analyses.[356] Also these assessments are based on the perceived relevance and usefulness of the traces as well as guidelines dictating, for example, how many DNA analyses can be run for a certain type of crime.[357]

---

[356] Baechler (2016). Study of Criteria Influencing the Success Rate of DNA Swabs in Operational Conditions: A Contribution to an Evidence-based Approach to Crime Scene Investigation and Triage, pp. 130–139; Pearson & Watson (2010). Digital Triage Forensics: Processing the Digital Crime Scene.
[357] There is ongoing research into the effect of this knowledge of limited resources on the selection and prioritization of traces while at the scene; see Lidén & Almazrouei (2021). Blood, Bucks and Bias: Reliability and Biasability of Crime Scene Investigators' Selection and Prioritization of Blood Traces.

In principle, these three stages are clearly separated over time. The decision to attend the scene precedes the actual attendance of the scene and the triaging decisions occur after the completion of the scene investigation. Yet, in practice, the stages are necessarily intertwined, for example because crime scene attendance and prioritization have decisive influences on the later stages. When scenes are not attended at all or attended using inadequate resources, the result can be a complete absence of physical traces. It can also be that deprioritized traces cannot be recovered as the scene has been released or, if an officer without appropriate forensic background has collected the traces, that the integrity of the traces is at risk (due to, for example, cross-contamination).[358] Similarly, the choices made during the investigation of the scene are oriented not only by what type of crime is suspected to have occurred, as decided before entering the scene, but also by the knowledge of what and how many analyses will be possible,[359] as decided after investigating the scene on the basis of applicable guidelines, and so on. Importantly, what guidelines are applicable will often depend on the initial preliminary categorization of the event as one or other crime.[360] This provides a constant link between the three stages. Being aware that limited resources will be dedicated to a case afterwards may impact on the decision-making during the actual collection of traces.

Before a crime scene is attended (Stage 1), the possibility of a crime having been committed, or is still being committed, is communicated somehow to, for example, emergency call responders or law enforcement personnel. This initial communication could entail anything from a phone call from homeowners who have returned after vacation and realized that someone broke into their home, to more urgent calls for help from people who have just witnessed a bomb blast. Regardless of how the possible crime is reported, it will always require an assessment on the part of the recipient, often a very rapid assessment, of what has happened and, based on that, what is the appropriate response. While such early assessments are thus required to enable effective decision-making and action, they are also sometimes premature and too specific given the limited information available at the time. Most importantly, reported incidents are regularly categorized as specific crimes at very early stages.[361] Such categorizations provide police officers, first responders, and other involved practitioners with contextual information that, for example, enables them to assess the urgency of attending the scene, whether there may be any immediate

---

[358] United Nationals Office on Drugs and Crime (UNODC) (2009). Crime Scene and Physical Evidence Awareness for Non-forensic Personnel.

[359] Lidén & Almazrouei (2023). Blood, Bucks and Bias: Reliability and Biasability of Crime Scene Investigators' Selection and Prioritization of Blood Traces.

[360] Ibid. These are preliminary findings in an ongoing research study, see Lidén & Almazrouei (2021). Blood, Bucks and Bias: Reliability and Biasability of Crime Scene Investigators' Selection and Prioritization of Blood Traces.

[361] van den Eeden, de Poot, & van Koppen (2017). From Emergency Call to Crime Scene: Information Transference in the Criminal Investigation, pp. 79–89.

threats still present at the scene, as well as what kind of traces may need to be collected. Also, across many jurisdictions,[362] such categorizations will also make different crime specific protocols applicable.[363] Such protocols impact on how crime scene investigations are conducted since they outline, based on experience from previous cases and with varying degrees of scientific support, which traces to collect and how many can be sent for forensic analysis, just one aspect among many a given protocol may cover. Also, the initial assessment of the gravity of the crime is directly relevant to which resources are allocated, when, by whom, how many investigators should attend, and so on. Hence, while an initial categorization is by necessity formed on limited information, it simultaneously sets the frame for the entire investigation.[364] Arguably, this constitutes a confirmation bias in itself. More specifically, from the initial report comes an initial hypothesis about what has happened and this dictates which protocols to be applied should the hypothesis be true. Hence, this builds on the logic 'If the hypothesis is true, what traces do we expect to find? And how should we work to find them?' Such strategies for scene investigations have similarities with the confirmation strategy which Wason discovered in the 1960s among his participants who were faced with the '2-4-6 task' (Chapter 2.2).[365] As a reminder, Wason noted that most participants generated a series of numbers that potentially could confirm their hypothesis of what the rule was, while far fewer generated numbers that were inconsistent with the rule and therefore potentially could falsify their hypothesis.[366] Before even beginning a crime scene investigation it is impossible to know what will be found on the scene as well as whether or not forensic analyses will confirm initial categorizations/information. It could therefore be argued that even using such a strategy will enable disconfirmation, yet notably, Wason's participants were unaware of future results. This is in no way required for a confirmation bias to be at play. To falsify a hypothesis, it is not necessarily sufficient that, for example, a forensic test has a negative outcome; the DNA found on the crime scene may not be a match with a suspect, but investigators can still maintain their beliefs that this is the case. Rather, falsifying a hypothesis requires more active evaluation. In other words, it is about asking questions like 'If this hypothesis is incorrect, what evidence would we expect to find? If an alternative hypothesis is correct, what evidence would we expect to find?' Hence, to incorporate such active falsification attempts is largely left to the

---

[362] The National Forensic Science Technology Center (NFSTC) (2013). Crime Scene Investigation—A Guide for Law Enforcement; The Association of Chief Police Officers (ACPO) (2006). Murder investigation manual; Polisens Metodstöd för Utredning av Grova Våldsbrott (PUG).
[363] Lidén & Almazrouei (2021). Blood, Bucks and Bias: Reliability and Biasability of Crime Scene Investigators' Selection and Prioritization of Blood Traces.
[364] van den Eeden, de Poot, & van Koppen (2017). From Emergency Call to Crime Scene: Information Transference in the Criminal Investigation, pp. 79–89.
[365] Wason (1960). On the Failure to Eliminate Hypotheses in a Conceptual Task, pp. 129–140.
[366] Wason (1960). On the Failure to Eliminate Hypotheses in a Conceptual Task, pp. 129–140.

individual CSIs attending the scene. In practice, these CSIs will often be limited by the initial categorization/information, both in terms of resources and in terms of cognition.[367]

The minute the police and the CSIs arrive at an indicated address (Stage 2) they have to start making decisions, including what areas should be considered part of the crime scene and therefore be taped off.[368] This sets the frame for the investigation in a tangible way. It also, potentially, constitutes the starting point of a confirmation bias. Not only does it set a boundary in relation to the cluster of emergency medical services (EMS) vehicles, spectators standing around on the street, and the associated contamination but it also sets the limit for what is considered relevant areas to examine. Hence, the taping off of a scene is already a limitation on what information is sought, based on an available hypothesis about what has happened (Stage 1). During the actual collection of traces at the area determined to constitute the crime scene, it is common that CSIs will be unable to secure every trace. This is the case not least in fact-rich cases[369] like core international crimes or even cases concerning murders, gross violence, or large-scale financial crimes. By necessity, CSIs have to limit what traces are sought, secured, and subsequently sent to the forensic laboratory.

The number of items that could potentially constitute important traces is sometimes very high and even if the scene is examined multiple times by several different investigative teams, there may still be relevant traces left. For example, in the Ayyash et al. case, no fewer than four investigative teams from four different countries—Lebanon, Switzerland, the Netherlands, and Spain—examined the scene.[370] Even 15 months after the explosion, and even after the scene had already been searched by the Lebanese, Swiss, and Dutch forensic teams, the Spanish team still found evidentiary material including bone fragments, clothing, wiring, electronic circuits, and parts of vehicles.[371] The area considered the crime scene was an 11,000 square metre site covered with rubble, and relevant evidence may have been as small as a finger nail.[372] Also, vehicle parts belonging to the vehicle used to carry the bomb were found at the bottom of swimming pools as well as in the sea.[373]

---

[367] van den Eeden, de Poot, & van Koppen (2017). From Emergency Call to Crime Scene: Information Transference in the Criminal Investigation, pp. 79–89; Lidén & Almazrouei (2021). Blood, Bucks and Bias: Reliability and Biasability of Crime Scene Investigators' Selection and Prioritization of Blood Traces. It is also part of a wider framework of psychological research into framing and anchoring effects; see, for example, Tversky & Kahneman (1981). The Framing of Decisions and the Psychology of Choice, pp. 453–458; and Tversky & Kahneman (1974). Judgment under Uncertainty: Heuristics and Biases, pp. 1124–1130.
[368] Gardner (2012). Practical Crime Scene Processing and Investigation, p. 63.
[369] Agirre Aranburu & Bergsmo (2020). Investigative Bottlenecks and the Mindset of Quality Control, pp. 1–24.
[370] Ayyash et al. Case, Trial Chamber, STL-11-01/T/TC, pp. 349–362.
[371] Ayyash et al. Case, Trial Chamber, STL-11-01/T/TC, p. 363.
[372] Ayyash et al. Case, Trial Chamber, STL-11-01/T/TC, p. 363.
[373] Ayyash et al. Case, Trial Chamber, STL-11-01/T/TC, p. 347.

Hence, while limiting a crime scene is necessary, even with much smaller and far less complex scenes,[374] often there will not be any chance of repeat investigations. In other words, CSIs might just get one chance to secure all the relevant traces. After that, traces may be removed, added, damaged, or contaminated, making it impossible to restore the scene to its original state at a later time. Therefore, evaluation and selection processes brought into play while at the crime scene are crucial for the accuracy of the subsequent investigations and proceedings.

Hence, while some selection and prioritization are inherent in all crime scene investigations, research also suggests that the information CSIs receive before they enter a crime scene significantly affects their selection and evaluation processes while they are at the scene. Categorizations of the likely crime to have occurred, made prior to the investigation, result not only in different protocols being applied which set the frame for how many traces can be collected but they also trigger expectations on what is to be found. Expectations are indeed powerful in directing attention and effort and this often happens subconsciously,[375] in line with the theory of confirmation bias. Prior categorizations in terms of crime type will influence which traces CSIs expect to find, and similarly are expected to look for; that is, investigators may only or primarily search for evidence that is expected to be present if the prior information is true.[376] This confirmatory biased way of testing hypotheses may make CSIs inattentive to evidence that would be expected if the prior information was incorrect and/or another hypothesis was correct. For instance, CSIs who believe that a deceased individual has committed suicide may search for and even find antidepressants but fail to search for and secure fingerprints on a door handle, or marks from tools that were used to enter a home.[377] This is all the more important considering that the distinction between a suicide and a homicide is complicated in many cases. To illustrate, in some high-volume blood scenes where deceased individuals with multiple stab wounds are

---

[374] van den Eeden, de Poot, & van Koppen (2017). From Emergency Call to Crime Scene: Information Transference in the Criminal Investigation, pp. 79–89; Lidén & Almazrouei (2021). Blood, Bucks and Bias: Reliability and Biasability of Crime Scene Investigators' Selection and Prioritization of Blood Traces.

[375] Cooley & Turvey (2021). Observer Effects and Examiner Bias: Psychological Influences on the Forensic Examiner, pp. 61–68; Kassin, Dror, & Kukucka (2013). The Forensic Confirmation Bias: Problems, Perspectives, and Proposed solutions, pp. 42–52; Risinger et al. (2002). The Daubert/Kumho Implications of Observer Effects in Forensic Science: Hidden Problems of Expectation and Suggestion, pp. 1–56; Saks et al. (2003). Context Effects in Forensic Science: A Review and Application of the Science of Science to Crime Laboratory Practice in the United States, pp. 77–90.

[376] van den Eeden, de Poot, & van Koppen (2017). From Emergency Call to Crime Scene: Information Transference in the Criminal Investigation, pp. 79–89; Lidén & Almazrouei (2021). Blood, Bucks and Bias: Reliability and Biasability of Crime Scene Investigators' Selection and Prioritization of Blood Traces.

[377] van den Eeden, de Poot, & van Koppen (2017). From Emergency Call to Crime Scene: Information Transference in the Criminal Investigation, pp. 79–89.

encountered, it can be incredibly difficult to decide whether it was at all possible for the deceased to inflict the injuries themselves or not. While suicide by self-stabbing is fairly unusual,[378] there may be circumstances such as hesitation marks,[379] primarily horizontal stab wounds,[380] documented suicidal tendencies,[381] and a lack of signs of struggle or defence wounds[382] that may indicate suicide. The sheer volume of the blood and the number of stab wounds, however, make it questionable whether the harm could really have been self-inflicted, despite any drug intake, mental illness, etc.[383] Hence, world knowledge and information from previous experiences can be used to interpret new situations.[384] Schemas like these can effectively guide CSI attention to areas or aspects that are thought to be relevant based on previous experiences.[385] However, CSIs sometimes allow these initial impressions to become fixed despite the discovery of additional information or evidence that contradicts their hypothesis. This refusal to consider other viable hypotheses of what happened can hamstring the investigation and hinder the administration of justice.[386] In addition, what is perceived may be incorrectly interpreted in a way consistent with the pre-existing schema.[387] Hence, although CSIs may be assisted by contextual case and base rate information, it can also bias their decisions as it may make them less open-minded towards alternative, less likely scenarios.[388]

---

[378] Start, Milroy, & Green (2012). Suicide by Self-stabbing; Konopka, Bolechała, & Strona (2003). Chest Stab Wound Comparison in Suicidal and Homicidal Cases; Abdullah, Nuernberg, & Rabinovici (2003). Self-inflicted Abdominal Stab Wounds; Karger, Niemeyer, & Brinkmann (2000). Suicides by Sharp Force: Typical and Atypical Features; Schnider et al. (2009). Injuries Due to Sharp Trauma Detected by Post-mortem Multislice Computed Tomography (MSCT): A Feasibility Study; Singh & Lathrop (2008). Youth Suicide in New Mexico: A 26-year Retrospective Review.

[379] Mazzolo & Desinan (2005). Sharp Force Fatalities: Suicide, Homicide or Accident? A Series of 21 Cases; Vanezis & West (1983). Tentative Injuries in Self Stabbing; Betz, Tutsch-Bauer, & Eisenmenger (1995). Tentative Injuries in a Homicide.

[380] Karlsson (1999). Multivariate Analysis ('Forensiometrics')—A New Tool in Forensic Medicine. Differentiation between Firearm-related Homicides and Suicides; Ormstad et al. (1986). Patterns in Sharp Force Fatalities—A Comprehensive Forensic Medical Study.

[381] Olajossy, Wysocka, & Chuchra (1985). Study of an Atypical Suicidal Attempt.

[382] Start, Milroy, & Green (1992). Suicide by Self-stabbing; Konopka, Bolechała, & Strona (2003). Chest Stab Wound Comparison in Suicidal and Homicidal Cases; Fukube et al. (2008). Retrospective Study on Suicidal Cases by Sharp Force Injuries.

[383] Olajossy, Wysocka, & Chuchra (1985). Study of an Atypical Suicidal Attempt; Vennemann (2001). Suicide by More than 90 Stab Wounds Including Perforation of the Skull; Kondo & Ohshima (1995). Retrospective Investigation of Medico-legal Autopsy Cases involving Mentally Handicapped Individuals.

[384] Van den Eeden, de Poot, & van Koppen (2018). The Forensic Confirmation Bias: A Comparison Between Experts and Novices, p. 120.

[385] Tuckey & Brewer (2003). How Schemas Affect Eyewitness Memory over Repeated Retrieval Attempts, pp. 785–800.

[386] Gardner (2012). Practical Crime Scene Processing and Investigation, pp. 85–86; De Poot et al. (2004). Portrait of Detectives: About Dilemmas in the Criminal Investigation.

[387] De Poot et al. (2004). Portrait of Detectives: About Dilemmas in the Criminal Investigation.

[388] Christensen et al. (1991). Framing Bias among Expert and Novice Physicians, pp. 76–78; Dror (2011). The Paradox of Human Expertise: Why Experts Get it Wrong, pp. 177–188.

Adding to the risk of confirmation bias, there is a documented risk that experts, including CSIs, can be overly confident in their skills[389] (see more about this in relation to prosecutors in Chapter 4.2). Although experts usually outperform novices in understanding the deep structure of a problem, they sometimes overlook details.[390] Research from the Dutch setting suggests that experienced criminal investigators underestimate the effect of expectations/categorizations.[391] In fact, expectations can be very powerful and may impact on how experienced CSIs investigate a crime scene. This was illustrated in a study with Dutch CSIs examining an ambiguous mock crime scene; a home in which a female was found dead, hanging in the stairwell.[392]

Before entering the mock crime scene, the Dutch CSIs received one of three possible kinds of advance information, which indicated that (i) the victim had committed suicide, (ii) was murdered, or (iii) they received no prior information at all. Then, using a 360-degree panoramic photograph, the CSIs examined the scene in 360 degrees as they walked through it and also looked at detailed photographs, some with small forensic traces, such as blood on a door handle and hairs around the victim's neck that were longer and of a different colour than the victim's hair. The influence of prior information was measured at three different times in the investigation: (i) the CSIs' initial assessment of the scene (first impression), (ii) during the investigation, more specifically, which traces they wanted to secure and which five traces they wanted to send to the forensic laboratory for further analysis, and (iii) when they were finished with the investigation, they were asked to indicate the most likely scenario. Effects of the prior information were found for all three measures, although not all reached a threshold of significance. Among the CSIs looking at the scene as a suicide, 89 per cent stated that their first impression was suicide whereas the corresponding percentage in the murder condition was 55 per cent ($p = 0.09$). Also, participants in the murder scenario secured significantly more traces compared to those secured in the suicide scenario and participants who mentioned murder as the most likely scenario secured the hairs around the victim's neck significantly more often. Also, for their assessments of most likely scenario, CSIs in the murder scenario more often stated that the crime was murder (60 per cent) than the participants in the suicide condition (26 per cent), ($p = 0.33$).

Prior information may also narrow CSIs' collection of evidence as it impacts on their perceptions of which items are to be considered traces and possible evidence that are useful and necessary to bring the investigation forward. For example, a

---

[389] Chi (1978). Knowledge Structure and Memory Development, pp. 73–96.
[390] Adelson (1984). When Novices Surpass Experts: The Difficulty of a Task May Increase with Expertise, pp. 483–495.
[391] van den Eeden, de Poot, & van Koppen (2017). From Emergency Call to Crime Scene: Information Transference in the Criminal Investigation, pp. 79–89.
[392] van den Eeden, de Poot, & van Koppen (2016). Forensic Expectations: Investigating a Crime Scene with Prior Information, pp. 475–481.

knife might not be of any interest at all in a suspected suicide but a possible murder weapon in a murder case. If expectations set the frames for what falls under consideration as a relevant trace, as well as whether this trace can be analysed given the available resources, it is not difficult to see how a trace which could potentially change the crime classification might be overlooked. It is also likely that the prior information triggers rules of thumb of what will be possible to achieve by securing a certain trace. For example, a CSI who examines a burned-out car may find a cigarette butt on the ground outside the car, which has been left there for a couple of days before the investigation.[393] This could clearly provide relevant DNA but the CSI decides to not collect the trace, reasoning that '[e]ven if you get a match on that, what would that mean?'[394] The cigarette butt could have been left there by the perpetrator but also by anyone else who may have taken interest in the burned-out car over recent days. Hence, this is a predictive assessment of what will be deprioritized after the investigation or discounted in court as non-indicative of guilt.

After the collection of traces (Stage 3), during the so-called *triage* process, further selection will be conducted based on resources and priorities, as well as the perceived usefulness of conducting possible forensic analyses. For example, a bloody fingerprint can be sent for DNA or fingerprint analysis but not both as each analysis disables the other.[395] There may also be traces which have been collected but it is uncertain whether they will be possible to analyse. This is the case with, for example, partial or smudged fingerprints that may or may not be identifiable.[396] Such judgment calls are likely to be influenced by what is believed to have happened, suggesting that an initial hypothesis may impact decision-making also at this stage. Sometimes the selection is not even related to what analysis can be conducted or is likely to be successful but more purely on whether it is considered relevant and necessary for the prosecutor to be able to press charges and/or for obtaining a conviction. This will entail a risk that other relevant analyses are never conducted or only conducted much later when someone may have been wrongfully imprisoned for years. For example, in a Swedish murder case, The Sabri case, bloodstain pattern analysis conducted 29 years after a murder conviction against Mr Sabri became crucial evidence for the reopening of the case. Drastically, with a retracted confession and an alternative hypothesis presented by Mr Sabri, the blood left on his T-shirt at the time of the murder now came into different light. As described below, the original proceedings seem to have been biased by Mr Sabri's confession.

---

[393] Kruse (2015). The Social Life of Forensic Evidence, p. 91.
[394] Kruse (2015). The Social Life of Forensic Evidence, p. 91.
[395] Kruse (2020). Swedish Crime Scene Technicians: Facilitations, Epistemic Frictions and Professionalization from the Outside, pp. 67–83.
[396] Kruse (2015). The Social Life of Forensic Evidence, p. 99.

In 1986, in Spånga, a suburb to Stockholm, a 15-year-old man, Samir Sabri, confessed to having murdered his stepmother through several stab wounds to her chest and abdomen in the home where both of them, as well as Samir's father and brother, lived.[397] Shortly thereafter he was convicted and sentenced to closed psychiatric care.[398] Samir then retracted his confession stating that his father had told him to take on responsibility for the murder. Samir had accepted this and, to make his confession credible he had, for example, laid down on the bed where the stepmother's body had left lots of blood and intentionally pressed his chest to the bed to leave blood impressions on it.[399] While his t-shirt was never forensically analysed in the original investigation, the expert reports from 2015 noted that the T-shirt did not have any stains from blood spatter, but rather from gory bed linen.[400] Given the large amount of blood that the stepmother had lost, there should reasonably have been blood spatter on the perpetrator's clothes, yet this was missing.[401] Since this was consistent with Samir's new version of events and because he had previously been convicted largely on the basis of his confession, he was granted a new trial[402] and acquitted in 2016.[403]

Since Mr Sabri had confessed to the crime, and confessions are powerful evidence that can easily trigger a confirmation bias (Sections 3.5.1.2 and 3.5.4.2), it is likely that, in 1986, it was considered irrelevant for the progress of the case to conduct bloodstain pattern analysis of the blood found on Mr Sabri's T-shirt. The more general presence of blood on his T-shirt was, seemingly, noted but presumably this was considered consistent with his confession. However, the patterns were never examined. What these patterns would have been expected to look like, should the hypothesis be wrong, was, it seems, not a question that was asked or further probed in the original investigation.

In sum, the risk of confirmation bias does not only pertain to the initial trace collection on a crime scene but has to be understood in relation to the stages before and after this. Regardless of jurisdiction and suspected crime type, effective bias mitigation requires considerations pertaining to all three stages as well as the interplay between them.

---

[397] Stockholm District Court, Case No. B 322/86.
[398] Stockholm District Court, Case No. B 322/86.
[399] Svea Court of Appeal, Case No. Ö 7110-15, p. 8.
[400] Svea Court of Appeal, Case No. Ö 7110-15, p. 4.
[401] Svea Court of Appeal, Case No. Ö 7110-15, p. 4.
[402] Svea Court of Appeal, Case No. Ö 7110-15.
[403] Svea Court of Appeal, Case No. Ö 7110-15.

3.5.3.3 Mitigating Bias
3.5.3.3.1 Contextual Information Management (CIM)
Since there is a risk that CSI's search, interpretation, and collection of traces are biased by investigative hypothesis or other contextual information,[404] there is good reason to consider seriously what information should be made available to CSIs before they enter a scene. This is referred to as contextual information management (CIM) and has previously been discussed and evaluated primarily in relation to forensic analysis.[405] Hence, CIM as a debiasing technique will be addressed more in detail in Section 3.5.4.4.1 on forensic analysis. However, the task of a so-called context manager in relation to crime scene investigations is to decide essentially on two questions: (i) which contextual information is relevant for the CSIs to know, and (ii) whether this information is potentially biasing. If the information is potentially biasing but still relevant, one potential solution is to postpone disclosure of that information so that a CSI first examines the crime scene without the information, and then with it, or if that is not possible, with two CSIs, one who is aware and one who is unaware of this information. The latter option thus combines contextual information management with having multiple CSIs at the scene (Section 3.5.3.3.2).

3.5.3.3.2 Multiple CSIs
In line with experimental results suggesting that decision-makers are more critical in relation to decisions made by others than those made by themselves,[406] there are other small-scale empirical evaluations suggesting that having more than one CSI attend the scene (two or three) can be functional as a debiasing technique.[407] For example, having multiple CSIs can facilitate a more diversified collection of evidence, and for this purpose, structured search strategies are sometimes also recommended (Section 3.5.3.3.3).

3.5.3.3.3 Structured strategies for trace collection
Today there are published guidelines specifying structured search strategies such as screening the crime scene by investigators walking in circles or in lines through

---

[404] van den Eeden, de Poot, & van Koppen (2016). Forensic Expectations: Investigating a Crime Scene with Prior Information, pp. 475–481.

[405] Osborne & Taylor (2018). Contextual Information Management: An Example of Independent Checking in the Review of Laboratory-based Bloodstain Pattern Analysis, pp 226–231.

[406] Lidén, Gräns, & Juslin, 'Guilty, No Doubt': Detention Provoking Confirmation Bias in Judges' Guilt Assessments and Debiasing Techniques, pp. 219–247; Lidén, Gräns, & Juslin, The Presumption of Guilt in Suspect Interrogations: Apprehension as a Trigger of Confirmation Bias and Debiasing Techniques, pp. 336–354.

[407] Sutto, Trueman, & Moran (2017). Crime Scene Management: Scene Specific Methods; Gupta et al. (2016). A Heuristic for Maximizing Investigation Effectiveness of Digital Forensic Cases involving Multiple Investigators; Granér & Kronkvist (2015). The Past, the Present and the Future of Police Research.

the scene.[408] While it seems likely that such structured searches could prevent CSIs from simply following their gut feeling on what specific parts of the scene need closer attention, it should be emphasized that structured searches have not been empirically evaluated as debiasing techniques. For example, in practice, CSIs may be reluctant to conduct these kinds of searches due to fear of contaminating the scene. Moreover, even if this kind of search strategy focuses CSIs' attention to parts of the crime scene they may have ignored, they must still assess which traces are relevant to secure.[409] Thus, the selection and evaluation of traces may still be biased even if the search is not. This highlights the need to evaluate debiasing techniques together rather than separately. Ideally, for crime scenes this would entail contextual information management (CIM), having multiple CSIs examine the scene, and structured searches. This would enable not only knowledge of how the techniques work together in practice but also whether some of the techniques appear more promising than others. Today, CIM appears the most promising technique, but it is also the technique that has attracted most attention.

Additionally, the practical reality of limited resources needs to be taken into account. For example, research should examine the added value versus cost of collecting additional evidence, with the aim of maximising the value of evidence collection.[410] It is today not uncommon that there is a 'trace funnel'[411] whereby a significant amount of evidence is gathered but not subsequently used in court. As illustrated by the case against Mr Sabri (Section 3.5.3.2), evidence that is not made part of the initial process can come to radically new light when circumstances change, for example because convicted individuals retract their confessions. In this case, it was decisive that Mr Sabri's T-shirt (by mistake) had been kept and could still be analysed. Without the T-shirt, it is unlikely that Mr Sabri would have been acquitted. This highlights the fact that the interaction between the different stages of a crime scene investigation, here primarily Stages 2 and 3 (Section 3.5.3.2), needs to be considered not only when trying to understand why confirmation bias may be at play but also as part of debiasing attempts. It is of little use that traces are collected in an unbiased way from the scene if the traces are never analysed. Whether the traces are analysed or not is a result of priorities, available resources as well as what guidelines (including timelines) for storing

---

[408] De Gruijter, de Poot, & Elffers (2016). Reconstructing with Trace Information—Does Rapid Identification Information Lead to Better Crime Reconstructions?, pp. 1–16; De Gruijter & de Poot (2018). The Use of Rapid Identification Information at the Crime Scene: Similarities and Differences between English and Dutch CSIs; Van Amelsvoort, Groenendal, & van Manen (2004). Werkwijze bij het onderzoek op de Plaats Delict (PD), pp. 72–83; Gardner (2012). Practical Crime Scene Processing and Investigation; Weston (2009). Criminal Investigation: Basic Perspectives.
[409] Lee & Pagliaro (2013). Forensic Evidence and Crime Scene Investigation.
[410] Bitzer et al. (2015). Science and Justice Utility of the Clue—From Assessing the Investigative Contribution to Forensic Science to Supporting the Decision to Use Traces, pp. 509–513; Van Asten (2014). Science and Justice on the Added Value of Forensic Science and Grand Innovation Challenges for the Forensic Community, pp. 170–179.
[411] Ribaux et al. (2017). Expressing the Value of Forensic Science in Policing, pp. 489–501.

and destructing traces are applicable.[412] Subsequently, legal and policy questions will interact with debiasing attempts, and together this will decide whether and to what extent crime scene investigations can help promote the accuracy of criminal investigations and proceedings.

3.5.3.3.4 Technological advances
Since technological advances are rapid and their use in criminal investigations is increasing, such advances should be discussed; in particular whether *Rapid Identification Technologies (RI)* and *3D laser scanning/3D point cloud technology* can help mitigate confirmation bias during crime scene investigations.

Rapid identification technologies (RI) are methods that are still being developed and tested and which allow CSIs to analyse DNA[413] and fingerprints[414] already when first attending the crime scene.[415] Another promising development is a spectral camera that can be used to detect blood on visually problematic places such as dark surfaces and also provide an indication of the age of the bloodstain.[416] Such techniques allow CSIs to test several hypotheses while they are still at the crime scene.[417] Although these techniques hold some promise, research thus far indicates that CSIs seem to integrate results only or primarily if they are in line with their expectations.[418] This is a clear demonstration of confirmation bias. Also, researchers noted that experienced CSIs using the camera tended to focus on dark surfaces rather more than other surfaces to find traces suitable for the rapid identification technique.[419] While this can be a positive step, it also constitutes a risk of overlooking other possibly important traces. Evidently, CSIs' attention can change, depending on their goals and when using the technology, their goal may be more to find traces suitable for the technology rather than to conduct a broader search and examination of the scene.[420]

---

[412] For example, for the United Kingdom, see National Police Chief's Council (NPCC). Retention, Storage and Destruction of Material and Records Relating to Forensic Examination.
[413] Lounsbury, Bienvenue, & Landers (2010). Sample-to—Result STR Genotyping Systems; Mapes, de Poot, & Kloosterman (2015). DNA in the Criminal Justice System: The DNA Success Story in Perspective, pp. 851–856.
[414] Kurpershoek (2009). Indicatief Onderzoek: Steeds Sneller, pp. 32–35.
[415] Kurpershoek (2009). Indicatief Onderzoek: Steeds Sneller, pp. 32–35.
[416] De Gruijter, de Poot, & Elffers (2016). The Influence of New Technologies on the Visual Attention of CSIs Performing a Crime Scene Investigation, pp. 1–9.
[417] de Gruijter, de Poot, & Elffers (2016). Reconstructing with Trace Information: Does Rapid Identification Information Lead to Better Crime Reconstructions?, pp. 88–103; de Gruijter, Nee, & de Poot (2017). Identification at the Crime Scene: The Sooner, the Better? The Interpretation of Rapid Identification Information by CSIs at the Crime Scene, pp. 296–306.
[418] de Gruijter, de Poot, & Elffers (2016). Reconstructing with Trace Information: Does Rapid Identification Information Lead to Better Crime Reconstructions?, pp. 88–103; de Gruijter, Nee, & de Poot (2017). Identification at the Crime Scene: The Sooner, the Better? The Interpretation of Rapid Identification Information by CSIs at the Crime Scene, pp. 296–306.
[419] Edelman, van Leeuwen, & Aalders (2013). Hyperspectral Imaging of the Crime Scene for Detection and Identification of Blood Stains.
[420] Edelman, van Leeuwen, & Aalders (2013). Hyperspectral Imaging of the Crime Scene for Detection and Identification of Blood Stains; Chun & Wolfe (2008). Visual Attention, pp. 272–310.

Three-dimensional laser scanning and 3D point cloud technology are trace and crime portrait simulation systems drawing on artificial intelligence.[421] So far, they have been used, for example, for reconstructing the crime scene from scene photos,[422] simulating dynamic behaviour,[423] and analysing bullet trajectory.[424] Such possibilities can enable CSIs to experiment with different hypotheses regarding a certain course of event. This, however, demands that the sources of errors pertaining to the technology itself are better researched. Furthermore, 3D laser scanning and 3D point cloud technology hold some promise when it comes to extracting traces that require no contact. For example, when shoe prints on snow are to be secured, the traditional methods are to use sulphur which is injected into the shoe print, cools off, and forms a an imprint, but at the risk of some damage done to the original shoe print.[425] Alternatively, photos of the shoe print are taken but these provide incomplete information since they do not capture the angle and depth of the shoe print.[426] With 3D laser scanning technology, the characteristics of the shoe print, including angle and depth, will be captured in the resulting mould and since the technology is non-contact, the technology will not impact on the original shoe print. Improved methods for capturing such traces can enable more well-founded decision-making during the triage, for example because shoe prints are not excluded from analysis because the quality of the prints are considered too low. This is essential as confirmation bias is stronger in relation to ambiguous material.[427] Similarly, when the actual analysis of the prints is conducted, the improved quality should help forensic analysts make more accurate decisions.

As always when it comes to humans using technology, it is also important to consider what this means for human cognition. Even if the technologies in themselves were foolproof, there would still be a human in the loop to make decisions, set priorities, and conduct evaluations, and if this human is biased, then the outcome may still be inaccurate. This means that technological advances are not a guaranteed solution to human sources of error. While they can assist humans to a certain extent (e.g. obtaining more complete shoe prints from a scene), technological

---

[421] Liu (2019). Three-dimension Point Cloud Technology and Intelligent Extraction of Trace Evidence at the Scene of Crime; Puentes, Taveira, & Madureira (2009). Three-dimensional Reconstitution of Bullet Trajectory in Gunshot Wounds: A Case Report, pp. 407–410.
[422] Cavagnini, Sansoni, & Trebeschi (2009). Using 3D Range Cameras for Crime Scene Documentation and Legal Medicine.
[423] Cai, Liu, Ma, & Chen (2011). Applications of 3D Laser Scanning Technology in Reconstruction of Criminal Scene, pp. 51–54.
[424] Puentes, Taveira, & Madureira (2009). Three-dimensional Reconstitution of Bullet Trajectory in Gunshot Wounds: A Case Report, pp. 407–410.
[425] Liu (2019). Three-dimension Point Cloud Technology and Intelligent Extraction of Trace Evidence at the Scene of Crime.
[426] Liu (2019). Three-dimension Point Cloud Technology and Intelligent Extraction of Trace Evidence at the Scene of Crime.
[427] Osborne & Zajac (2015). An Imperfect Match? Crime-related Context Influences Fingerprint Decisions, pp. 126–134.

advances can also result in more errors or other types of errors, for example because humans trust the technology too much. Also, the technology often changes the type of decisions that humans have to make,[428] but the sources of errors in their decision-making are still there, including compelling hypotheses that are difficult to shake. Hence, when considering technological advances as potential debiasing techniques, it is essential also to consider the interaction between the technology and the human, and how this might impact on the errors committed.

3.5.3.4 Conclusion

Since crime scenes are often a main source of crime-relevant information and at the same time are often transient, complex, ambiguous or even contradictory, the selection and prioritization of traces to be sent for forensic analysis are difficult but incredibly important tasks. Confirmation bias can clearly impact very negatively on CSIs' abilities to conduct these tasks properly. Early categorizations of incidents as specific crime types, and other contextual information, can trigger a confirmation bias that impacts (subconsciously) on how CSIs examine the scene, prioritize different traces, and so on. Since such categorizations also affect the resources available and what type of traces CSIs are expected to secure from a scene, their information processing is limited also in this regard. Hence, to understand whether and how confirmation bias may manifest it is essential that not only the actual trace collection at the scene is examined but also what happens before and after the trace collection. For example, the importance of triage processes in creating a confirmation bias present at the crime scene is clearly under-researched.

When it comes to mitigation strategies, the research available suggests that CIM is advisable. There are also less well-researched techniques that hold some promise, including having multiple CSIs examine the scene, for example with and without knowledge of potentially biasing contextual information. While structured searches for information, such as walking in lines and circles, have been mentioned in a few guidelines, such searches may be associated with practical difficulties (e.g. contamination risk) and have not been empirically evaluated as debiasing techniques. Similarly, technological advances may hold some promise but the few evaluations that have been conducted in relation to RITs show that they may exacerbate confirmation bias. Even less is known about 3D laser scanning and 3D point cloud technology as debiasing techniques. It appears that the possibility of reconstructing scenes to test alternative scenarios and to secure more complete non-contact traces (e.g. shoe prints in snow) hold promise and should be further evaluated, taking the human–technology interaction into account.

---

[428] Dascal & Dror (2005). The Impact of Cognitive Technologies—Towards a Pragmatic Approach, pp. 451–457; Dror & Harnad (2008). Cognition Distributed: How Cognitive Technology Extends our Minds.

3.5.4 Forensic Analysis

3.5.4.1 Introduction

Since there are many selection processes before, during, and after a crime scene investigation (Section 3.5.3), it is clear that not all traces present at a crime scene will be sent for forensic analyses. The traces may have been overlooked or deprioritized and therefore left at the scene, now potentially damaged, contaminated, or removed by individuals, the weather, and so on. Another possibility is that traces have been secured and are stored with the police or at the forensic lab but have not been prioritized for analysis due to, for example, limited resources and/or that they have been considered irrelevant given the focus of the investigation. Pursuant to applicable laws and/or guidelines, there is also a risk that stored traces are destroyed as time passes by. Consequently, even if the results of the forensic examinations that are in fact conducted are totally free from bias the analysis may still be misrepresentative since there may be relevant traces that were never analysed. Depending on which hypothesis or hypotheses are being evaluated, investigators or prosecutors will ask the forensic lab to conduct certain analyses in relation to certain traces. The questions they ask will dictate the answers they get. Had different questions been asked in relation to the same traces or other traces from the same case, the results and conclusions from the forensic analyses, as well as their implications for the investigation in a wider sense, may very well have been completely different. Such narrowing of the forensic analyses of traces considered of primary importance to the investigation is, certainly, problematic in itself.

Adding significantly to the potentially distorting power of forensic evidence is the fact that forensic examiners, unsurprisingly, are not immune to confirmation bias. Today, there is fairly extensive research into the forensic field to indicate the prevalence of a so-called forensic confirmation bias,[429] not least in criminalistics (Section 3.5.4.2), but also in forensic medicine (Section 3.5.4.3) and forensic anthropology (Section 3.5.4.4). Overall, this research suggests that these forensic examiners' observations and conclusions pertaining to evidence are tainted by the contextual information available to examiners at the time of the examination.[430] To mitigate this bias, measures have been suggested, including contextual information management (Section 3.5.4.4.1), linear sequential unmasking (Section 3.5.4.4.2), independent review (Section 3.5.4.4.3), and advanced technology (Section 3.5.4.4.4).

---

[429] Kassin, Dror, & Kukucka (2013). The Forensic Confirmation Bias: Problems, Perspectives, and Proposed Solutions, pp. 42–52.
[430] Cooper & Meterko (2019). Cognitive Bias in Research in Forensic Science: A Systematic Review, pp. 35–46.

3.5.4.2 Understanding Bias—Criminalistics

In criminalistics, forensic confirmation bias has been found in a range of different types of assessments such as fingerprint analysis,[431] comparisons of shoe prints,[432] bite marks,[433] bullets,[434] and handwriting samples.[435] It has also been noted in relation to DNA mixtures,[436] bloodstain pattern analysis (BPA),[437] dog detection evidence,[438] arson investigations,[439] and a range of forensic reconstructions.[440] There is also emerging research into the risks of bias in digital forensics,[441] an increasingly important area.[442] Research on confirmation bias in this field examines, for example, how contextual information such as inferences made by others[443] or information found on a digital device, for example Internet search logs,[444] influence the digital forensics practitioners' (DFP) perceptions of images, documents, or chat conversations found on the same digital device.[445] To illustrate this, in one study contextual information seems to have biased the DFPs' observations of 11 crime relevant traces (e.g. email content, documents, chats) on a digital device, some of them relatively easy to find and some of them requiring

---

[431] Osborne & Zajac (2015). An Imperfect Match? Crime-related Context Influences Fingerprint Decisions, pp. 126–34.

[432] Kerstholt, Paashuis, & Sjerps (2007). Shoe Print Examinations: Effects of Expectation, Complexity and Experience, pp. 30–34.

[433] Osborne et al. (2014). Does Contextual Information Bias Bitemark Comparisons?, pp. 267–73.

[434] Kerstholt et al. (2010). Does Suggestive Information Cause a Confirmation Bias in Bullet Comparisons?, pp. 138–42.

[435] Kukucka & Kassin (2014). Do Confessions Taint Perceptions of Handwriting Evidence? An Empirical Test of the Forensic Confirmation Bias, pp. 1–15.

[436] Dror & Hampikian (2011). Subjectivity and Bias in Forensic DNA Mixture Interpretation, pp. 204–208; Lynch (2003). God's Signature: DNA Profiling, the New Gold Standard in Forensic Evidence, pp. 93–97; Kloosterman, Sjerps, & Quak (2014). Error Rates in Forensic DNA Analysis: Definition, Numbers, Impact and Communication, pp. 77–85.

[437] Osborne, Zajac, & Taylor (2014). Bloodstain Pattern Analysis and Contextual Bias. In Jamieson and Moenssens (Eds). Wiley Encyclopedia of Forensic Science, pp. 1–8; Laber et al. (2014), Reliability Assessment of Current Methods in Bloodstain Pattern Analysis.

[438] Lit, Schweitzer, & Oberbauer (2011). Handler Beliefs Affect Scent Detection Dog Outcomes, pp. 387–94; Minhinnick (2016). Statistical Reliability Confounders and Improvement in Advanced Dog Training: Patterns, Routines, Targets, Alerts, Distractors, Reinforcement, and Other Issues. In Jezierski, Ensminger, & Papet (Eds.). Canine Olfaction Science and Law: Advances in Forensic Science, Medicine, Conservation, and Environmental Remediation, pp. 197–212.

[439] Bieber (2017). Measuring the Impact of Cognitive Bias in Fire Investigation, pp. 1–13.

[440] Levin et al. (2019). A Comparison of Thresholding Methods for Forensic Reconstruction Studies Using Fluorescent Powder Proxies for Trace Materials, pp. 431–42; Carew et al. (2019). A Preliminary Investigation into the Accuracy of 3D Modelling and 3D Printing in Forensic Anthropology Evidence Reconstruction, pp. 342–52.

[441] Sunde & Dror (2019). Cognitive and Human Factors in Digital Forensics: Problems, Challenges, and the Way Forward, pp. 101–08; Sunde (2017). Non-Technical Sources of Errors When Handling Digital Evidence within a Criminal Investigation.

[442] McDermott, Koenig, & Murray (2021). Open Source Information's Blind Spot: Human and Machine Bias in International Criminal Investigations, pp. 1–21.

[443] Zapf & Dror (2017). Understanding and Mitigating Bias in Forensic Evaluation: Lessons from Forensic Science, pp. 227–38.

[444] Sunde & Dror (2019). Cognitive and Human Factors in Digital Forensics: Problems, Challenges, and the Way Forward, pp. 101–108.

[445] Sunde (2021). Human Factors Impacting Digital Forensics Investigations.

more in-depth examination.[446] Participants who were led to believe in guilt made more observations (found more of the traces) than those who were led to believe in innocence.[447] This contextual information did not impact significantly on the interpretations of those observations or the conclusions drawn from them, but much variation between different observers was found.[448] Given the pace of technological developments and the fact that it is today uncertain what is being done in terms of quality control in this field,[449] the need for further research is pronounced.

The research available today suggests that forensic confirmation bias can be triggered by analysts' knowledge of contextual information including, for example, that the suspect has been identified by witnesses,[450] the results of other forensic analyses,[451] the implications that their analysis will have for the investigation,[452] or that the suspect has confessed.[453]

The effect of knowing that a suspect has been identified by witnesses was tested in 1984 by Miller.[454] He instructed his participants to compare a forged check against handwriting samples from one or more suspects.[455] Among the participants who were unaware of the witness identifications, all correctly concluded that none of the suspect had authored the forged check. In contrast, among participants who were aware of the witness identifications, 67 per cent incorrectly concluded that the suspect in question had forged the signature. This is particularly relevant considering that witness identifications in themselves can be biased, for example due to how a suspect line-up has been conducted (Section 3.5.2).

In 2006, Dror and colleagues demonstrated similar effects as those found in relation to the handwriting samples but this time in fingerprint experts.[456] Five

---

[446] Sunde & Dror (2021). A Hierarchy of Expert Performance (HEP) Applied to Digital Forensics: Reliability and Biasability in Digital Forensics Decision Making, pp. 1–11.

[447] Sunde & Dror (2021). A Hierarchy of Expert Performance (HEP) Applied to Digital Forensics: Reliability and Biasability in Digital Forensics Decision Making, pp. 1–11.

[448] Sunde & Dror (2021). A Hierarchy of Expert Performance (HEP) Applied to Digital Forensics: Reliability and Biasability in Digital Forensics Decision Making, pp. 1–11.

[449] Sunde p. 4.

[450] Miller (1984). Bias among Forensic Document Examiners: A Need for Procedural Change, pp. 407–411.

[451] Stevenage & Bennett (2017). A Biased Opinion: Demonstration of Cognitive Bias on a Fingerprint Matching Task through Knowledge of DNA test results, pp. 93–106; Dror & Charlton (2006). Why Experts Make Errors, pp. 600–616; Dror, Charlton, & Peron (2006). Contextual Information Renders Experts Vulnerable to Making Erroneous Identifications, pp. 74–78; Dror et al. (2012). The Impact of Human-Technology Cooperation and Distributed Cognition in Forensic Science: Biasing Effects of AFIS Contextual Information on Human Experts, pp. 343–352.

[452] Dror & Hampikian (2011). Subjectivity and Bias in Forensic DNA Mixture Interpretation, pp. 204–208.

[453] Kukucka & Kassin (2013). Do Confessions Taint Perceptions of Handwriting Evidence? An Empirical Test of the Forensic Confirmation Bias, pp. 1–15.

[454] Miller (1984). Bias among Forensic Document Examiners: A Need for Procedural Change, pp. 407–411.

[455] Miller (1984), Bias among Forensic Document Examiners: A Need for Procedural Change, pp. 407–411.

[456] Dror & Charlton (2006). Why Experts Make Errors, pp. 600–616; Dror, Charlton, & Peron (2006). Contextual Information Renders Experts Vulnerable to Making Erroneous Identifications, pp. 74–78.

experienced fingerprint examiners were provided with sets of prints that they, unknowingly, had themselves judged as a match several years earlier. When the experts were told that the prints were taken from a high-profile misidentification case, the misidentification of Brandon Mayfield as perpetrator of the Madrid train bombings on 11 March 2004, four out of five concluded that the prints did not match. Although this sample size is very small, similar results have been found in a range of studies with larger samples of experts,[457] summarized in a meta-analysis in 2008.[458] This research confirms the bias in relation to fingerprints and there are also single studies suggesting that the tendency increases with emotional intensity (manipulated using emotional photographs from crime scenes).[459] These studies furthermore illustrate that the effects seem to occur primarily in relation to ambiguous fingerprints.[460]

In 2011, Dror and Hampikian described a gang rape case in Georgia in which three of the assailants accepted a plea bargain to testify against the two other suspects.[461] Under state law, the testimony was inadmissible without corroborating evidence. Aware of this evidentiary rule, DNA analysts concluded that a complex DNA mixture taken from the victim's body originated from the two other men. The establishment of this corroborating fact was essential to the prosecution of the suspects that claimed they were innocent. In order to examine whether the awareness of the rule might have biased the analysts' conclusions, the same DNA mixture was later presented to 17 other DNA analysts who were unaware of the case information. Twelve of these concluded that the DNA sample in fact excluded the two other suspects, four judged the sample as inconclusive, and only one agreed with the original conclusion, that is, that the sample matched the DNA of the other two suspects. Since this study is not a controlled experiment, care should be taken in the interpretation of the results. It is unknown which information apart from the evidentiary rule, and its relevance, was provided to the DNA analysts in the actual criminal case. Other information or circumstances might have contributed to their interpretation of the samples as well. However, the study demonstrates that most of the DNA analysts who examined the samples unaware of the relevance of the

---

[457] Dror & Charlton (2006). Why Experts Make Errors, pp. 600–616.

[458] Dror & Rosenthal (2008). Meta-analytically Quantifying the Reliability and Biasability of Forensic Experts, pp. 900–903.

[459] Osborne & Zajac (2015). An Imperfect Match? Crime-related Context Influences Fingerprint Decisions, pp. 126–134; Dror et al. (2005). When Emotions Get the Better of Us: The Effect of Contextual Top-down Processing on Matching Fingerprints, pp. 799–809.

[460] Osborne & Zajac (2015). An Imperfect Match? Crime-related Context Influences Fingerprint Decisions, pp. 126–134; Cole (2002). Suspect Identities: A History of Fingerprinting and Criminal Identification; Phillips, Saks, & Peterson (2001). The Application of Signal Detection Theory to Decision-making in Forensic Science, pp. 294–308; Risinger et al. (2002). The Daubert/Kumho Implications of Observer Effects in Forensic Science: Hidden Problems of Expectation and Suggestion, pp. 1–56.

[461] Dror & Hampikian (2011). Subjectivity and Bias in Forensic DNA Mixture Interpretation, pp. 204–208.

evidentiary rule in the case made interpretations contrary to those made by the analysts in the actual case. Thus, even if it is not certain that this knowledge was the only factor that caused the analysts' different interpretations, it appears to have at least contributed. Cognitive contamination of forensic examiners is not limited to the impact of knowing irrelevant case information but emerges from a whole spectrum of sources.[462] Such sources are, for example, that analysts work 'backwards' from the suspect to the evidence and that base rates cause expectations impacting on the examination.[463]

In 2014, Kukucka and Kassin found that knowledge of a suspect's confession made analysts more likely to conclude that handwriting samples matched.[464] Thus, analysts with knowledge of a confession would, to a greater extent than those without such knowledge, provide evidence implicating the suspect.[465] While the effect of confessions, just like other experimental manipulations, has not been tested specifically with all possible types of forensic analyses, this research highlights a risk of such a bias in relation to other evidence too. This is because many forensic assessments, just like handwriting comparisons, involve visual comparisons between a pattern found on the crime scene and a suspect sample,[466] such as comparisons of shoe prints,[467] bite marks,[468] tool marks, and bullets.[469] Furthermore, these patterns may be distorted, partial, or consistent with several types of shoes, tools, tyres, and so on. There are multiple cases from national jurisdictions which highlight the possibility of a forensic confirmation bias following a confession. Notably, in all these cases, the confessions were most likely to have been false and the forensic evidence was therefore an important step in the subsequent (acknowledged) wrongful confessions.

For example, in the Tair Rada case, a 13-year-old Israeli girl was found dead in a school bathroom.[470] Roman Zadorov, who had worked at the school at the relevant time, was identified as the suspect. During his first interviews, Mr Zadorov consistently denied all responsibility, then, the police, falsely, told him that his DNA

---

[462] Dror (2013). Practical Solutions to Cognitive and Human Factor Challenges in Forensic Science, pp. 1–9.
[463] Dror (2013). Practical Solutions to Cognitive and Human Factor Challenges in Forensic Science, pp. 1–9.
[464] Kukucka & Kassin (2013). Do Confessions Taint Perceptions of Handwriting Evidence? An Empirical Test of the Forensic Confirmation Bias, pp. 1–15.
[465] Kukucka & Kassin (2013). Do Confessions Taint Perceptions of Handwriting Evidence? An Empirical Test of the Forensic Confirmation Bias, pp. 1–15.
[466] Dror & Cole, The Vision in 'Blind' Justice: Expert Perception, Judgment, and Visual Cognition in Forensic Pattern Recognition, pp. 161–167.
[467] Kerstholt, Passhuis, & Sjerps (2007). Shoe Print Examinations: Effects of Expectation, Complexity and Experience, pp. 30–34.
[468] Osborne et al. (2014). Does Contextual Information Bias Bitemark Comparisons?, pp. 267–273.
[469] Kerstholt et al. (2010). Does Suggestive Information Cause a Confirmation Bias in Bullet Comparisons, pp. 138–142.
[470] Nazareth District Court, February 2014, Israel Supreme Court, December 2015.

had been found on the crime scene and that Tair's blood had been found on his clothes. They had him imprisoned together with an informant who gained his trust and who made him speculate about his involvement in the crime, while repeatedly stating that he did not trust his own memory. After further police questioning, Mr Zadorov confessed. The police also provided Mr Zadorov with details about how the crime happened, which he then could incorporate into the re-enactment of the killing. For example, Mr Zadorov illustrated how he, after having killed Tair, had locked the toilet cubicle door and climbed out from it, which was considered guilty knowledge, facts that only the perpetrator could have known.[471] However, at this point it had been made clear that there was no DNA to tie Mr Zadorov to the murder and therefore forensic examiners reanalysed the photos from the crime scene. In the process of reanalysing the photos, the former head of the forensic lab, Mr Rosengarten, described how, suddenly, when examining bloodstains on Tair's pants, he: 'saw shoe prints that simply cried out'.[472] These shoe prints, that no other examiner had claimed to see before, were then matched to Mr Zadorov's shoes by the Israeli forensic lab.

The defence hired a world-leading expert, Mr Bodziak, for a second opinion on the marks and he concluded that it was uncertain whether the marks were shoe prints at all. However, the judges in the first instance, the Nazareth District Court, trusted their own judgments regarding the marks and subsequently convicted and sentenced Mr Zadorov to life in prison. The conviction was upheld on appeal and the Supreme Court in Jerusalem did not try the case. In May 2021, after Mr Zadorov had spent more than 11 years in prison, new evidence, including forensic evidence—a hair found on Tair's body which did not belong to Mr Zadorov—has resulted in a retrial being ordered by the Supreme Court.[473] Since then, Mr Zadorov was released to house arrest and the Nazareth District Court Judge Asher Kula allegedly made a rare pre-verdict statement believed to indicate that the Court would acquit Mr Zadorov.[474] However, currently the final outcome is unknown.

In the Tair Rada case it seems fairly likely that Mr Zadorov's confession impacted on the forensic examiner's 'sudden' observation that there were shoe prints at the scene, as well as the matching of those prints to Mr Zadorov's shoes. There are many other cases in which it is likely that false confessions have been elicited, but their impact on the forensic analyses conducted in the cases has never been analysed in detail. This includes landmark cases such as the Engin Raghip case in

---

[471] Appleby, Hasel, & Kasin (2013). Police-induced Confessions: An Empirical Analysis of their Content and Impact, pp. 111–128; Alceste, Jones, & Kassin (2020). Facts Only the Perpetrator Could Have Known? A Study of Contamination in Mock Crime Interrogations, pp. 128–142.

[472] Rosengarten, cited in 'Shadow of Truth'.

[473] The Times of Israel (2021). Supreme Court orders Retrial of Convicted Killer of 13-year-old Tair Rada.

[474] Bob (2022). Prosecution Retrial of Zadorov may be on the Ropes. See also The Jerusalem Post (2022). Criminal Law Expert: Roman Zadorov will be Acquitted in Tair Rada Murder Case.

1991, one of the so-called Tottenham Three, which has been extremely influential in broadening the criteria for the admissibility of psychological evidence in the English courts.[475] There are also similar landmark cases from Northern Ireland, including PK's confession in relation to the so-called IRA funeral murders.[476] PK was one of many persons who was arrested and interviewed about the murders; the police challenged his account and told him they had evidence that implicated him. In repeated interviews, they suggested false propositions and PK gradually began to incriminate himself, leading up to a confession. PK and two other men were convicted by the Belfast Crown Court. It later came to light that PK, due to high levels of anxiety and compliance, was at a disadvantage in having to cope with the police interview, and this explains why he confessed falsely. However, the most famous examples globally are US cases that have gained enormous media attention, including, for example, the 'Central Park Five'[477] and Brendan Dassey who remains convicted of the murder of photographer Theresa Halbach in Manitowoc County, Wisconsin in 2005.[478] While both these cases drew worldwide attention, not least through the Netflix depictions of the cases,[479] there are also far less well-known cases. This includes Stefan Kiszko who confessed to having murdered a schoolgirl in north-west England in 1975,[480] Lorenzo Montoya who confessed to having participated in the beating and death of a woman in her home in Denver, Colorado,[481] and Samir Sabri who confessed to murdering his stepmother in Sweden in 1986.[482] In fact, research implies that known cases of false confessions are only the tip of the iceberg.[483] If forensic analysts confirm false confessions through their analysis, not because of the evidence per se but because the false confessions make the analysts perceive of the evidence differently and their analysis, in turn, provides false corroboration, this considerably increases the risk of a false positive.

The connection between confessions and confirmation bias is essential not only because a confession can result in a confirmation bias in a forensic analyst but confirmation bias can also be the reason why a suspect confesses in the first place. As discussed in Section 3.5.1, confirmation bias can be triggered at

---

[475] Gudjonsson & Haward (1998). Forensic Psychology: A Guide to Practice.
[476] Gudjonsson (1999). The IRA Funeral Murders: The Confession of PK and the Expert Psychological Testimony, pp. 45–50.
[477] The 'Central Park Five' is the common description of five teenaged boys who confessed falsely, in coercive interviews by New York police officers, to raping a jogger in Central Park in 1989; see, for example, Weiser (), 5 Exonerated in Central Park Jobber Case Agree to Settle Suit for $ 40 Million.
[478] Dassey v. Dittmann, 877 F.3d 297 (7th Cir. 2017) holding four to three that the State Court findings of voluntariness were not so unreasonable that they could be set aside on federal habeas. Dassey was 16-year-old when he after earlier interviews provided a statement inculpating himself in a murder, adopting some accurate details that law enforcement officers provided but getting other details wrong.
[479] See Netflix, When They See Us and Netflix, Making a Murderer: Plight of the Accused.
[480] Rose & Panter (1997). Innocents: How Justice Failed Stefan Kiszko and Lesley Molseed.
[481] Gaines (2018). Presupposition as Investigator Certainty in Police Interrogation: The Case of Lorenzo Montoya's False Confession.
[482] Svea Court of Appeal, Case No. Ö 7110-15, p. 8.
[483] Gudjonsson (2002). The Psychology of Interrogations and Confessions: A Handbook.

relatively early stages of an investigation, sometimes already by the time a suspect is named, and this can result in guilt-presumptive or even confrontative questioning of the suspect. In essence, this means that a sufficiently strong guilt hypothesis can generate a false confession, the false confession will cognitively contaminate the forensic analyst, who then is more likely to provide corroborating evidence. Furthermore, as outlined in Section 3.5.1, it is also possible that a witness will provide corroborating evidence when informed about a suspect's confession, while this wouldn't have been the case had the witness not known about the confession. This is sometimes referred to as *corroboration inflation*[484] or *bias snowball effect*,[485] that is, that different items of biased evidence can bias each other. Specifically, Dror and colleagues distinguish between two different effects: (i) *the bias cascade effect*, when irrelevant information cascades from one stage to another, for example from the initial evidence collection to the evaluation and interpretation of the evidence; and (ii) *the bias snowball effect*, when the irrelevant information is not only cascading from one stage to another but the bias also increases as irrelevant information from a variety of sources is integrated and influences each other. Clearly this is not only relevant in relation to confessions but other types of evidence too. For example, a forensic examiner comparing bite marks may be influenced by the knowledge that fingerprint evidence indicates that the suspect is guilty.[486] Similarly, eyewitnesses can change their testimony after learning that forensic evidence suggested that a fire was not accidental but the result of arson.[487] When different pieces of evidence influence one another their value and reliability is clearly diminished while the total distorting power increases as more and more evidence is affected by, and affects, other lines of evidence.[488] Consequently, the premises for the judges' evaluation are distorted. While judges are likely to perceive of the different evidence items as independent corroboration, the evidence items are, in fact, interdependent and may stem from a premature hypothesis about what has happened, which is often

---

[484] Kassin (2012). Why Confessions Trump Innocence, pp. 431–445.
[485] Dror et al. (2017). The Bias Snowball and the Bias Cascade Effects: Two Distinct Biases that may Impact Forensic Decision Making, pp. 832–833.
[486] Hasel (2013). Evidentiary Independence—How Evidence Collected Early in an Investigation Influences the Collection and Interpretation of Additional Evidence, pp. 142–159; Hasel & Kassin (2009). On the Presumption of Evidentiary Independence: Can Confessions Corrupt Eyewitness Identifications? pp. 122–126; Marion et al. (2016). Lost Proof of Innocence: The Impact of Confessions on Alibi Witnesses, pp. 65–71.
[487] Hasel (2013). Evidentiary Independence—How Evidence Collected Early in an Investigation Influences the Collection and Interpretation of Additional Evidence, pp. 142–159; Hasel & Kassin (2009). On the Presumption of Evidentiary Independence: Can Confessions Corrupt Eyewitness Identifications? pp. 122–126; Marion et al. (2016). Lost Proof of Innocence: The Impact of Confessions on Alibi Witnesses, pp. 65–71.
[488] Dror et al. (2017). The Bias Snowball and the Bias Cascade Effects: Two Distinct Biases that may Impact Forensic Decision Making, pp. 832–833.

the case in suspect-driven investigations (Section 3.2.1). The overall result is a less accurate and legitimate criminal investigation.

Given the width of the research conducted into forensic confirmation bias it may seem as if this subfield has already evaluated all relevant types of forensic analysis that criminal investigations entail. However, this notion is not only inaccurate but also to a certain extent misleading.[489] For example, the existing research largely leaves out forensic analysis that is more often conducted in the context of international criminal justice, for example crime pattern analysis. Many of the core international crimes require a systematic element to the criminal conduct. For instance, to prove that a crime against humanity has been committed, the prosecutor has to prove that murders, deportations, rapes, and/or other acts were 'committed as part of a widespread or systematic attack directed against any civilian population', pursuant to Article 7 of the Rome Statute of the ICC. Similarly, for genocide by killing it is required that the acts were 'committed with intent to destroy, in whole or in part, a national, ethnical, racial or religious group', following Article 6 of the Rome Statute of the ICC.

Hence, crime pattern analysis is conducted in order to assess whether a large number of incidents can be characterized as a pattern and this is only possible if they share certain common features relating to perpetrators, victims, geographical, chronological distribution, and so on.[490] In this aggregation of multiple incidents into a (potential) pattern, there is, just like with other complex cognitive tasks, ample room for confirmation bias.[491] Similarly, there are also important developments in digital forensics, for example the usage of digital open source information and satellite imagery,[492] which need to be explored. Apart from this, there is also one type of forensic evidence which is not only common to both national and international jurisdictions but also highly influential, namely forensic medical opinions, which, compared to criminalistics, is understudied. However, given the status of this evidence type, the next section will discuss the early research that has been conducted into this field as well as case studies highlighting different possible manifestations of confirmation bias in the decision-making processes of forensic doctors.

---

[489] Note also null findings from two Dutch studies: Kerstholt, Paashuis, & Sjerps (2007). Shoe Print Examinations: Effects of Expectation, Complexity and Experience, pp. 30–34; Eikelboom et al. (2010). Does Suggestive Information Cause a Confirmation Bias in Bullet Comparisons? pp. 138–142.

[490] Agirre Aranburu (2010). Sexual Violence beyond Reasonable Doubt: Using Pattern Evidence and Analysis for International Cases, pp. 609–627.

[491] Lidén (2020). Confirmation Bias in Investigations of Core International Crimes: Risk Factors and Quality Control Techniques, pp. 461–528.

[492] McDermott, Koenig, & Murray (2021). Open Source Information's Blind Spot: Human and Machine Bias in International Criminal Investigations, pp. 85–105.

3.5.4.3 Understanding Bias—Forensic Medicine

It is a positive thing if the forensic doctor on site has a reasonable level of paranoia.[493]

                                                    Forensic doctor Brita Zilg, 2020

Forensic doctors, just like forensic analysts and the remaining human population, stand a risk of becoming biased in their decision-making processes.[494] It is no secret that the statements of forensic doctors regarding, for example, cause of death (COD) or the origins of injuries, can be very powerful evidence. Not only can forensic medical opinions steer investigations in a certain direction because they suggest a certain perpetrator or crime type, they can also be considered decisive proof of guilt in court, for example because they provide a specific time period within which a crime must have taken place.[495] In some cases, such evidence can narrow down the possible perpetrators to just one person. In fact, in 1906, Hans Gross noted that '[o]f all the experts an Investigating Officer has to deal with the most important and the most frequently questioned are medical jurisprudents; with them therefore the Investigating Officer should enter into very intimate relations.'[496] The authoritative status as well as the potentially great distorting power of a forensic medical opinion have been pointed out.[497] Furthermore, real cases confirm these notions, not least cases involving 'Shaken Baby' syndrome. These cases are found in various national jurisdictions and, in them, forensic doctors have concluded, without sufficient scientific evidence,[498] that babies' injuries were specific of child abuse such as Shaken Baby Syndrome (SBS) or Abusive Head Trauma (AHT).[499] Adding more to the risk of error, such evidence has sometimes been used by the police or prosecution as leverage to gain a confession from the parent who was last with the baby.[500] This has proven to be effective since the forensic medical opinion not only specifies the way in which the injuries must have arisen but also within what time frame. This makes it difficult for a parent who was alone with the baby during that time to come up with any other plausible explanations. Evidently, such medical opinions offer persuasive hypotheses about guilt that may have triggered

---

[493] SVT Play (2020). Brottsjournalen.
[494] Dror et al. (2018). No One is Immune to Contextual Bias—Not Even Forensic Pathologists, pp. 316–317.
[495] Payne-James et al. (2011). Simpson's Forensic Medicine.
[496] Gross (1906). Criminal Investigation, A Practical Handbook for Magistrates, Police Officers and Lawyers, p. 155.
[497] Dror et al. (2021). Cognitive Bias in Forensic Pathology Decisions, pp. 1751–1757.
[498] Lynoe et al. (2016). Insufficient Evidence for 'Shaken Baby Syndrome'—A Systematic Review, pp. 1021–1027; The Swedish Agency for Health Technology Assessment and Assessment of Social Services (2016). Skakvåld—Triadens Roll vid Medicinsk Utredning av Misstänkt Skakvåld.
[499] Tuerkheimer (2014). Flawed Convictions, 'Shaken Baby Syndrome' and the Inertia of Injustice.
[500] The Swedish Supreme Court, Ö 1860-12 and Ö 2345-12.

confirmation bias in these cases. Lacking sufficient scientific expertise, such hypotheses will be difficult for legal actors to challenge sufficiently, resulting in a serious risk of error. Consequently, there are several acknowledged cases of wrongful convictions based on such medical evidence in Japan,[501] the United States,[502] the United Kingdom,[503] Norway,[504] and Sweden,[505] yet even until today, some forensic doctors maintain their belief in the shaken baby diagnosis and the specificity of the so-called triad.[506] The triad, that is, subdural haematoma in combination with retinal haemorrhage and encephalopathy, is believed by some to be specific for abusive head trauma/shaken baby syndrome, while this is greatly challenged by others.[507]

Confirmation bias in forensic doctors' decision-making can, however, entail many other types of assessment than those in shaken baby cases. Given the status of forensic medical opinions, it is somewhat surprising that potential bias and debiasing techniques in forensic doctors have not been examined to the same extent as the corresponding questions in criminalistics. The early research which is available suggests that history and contextual information can bias forensic doctors' interpretations of patterned injuries on the skin.[508] Furthermore, it seems that the ethnicity and role of a caregiver taken together can affect forensic doctors' determination of whether an infant death was an accident or intentional.[509] The research study examining ethnicity and the role of a caregiver generated many critical reactions among forensic doctors who claimed, for example, that the researchers tried to label forensic doctors as racists[510] and seriously misrepresented the data,[511] calling for the Journal of Forensic Sciences, to retract the paper.[512] These claims were rebutted after investigation and review.[513] However, there are also forensic doctors who have expressed awareness and concern about

---

[501] Shaken Baby Syndrome (SBS) Review Project Japan, and Osaka High Court overturning SBS conviction, linked on the SBS Review Project Japan's webpage.
[502] Burg (2012). Unconvicting the Innocent: The Case for Shaken Baby Syndrome Review Panels, pp. 657–694; Jenecke (2013). Shaken Baby Syndrome, Wrongful Convictions, and the Dangers of Aversion to Changing Science in Criminal Law, pp. 147–188.
[503] Goldsmith (2004). The Review of Infant Death Cases, Office of the Attorney General; Le Fanu (2005). Wrongful Diagnosis of Child Abuse—A Master Theory, pp. 249–254.
[504] Wester et al. (2021). Re-evaluation of Medical Findings in Alleged Shaken Baby Syndrome and Abusive Head Trauma in Norwegian Courts Fails to Support Abuse Diagnosis, pp. 1–14.pp. 511–537.
[505] Lidén (2021). Resning i brottmål i Sverige, pp. 509–537.
[506] Narang et al. (2016). Acceptance of Shaken Baby Syndrome and Abusive Head Trauma as Medical Diagnoses, pp. 273–278.
[507] Ibid.
[508] Oliver (2017). Effect of History and Context on Forensic Pathologist Interpretation of Photographs of Patterned Injury of the Skin, pp. 1500–1505.
[509] Dror et al. (2021). Cognitive Bias in Forensic Pathology Decisions, pp. 1751–1757.
[510] Peterson et al. (2021). Letter to the Editor, Commentary on: Dror, Melinek, Arden, Kukucka, Hawkins & Carter, pp. 1–2.
[511] Gill et al. (2021). Letter to the Editor, Commentary on; Dror, Melinek, Arden, Kukucka, Hawkins, Carter et al. Cognitive bias in Forensic Pathology Decisions, pp.
[512] Peath (2021). JFS Editor-in-Chief Preface.
[513] Peath (2021). JFS Editor-in-Chief Preface.

the risk of bias, including Thiblin and Michard,[514] Walong and Oduor,[515] as well as Parry,[516] even if awareness in itself is unlikely to suffice as a debiasing technique (Section 2.2.1).

There is also ongoing research examining the prevalence of bias in, for example, assessments of ligature marks around a deceased individual's neck.[517] Similarly, research investigates the effect on forensic doctors' decision making of knowing only one hypothesis; the one presented by the prosecution, or also knowing an alternative hypothesis presented by the defence.[518]

From the cited research, as well as research into bias in forensic doctors' decision-making outside criminal cases (e.g. in histopathological tumour grading),[519] it appears as though forensic doctors are impacted by similar types of contexts as forensic analysts, yet since the assessments made by forensic doctors are inherently different and also have different implications for criminal case procedure, they should be studied and discussed separately. To illustrate possible manifestations of confirmation bias and to emphasize the need for further research in the field, the following outlines three case studies which reinforce the need for a 'reasonable level of paranoia',[520] which may in fact be an asset in a forensic doctor.

Case Study 1: Homicide or struck by lightning?
After two Indian goat herders did not return from their routine morning herding activity, their family members and villagers initiated a search and found their two dead bodies underneath a tree, as illustrated in Figure 3.2.[521]

The family members of the two deceased men filed a police report alleging that someone in the rural area had killed the men. However, the men had no visible injuries on their bodies, at first confusing the criminal investigators regarding the cause of death. Later, when examining the scene more closely, investigators made a few observations they considered relevant, namely that the men both held towels with rigor mortis above their heads, as illustrated in Figures 3.2 and 3.3), and tree bark was damaged, as illustrated in Figure 3.4.

---

[514] Thiblin & Michard (2014). Rättsmedicin i Teori och Praktik: En Guide För Läkare och Jurister.
[515] Walong & Oduor (2019). A 26-year-old Female Presenting with a Fatal Stroke Due to Embolism of Cardiac Myxomatous Neoplasm Diagnosed at Forensic Autopsy Service: A Case Report, pp. 1–4.
[516] Parry (2019). Keeping an Open Mind at Autopsy: Perspective from Veterinary Pathology, pp. 1–5.
[517] Lidén, Dror, & Melinek (2022). Homicide or Suicide? Reliability and Biasability of Forensic Pathologists' Assessments of Ligature Marks.
[518] Lidén et al. (2022). The Role of Alternative Hypotheses in Reducing Bias in Forensic Medical Experts' Decision Making.
[519] Fandel et al. (2008). Do We Truly See What We Think We See?, pp. 193–200.
[520] SVT Play (2020). Brottsjournalen.
[521] This case study has been published by Moorthy (2019). Suspicious Death—Crime Scene Evidence Indicated the Cause of Death: An Interesting Multiple Death Case Report, pp. 5–7.

CONFIRMATION BIAS IN SPECIFIC INVESTIGATIVE SETTINGS 115

Figure 3.2 Two men found deceased underneath a tree in a rural area in India. Reprinted with Permission of the copyright holder.
© 2021 Nataraja Moorthy T.

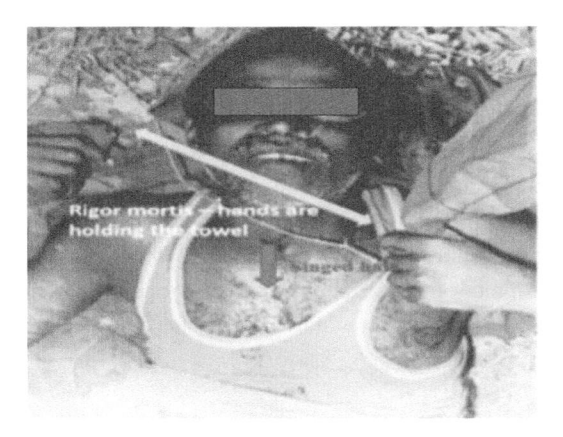

Figure 3.3 One of the two deceased men holding a towel above his head with rigor mortis. Reprinted with permission of the copyright holder. © 2021 Nataraja Moorthy T.

Furthermore, it was well-known to investigators that lightning is a common weather phenomena in the relevant area and that accidental deaths due to lightning are reported every now and then.[522] Together these circumstances suggested to the investigators that the men had held the towels above their heads to shield

---

[522] Moorty (2019). Suspicious Death—Crime Scene Evidence Indicated the Cause of Death: An Interesting Multiple Death Case Report, p. 5.

Figure 3.4 Charred mark on the trunk of the tree underneath which the two deceased men were found. Reprinted with Permission of the Copyright Holder. © 2021 Nataraja Moorthy T.

themselves from the rain while running to take cover underneath the tree where they were struck by lightning which hit the tree and then had raced down the trunk, leaving the marks. The forensic doctor who conducted the autopsy confirmed the investigators' suspicion that the COD was death by lightning.

Cases like this raise questions as to what information should be communicated to forensic doctors. It is unknown whether the men in this case displayed any typical signs of having been struck by lightning. Such signs are, for example, dendrites, fern-like redness from heat-coagulated blood as well as burns from metallic objects such as a button on trousers.[523] It is also unknown whether and to what extent the forensic doctor made the assessment based on the contextual information from the scene, or if the forensic doctor would have reached another conclusion without such contextual information.

Case Study 2: Homicide or cardiac myxoma?
A Kenyan case from 2019 illustrate that even if contextual information can bias forensic doctors' decision-making, absence of contextual information such as details of the deceased's individual's clinical history can also lead them to overlook essential information.[524] Exactly how much information forensic doctors should know is often a difficult assessment.[525] In this case, a 26-year-old female had a sudden and unexpected death six weeks after delivering a baby, and prior to this she had

---

[523] See, for example, Pincus et al. (2015). Lightning Deaths: A Retrospective Review of New Mexico's Cases, 1977–2009, pp. 66–71.
[524] Walong & Odour (2019). A 26-year-old Female Presenting with a Fatal Stroke due to Embolism of Cardiac Myxomatous Neoplasm Diagnosed at a Kenyan Forensic Autopsy Service: A Case Report, pp. 1–4.
[525] Thiblin & Michard (2014). Rättsmedicin i Teori och Praktik: En Guide för Läkare och Jurister.

recurrent undiagnosed transient ischaemic attacks, which were never investigated. On the day of her death, the woman had an argument with her spouse after which she was unable to talk or move and she also had right-sided weakness. Twelve hours later she died in hospital, her spouse was arrested, and a murder investigation was initiated. According to the first autopsy, performed 72 hours after her death, there was no evidence of external trauma but instead findings suggesting that the COD was cardiac myxoma, that is intracardiac neoplasms that frequently embolize resulting in cerebral infarcts (strokes) and tumour emboli to the cerebral arteries.[526] The spouse was released. However, since the deceased woman's siblings were unsatisfied with the autopsy findings, they sought the opinion of an independent forensic doctor whose hypothesis was that traumatic injury may have contributed to embolization of the cardiac myxoma. Because of this, another autopsy was performed by two independent forensic doctors, yet this autopsy showed no evidence of trauma. Therefore, the hypothesis that chest trauma contributed to tumour fragmentation and embolization could not be supported. The consensus among the forensic doctors was that this was a natural death. Cardiac myxomas may present as sudden unexpected death and may therefore well confound homicide investigations. Because histopathology and keen systematic evaluation are rarely performed in African forensic autopsies, these diagnoses are frequently missed.[527] The rate of maternal mortality due to strokes are 30 per 100,000 in developed countries.[528] The rates in eastern Africa are unknown but are postulated to be higher, not least because persons of African descent have higher incidences of stroke.[529]

Case Study 3: Death due to self-inflicted acute alcohol poisoning (AAP) or homicide through cyanide poisoning?
In 2019, Swedish courts dealt with murder charges against a woman whom the media referred to as the 'Cyanide Woman'. She was believed to have poured a deadly amount of cyanide into a drink she had served to the man with whom she lived, resulting in his death.[530] Due to the deceased man's acknowledged issues with alcohol, the lack of visible injuries, and other factors, acute alcohol poisoning (AAP) had previously been presumed to be the COD. In fact, this presumption seems to have dominated the investigation for quite some time. Only after repeated attempts did the daughter of the deceased man manage to initiate a post-mortem

---

[526] Walong & Oduor (2019). A 26-year-old Female Presenting with A Fatal Stroke due to Embolism of Cardiac Myxomatous Neoplasm Diagnosed at a Kenyan Forensic Autopsy Service: A Case Report, pp. 1–4.
[527] Walong & Oduor (2019). A 26-year-old Female Presenting with A Fatal Stroke due to Embolism of Cardiac Myxomatous Neoplasm Diagnosed at a Kenyan Forensic Autopsy Service: A Case Report, pp. 1–4.
[528] Swarts et al. (2017). The Incidence of Pregnancy-related Stroke: A Systematic Review and Meta-Analysis, pp. 687–697.
[529] Sells & Feske (2017). Stroke in Pregnancy, pp. 669–678.
[530] Svea Court of Appeal, B 6615-19.

forensic toxicological assessment with the purpose of detecting any poison[531] in her father's body. Subsequently, when a forensic toxicologist finally re-examined the body, a deadly amount of cyanide was found, confirming the daughter's suspicions and contradicting the initial hypothesis of excessive alcoholic intoxication. The new findings resulted in formalized suspicions against the woman who was convicted by the District Court[532] and the conviction was upheld on appeal.[533]

Had the daughter of the deceased man not insisted, it is unlikely that the alternative hypothesis of poisoning would have been examined at all. Consequently, the main hypothesis of excessive alcohol consumption would not have been sufficiently challenged. This emphasizes the strength of an initial hypothesis and how forensic medical opinions can vary depending on what questions the examiners are asked to look into. In real-life criminal cases, forensic medical examinations are of course not conducted in a vacuum but requested and specified by the police and the prosecution. Since these actors often, in many jurisdictions, have a duty to examine incriminating and exonerating circumstances equally, it can be questioned whether and to what extent it is their or the defence's responsibility to include alternative hypotheses in their requests for medical opinions. Although it may vary in different legal systems and in different types of cases, the defence may have limited resources to conduct own investigations and/or limited access to state-level trusted forensic expertise.[534] In practice, this is likely to limit the possibilities of introducing and properly evaluating alternative hypotheses to that cited in the original proceedings, and it is not necessarily easier to introduce an alternative thereafter. When it comes to poison specifically, the situation can of course also be the opposite to that in the Swedish case. While someone did die under the influence of toxins, as determined through toxicological assessment, the real cause of death may in fact be something else such as a car accident or a fall from a height.[535] Contrary to the situation in the Swedish cyanide case, this could in fact mean that someone who is suspected of having poisoned a deceased individual is in fact not responsible for the deceased's death, even though that person might have intended to kill the deceased individual.

There is a range of other possible forensic medical assessments in relation to which confirmation bias may arise. For example, early research illustrates a confirmation

---

[531] Torrance (2016). Forensic Toxicology, in White, Crime Scene to Court, The Essentials of Forensic Science, p. 447.
[532] Norrtälje District Court, B 1268-18.
[533] Svea Court of Appeal, B 6615-19.
[534] Thiblin, Wennström, & Allen (2012). Let the Defence Have Access to Forensic Expertise Too, pp. 1–2.
[535] Torrance (2016). Forensic Toxicology. In White, Crime Scene to Court, The Essentials of Forensic Science, p. 445.

bias in forensic odontologists radiographic matching decisions.[536] These decisions are used as a basis for forensic age estimations (FAEs), which are of considerable importance in all jurisdictions. In the context of criminal investigations and proceedings, age estimations are crucial, for example because many crimes require that an individual is legally classified as a child, such as child trafficking, child pornography, conscripting or enlisting child soldiers, and rape or sexual exploitation of a child. When it comes to age estimations of child soldiers in particular, establishing whether someone has reached 15 years does not only determine whether a crime has been committed but it can also potentially change the status of the individual from a victim to a perpetrator.[537] Also, age estimations can be decisive in the determination of whether an individual found guilty of a crime is exempt from the death penalty[538] as well as other questions relating to sentencing (severity and length).[539] Although the more specific forensic methods used vary greatly across different jurisdictions,[540] the three most common ones among EU states are assessments including the hand or wrist (bone age),[541] teeth (dental age),[542] and collarbone (also bone age).[543] All these assessments have similarities with other forensic assessments where confirmation bias has been studied and documented. For example, X-ray interpretation is a visual assessment, just like fingerprint or handwriting examination, and X-rays can often be ambiguous, something that is known to increase the risk of confirmation bias.[544] In fact, bias and related cognitive phenomenon such as inattentional blindness have been noted in other types of radiological assessments.[545] Hence, there is good reason to, empirically and systematically, evaluate and be aware of the risk of confirmation bias in FAEs.

---

[536] Chiam et al. (2021). The Biasing Impact of Irrelevant Contextual Information on Forensic Odontology Radiograph Matching Decisions, pp. 1–8.
[537] Lidén (2020). Child Soldier or Soldier? Estimating Age in Cases of Core International Crimes: Challenges and Opportunities.
[538] Hood & Hoyle (2012). The Death Penalty: A Worldwide Perspective.
[539] Schwarts (2012). Age-appropriate Charging and Sentencing; McGrath (2016). Intersection of Indigenous Status, Sex and Age in Sentencing Decisions in the New South Wales Children's Court; Steffensmeier, Kramer, & Ulmer (1995). Age Differences in Sentencing.
[540] The Council of Europe Children's Rights Division (2017). Age Assessment: Council of Europe Member States' Policies, Procedures and Practices Respectful of Children's Rights in the Context of Migration; European Asylum Support Office (EASO) (2018). Practical Guide on Age Assessment, EASO Practical Guide Series, p. 33.
[541] Doyle et al. (2019). Guidelines for Best Practice: Imaging for Age Estimation in the Living, pp. 38–49.
[542] Doyle et al. (2019). Guidelines for Best Practice: Imaging for Age Estimation in the Living, pp. 38–49.
[543] Schmeling et al. (2008). Criteria for Age Estimation in Living Individuals, pp. 457–460; Schmeling et al. (2016). Forensic Age Estimation: Methods, Certainty, and the Law, pp. 44–50.
[544] Osborne & Zajac (2015). An Imperfect Match? Crime-related Context Influences Fingerprint Decisions, pp. 126–134; Mossman (2013). When Forensic Examiners Disagree: Bias, or Just Inaccuracy?
[545] Gunderman (2009). Biases in Radiologic Reasoning, pp. 561–564; Lee et al. (2013). Cognitive and System Factors Contributing to Diagnostic Errors in Radiology, pp. 611–617; Busby, Courtier, & Glastonbury (2017). Bias in Radiology: The How and Why of Misses and Misinterpretations, pp. 236–247; Drew & Wolfe (2013). The Invisible Gorilla Strikes Again: Sustained Inattentional Blindness in Expert Observers, pp. 1848–1853.

3.5.4.4 Understanding Bias—Forensic Anthropology

In 1988, one of the most extensive police inquiries in Norwegian history was initiated following the disappearance of the nine-year-old girl Therese Johanessen.[546] About 11,000 people were questioned and 4,000 vehicles were searched for any information about what might have happened to Therese, but in 1989 the inquiry had not generated suspicions against any particular person and the magnitude of the inquiry gradually subsided,[547] clearly a disappointing development in a missing person case, particularly one regarding a child.

In 1993, the investigation into Therese's disappearance was brought to life again following Mr Bergwall's confessions pertaining to more than 30 murders, including the murder of Therese.[548] There were many circumstances that should have raised doubts regarding the accuracy of Mr Bergwall's confessions, for example that the confessions were elicited during therapy when he was in forensic psychiatric care,[549] and two of the individuals he claimed he had murdered turned out to be alive.[550] Regardless of this, the investigators focused fairly one-sidedly on obtaining evidence that could confirm Mr Bergwall's guilt. In the Therese Johanessen case, Mr Bergwall told investigators that he had disposed and buried Therese's remains in a forest region near Drammen where Therese lived with her mother.[551] Consequently, the Norwegian police conducted a massive search in the forest region and emptied an entire forest lake in the search for Therese's remains.[552] Small pieces of organic material were finally identified (see Figure 3.5) and when confronted with them, Mr Bergwall told investigators that he had dismembered Therese's body using a saw and that the pieces might come from her thighbone.[553]

The two forensic experts who examined the organic material concluded that they, most probably, were human bone originating from a young person and that the pieces also showed traces of a cutting object.[554] One of the experts added that the appearance of the cut indicated that a saw had been used[555] and that the bone's overall appearance suggested that it came from an upper arm or a thighbone.[556] Unsurprisingly, Mr Bergwall was convicted of the murder of Therese and was sentenced to continued forensic psychiatric care.[557] However, 13 years later when he

---

[546] Hedemora District Court, B 100/97 pp. 3–13.
[547] Hedemora District Court, B 100/97 pp. 3–13.
[548] Swedish Government Official Reports, Rapport från Bergwallkommissionen, SOU 2015:52, p. 29.
[549] The Swedish Government Official Reports, SOU 2015:52 and Hedemora District Court, B 100/97 pp. 3–4.
[550] The Swedish Government Official Reports, SOU 2015:52.
[551] Hedemora District Court, B 100/97 pp. 3–4.
[552] Hedemora District Court, B 100/97 pp. 3–4.
[553] Hedemora District Court, B 100/97 pp. 8, 15–16.
[554] Hedemora District Court, B 100/97 pp. 8, 15–16.
[555] Hedemora District Court, B 100/97 pp. 8, 15–16.
[556] Hedemora District Court, B 100/97 pp. 15–16.
[557] Hedemora District Court, B100/9, p. 1.

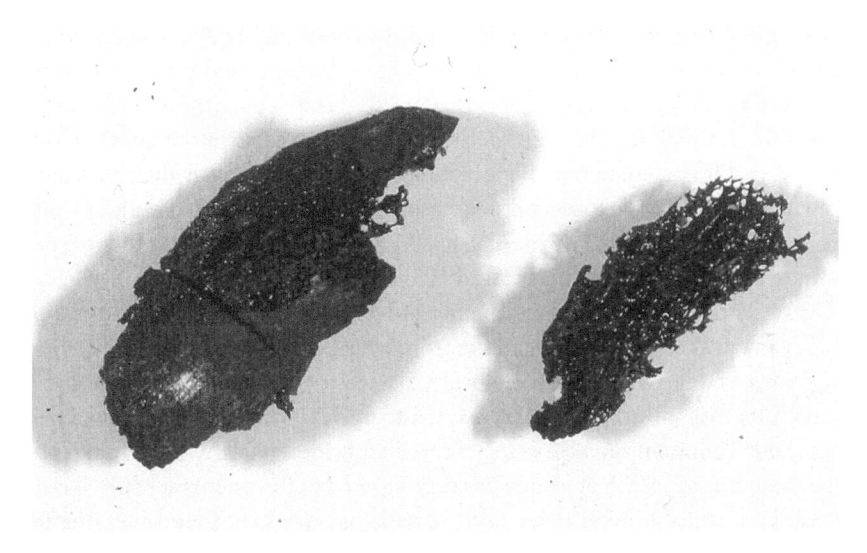

Figure 3.5 Organic material found in the Norwegian Forest Area in the Therese Johanessen case. Reprinted with permission from the copyright holder.

retracted his confession, he was granted a new trial and acquitted.[558] Since Mr Bergwall had also retracted five other confessions pertaining to other murder cases, the case received enormous media attention pointing out many sources of error in the original investigations and proceedings.[559] As the inquiry in the Therese Johanessen case was resumed, other forensic experts re-examined the same pieces of organic material that were found in the Norwegian forest region in 1993 and concluded that they were not, in fact, human bone.[560] In 2019, the Cold Case Division at the Norwegian Criminal Investigation Service (Kripos), a special agency of the Norwegian Police Service, reported that the possibility of solving the case was very limited and that no further investigation was to be undertaken.[561]

Since the forensic assessments seem to have been dictated, or at least affected, by the context in which they were conducted, they illustrate that confirmation bias may be present also in forensic anthropological assessments (osteology). In the original proceedings, the experts who were aware of Mr Bergwall's confessions both reached the conclusion that the material was human bone and its appearance was consistent with Mr Bergwall's stated course of events. It is unknown whether

---

[558] Svea Court of Appeal, Ö 3293-10, Falun District Court, B 3585/10.
[559] Guillou (2008). Klockan Tickar om de Riktiga Mördarna ska Kunna Dömas; Andersson (2009). Quicks Erkännande—en Kopia av Efterlyst; Råstam (2010). Material som kunde Fria Quick Gömdes av Polisen.
[560] Svea Court of Appeal, Ö 3293-10, p. 4.
[561] Bjerkeseth et al. (2019). Moren till Therese vil aldrig gi opp jakten på svar.

Mr Bergwall provided his version first or did so only after knowing the results of the forensic assessment. However, as the context changed, and the overall media picture of Mr Bergwall was no longer that of a serial killer but instead that of a false confessor, the analysts who re-examined the material came to the opposite conclusion, that it was not human bone at all. In this case specifically the conclusions drawn by the forensic experts in the original proceedings resulted both in a false positive, the conviction of Mr Bergwall, and the inability to identify the real perpetrator after so much time had passed.

Apart from assessments as to whether bone is human or not, forensic anthropology involves assessments including from what part of the human body a bone originates, as well as the likely biological sex, ancestry, and age of the individual.[562] As such, forensic anthropological assessments are often vital to criminal cases since these fairly commonly involve searches for missing individuals who are found only after long time spans when a body has decomposed to the extent that only skeletal remains are available for analysis. Skeletal remains can also be found after fires following arson, airline disasters, attempts to eliminate a deceased victim's body, etc.

Research within the field of forensic anthropology has identified a confirmation bias in evaluations of biological sex and ethnicity based on morphological (visual) assessments of skeletal remains.[563] Specifically, this research implies that forensic anthropologists were biased by contextual information suggesting a certain biological sex and ethnicity, and this affected how they perceived the skeletal remains. Furthermore, the presence of gender-specific clothing at a scene biased morphological sex-estimation observations and conclusions.[564] Also, the order in which different skeletal material is analysed seem to have a biasing effect.[565] Furthermore, research suggests that anthropologists' (visual) assessments of whether skeletal remains have been exposed to trauma are biased by contextual information, such as where the remains were found; a mass grave, indicating a high probability of trauma, or an archaeological site, indicating a relatively low probability of trauma.[566] Such morphological non-metric assessments are associated with a fairly high level of interpretation relative to metric methodologies,

---

[562] Christensen, Passalacqua, & Bartelink (2019). Forensic Anthropology—Current Methods and Practice, pp. 1–2.

[563] Nakhaeizadeh, Hanson, & Dozzi (2014). The Power of Contextual Effects in Forensic Anthropology: A Study of Biasability in the Visual Interpretations of Trauma Analysis on Skeletal Remains, pp. 1177–1183; Nakhaeizadeh et al. (2017). Cascading Bias of Initial Exposure to Information at the Crime Scene to the Subsequent Evaluation of Skeletal Remains, pp. 403–411.

[564] Nakhaeizadeh et al. (2017). Cascading Bias of Initial Exposure to Information at the Crime Scene to the Subsequent Evaluation of Skeletal Remains, pp. 403–411.

[565] Davidson, Rando, & Nakhaeizadeh (2019). Cognitive Bias and the Order of Examination on Skeletal Remains; Klales & Lesciotto (2016). The 'Science of Science': Examining Bias in Forensic Anthropology.

[566] Nakhaeizadeh, Hanson, & Dozzi (2013). The Power of Contextual Effects: A Study of Biasability in Visual Interpretations of Trauma Analysis on Skeletal Remains, pp. 1177–1183.

that is, methodologies using actual measurements as a basis for conclusions.[567] Consequently, metric assessments are usually considered less susceptible to bias than non-metric assessments.[568] However, more recent research suggests that forensic anthropological sex determinations are prone to bias, even when based on metric measurements.[569] Specifically, forensic anthropologists/trained osteologists conducted sectioning point-based sex estimation based on a femur[570] including both continuous data (measurements) and categorical perception (categorization into discrete decisions: male/female). They were presented with contextual information; photos from the scene showing either female or male clothing. Even though the femur originated from a male anatomical skeleton, 78.5 per cent of the forensic anthropologists who were exposed to female clothes categorized the individual as female (conclusion), although no significant differences were seen in their measurements (observations) compared to the anthropologists who were exposed to male clothes.[571]

It is easy to see how confirmation bias in forensic anthropological assessment can set a criminal investigation off in a completely erroneous direction. This was fairly obvious in the Therese Johanessen case but since forensic anthropology also includes a range of other types of assessments, many other potential errors may be made. For example, an erroneous assessment of whether skeletal remains belong to a male or a female individual can lead investigators to believe that they have identified a victim when, in fact, they have not. Vice versa, they may overlook the possibility that skeletal remains originate from a specific missing person. Both types of errors are clearly detrimental to the accuracy of the criminal investigation, and are risk factors both in relation to false positives and false negatives.

3.5.4.5 Mitigating Bias

The potentially strong distorting power of forensic confirmation bias is, or should be, a strong incentive for forensic laboratories and forensic doctors' clinics to find proper ways to avoid exposure to *irrelevant* potentially biasing contextual information. Simultaneously, *relevant* potentially biasing contextual information needs to be used wisely. Hence, bias mitigation is not about completely isolating forensic analysts or forensic doctors from the outside world, including, for example, investigators and prosecutors, the media, or even their colleagues. Rather, it is about

---

[567] Hartley, Powanda Winburn, & Dror (2021). Metric Forensic Anthropology Decisions: Reliability and Biasability of Sectioning-Point-Based Sex Estimates, pp. 1–12.
[568] Winburn (2018). Subjective with a Capital S? Issues of Objectivity in Forensic Anthropology, pp. 21–37; Walker (2005). Greater Sciatic Notch Morphology: Sex, Age, and Population Differences; Pietrusewsky (2008). Metric Analysis of Skeletal Remains: Methods and Applications.
[569] Hartley, Powanda Winburn, & Dror (2021). Metric Forensic Anthropology Decisions: Reliability and Biasability of Sectioning-Point-Based Sex Estimates, pp. 1–12.
[570] France (1998). Observation and Metric Analysis of Sex in the Skeleton, pp. 163–186.
[571] Hartley, Powanda Winburn, & Dror (2021). Metric Forensic Anthropology Decisions: Reliability and Biasability of Sectioning-Point-Based Sex Estimates, pp. 1–12.

managing and mitigating the risk of bias through debiasing techniques. In the field of forensic analysis, four main debiasing techniques have appeared in the research available so far. These techniques are (i) contextual information management (CIM), (ii) linear sequential unmasking (LSU), (iii) changing decision-maker/ independent verification, and (iv) usage of technological advances. While these techniques will be addressed separately, they can be used both on their own or combined depending on the case specific circumstances as well as organizational factors.

3.5.4.5.1 Contextual Information Management (CIM)
For forensic analysts and doctors to understand what they are asked to do, at least some type of communication with investigators and prosecutors is clearly necessary. Hence, such communication cannot, and should not, be fully removed. However, it is essential to exercise caution in this communication. Furthermore, the caution needs to be exercised at both ends. Investigators and prosecutors need to consider carefully which specific questions they request analysts and forensic doctors to answer as well as which case information they provide.[572] At the same time, analysts and forensic doctors also need to be careful regarding which information they ask for or obtain themselves from case files or other sources of information.

While research in this area started with proposals for so-called blind testing,[573] the recommendations today are more elaborate and detailed. More specifically, it is recommended to have a context manager, an individual who serves as a gateway between the two and who mitigates bias by considering essentially two questions: (i) whether the contextual information is relevant for the analysis to be conducted, and (ii) whether the information is potentially biasing. This results in the four possible outcomes illustrated in Table 3.3.[574] The table also outlines the measures suggested in relation to the four different categories of information. The top left category of potentially biasing but task-relevant information ought to be of interest in many criminal investigations. This category is also associated with the most in-depth and detailed bias mitigating measure, that is, to avoid immediate full disclosure of information and instead postpone disclosure using so-called linear sequential unmasking (LSU), which will be addressed in detail in Section 3.5.4.4.2. It should also be noted, however, that not all types of contextual information can be neatly contained and 'put on hold' in criminal investigations. This is the situation, for example, in high-profile cases with massive media exposure.

---

[572] Kassin, Dror, & Kukucka (2013). The Forensic Confirmation Bias: Problems, Perspectives, and Proposed Solutions, p. 50.
[573] Kassin, Dror, & Kukucka (2013). The Forensic Confirmation Bias: Problems, Perspectives, and Proposed Solutions, pp. 42–52.
[574] Osborne & Taylor (2018). Contextual Information Management: An Example of Independent-Checking in the Review of Laboratory-Based Bloodstain Pattern Analysis, pp. 226–231.

Table 3.3 Measures suggested based on task relevance and the potentially biasing effect of contextual information.

Information	Task relevant	Task irrelevant
Biasing	Postpone disclosure (linear sequential unmasking, LSU)	No disclosure
Not biasing	Disclosure	Disclosure unnecessary

> REMARKS:
> The above listed suspect is the person who pulled the trigger, making every effort to place him in the truck. One witness riding in the truck was too drunk to make an identification.
> NAME OF PERSON REQUESTING EXAMINATION: Det. ███████ DATE ███████

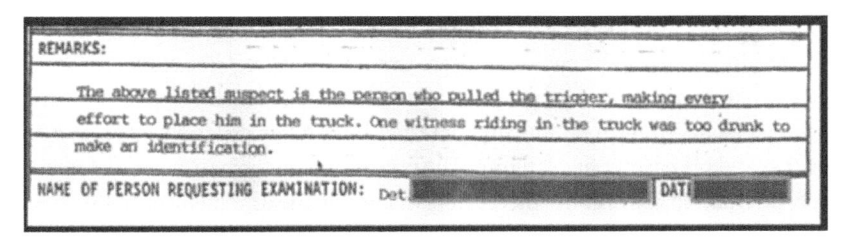

Figure 3.6 Evidence submission form from homicide case containing irrelevant and potentially biasing information. Reprinted with permission from the copyright holder.

In national jurisdictions, this could entail, for example, alleged acts of terrorism, murders, crimes against children, or other crimes that generate public outrage. In international jurisdictions it is more or less a constant, given the gravity of the crimes dealt with and/or the often powerful status of the suspects. The recommendation then, rather than LSU, would be to obtain independent review, that is, to have a second decision-maker, blind to the contextual information, conduct the same analysis, addressed more in detail in Section 3.5.4.4.3.

Some types of information should be fairly easy to categorize. Figure 3.6 shows remarks made by a requestor (i.e. a police officer or prosecutor) in an evidence submission form, a form that referring agencies like police departments use to submit evidence and requests for forensic analysis. This evidence submission form was submitted in a homicide case, the details of which have been omitted here to protect the integrity of the individuals involved. The remarks made offer a clear example of irrelevant and potentially biasing information that should not be disclosed.

These remarks explicitly communicate the requestor's hypothesis, not only that the suspect is guilty but also which more specific role the suspect played in the crime ('the listed suspect is the person who pulled the trigger'). Also, the remarks appear to be more a call for help from the analyst to ensure that the suspect can be brought to justice rather than a request for an objective investigation ('making every effort to place him in the truck' and noting that the witness riding in the truck 'was too drunk to make an identification'). This is likely to put some pressure on the analyst to reach the conclusion suggested by the requestor. The progress of the case is described by the requestor as more or less fully dependent on the analyst's findings. While analysts may of course consciously attempt to distance themselves from a requestor's hypothesis and actively try to remain neutral, such efforts are most likely to be insufficient given the more or less subconscious nature of confirmation bias.

Yet, the distinction between the categories 'biasing and irrelevant information' on the one hand and 'biasing and relevant information' on the other hand is far from evident in every single case. Some types of information may be relevant because they cause analysts or forensic doctors to think of possibilities they otherwise may never have considered. For example, a man was found deceased in his car and next to him, on the passenger seat, there was a note saying 'Bee stung'.[575] The deceased man had regular contact with a physician due to an HIV-infection and the physician believed the man was suicidal since he recently experienced great financial loss and his partner had left him. The note found on the passenger seat was initially interpreted as a cryptic suicide note that might mean something to his friends and family. However, the forensic examiners decided to look for signs of an allergic reaction and found such signs in a microscopic examination of his respiratory tract. The subsequent analysis showed that the likely cause of death was high levels of bee poison resulting in a strong anaphylactic shock. Since there were no signs of a bee sting on the man's body, they would not have come to the same conclusion if they did not know about the 'suicide note'. Similarly, in Case study 2 (Section 3.5.4.3) the deceased woman's clinical history was relevant to the determination that she had suffered from cardiac myxoma rather than having been murdered. Vice versa, there are also examples in which omission of information entails a risk that the forensic doctor overlooks crime-relevant symptoms.[576] To illustrate, in a suspected murder case knowing that a deceased person had undergone heart surgery due to coronary artery disease lead the forensic doctor to conclude initially that the person had suffered a sudden cardiac death since no injuries were visible on the deceased man's body.[577] This contextual information also made the forensic doctor interpret the man's crushed liver and the big hole found in his diaphragm as results of the violent cardiac pulmonary resuscitation (CPR), thus still consistent with the sudden cardiac death hypothesis. It was not until the forensic doctor also discovered that the man's spine was broken that the forensic doctor abandoned this hypothesis. A police investigation was initiated and resulted in the conclusion that the man's body had been crushed by equipment at the lumber mill.

---

[575] Thiblin & Michard (2014). Rättsmedicin i Teori och Praktik—En Guide för Läkare och Jurister, p. 81.
[576] Thiblin & Michard (2014). Rättsmedicin i Teori och Praktik—En Guide för Läkare och Jurister, pp. 48–49.
[577] Thiblin & Michard (2014). Rättsmedicin i Teori och Praktik—En Guide för Läkare och Jurister, pp. 48–49.

Since it is not necessarily self-evident in every given situation to which category the information of interest belongs, in cases of doubt it makes sense to follow the overall recommendation to exercise caution. This would in many situations imply that the information should be treated as *task relevant*, to ensure that important findings are not missed, *but also potentially biasing* and that it should therefore be subjected to postponed disclosure including LSU.[578] If, for example, the disclosure of potentially biasing information is postponed until after the examiner has first analysed, for example, prints without any such information, any deviations in their assessments following the disclosure would need to be explained. Alternatively, the evidence should be subjected to independent review/change of decision-maker.

Notably, there are also examples which highlight that confirmation bias is not always triggered by too much information, or the wrong type of information. It can also be triggered by the fact that insufficient information is communicated. This is because the questions asked by investigators and prosecutors dictate what answers are provided by forensic analysts and forensic doctors. For example, in a Swedish murder case from 2008, Mr Westlund was suspected of having killed his wife, Agneta, using a lawn mower.[579] The 'lawn mower hypothesis' came about, for example, because the deceased woman had deep cuts on her legs with grass pressed inside of the cuts.[580] The suspect denied all involvement and put forward the alternative hypothesis to investigators that his wife might have been attacked and killed by a moose,[581] the 'moose hypothesis'. However, the first request to the forensic doctor only asked for an examination into whether the wounds were consistent with the lawn mower hypothesis. Hence, the request did not mention the moose hypothesis at all.[582] Subsequently, the forensic doctor provided an answer regarding the lawn mower hypothesis in the autopsy report, namely that '[m]ost of the injuries and the existence of grass deep inside the cut on the right leg are consistent with that AW [Agneta; own addition] has been run over by a lawn mower. The findings strongly suggest that the death was caused by another person.'[583]

Following this, and awaiting the result of the analysis of blood found underneath the lawn mower, which later turned out to be blood from a small animal rather than a human,[584] Mr Westlund was detained and remained the main suspect. Only after

---

[578] Krane et al. (2008). Sequential Unmasking: a Means of Minimizing Observer Effects in Forensic DNA Interpretation, pp. 1006–1007; Dror et al. (2015). Letter to the Editor: Context Management Toolbox: A Linear Sequential Unmasking (LSU) Approach for Minimizing Cognitive Bias in Forensic Decision Making, pp. 1111–1112.
[579] Kalmar District Court, B 2994-08.
[580] Autopsy report 20080910.
[581] Kalmar Police Authority, Detention Memo, Ref. No. 0800-K19154-08, Interview 2008-09-06, 13:20–14:35, p. 12.
[582] Autopsy report 20080910.
[583] Autopsy report 20080910.
[584] Directive from the prosecutor/Record from meeting, 2008-12-04; Email correspondence between prosecutor and police officer, 2008-10-16; Directive from the prosecutor, 2008-11-28, Directive from the prosecutor, 209-01-23; Kalmar Prosecution Authority, Decision to dismiss Ingemar Westlund as a suspect, 2019-01-28, Case No. AM-138010-08.

he had been detained for approximately four months did the prosecutor request a medical evaluation of whether Agneta's injuries were consistent with the moose hypothesis.[585] The forensic doctor confirmed that the injuries were 'consistent with an attack by a deer or similar'.[586] Following this, and after large amounts of moose saliva and hair had been found on Agneta's body, Mr Westlund was set free and was no longer considered a suspect.[587]

Although the responsibilities of the prosecution and defence vary across different jurisdictions, it can be argued that any prosecutor who has a duty to investigate incriminating and exonerating circumstances equally has an accompanying responsibility to request forensic examination into alternative hypotheses. In Mr Westlund's case specifically, he had proposed the moose hypothesis in his first police interview. Specifically, he stated he had heard 'loud splashes',[588] possibly from a moose getting in the lake nearby where he found his wife. He also repeated this possibility in all subsequent interviews. Thus, while the moose hypothesis may have come across as unlikely, comical, or even a guilty man's desperate attempt to free himself of suspicion, there are reasons to suggest that the moose hypothesis should have been included in the first request to the forensic doctor conducting the autopsy. If a prosecutor, for one reason or another, does not request examinations into a known alternative hypothesis, then the introduction of such hypotheses will be left to the defence. The extent to which the defence is successful in this regard will depend on whether and to what extent forensic laboratories or forensic doctors are obliged to conduct examination into a hypothesis suggested by the defence. It is also dependent on whether the defence has financial resources to hire their own experts, the credibility of those experts vis-à-vis the experts hired by the prosecution, and so on. At the very least, defence attorneys have good reason to argue that forensic examinations focusing on the prosecution hypothesis exclusively are insufficient for a conviction, since this creates reasonable doubt. It can be argued whether and to what extent judges who are not presented with such arguments should request information about how the analysis was conducted themselves. Asking such questions during hearings, and/or raising such issues in written verdicts, for example as a reason for an acquittal, can have positive directing effects on forensic analysis routines. Furthermore, it can be discussed whether, during the investigative phase, and in situations where alternative defence hypotheses are not presented, whether a context manager should act in some capacity. At least some

---

[585] Directive from the prosecutor, 2009-01-23, Case No. AM-138010-08 and Forensic Medical opinion 20090123.
[586] Forensic medical opinion 20090123.
[587] Kalmar Prosecution Authority, Decision to dismiss Ingemar Westlund as a suspect, 2019-01-28, Case No. AM-138010-08.
[588] Kalmar Police Authority, Detention Memo, Ref. No. 0800-K19154-08; Interrogation 2008-09-05, 22:55-23:15, pp. 5–6.

of the case material, including interviews with suspects, may be readily available to them, and yet if context managers actively search for alternative hypotheses on their own initiative, they not only go beyond the request made by the investigators/prosecutor but also risk impacting on the criminal investigation either to the accused's disadvantage or advantage. Context managers cannot reasonably know what the result of such an investigation would be. One possibility for a context manager would be to ask whether the defence has any hypothesis to be examined, or to state clearly in the medical opinion that the injuries had only been examined in relation to the suggested hypothesis and that they may also be consistent with other hypotheses which have not been examined. To what extent such an approach will be effective in practice depends on to what extent prosecutors and judges are receptive to such communications.

In some jurisdictions there is guidance to be found on the topic of what information is task relevant. For example, the US National Commission on Forensic Science has issued a statement in this regard.[589] More specifically, the Commission considers information task relevant if it is necessary to draw conclusions: (i) about the propositions in question, (ii) from the physical evidence that has been designated for examination, and (iii) through the correct application of an accepted analytic method by a competent analyst.[590] If a piece of information does not meet all three criteria, then it is considered irrelevant to the task at hand. To illustrate what it considers task irrelevant, The Commission uses the following examples: information about a suspect's criminal history, a suspect's confession, implications of guilt by other evidence at the crime scene such as DNA evidence and information relating to another latent print examiner's conclusions regarding the prints found on another item at the crime scene. Authorities in the United States[591] as well as in other countries such as the United Kingdom[592] have offered similar views and recommendations, although with varying levels of details and specification.[593]

Forensic analysts and forensic doctors can receive contextual information in many ways. This includes evidence submission forms, personal communications via email and phone as well as through media reports. Depending on what the source of the contextual information is contextual information management will have to take different shapes.

---

[589] National Commission on Forensic Science (2015). Ensuring That Forensic Analysis is Based Upon Task-relevant Information.
[590] National Commission on Forensic Science (2015). Ensuring That Forensic Analysis is Based Upon Task-relevant Information.
[591] President's Council of Advisors on Science and Technology (2016). Report to the President: Forensic Science in Criminal Courts: Ensuring Scientific Validity of Feature-comparison Methods, Executive Office of the President of the United States.
[592] Forensic Science Regulator (2015). Cognitive Bias Effects Relevant to Forensic Science Examinations.
[593] Dror et al. (2015). Letter to the Editor—Context Management Toolbox: A Linear Sequential Unmasking (LSU) Approach for Minimizing Cognitive Bias in Forensic Decision Making, pp. 1111–1112.

Evidence submission forms are one of the primary ways in which referring agencies and analysts or forensic doctors communicate. For a context manager, it is therefore relevant not only what information requestors add to these forms (see the examples above) but also what type of information the blank forms request from referring agencies. Research based on evidence submission forms from 113 US crime laboratories, representing 47 US states and the federal jurisdiction, suggest that a relatively large proportion of these forms, in fact, request potentially biasing irrelevant information.[594] The sample of evidence submission forms used in this study are used by 70.8 per cent of identified crime laboratories in the US. To illustrate, 45.4 per cent of the forms request information regarding the suspect's race or ethnicity, which is problematic since this may influence the decision-making. For example, research with mock jurors suggest that African-American defendants are more likely to be found guilty and given lengthier sentences than Caucasian defendants.[595] Also, 42.3 per cent of the forms request information regarding whether the suspect has an FBI or state identification number, associated with, although not equated with, having a criminal history.[596] Many forms, 47.4 per cent, contained a broad prompt requesting additional information, considerations, or comments, leaving room for the sort of remarks illustrated in the homicide case above. Also, 8.2 per cent of the forms requested previous forensic analyses that had been conducted on the submitted evidence, which is known to be a biasing factor. Single forms also asked for information like: 'What are you trying to establish with the evidence?' or whether the suspect was considered a 'serious violent felon' a 'flight risk' or whether the case concerned an 'officer involved shooting'.[597] It is possible that some types of information such as being labelled a flight risk may be relevant as regards the urgency of the case but it can also be potentially biasing. Hence, the evidence submission forms themselves may prompt biasing information and a context manager should review forms in light of the research on forensic confirmation bias. If it is considered necessary to include such requests then the context manager will also have to monitor the information that referring agencies add in these fields and consider whether that information needs to be disclosed, as well as when.

Personal communication can be initiated from either party and this is sometimes beyond the control of a context manager. Hence, CIM models also presuppose personal responsibility for the individual forensic examiners, investigators,

---

[594] Gardner et al. (2019). Do Evidence Submission Forms Expose Latent Print Examiners to Task-irrelevant Information? pp. 236–242.

[595] Johnson et al. (1995). Justice is Still Not Colorblind: Differential Racial Effects of Exposure to Inadmissible Evidence, pp. 893–898; DeSantis & Kayson (1997). Defendant's Characteristics of Attractiveness, Race, and Sex and Sentencing Decisions.

[596] Gardner et al. (2019). Do Evidence Submission Forms Expose Latent Print Examiners to Task-irrelevant Information, p. 239.

[597] Gardner et al. (2019). Do Evidence Submission Forms Expose Latent Print Examiners to Task-irrelevant Information, pp. 236–242.

and prosecutors. Such responsibility presupposes, in turn, sufficient knowledge of the potentially biasing effect that communications may have. It is possible, especially in difficult or ambiguous cases, that well-meaning forensic examiners feel tempted to ask for more information to guide their analysis. Vice versa, in for example high-profile cases, well-meaning investigators and prosecutors may feel tempted, on their own initiative, to provide more information to ensure that nothing is missed during the forensic examination. In some situations, asking for/providing additional information would not serve any legitimate purpose. Fingerprint examiners must reasonably be able to perform their jobs without knowledge about whether the suspect has confessed or has an alibi, etc. Likewise, DNA analysts are probably fully capable of carrying out their jobs unaware of the huge implications their results may have in relation to evidentiary rules. However, not knowing what the defence's perspective is, or not knowing that the deceased has allergies, for example, can result in important aspects being overlooked. Between different jurisdictions, as well as between different types of cases, there is variation in how much information is provided in case files and also to what extent examiners and investigators/prosecutors communicate with each other.

When it comes to information from the media specifically, this is probably inevitable, especially in high-profile cases. From the point of view of a context manager, the most reasonable response is to ask for second opinions by examiners in other countries or geographical areas where blinding to medial information is possible. Should such examiners reach different conclusions, one possible explanation of this is that the first examiner, often subconsciously, was biased by the contextual information. Although potentially detrimental to the administration of justice, it is indeed rational and unsurprising that individuals consciously or subconsciously make use of the information they can access.

Overall, it is also important to consider the information flow to crime laboratories or forensic medical units, which is dependent on organizational context. It is fairly common for laboratories to be part of the police and/or prosecution authorities; this is the case for example in Sweden[598] and several US states.[599] In fact, among survey crime laboratories in the United States, 79 per cent were located within law enforcement or public safety agencies and 57 per cent would only examine evidence submitted by law enforcement officials. However, labs are organizationally separated from law enforcement in for example the United Kingdom where private forensic science providers are hired, with associated difficulties but of a different kind.[600] Close organizational links to the police and prosecution can create contextual influences, more or less pronounced, that pull forensic scientists

---

[598] The Swedish Government Official Reports, SOU 2012:13.
[599] Bernstein (1996). Junk Science in the United States and the Commonwealth; Gianelli (1993). Independent Crime Laboratories: The Problem of Motivational and Cognitive Bias.
[600] House of Lords (2019). Science and Technology Select Committee, Forensic Science and the Criminal Justice System: A Blueprint for Change.

away from strict neutrality and towards findings more influenced by the parties they serve. In fact, the risk of an 'inbred bias'[601] following the crime lab's organizational affiliation with law enforcement agencies have been pointed out by courts,[602] politicians,[603] prosecutors,[604] investigators,[605] scholars,[606] and reporters.[607] The National Academy of Sciences (NAS), in its report 'Strengthening Forensic Science in the United States: A Path Forward', warned that such a lack of independence could hamper objectivity of forensic science.[608] Certainly, if forensic analysts (perceive that they) are, factually and/or organizationally, part of law enforcement, this can impact their perceptions of their own roles in the criminal justice system. Research in the US setting implies that forensic examiners may have biasing base rate expectations already on the basis of working in the context of criminal proceedings.[609] In addition, according to an interview study with fingerprint examiners from a variety of law enforcement agencies, examiners recurrently expressed individual satisfaction with their jobs when helping to catch criminals and solve crimes, and this may motivate findings in investigations consistent with guilty verdicts, particularly in high-profile or long-running cases.[610] Clearly such aspects should be taken into account by the context manager. From this perspective, context management is more of an enterprise than an occasional check of incoming evidence submission forms. Protocols will need to be established that are organization specific and which also minimize impact on the regular workflow. However, it is also clear that some of the potential risk factors such as the organizational affiliations between forensic labs and law enforcement cannot be fully addressed by a context manager but are instead questions of a political nature.

In sum, while context management is certainly necessary and has demonstrated effects for bias mitigations, it is today unknown whether and to what extent context

---

[601] Starrs (1993). The Seamy Side of Forensic Science: The Mephitic Stain of Fred Salem Zain, pp. 1 and 8, cited in Gianelli (1993). Independent Crime Laboratories: The Problem of Motivational and Cognitive Bias.

[602] Court of Appeal, Criminal Division, R v. Ward, 1993, 96 Crim. App. 1, 68 UK ('Forensic scientists may become partisan').

[603] Ellis (2004). Want Tough on Crime? Start by Fixing HPD Lab. Ellis was a Texas State senator at the time he wrote the editorial ('When crime labs are operating within a police department, examiner bias can undermine the integrity of scientific results').

[604] Bales (2000). Turning the Microscope Back on Forensic Scientists.

[605] Thomson (1974). Bias and Quality Control in Forensic Science: A Cause for Concern.

[606] Starrs (1993). The Seamy Side of Forensic Science: The Mephitic Stain of Fred Salem Zain, Gianelli (1993). Independent Crime Laboratories: The Problem of Motivational and Cognitive Bias.

[607] Mills et al. (2004). When Labs Falter, Defendants Pay: Bias Toward Prosecution Cited in Illinois Cases, Teichroeb, Crime Labs Too Beholden to prosecutors, Critics Say.

[608] Committee on Identifying the Needs of the Forensic Science Community (2009). Strengthening Forensic Science in the United States: A Path Forward.

[609] Peterson, Mihajlovic, & Gilliland (1984). Forensic Evidence and the Police: The Effects of Scientific Evidence on Criminal Investigations, pp. 1–266. See, however, also Oaksford & Chater (2007). Bayesian Rationality: The Probabilistic Approach to Human Reasoning, pp. 76–83.

[610] Charlton, Fraser-Mackenzie, & Dror (2010). Emotional Experiences and Motivating Factors Associated with Fingerprint Analysis, pp. 385–393.

management takes place in jurisdictions across the world. It has been documented in single countries and for certain types of analyses. For example, in Australia, the Victoria Police Forensic Services Department has introduced a system of contextual information management for handwriting examinations.[611] Needless to say, the need to incorporate context management on a more systematic and comprehensive level is an essential part of bias mitigation.

3.5.4.5.2 Linear Sequential Unmasking (LSU)

Since initial information can create powerful first impressions that are difficult to override,[612] varying the order in which the information is presented can impact on decision outcome.[613] The aim of LSU is to prevent analysts from using an initial piece of information such as a suspect sample as a guide that directs their attention to certain matching features of the crime scene sample, while downplaying or even disregarding features that do not match.[614]

LSU was first developed to minimize bias in forensic DNA interpretation specifically[615] and was then expanded to other comparative forensic domains like handwriting and fingerprint analysis and ballistics.[616] The limitation to comparative forensic domains was centred around the idea that the bias would manifest in the matching process, however many forensic assessments are not necessarily based on comparisons. This includes, for example, forensic medicine and digital forensics. Therefore, researchers have expanded the mitigation strategy in the so-called LSU-Expanded (LSU-E) to non-comparative assessments that nevertheless entail biasing information that can create problematic expectations.[617] Importantly, just as with context management overall, the idea with LSU is not to deprive experts of the information they need but rather to minimize bias by providing that information in the optimal sequence. The principle is fairly straightforward: the analyst should always begin with the actual data/evidence such as a deceased body or a fingerprint on a scene and only thereafter consider contextual information such as what was said in

---

[611] Found & Ganas (2013). The Management of Domain Irrelevant Context information in Forensic Handwriting Examination Casework, pp. 154–158.
[612] Darley & Gross (1983). A Hypothesis-confirming Bias in Labelling Effects, pp. 20–33.
[613] Hovland (1957). The Order of Presentation in Persuasion, Asche (1964). Forming Impressions of Personality; Davidson, Rando & Nakhaeizadeh (2021). Cognitive Bias and the Order of Examination in Forensic Anthropological Non-metric Methods: A Pilot Study, pp. 1–17.
[614] Nickerson (1998). Confirmation Bias: A Ubiquitous Phenomenon in Many Guises, pp. 175–220; Barry & Halfmann (2016). The Effect of Mindset on Decision-making, pp. 49–74.
[615] Krane et al. (2008). Sequential Unmasking: A Means of Minimizing Observer Effects in Forensic DNA Interpretation, pp. 1006–1107.
[616] Dror et al. (2015). Context Management Toolbox: A Linear Sequential Unmasking (LSU) Approach for Minimising Cognitive Bias in Forensic Decision Making, pp. 1111–1112.
[617] Dror & Kukucka (2021). Linear Sequential Unmasking-Expanded (LSU-E): A General Approach for Improving Decision Making as well as Minimizing Noise and Bias, pp. 1–5.

an interview regarding the cause of death or the suspects fingerprint.[618] LSU-E provides three criteria for determining the optimal exposure sequence; biasing power, objectivity, and relevance. The order of information needs to be weighed against the potential benefit it can provide. This is exemplified in the expert testimony in a trial regarding the death of Mr Floyd, with charges against police officer Mr Chauvin. The forensic doctor Mr Baker testified that he had intentionally chosen not to watch the video of Mr Floyd's death before conducting the autopsy as he did not want the video to bias the autopsy in the sense that it might lead him 'down one path or another'.[619]

It is likely that LSU will promote more comprehensive initial forensic examinations, where analysts and doctors may discover details that would not have been discovered if two samples were compared simultaneously or two pieces of information were integrated into a single source. A critical view is that a comparison (LSU) or integration of the information (LSU-E) will have to be carried out sooner or later, and that it therefore is uncertain whether this mitigates bias in analyst's final judgments. Even if the comparison is carried out later than usual, there is still a risk that the analyst reassesses the initial examination in the light of the suspect sample. Such assessments may also result in an analysis that is driven by similarities alone rather than both similarities and differences. This is where the documentation of the process comes in. Central to LSU and LSU-E is that reasons for deviations from the initial assessment are documented. This facilitates the detection of whether and when in the decision-making process examiners changed their minds as well as analysis of why, including the risk of bias. However, in practice, it seems that the process of deciding an appropriate exposure sequence may sometimes, at least in more complex cases, require the assistance of a context manager. Also, the analysis of what happens during the process of LSU is likely to be facilitated with comparison to an independent reviewer/second decision-maker.

3.5.4.5.3 Independent review/changing decision-maker
Some of the most blatant cases of incorrect forensic assessments in the past were carried out by experts working in isolation. A well-known example is the Canadian child forensic doctor, Dr Randal Smith, whose assessments resulted in a number of custodians who were wrongfully convicted of child murder.[620] A public inquiry led by Justice Goudge found that Dr Randal Smith, while testifying in court, had made false and misleading statements and had also exaggerated his expertise.[621] One of the

---

[618] Dror & Kukucka (2021). Linear Sequential Unmasking-Expanded (LSU-E): A General Approach for Improving Decision Making as well as Minimizing Noise and Bias, pp. 1–5.
[619] CNN, Medical examiner: I 'intentionally chose not' to view videos of Floyd's death before conducting autopsy, 9 April 2021.
[620] O'Hara (2001). Dead Wrong: How the Faulty Findings of an Eminent Pathologist Led to Erroneous Murder Charges and Ruined Lives; Thiblin, & Michard, Rättsmedicin i teori och praktik, p. 30.
[621] CBC (2009). Dr Charles Smith: The Man Behind the Public Inquiry.

convicted parent's defence counsels argued that Dr Randal Smith had acted more like a prosecutor than a forensic doctor.[622]

One could argue that, generally speaking, it cannot possibly be that risky for forensic experts to work on their own. Experienced forensic experts without any stakes in a given case are able to be self-critical enough to prevent miscarriages of justice. Surely Dr Randal Smith's case must have been an outlier. However convinced one may be that one's own expertise, extensive experience, and conscious efforts are sufficient, this is contradicted both by real cases and by research. Furthermore, not only is a second decision-maker necessary but this decision-maker also needs to be truly independent and blind to the conclusions of the first decision-maker. This is probably easier to accomplish if the second decision-maker is from another lab or forensic medical unit than that of the first decision-maker.

In the investigation following the Madrid train bombings on 11 March 2004 when bombs exploded at three commuter trains, fingerprints were found, and through the FBI's forensic analysis, Mr Mayfield, a Portland lawyer, became the main suspect.[623] The first fingerprint examiner made three repeated analyses and came to the same conclusion. Three other examiners, of which one was an appointed court expert, confirmed that the fingerprints originated from Mr Mayfield. The three latter examiners carried out their analysis knowing that the first examiner had made a positive identification.[624] Later on, Spanish authorities carried out a fingerprint analysis resulting in Mayfield being ruled out as a suspect and the fingerprints were instead matched to an Algerian citizen.[625] As if that was not enough, four out of five experts included contradicted their own previous conclusions.[626] Unknowingly, the experts re-examined matches they themselves had made in real investigations, but this time under the (false) premise that the fingerprints were known to have formed the basis of the false identification of Mr Mayfield as the Madrid train bomber. This time four out of five experts concluded that the fingerprints did not match.[627]

There are four main observations to be made in relation to the fingerprint examinations following the Madrid train bombings. First, the first FBI examiner was clearly unable to challenge his own conclusions. Through the first analysis, this examiner had already declared a standpoint which seem to have made it impossible

---

[622] CBC (2009). Dr Charles Smith: The Man Behind the Public Inquiry.

[623] Stacey (2005). A Report on the Erroneous Fingerprint Individualization in the Madrid Train Bombing Case, pp. 709–711.

[624] Giannelli (2010). Cognitive Bias in Forensic Science; Gianelli (2007). Confirmation Bias in Forensic Testing, pp. 22–23.

[625] Giannelli (2010). Cognitive Bias in Forensic Science; Gianelli (2007). Confirmation Bias in Forensic Testing, pp. 22–23.

[626] Dror & Charlton (2006). Why Experts Make Errors, pp. 600–616; Dror, Charlton, & Peron (2006). Contextual Information Renders Experts Vulnerable to Making Erroneous Identifications, pp. 74–78.

[627] Dror & Charlton (2006). Why Experts Make Errors, pp. 600–616; Dror, Charlton, & Peron (2006). Contextual Information Renders Experts Vulnerable to Making Erroneous Identifications, pp. 74–78.

for the examiner to come to another conclusion. Secondly, since the three other FBI examiners were aware of the first examiner's conclusion, they may have been affected by a subconscious tendency to confirm the first examiner's conclusion.[628] Thirdly, it was only when an external lab in Spain conducted the examinations, and then with a second suspect having been identified, that the first examiner's conclusion was contradicted. Fourthly, the bias apparent in the fingerprint examination was neither the result of unusual circumstances nor something unidirectional. Also the experts included in the research study seem to have been impacted by the contextual information, but this time in the opposite direction; to contradict matches they themselves had already made in real investigations. This illustrates the strong influence contextual information can have even in highly motivated experienced experts without any stakes in reaching a certain conclusion.

Hence, known cases of erroneous forensic analysis seem to suggest that the ideal type of review is a full re-examination by an independent expert who is truly blind in relation to the conclusions drawn by the first expert. This has also been confirmed in research.[629] Certainly, such fully independent in-depth review is more resource intensive than, for example, a more superficial review or even administrative check by a colleague in the same lab.[630] Yet, when independent experts engage genuinely and fully autonomously with the evidence, they are far more likely to detect critical errors than colleagues who, in practice, act only as verifiers, however well-meaning.[631] Some deviation between experts is expected on the basis of the difficulty of some forensic assessments and the nature of human cognition.[632] This type of disagreement can be hugely beneficial to the quality of the decision making process, if incorporated appropriately. In some contexts, for example forensic age estimations (FAEs) there are, in some jurisdictions, in fact decision making rules regarding how many experts have to agree to reach a certain conclusion.[633]

3.5.4.5.4 Technological advances

Just like with crime scenes, the field of forensic analysis has seen an increased usage of technology and therefore also increased human-technology cooperation. Following developments in other fields, among the most influential are so-called *cognitive technologies,* that is, systems that can carry out cognitive operations

---

[628] Giannelli (2010). Cognitive Bias in Forensic Science; Gianelli (2007). Confirmation Bias in Forensic Testing, pp. 22–23.
[629] Lidén & Dror (2020). Expert Reliability in Legal Proceedings: 'Eeny, Meeny, Miny, Moe, With Which Expert Should We Go?', pp. 37–46.
[630] Horsman & Sunde (2020). Part 1: The Need for Peer Review in Digital Forensics, p. 6.
[631] Horsman & Sunde (2020). Part 1: The Need for Peer Review in Digital Forensics, p. 6.
[632] Lidén & Dror (2020). Expert Reliability in Legal Proceedings: 'Eeny, Meeny, Miny, Moe, With Which Expert Should We Go?', pp. 37–46.
[633] Mostad & Tamsen (2019). Error Rates for Unvalidated Medical Age Assessment Procedures, pp. 613–623.

that were once the sole domain of humans.[634] The most fundamental examples of a cognitive technologies is using a computer to store information rather than memorizing it, or using a calculator rather than doing the math.[635] There is also an increased reliance on technology that requires humans and technology to become more and more intertwined and collaborate with one another. This is the case not least when it comes to digital forensics and digital evidence such as software used to collect and convert data from a suspect's cell phone[636] or databases used to search for links between crimes or crime patterns.[637] This creates what is referred to as *distributed cognition*, that some traditionally human cognitive operations are offloaded onto technology.[638] Distributed cognition enables increased performance and abilities in humans[639] but simultaneously affects human cognition.[640] On the one hand, it is clear that technology can help reduce cognitive load (Chapter 2.2.2.1) because technology (e.g. software) can conduct, for example, advanced statistical analysis that humans are unable to do. As such, it may have debiasing potential. On the other hand, since the technology also changes the quality of the cognitive tasks conducted by human examiners, the potential bias introduced by them needs to be addressed more fully in research.

In many forensic fields, including forensic anthropology, practitioners currently use software programs like FORDISC 3.0 to calculate sex-estimation probabilities.[641] These are more statistically sound than sectioning point approaches.[642] Hence, there is technological support to enable sex-estimation approaches that generate probabilities rather than arbitrarily defined categories like 'probable female' or 'indeterminate'.[643] So far, this has come across as an important tool for bias mitigation in sex estimation specifically. This is because this kind of software synthesizes metric data from multiple skeletal elements, generating

---

[634] Dror (2007). Cognitive Technologies and the Pragmatics of Cognition, p. 186.
[635] Dror et al. (2012). The Impact of Human-Technology Cooperation and Distributed Cognition in Forensic Science: Biasing Effects of AFIS Contextual Information on Human Experts, pp. 343–352.
[636] SWGDE (2018). Establishing Confidence in Digital Forensic Results by Error Mitigating Analysis, 20 November 2018, Sunde (2021). Dataetterforskare—Mennesker eller maskiner.
[637] Lidén (2020). Confirmation Bias in Investigations of Core International Crimes: Risk Factors and Quality Control Techniques, p. 496.
[638] Dror & Harnad (2008). Offloading Cognition onto Cognitive Technology. In Dror & Harnad (Eds). Cognition Distributed: How Cognitive Technology Extends our Minds, pp. 1–23.
[639] Dror & Harnad (2008). Offloading Cognition onto Cognitive Technology In Dror & Harnad (Eds). Cognition Distributed: How Cognitive Technology Extends our Minds, pp. 1–23.
[640] Dror (2007). Land Mines and Gold Mines in Cognitive Technologies. In Dror (2007). Cognitive Technologies and the Pragmatics of Cognition, pp. 1–7.
[641] Jantz & Ousley (2005). FORDISC 3: Computerised Forensic Discriminant Functions, Version 3.0 Knoxville.
[642] Hartley, Powanda Winburn, & Dror (2021). Metric Foensic Anthropology Decisions: Reliability and Biasability of Sectioning-Point-Based Sex Estimates.
[643] Tallman, Kincer, & Plemons (2021). Centering Transgender Individuals in Forensic Anthropology and Expanding Binary Sex Estimation in Casework and Research.

probability-based statements. Similarly, in forensic anthropology, as in forensic medicine[644] and forensic genetics,[645] there is increased use of artificial intelligence.[646] While these have potential in reducing cognitive load and conducting operations that humans would struggle to undertake, it remains to be seen whether and how they affect the risk of bias. Answering such questions should be a priority in future research.

Just as with artificial intelligence, Automated Fingerprint Identification System (AFIS) enables rapid analysis of large amounts of data. Specifically, AFIS is a computerized system that extracts and stores individual characteristics of digitized fingerprints.[647] In criminal investigations, it is used to search unknown fingerprints or partial marks against the known fingerprints stored in a database. This includes a repository of millions of known fingerprints against which automated searches can be conducted in seconds, and as such it has been described as an 'extremely powerful forensic tool'.[648] This also means that when AFIS suggests matches to a set of candidate prints to the human examiners, the result can come across fairly persuasive. For example, in the Madrid bomber case, the ability to locate similar prints was a result of an AFIS search of millions of prints.[649] Presented with such a similar print, a human examiner can easily be persuaded and forget about the increased likelihood of seeing two similar prints from different sources as a result of searching the large AFIS database.[650] Hence, while AFIS is capable of introducing other alternative suspects, potentially challenging the main hypothesis in a suspect-driven investigation, the AFIS result can in itself become a biasing factor. As pointed out by Dror and Mnookin, 'AFIS does change in important ways the cognitive tasks in which latent fingerprint experts are engaged'.[651] The consequences of distributed cognition still need to be further evaluated.

---

[644] Thurzo et al. (2021). Use of Advanced Artificial Intelligence in Forensic Medicine, Forensic Anthropology, and Clinical Anatomy, p. 1545.

[645] Hwa et al. (2019). Massively Parallel Sequencing Analysis of Nondegraded and Degraded DNA Mixtures using the ForenSeq System in Combination with EuroForMix Software, 25–37; Götz et al. (2017). GenoProof Mixture 3—New Software and Process to Resolve Complex DNA Mixtures, e549–e551; Alladio et al. (2018). DNA Mixtures Interpretation—A Proof of Concept Multi-software Comparison Highlighting Different Probabilistic Methods' Performances on Challenging Samples, pp. 143–150.

[646] Thurzo et al. (2021). Use of Advanced Artificial Intelligence in Forensic Medicine, Forensic Anthropology, and Clinical Anatomy, p. 1545.

[647] Dror et al. (2011). The Impact of Human-Technology Cooperation and Distributed Cognition in Forensic Science: Biasing Effects of AFIS Contextual Information on Human Experts, pp. 343–352.

[648] Dror et al. (2011). The Impact of Human-Technology Cooperation and Distributed Cognition in Forensic Science: Biasing Effects of AFIS Contextual Information on Human Experts, p. 344.

[649] Stacey (2004). Report on the Erroneous Fingerprint Individualization Bombing Case, pp. 706–718; Office of the Inspector General (OIG) (2006). Oversight and Review Division U.S. Department of Justice. A Review of the FBI's Handling of the Brandon Mayfield Case.

[650] Dror & Mnookin (2010). The Use of Technology in Human Expert Domains: Challenged and Risks Arising from the Use of Automated Fingerprint Identification Systems in Forensics, pp. 47–67; Dror et al. (2011). The Impact of Human-Technology Cooperation and Distributed Cognition in Forensic Science: Biasing Effects of AFIS Contextual Information on Human Experts, pp. 343–352.

[651] Dror & Mnookin (2019). The Use of Technology in Human Expert Domains: Challenges and Risks Arising from the Use of Automated Fingerprint Identifications Systems in Forensics, pp. 8–9.

3.5.4.6 Conclusion

While forensic analysis entails a range of distinct assessments stemming from multiple scientific fields, there is always a human examiner in the loop and an associated risk of confirmation bias. This is essential given that forensic evidence, particularly evidence such as DNA or medical opinions, is often considered the most reliable type of evidence available in criminal cases. Nevertheless, confirmation bias has been found repeatedly in this field, not least in criminalistics that has gained most scientific attention research to date. In anthropological assessments of sex, age, and ancestry, confirmation bias has been demonstrated on repeated occasions. When it comes to forensic doctors, there is today little research conducted relative to the other fields, and this should be a priority for future research. For example, it is evident how biased medical opinions about the COD can completely distort both the investigations and the proceedings.

To introduce contextual information management seems to be a necessary starting point in mitigating bias, whether in criminalistics, medicine, or anthropology. The experts themselves work under time pressure, often with complex cases and, like the remaining human population, they have a bias blind spot. Also, because deciding what contextual information should be available requires actually taking part of the contextual information, it would defeat the purpose of CIM if the experts themselves were to make these decisions. It is therefore essential to have assigned context managers. These managers will provide direct links to other debiasing techniques because they will decide, for example, when LSU or independent review is appropriate. In addition, technological advances have some debiasing potential, for example because they can reduce the cognitive load forensic examiners bear. This is evident with software that enable instantaneous analysis of large amounts of data including AFIS or AI-based approaches. Yet, since the interaction between humans and technology also affects the quality of human decision-making, more research is needed into whether and to what extent technological advances can trigger confirmation bias or in other ways impact on how confirmation bias is manifested.

4
Confirmation Bias in Criminal Litigations

4.1 Introduction

When a criminal investigation comes to the point at which legal actors have to decide how to proceed, confirmation bias may already have had a great impact on, for example, preliminary legal classifications and what evidence is available. As illustrated in the previous chapters, there is a risk of confirmation bias in relation to all evidence types, that is, interviews, line-ups, crime scene investigations and forensic analysis (criminalistics, forensic medicine, and forensic anthropology). Indeed, prosecutors, as leaders of the inquiry, may very well have contributed to one-sided investigations because they themselves have a confirmation bias, manifested in, for example, overconfident leadership. Across jurisdictions, both prosecutors' and judges' involvement in inquiries vary due to legal and historical factors.[1] Hence, the extent to which they can influence the scope of the inquiry also varies. Regardless, the risk that prosecutors and judges make their decisions on the basis of biased evidence is constant. This is not necessarily apparent to them. For example, prosecutors deciding whether to press charges may do so primarily or solely on the basis of evidence confirming an investigative hypothesis, not because there is no evidence contradicting the hypothesis but because no such evidence has been sought and collected. Alternatively, such evidence has been found but downgraded as irrelevant. This can make prosecutors more inclined to prosecute since they perceive of the evidence against the suspect as stronger and less ambiguous than it really is. Similarly, a judge who is presented with such one-sided evidence may assess that there is reasonable suspicion and detain the suspect before the trial, or even vote for a conviction following the main hearing. In the described situations, the very fundament of prosecutors' and judges' decision-making is flawed. This means that these actors will sometimes be unable to exercise the control function they are meant to exercise.

Another circumstance that can impair prosecutors and judges' abilities to exercise their intended control function is that they may themselves develop a confirmation bias that impacts on their decision-making in pre-trial and trial phases. This is unsurprising as it merely confirms that prosecutors' and judges' are part of the human population. Nevertheless, it also means that there is a risk of biased

---

[1] See, for example, Lidén, Gräns, & Juslin (2018). From Devil's Advocate to Crime Fighter: Confirmation Bias and Debiasing Techniques in Prosecutorial Decision-making, pp. 494–526.

decisions on the basis of already one-sided evidence, potentially a significant mechanism in the production of false positives and negatives. The following chapters outline possible manifestations and ways to counter confirmation bias in prosecutors' (Section 4.2) and judges' (Section 4.3) decision-making.

4.2 Prosecutorial Decision-making

4.2.1 Introduction

While prosecutors' more specific roles vary across jurisdictions, they regularly hold tremendous powers as leaders of criminal investigations as well as the defendant's counterparty in court. Prosecutors not only set the frames for who to investigate, on what charges, using which tactics but also what sentence to seek upon conviction, etc. These frames can also come to dictate the investigation in the sense that prosecutors, in practice, and despite obligations to investigate incriminating and exonerating circumstances equally, only seriously consider one preferred hypothesis. Legal demands on prosecutors require them to remain balanced and neutral, critically evaluating and actively challenging investigative hypothesis as their own 'Devil's Advocates'. They are expected to be simultaneously determined, hard-working, and effective 'crime fighters'. Arguably, fulfilling all these roles at the same time is cognitively untenable.[2] Even among prosecutors with incredibly high professional standards, their parallel roles will, in practice, be difficult to fulfil. This is because prosecutors, on the basis of being human beings, will struggle to consider more than one hypothesis at once.

Given that prosecutors' decisions are greatly influential for criminal proceedings, confirmation bias in their decision-making has strong ties to both false positives and false negatives. Hence, the following sections examine different manifestations of confirmation bias in prosecutors. This includes, not least, overconfident leadership (Section 4.2.2.1) which will affect, for example, what evidence is available for decision-making. It also entails pre-trial decisions (Section 4.2.2.2) and the charging decision (Section 4.2.2.3) as triggers of confirmation bias. Furthermore, possible mitigation measures will be examined like changing decision-maker (Section 4.2.3.1) as well as Devil's Advocate procedures, Red Teams, and Evidence Review Boards (Section 4.2.3.2).

---

[2] Lidén, Gräns, & Juslin (2018). From Devil's Advocate to Crime Fighter: Confirmation Bias and Debiasing Techniques in Prosecutorial Decision-making, pp. 494–526; Green & Roiphe (2017). Rethinking Prosecutor's Conflicts of Interest, pp. 464–5387; Heuman (2004), Domarens och åklagarens skyldighet att vara objektiva, pp. 42–52; Jacobson, (2008). 'We Can't Just Do It Any Which Way'"— Objectivity Work among Swedish prosecutors, pp. 46–68; Lindberg (1997). Om Åklagaretik; O'Brien, (2009). A Recipe for Bias: An Empirical Look at the Interplay Between Institutional Incentives and Bounded Rationality in Prosecutorial Decision-making, pp. 1000–1049.

4.2.2 Understanding Bias

4.2.2.1 Overconfident leadership

In my prosecutor's office, we not only routinely told forensic scientists what answer we sought from their analysis and the time by which we needed it, but in some instances indicated that it was important because a 'match' would be crucial to getting a conviction. This no doubt put great pressure on the forensic scientists to confirm our theories of the case, and created strong confirmation biases... I told the handwriting expert that I needed him to confirm that the signatures on all the documents matched the defendant's, and I made it clear that this was important because trial was starting and I needed the answers ASAP... At the time, I, and I believe others in my office, felt that there was nothing wrong with this practice. I was completely unaware of the effects of confirmation bias, as most prosecutors and police officers remain equally ignorant today. And we all believed that our defendants were 100 per cent guilty. We knew that the signatures were made by the defendant even before we had an expert examine them. And in a ballistics case we believed that of course the bullet came from the defendant's gun.[3]

Mark Godsey, former federal prosecutor in New York City, today advocating for the innocent within the auspices of the Ohio Innocence Project, provides multiple examples of how confirmation bias manifested itself in the investigations in which he was involved. This includes how his office communicated explicit expectations to forensic scientists to confirm the office's theories through their analysis. Overall, Mr Godsey's account illustrates how confirmation bias can take the shape of very directive, demanding and indeed over-confident, leadership, even impacting on the decision-making of other practitioners. It is likely that Mr Godsey's ability to see such tendencies has benefited greatly from his marked change of professional role. From critical reviews of prosecutors in other jurisdictions, it seems that such conduct is not necessarily unusual.[4]

As highlighted by Mr Godsey's account, prosecutors can themselves be sources of contextual information that potentially biases forensic analysts (Chapter 3.5.4.2). This increases the odds that forensic analysts will provide the corroborating evidence necessary to press charges and/or get a conviction in court. Such influence may also be exerted on, for example, forensic doctors, who may subconsciously tend to 'observe' more hypothesis confirming instances on a dead body and

---

[3] Godsey (2017). Blind Injustice: A Former Prosecutor Exposes the Psychology and Politics of Wrongful Convictions, pp. 99–100.

[4] See, for example, Innocence Project (2016). Prosecutorial Oversight: A National Dialogue in the Wake of Connick v. Thompson; Innocence Project (2010). New Report; Prosecutorial Misconduct and Wrongful Convictions; Sullivan & Possley (2015). The Chronic Failure to Discipline Prosecutors for Misconduct: Proposals for Reform, pp. 881–945; Schnurbush (2012). Wrongful Convictions: A Conceptual Framework for Understanding Police and Prosecutor Misconduct, pp. 1–139; Grissom (2017). Death Row Inmate Seeks to Halt Execution for Dallas-area Murders, Alleges Prosecutor Misconduct.

therefore be more likely to confirm the prosecutor's hypothesis in their medical statements (Chapter 3.5.4.3). Since the defence's access to forensic examinations may vary following legislation and/or financial components,[5] it is possible that any alternative hypothesis thought of at the time of the forensic examination will never be evaluated. Hence, it is very uncertain whether the defence can offer a sufficiently strong challenge in this regard. It is easy to see how this increases the risk of a false positive.

And yet, the potential influence of confirmation bias in prosecutors' leadership is not limited to forensic evidence. Prosecutors' 'tunnel-vision'—or even 'goal-orientation'—can manifest in a more general tendency to only, or primarily, wanting to prove that the case theory is correct. This results in a focus on finding the evidence proving the theory rather than conducting a broad and impartial investigation; that is, a suspect- or hypothesis-driven investigation (Chapter 3.2.1). Such tendencies have been noted in both international and national jurisdictions. The role of the prosecutor in producing such one-sided investigations is captured well in a former International Criminal Court (ICC) attorney's description of the first Prosecutor of the ICC, Mr Luis Moreno-Ocampo. The ICC attorney, in an interview with a *New York Times Magazine* journalist described that 'He would see the leader of a state and say: "There must be evidence out there. Go get it for me"'.[6] Logically speaking, there can be lots of hypothesis-consistent evidence even in relation to hypotheses that are incorrect. However, with an overconfident leadership such as that described, it is unlikely that the prosecution will sufficiently challenge its hypothesis. If the prosecution does realize that the hypothesis is incorrect this may happen only at a very late stage, with associated complications in terms of lost evidence, wrongful suspicions against innocent individuals, and so on. This is exemplified by multiple cases from national jurisdictions, for example the Norfolk Four case described below.[7]

In the investigation following the murder of Michelle Bosko in Norfolk, Virginia, in the United States, no less than four false confessions were elicited.[8] According to a witness statement, Mr Williams had taken a sexual interest in Michelle and he therefore became the primary suspect.[9] After being told (falsely) that he failed a polygraph test,[10] and having been threatened with the death penalty

---

[5] See, for example, John Murray v. United Kingdom, judgment of 8 February 1998, ECtHR; Öster (2015). Riskabelt att Göra Egna Undersökningar, Advokaten nr 9 2015.
[6] Verini (2016). The Prosecutor and the President, The New York Times.
[7] Leo & Ofshe (2010). From False Confession to Wrongful Conviction: Seven Psychological Processes, p. 12.
[8] Leo & Ofshe (2010). From False Confession to Wrongful Conviction: Seven Psychological Processes, p. 12.
[9] Leo & Ofshe (2010). From False Confession to Wrongful Conviction: Seven Psychological Processes, p. 12.
[10] Leo & Ofshe (2010). From False Confession to Wrongful Conviction: Seven Psychological Processes, p. 13.

as well as other coercive measures if he refused to confess,[11] Mr Williams finally gave in and confessed, yet his confession had major inconsistencies with the other evidence in the case, for example the autopsy report.[12] After Mr Williams had been told about the correct details and multiple revised confessions had been elicited from him,[13] the DNA analysis came back exculpating Mr Williams. Instead of abandoning or at least seriously questioning their hypothesis, the investigative team's hypothesis was expanded to include a co-perpetrator whom they claimed must have left DNA in Michelle's body. In the quest to locate this co-perpetrator, three other false confessions from three other individuals were elicited. These three individuals, Mr Williams, as well as three further individuals, in total seven individuals, were all imprisoned despite the fact that none of their DNA matched that found in Michelle's body.[14] After many years, the real perpetrator, Mr Ballard, confessed on his own initiative. Mr Ballard's statement contained accurate details of the crime not mentioned by any of the other defendants. Also, Mr Ballard's DNA matched that found in Michelle's body. While one would think that this hypothesis-inconsistent information would finally put the main hypothesis to rest, this was not the case. Once again, instead of abandoning their hypothesis, the prosecutor and investigators extended their hypothesis as to accommodate the new information. Specifically, they now believed that they had finally located the missing member of an eight-man gang-rape murder. They offered Mr Ballard a plea contingent on him implicating the others, which he accepted in order to avoid the death penalty. Some of the others also pled guilty to avoid receiving the death penalty while others were found guilty in their separate jury trials. Leo and Ofshe identified confirmation bias as a major contributing factor to the outcome in this case and explained it in the following way:

> With belief in guilt more firmly entrenched, investigators treat the confession as confirmation of their belief in the suspect's guilt rather than as a hypothesis to be tested against case evidence. Further investigation tends to stop, and the confession becomes the centerpiece of the case ... The formal presumption of innocence is replaced by an unshakable assumption of guilt that provided the context for interpretation of all other evidence. Inconsistent evidence tends to be ignored, dismissed as flawed, or reinterpreted as either irrelevant or supportive of guilt, by investigators, judges, juries, and prosecutors, who sometimes even suppress contradictory or exculpatory evidence, and, even when the suspect is definitely

---

[11] Leo & Ofshe (2010). From False Confession to Wrongful Conviction: Seven Psychological Processes, p. 14.
[12] Leo & Ofshe (2010). From False Confession to Wrongful Conviction: Seven Psychological Processes, p. 14.
[13] Leo & Ofshe (2010). From False Confession to Wrongful Conviction: Seven Psychological Processes, p. 14.
[14] Leo & Ofshe (2010). From False Confession to Wrongful Conviction: Seven Psychological Processes, p. 17.

exonerated, may refuse to acknowledge his innocence or admit any mistakes in the investigation or prosecution.[15]

Notably, similar remarks were made in the Swedish Government Official Report in relation to the eight murder convictions against Mr Bergwall, who had been convicted largely due to his confessions which were made in therapy while he was under psychiatric care. In addition, Mr Bergwall's confessions were often inconsistent with other evidence, for example regarding the location of the crime scenes,[16] how the victims were dressed, as well as their more specific injuries.[17] When the inconsistencies became apparent, Mr Bergwall was provided with the accurate details.[18] In some of these cases, forensic evidence such as fingerprints and hairs were found on the crime scene and known not to originate from Mr Bergwall.[19] After retracting his confession, Mr Bergwall was ultimately acquitted of all eight murders.[20] The Commission examining these cases on behalf of the Swedish Government noted that:

> The investigative measures undertaken after Sture Bergwall's confessions were largely focused on finding evidence supporting the notion that Bergwall was the perpetrator. That the prosecutor and investigators from the outset seem to have presumed that this hypothesis was correct resulted in that alternative scenarios were insufficiently investigated. Although there were factors in the investigation which by themselves should have raised doubts regarding the veracity of the confessions, this did not result in a widened perspective. On the contrary, such factors often resulted in additional investigation aimed at supporting the notion that Bergwall had committed the crimes or to illustrate why evidence suggesting something else did not have to be taken into serious consideration.[21]

One factor that may have exacerbated the risk of confirmation bias in the cases against Mr Bergwall was that the same prosecutor was in charge of all eight cases (Chapter 2.2.2.3). As expected from research pertaining, for example, to the bias blind spot, it is possible that the prosecutor was unable to see the shortcomings in the overall hypothesis in the cases: that Mr Bergwall was a serial killer.

As illustrated by the cited cases, confessions are 'extraordinarily persuasive evidence'.[22] In fact, former US Supreme Court Justice William Brennan observed that

---

[15] Leo & Ofshe (2010). From False Confession to Wrongful Conviction: Seven Psychological Processes, pp. 32–33.
[16] Swedish Government Official Report, SOU 2015:52, p. 394.
[17] Swedish Government Official Report, SOU 2015:52, p. 396.
[18] Swedish Government Official Report, SOU 2015:52, p. 396.
[19] Swedish Government Official Report, SOU 2015:52, p. 399–400.
[20] Swedish Government Official Report, SOU 2015:52.
[21] Swedish Government Official Reports, SOU 2015:52; Report from the Bergwall Commission, pp. 591–592. Author's own translation of the Swedish original text.
[22] Leo (2008). Police Interrogation and American Justice.

'no other class of evidence is so profoundly prejudicial',[23] a notion that is supported by research.[24] Therefore, confession evidence tends to define the case against a defendant, usually overriding any contradictory information or evidence of innocence.[25] Hence, the confession itself can trigger a confirmation bias and as such have a very powerful biasing effect.[26] As illustrated, this biasing effect extends to also other parts of the investigation. For example, forensic analysts who examine fingerprints and police officers interviewing a witness may be more likely to search for and evaluate information in hypothesis-consistent ways when aware of the suspects' confession. In fact, in aggregated case studies, confessions accounted for 14–60 per cent of documented wrongful convictions.[27] These numbers should be considered together with the finding that even defence attorneys sometimes seem to succumb to confirmation bias after learning that their client has confessed, as they may rule out the possibility of innocence.[28] Given that a defence attorney is presumed to function as a counterweight to the prosecutor, arguably with unequal arms in many jurisdictions and cases,[29] this is clearly problematic.

So far, the examination has focused on how confirmation bias in prosecutors can contribute to false positives. However, it is essential to keep in mind that confirmation bias in prosecutors can also result in false negatives. If the investigative hypothesis was in fact correct, prosecutors can still, due to overconfidence, fail to see and address weaknesses in the case before it is presented in court. Such weaknesses may come across clearly, even undeniably, to the judges. The risk of false negatives following confirmation bias may be particularly pronounced in fact-rich cases, concerning organized crime or core international crimes, for instance.[30] This is because such investigations often require evidence into complex hierarchical or command

---

[23] Colorado v. Connelly, 479 US 157 (1986), p. 182,
[24] Miller & Boster (1977). Three Images of the Trial: Their Implications for Psychological Research. In Sales (Ed.) Psychology in the Legal Process, pp. 19–38; Kassin & Sukel (1997). Coerced confessions and the Jury, pp. 27–46; Kassin & Neumann (1997). On the Power of Confession Evidence: An Experimental Test of the Fundamental Difference Hypothesis, pp. 460–484; Leo & Ofshe (1998) The Consequences of False Confessions: Deprivation of Liberty and Miscarriages of Justice in the Age of Psychological Interrogation, pp. 429–496, Drizin & Leo (2004). The Problem of False Confessions in the Post-DNA World, pp. 891–1007.
[25] Leo & Ofshe (1998) The Consequences of False Confessions: Deprivation of Liberty and Miscarriages of Justice in the Age of Psychological Interrogation, pp. 429–496.
[26] Leo & Davis (2010). From False Confession to Wrongful Conviction: Seven Psychological Processes, pp. 9–50.
[27] Bedau & Radelet, Miscarriages of Justice in Potentially Capital Cases, pp. 21–179; Scheck, Neufeld, & Dwyer (2000). Actual Innocence: Five Days to Execution and other Dispatches from the Wrongly Convicted; Gross et al. (2005). Exonerations in the United States, 1989 through 2003.
[28] Leo & Ofshe (2010). From False Confession to Wrongful Conviction: Seven Psychological Processes, p. 33.
[29] See, for example, John Murray v. United Kingdom, judgment of 8 February 1998, EctHR; Kuopila v. Finland, judgment of 27 April 2000; EctHR; Neumeister v. Austria, judgment of 7 May, 1974. See also van Dijk & van Hoof (2018). Theory and Practice of the European Convention on Human Rights, p. 476.
[30] See, for example, Agirre Aranburu & Bergsmo (2020). Investigative Bottlenecks and the Mindset of Quality Control, pp. 1–24.

structures but simultaneously, they are also associated with significant challenges with obtaining sufficient information, including state non-co-operation.[31] As such, prosecutors who are convinced of the accuracy of their hypothesis may be inclined to subconsciously fill in the gaps in their narratives. For example, in the ICC case *The Prosecutor v. Laurent Gbagbo and Charles Blé Goudé*, Judge Henderson remarked in his concurring opinion annexed to the majority's acquittal[32] that the prosecutor seemed 'to have started from the premise that her case theory is correct'.[33] Similarly, Judge Tarfusser, in his concurring opinion in the same case, went a step further in his observations as he stated: 'Day after day, document by document, witness after witness, the Prosecutor's case' has been revealed and exposed as a fragile, implausible theorem relying on shaky and doubtful bases, inspired by a Manichean and simplistic narrative of an Ivory Coast depicted as a "polarized" society . . . a caricatured "one-sided" narrative . . . .'[34] Trial Chamber I, by majority, Judge Herrera Carbuccia dissenting, had acquitted Mr Gbagbo and Mr Blé Goudé from all charges of crimes against humanity allegedly committed in Côte d'Ivoire in 2010–2011.[35] In March 2021, the Appeals Chamber confirmed, by majority, the acquittal decision, which is now final.[36] Hence, external observers who lack the commitment (Chapter 2.2) that prosecutors may have to a hypothesis become more critical evaluators of it. Should the case hypothesis have been correct, this will result in a false negative.

Research explains in more detail the close relationship between overconfidence and confirmation bias.[37] Put simply, individuals are overconfident because they favour positive rather than negative evidence[38] and tend to disregard evidence inconsistent with a preferred solution.[39] Hence, this can result in a risk of poor calibration between their confidence and accuracy judgments, that is an issue with *diagnostic calibration*.[40] As such, prosecutors may, in some instances, be more confident than accurate. This has a clear connection to false positives. In addition, their confidence may make them unable to see flaws in their arguments or evidence,

---

[31] See, for example, Agirre Aranburu (2010). Prosecuting the Most Responsible for International Crimes: Dilemmas of Definition and Prosecutorial Discretion, pp. 1–23.

[32] Trial Chamber I, Situation in the Republic of Côte d'Ivoire in the case of The prosecutor v. Laurent Gbagbo and Charles Blé Goudé, ICC-02/11-01/15, 16 July 2019.

[33] The Prosecutor v. Laurent Gbagbo and Charles Blé Goudé, Situation in Côte d'Ivoire, ICC-02/11-01/15, Annex B, § 79 Judge Henderson's reasons.

[34] Judge Cuno Tarfusser describing his observations in the courtroom. See ICC, Situation in Côte d'Ivoire, The Prosecutor v. Laurent Gbagbo and Charles Blé Goudé, Trial Chamber, Opinion of Judge Cuno Tarfusser, 16 July 2019, ICC-02/11-01/15-1263-AnxA, para. 12.

[35] Trial Chamber I, Situation in the Republic of Côte d'Ivoire in the case of The prosecutor v. Laurent Gbagbo and Charles Blé Goudé, ICC-02/11-01/15, 16 July 2019.

[36] The Appeals Chamber, Situation in the Republic of Cote D'Ivoire in the Case of the Prosecutor v. Laurent Gbagbo and Charles Blé Goudé, ICC.02/11-01/15 A.

[37] Koriat, Lichtenstein, & Fischhogg (1980). Reasons for Confidence, pp. 107–118.

[38] Koriat, Lichtenstein, & Fischhogg (1980). Reasons for Confidence, pp. 107–118.

[39] Koriat, Lichtenstein, & Fischhogg (1980). Reasons for Confidence, pp. 107–118.

[40] Lidén, 'Child Soldier or Soldier?': Estimating Age in Cases of Core International Crimes.

even if their hypothesis is in fact correct. From the point of view of the prosecution, the case is rock-solid but an outside observer, especially a judge ultimately responsible for the accused's right to due process, gets the opposite impression. This, in turn, has a clear connection to false negatives. The risk of overestimating the own case strength has been noted by Xabier Agirre Aranburu, Senior Coordinator, Office of the Prosecutor, at the ICC:

> It is not uncommon that officers that have been involved in the investigation overestimate the strength of the case, as they often work under internal and external pressure to 'show results' for incrimination. Prosecutions and investigations tend to attract assertive personalities, which may be necessary to lead complex projects and confront criminals, but it comes with a risk of insufficient self-reflection. As indicated by an experienced prosecutor "a tragic lack of humility" on the part of investigating and prosecuting officers is a key factor in cases of judicial miscarriage, the remedy for which may be simply to show 'humility and the ability to accept our human limitations'.[41]

The risk that prosecutors form hypotheses they cannot free themselves of may be exacerbated by the fact that their involvement often starts early on, sometimes as early as the decision to open an investigation. As discussed in the next section, throughout the course of the inquiry, they also make several pre-trial decisions regarding the suspect which entail preliminary assessments of the suspect's involvement in a crime.

4.2.2.2 Pre-trial Decisions

Before the suspect's guilt has been tried in Court, prosecutors are required by law to hypothesize about the suspect's guilt. For example, in an application for an arrest warrant, the ICC prosecutor shall summarize the evidence and other information which establish '*reasonable grounds*' to believe that a person has committed a crime within the jurisdiction of the Court, following Article 58(2)(b) of the Rome Statute of the ICC. There is also corresponding legislation in other jurisdictions. In fact, legislations concern a range of different types of pre-trial decisions, often in one way or another depriving suspects of their liberty, seizing their assets, secretly wire-tapping their phones, and so on. These decisions entail different types of assessments and standards of proof, such as 'sufficient suspicion', 'reasonable suspicion', and 'probable cause'.[42] As such, the decisions are more or less strongly related to the decision about whether to prosecute, and whether the court should convict.

---

[41] Agirre Aranburu, The Contribution of Analysis to the Quality Control in Criminal Investigation, p. 142, citing Mark Godsey (2017). Seeing and Accepting Human Limitations. In Blind Justice: A Former Prosecutor Exposes the Psychology and Politics of Wrongful Convictions, p. 213.
[42] Lidén, Gräns, & Juslin (2018). From Devil's Advocate to Crime Fighter: Confirmation Bias and Debiasing Techniques in Prosecutorial Decision-Making, pp. 494–526; Feeney (1998). German and

While prosecutors are, thus, required by law to hypothesize about the suspect's guilt, it does make them susceptible to confirmation bias. In fact, some studies suggest that confirmation bias can be triggered as early as when a prosecutor decides who should be investigated and using what tactics[43] or with the identification and/or arrest of a suspect.[44] Such premature narrowing of the inquiry can make prosecutors downgrade exculpatory evidence, for example by categorizing it as irrelevant.[45] It can also influence prosecutors' judgments on whether to press charges, what charges, what sentence to seek upon conviction, and so on.[46]

During the pre-trial phase, prosecutors also have to make decisions about the appropriate allocation of resources, which can exacerbate the risk of confirmation bias, as it introduces or adds to, for example, 'sunk cost effects'.[47] This refers to a tendency to keep investing resources even if the initial investment was flawed, or, in other words: 'throwing good money after bad'.[48] For example, in the context of international criminal justice, appropriate allocation of resources and time requires that investigation plans into certain lines of inquiry are adopted by the prosecution at a relatively early stage of the investigation. Whether and to what extent such investigation plans constitute a risk of bias depends on how open or closed they are and between cases there is variation in when, and on what bases, individuals are identified as suspects.[49] For example, in the first Darfur case,[50] the initial investigation plan adopted in 2005 did not identify any suspect, as this only happened a year into the trail and then on the basis of the ICC's evidence.[51] However,

---

American Prosecutions: An Approach to Statistical Comparison; Weigend (2019). The Potential to Secure a Fair Trial Through Evidence Exclusion: A German Perspective, pp. 61-92.

[43] Griffin (2001). The Prudent Prosecutor.

[44] Fahsing & Ask (2013). Decision-making and Decisional Tipping Points in Homicide Investigations: An Interview Study of British and Norwegian Detectives, pp. 155-165.

[45] Burke (2006). Improving Prosecutorial Decision-making: Some Lessons of Cognitive Science, pp. 1588-1631; Jonakait (1987) The Ethical Prosecutor's Misconduct, p. 550-567; McCloskey (1989), Convicting the Innocent, pp. 140-141; Wastell et al. (2012). Identifying Hypotehsis Confirmation Behaviors in a Simulated Murder Investigation: Implications for Practice, pp. 184-198; Yaroshefsky (1999), Cooperation with Federal Prosecutors: Experiences of Truth Telling and Embellishment, pp. 917-964.

[46] Davis (2001). The American Prosecutor: Independence, Power, and the Threat of Tyranny, pp. 393-465; Green (2003) Prosecutorial Ethics as Usual; Griffin (2001) The Prudent Prosecutor.

[47] Lidén, Confirmation Bias in Investigations of Core International Crimes: Risk Factors and Quality Control Techniques, pp. 10-11.

[48] Arkes (1996). The Psychology of Waste, p. 124.

[49] Lidén, Confirmation Bias in Investigations of Core International Crimes: Risk Factors and Quality Control Techniques, pp. 10-11.

[50] ICC, Situation in Darfur, Sudan, Presidency, Decision Assigning the Situation in Darfur, Sudan to Pre-Trial Chamber I, 21 April 2005, ICC-02/05-1; Schabas (2017). An Introduction to the International Criminal Court, p. 48.

[51] See, for example, Agirre Aranburu & Belli (2019). The ICC and the Darfur Investigation—Progress and Challenges. In Natarajan (Ed.), International and Transnational Crime and Justice, OTP, First Report of the Prosecutor of the ICC to the Security Council Pursuant to UNSCR 1593 (2005), 29 June 2005.

in the Kenya investigation,[52] suspects were identified early, in 2009, on the basis of prior investigations of two different fact-finding commissions. Thus, adopting an investigation plan is not necessarily a trigger of confirmation bias in itself, yet the possibility of bias stemming from an investigation plan is highlighted by the research suggesting that investigators' minds 'seize and freeze'[53] already with decisions about who should be investigated and using what tactics,[54] or with the identification[55] and/or apprehension or arrest of a suspect.[56]

In international criminal justice, there is also the focus on the most responsible perpetrators,[57] which is more unambiguously linked to suspect identification. Thus, this focus is a more potent risk factor than investigation plans, generally speaking.[58] The narrowing down of the investigation to one or a few responsible individuals may make prosecutors downgrade exculpatory evidence, for instance by categorizing it as irrelevant.[59]

Furthermore, the wider context in which the prosecutors make their pre-trial decisions is relevant. Apart from prosecutors often having wide discretion,[60] there may be emotions at play, particularly in high-profile cases,[61] and institutional as well as societal incentives require prosecutors to be tough on crime.[62] Some even speak of a certain institutional and political culture in the prosecution offices,[63]

---

[52] Nichols (2015). The International Criminal Court and the End of Impunity in Kenya, pp. 69–70, and information obtained through personal communication with current and former ICC officers at the CILRAP conference 'Quality Control in Criminal Investigation', 22–23 February 2019, New Delhi, India.

[53] Kruglanski & Webster (1996). Motivated Closing of the Mind: 'Seizing' and 'Freezing', pp. 263–83.

[54] Griffin (2001). The Prudent Prosecutor, pp. 259–307.

[55] Fahsing & Ask (2013). Decision-making and Decisional Tipping Points in Homicide Investigations: An Interview Study of British and Norwegian Detectives, pp. 155–65.

[56] Lidén, Gräns, & Juslin (2018). The Presumption of Guilt in Suspect Interrogations: Apprehension as a Trigger of Confirmation Bias and Debiasing Techniques, pp. 155–65.

[57] Agirre Aranburu (2009). Prosecuting the Most Responsible for International Crimes: Dilemmas of Definition and Prosecutorial Discretion. In González (Ed.), Protección Internacional de Derechos Humanos y Estado de Derecho, pp. 381–404.

[58] This focus is mandated at the ICC by, inter alia, the reference to 'degree of participation' as a sentencing factor; see ICC Rules of Procedure and Evidence, 9 September 2002, Rule 145(1)©.

[59] Burke (2006). Improving Prosecutorial Decision-making: Some Lessons of Cognitive Science, pp. 1588–631, Jonakait (1987). The Ethical Prosecutor's Misconduct. pp. 550–67; McCloskey (1989). Convicting the Innocent, pp. 140–41; Wastell et al. (2012). Identifying Hypothesis Confirmation Behaviors in a Simulated Murder Investigation: Implications for Practice, pp. 184–98; Yaroshefsky (1999). Cooperation with Federal Prosecutors: Experiences of Truth Telling and Embellishment, pp. 917–64.

[60] Babcock & Loewenstein (1997). Explaining Bargaining Impasse: The Role of Self-Serving Biases, pp. 109–126; Hobbs (1950). Prosecutor's Bias, An Occupational Disease; Levinson & Young. (2010). Different Shades of Bias: Skin Tone, Implicit Racial Bias and Judgments of Ambiguous Evidence, pp. 307–350.

[61] Lidén (2020). Emotions and Cognition in International Criminal Justice: An Exploration from Cognitive Biases to Emotional Intelligence, pp. 1–10; Wettergren & Bergman Blix (2016). Empathy and Objectivity in the Legal Procedure; The Case of Swedish Prosecutors, pp. 19–35.

[62] Hobbs (1950). Prosecutor's Bias, An Occupational Disease; O'Brien (2009). A Recipe for Bias: An Empirical Look at the Interplay Between Institutional Incentives and Bounded Rationality in Prosecutorial Decision-making, pp. 1000–1049.

[63] Medwed (2004). The Zeal Deal: Prosecutorial Resistance to Post-conviction Claims of Innocence, pp. 125–183.

which contribute to a 'conviction psychology'.[64] This makes it easy to see how, during the pre-trial phase, pressure may gradually build up to convict the suspect. If the aim, explicitly or implicitly, is to convict someone, it is also easy to see how this may be promoted by selective searches for and evaluation of information.[65] As discussed in Chapters 2.2.2.2 and 2.2.2.3 on motivational, social, and organizational explanations of confirmation bias, this bias can help goal and career fulfilment. Since prosecutors, just like other human beings, have such motivations, confirmation bias is to a certain extent built into criminal investigations and proceedings.

Yet, it should be noted that in a study with Swedish prosecutors ($n = 40$), the prosecutors' assessments *before* the prosecution decision did not show signs of confirmation bias.[66] In fact, these prosecutors seemed capable of acting as their own Devils' Advocates.[67] Also, their assessments *while* deciding about whether to prosecute were reasonably balanced. However, as will be discussed in the next section, their mindsets seemed to change with the charging decision, a result also found in other jurisdictions.

4.2.2.3 The Charging Decision

Some research suggests that prosecutors are able to remain fairly neutral throughout the course of an inquiry.[68] Possibly this is because prosecutors use this time period to evaluate carefully whether there are sufficient reasons to prosecute and thereby act as their own Devil's Advocates. Since prosecutors only press charges if they are sufficiently certain of the accused's guilt,[69] it is instead the charging decision that is associated with a significant psychological shift.[70] Regardless of their duties during the inquiry, with the charging decision 'prosecutors become crime fighters whose primary objective is to get defendants convicted'.[71]

---

[64] Fisher (1988). In Search of the Virtuous Prosecutor: A Conceptual Framework, pp. 197–261; Findley & Scott (2006). The Multiple Dimensions of Tunnel Vision in Criminal Cases, pp. 291–398.

[65] Klayman & Ha (1987). Confirmation, Disconfirmation and Information in Hypothesis Testing, pp. 211–228; Nickerson (1998), Confirmation Bias: A Ubiquitous Phenomenon in Many Guises, pp. 175–220; Wason & Johnson-Laird (1972). Psychology of Reasoning: Structure and Content; Lidén, Gräns, & Juslin (2018). From Devil's Advocate to Crime Fighter: Confirmation Bias and Debiasing Techniques in Prosecutorial Decision-Making, pp. 494–526.

[66] Lidén, Gräns, & Juslin (2018). From Devil's Advocate to Crime Fighter: Confirmation Bias and Debiasing Techniques in Prosecutorial Decision-making, pp. 494–526.

[67] Lidén, Gräns, & Juslin (2018). From Devil's Advocate to Crime Fighter: Confirmation Bias and Debiasing Techniques in Prosecutorial Decision-making, pp. 494–526.

[68] Burke (2006). Improving Prosecutorial Decision Making: Some Lessons of Cognitive Science, pp. 1588–1631,

[69] Freedman (1990). Innocence, Federalism, and the Capital Jury: Two Legislative Proposals for Evaluating Post-trial Evidence of Innocence in Death Penalty Cases, pp. 315–323; Gershman (2001). The Prosecutor's Duty to Truth, pp. 309–354.

[70] Ernberg, Tidefors, & Landström (2016). Prosecutors' Reflections on Sexually Abused Preschoolers and their Ability to Stand Trial, pp. 21–29; Lievore (2005). Prosecutorial Decisions in Adult Sexual Assault Cases, pp. 1–6; Wettergren & Bergman Blix (2016). Empathy and Objectivity in the Legal Procedure: The Case of Swedish Prosecutors, pp. 19–35.

[71] Lidén, Gräns, & Juslin (2018). 'From Devil's Advocate to Crime Fighter: Confirmation Bias and Debiasing Techniques in Prosecutorial Decision Making', pp. 1588–631.

The charging decision not only has an impact on the nature of the prosecutors' tasks, but these changes can also have a cognitive motivational impact because the charging decision makes them strive, primarily, to convince the court that the perpetrator committed the crime as charged. Such a focus is to a certain extent implied in the legal demands on their decision-making. Specifically, prosecutors should not initiate charges unless they have good reason to do so. The question is what this means for their ability to remain neutral throughout the court proceedings. What demands are applicable on prosecutors' decision-making after they've pressed charges and become the accused's counterparty varies in different jurisdictions. In the Swedish context, the law was fairly recently changed to emphasize the fact that prosecutors are to remain neutral after having pressed charges, not just during the criminal investigation, in accordance with the Swedish Code of Judicial Procedure 45 ch. 3a §. Research with Swedish prosecutors suggests that the charging decision itself (*ceteris paribus*) biased prosecutors.[72] For example, prosecutors who decided to prosecute were less likely to undertake additional investigation. Furthermore, the investigation they did undertake was primarily aimed at confirming the defendant's guilt. This has been noted in research pertaining to other jurisdictions as well.[73]

There is also other research suggesting that taking on the role as the defendant's counterparty in court results in a subconscious focus on getting the defendant convicted. In their study, Engel and Glöckner assigned some participants the role of prosecutors.[74] These participants downplayed conflicting evidence more than participants in the defence role did, and still wanted the defendant to be convicted even when they were offered 100 euros if their decisions regarding the suspect's guilt were accurate. This is important since with the charging decision, prosecutors are likely to act in accordance with what they perceive is mandated by their role as the defendant's counterparty.[75] Also, prosecutors are likely to feel accountable for their decision to charge a suspect, which increases the risk of defensive bolstering; that is, tenaciously holding on to a previous position even in the face of contrary evidence.[76] Furthermore, at this stage, prosecutors have been required to construct a relatively well-shaped narrative to explain an event.[77] For example, a prosecutor

---

[72] Lidén, Gräns, & Juslin (2018). 'From Devil's Advocate to Crime Fighter: Confirmation Bias and Debiasing Techniques in Prosecutorial Decision Making', pp. 1588–631.

[73] Davis (2001). The American Prosecutor: Independence, Power, and the Threat of Tyranny, pp. 393–465; Green (2003). Prosecutorial Ethics as Usual; Griffin (2001). The Prudent Prosecutor.

[74] Engel and Glöckner (2013). Role-induced Bias in Court: An Experimental Analysis, pp. 272–284.

[75] Haney, Banks, & Zimbardo (1973). Study of Prisoners and Guards in a Simulated Prison, pp. 1–17; Thompson & Loewenstein (1992). Egocentric Interpretation of Fairness and Interpersonal Conflict, pp. 176–197.

[76] Lerner & Tetlock (1999) Accounting for the Effects of Accountability, pp. 255–275; O'Brien (2009). A Recipe for Bias: An Empirical Look at the Interplay between Institutional Incentives and Bounded Rationality in Prosecutorial Decision Making, pp. 1000–1049.

[77] Wagenaar, van Koppen, & Crombag (1993). Anchored Narratives: The Psychology of Criminal Evidence.

recognizes a killing as drug related or stemming from a domestic dispute and these so-called pattern-matching models influence which information they attend to.[78]

That the research seems to suggest different points in time at which confirmation bias may arise is an indication that more research is needed. In real-life criminal cases it is, however, also expected that confirmation bias may manifest at different points and in different ways across different jurisdictions and different cases. This is expected on the basis that prosecutors in different jurisdictions have somewhat different roles and levels of discretion.[79] In European countries, the historically important distinction between the investigative and the trial phase, where the investigation was often carried out by an examining magistrate whereas the indictment was issued and presented by a public prosecutor, is maintained to different extents to this day.[80] Swedish prosecutors' involvement in the investigative phase does not disqualify them from also acting in court,[81] even though this has been criticized.[82] Dutch prosecutors are involved both in the investigative and trial phase.[83] Similar to Swedish prosecutors, Dutch prosecutors are formally responsible for all aspects of the criminal investigation.[84] However, unlike Swedish prosecutors, Dutch prosecutors may, for more serious crimes, apply to an investigative judge for a preliminary judicial investigation (but the decision to institute criminal proceedings is exclusively reserved for the prosecutors).[85] Dutch prosecutors have been described as possessing 'enormous powers'.[86] In France, it has been considered necessary to counterbalance prosecutors' powers by having an investigative judge with an influential role, for example when it comes to coercive measures.[87] This is quite different from the roles of US prosecutors, not only because US prosecutors are often generally elected rather than appointed[88] but also because the prosecutors do not generally play a role in the investigative phase.[89] Hence, decisions about what crimes

---

[78] Bilalić, McLeod, & Gobet (2008). Why Good Thoughts Block Better Ones: The Mechanism of the Pernicious Einstellung (Set) Effect, pp. 652–661; Epelboim & Suppes (2001). A Model of Eye Movements and Visual Working Memory During Problem Solving in Geometry, pp. 1561–1574; Hecht & Proffitt (1995). The Price of Expertise: Effects of Experience on the Water-Level Task, pp. 90–95.

[79] Gilliéron (2013). Public Prosecutors in the United States and Europe—A Comparative Analysis with Special Focus on Switzerland, France, and Germany; Griffin (2001). The Prudent Prosecutor.

[80] Lidén, Gräns, & Juslin (2019). From Devil's Advocate to Crime Fighter: Confirmation Bias and Debiasing Techniques in Prosecutorial Decision-Making, pp. 494–526; Gilliéron (2013). Public Prosecutors in the United States and Europe—A Comparative Analysis with Special Focus on Switzerland, France, and Germany.

[81] The Swedish Government Bill, Prop. 2000/01:92 p. 20.

[82] Jacobson, (2008). 'We Can't Just Do It Any Which Way'——Objectivity Work among Swedish prosecutors, pp. 46–68; Lindberg (1997). Om Åklagaretik.

[83] Tak (2012). The Dutch Prosecutor. In Luna & Wade, The Prosecutor in Transnational Perspective.

[84] Tak (2012). The Dutch Prosecutor. In Luna & Wade, The Prosecutor in Transnational Perspective.

[85] Tak (2012). The Dutch Prosecutor. In Luna & Wade, The Prosecutor in Transnational Perspective

[86] Tak (2012). The Dutch Prosecutor. In Luna & Wade, The Prosecutor in Transnational Perspective.

[87] Gilliéron (2013). Public Prosecutors in the United States and Europe—A Comparative Analysis with Special Focus on Switzerland, France, and Germany.

[88] Jacoby (1980). The American Prosecutor, A Search for Identity; Ramsey (2002). The Discretionary Power of 'Public' Prosecutors in Historical perspective, pp. 1309–1393.

[89] Gilliéron (2013). Public Prosecutors in the United States and Europe—A Comparative Analysis with Special Focus on Switzerland, France, and Germany.

are investigated and who is arrested fall under police discretion.[90] Depending on state jurisdiction, even the decision to charge a suspect, at least for misdemeanours, is sometimes left to the police.[91] Thus, in such situations, the prosecutor's office receives the case only after charges against the individual have already been filed. It also varies whether a single prosecutor is responsible for a case from start to finish (vertical model) or whether different sections of the attorney's office process the same case at different stages (horizontal model).[92] Often this is related to the size of the office, with small and medium-size offices more often following the horizontal model and larger offices more often following the vertical model as the larger offices have different specialized sections that deal with specific types of crime.[93] Thus, across different legal contexts, there are different ideas about when a prosecutor is to become involved, and whether there is a need to include another decision-maker, such as the investigative judge or another prosecutor. To empirically evaluate the ideas about when a prosecutor is to become involved, research needs to divide prosecutorial decision into different stages. This enables detection of when and how the bias might arise. So far, empirical research which has made this distinction between different stages is still sparse.[94]

4.2.3 Mitigating Bias

4.2.3.1 Changing decision-maker

In line with findings about the debiasing effect of changing decision-makers in police interviews with suspects (Chapter 3.5.1.5.2) as well as in judges' decision-making (Chapter 4.3.3.1), it is possible that changing the decision-maker, for example between the decision to prosecute someone and the trial phase, will be effective as a debiasing technique. This technique has so far only been evaluated at an earlier stage, that is, after a prosecutor's decision to arrest someone and the charging decision.[95] Since according to the relevant study, no bias was triggered by the arrest decision, the potentially debiasing effect of changing decision-maker could not be properly evaluated.[96] Keeping this caveat in mind, it is likely, given the

---

[90] Harris (2011). The Interaction and Relationship Between Prosecutors and Police Officers in the US and hos this Affects Police Reform Efforts; Weigend (1978). Anklagepflicht und ermessen. Die stellung der Staatsanwalts Zwischen Legalitätsu. Opportunitätsprinzip nach Deutschem und Amerikanischmen Recht.
[91] Abadinsky (1998). Law and. Justice, An Introduction to the American Legal System.
[92] Abadinsky (1998) Law and. Justice, An introduction to the American Legal System.
[93] Gramckow (2008). Prosecutor Organization and Operations in the United States.
[94] See, however, Lidén, Gräns, & Juslin (2019). From Devil's Advocate to Crime Fighter: Confirmation Bias and Debiasing Techniques in Prosecutorial Decision-Making, pp. 494–526,
[95] Lidén, Gräns, & Juslin (2018). From Devil's Advocate to Crime Fighter: Confirmation Bias and Debiasing Techniques in Prosecutorial Decision-Making, pp. 494–526.
[96] Lidén, Gräns, & Juslin (2018). From Devil's Advocate to Crime Fighter: Confirmation Bias and Debiasing Techniques in Prosecutorial Decision-Making, pp. 494–526.

previous research findings as well as the social explanations of confirmation bias, that a change of decision-maker is beneficial in prosecutorial decision-making as well. Clearly, this is a variable to take into consideration in prosecution offices when considering prosecution models, for example whether a single prosecutor is responsible from a case from start to finish (vertical model) or whether different sections/prosecutors handle the same case at different stages (horizontal model) or a mix between these models.[97] As pointed out above, in the United States, this choice has often depended on the size of the prosecution's office, where small and medium-size offices are more likely to follow the horizontal model, while larger offices that consist of different specialized sections that handle specific types of crime more often follow the vertical model.[98] Also, at the ICC Office of the Prosecutor (OTP) a vertical prosecution model has been implemented since 2013, giving the direction of its teams at all stages of investigation and prosecution to the prosecutions division.[99] This means that a senior trial lawyer is in charge of each team starting from the investigation and the same person will also lead the case in court.[100] This development was in line with recommendations from a group of experts.[101]

The vertical model is often considered advantageous in practice. This is because, for example, it is believed to promote continuity and it also limits the number of different people that victims encounter through the court process.[102] However, simultaneously, it entails a substantial risk that prosecutors and investigators, who have been working with the investigation from outset of a case, fail to reason independently of an investigative hypothesis. In line with social explanations of confirmation bias (Chapter 2.2.2.3), vertical models are a risk factor for confirmation bias, not least considering the bias blind spot.

4.2.3.2 Devil's Advocates, Red Teams, and Evidence Review Boards
For the same reasons that changing decision-maker is likely to enable a more critical review of the evidence, having a Devil's Advocate, a Red Team, or an Evidence Review Board has some potential as debiasing techniques;[103] that is, an individual or a group of individuals, explicitly tasked to review the evidence critically, has

---

[97] Weimer (1980). Vertical Prosecution and Career Criminal Bureaus: How Many and Who? pp. 369–378.
[98] Gramckow (2008). Prosecutor Organization and Operations in the United States.
[99] Lidén (2020). Confirmation Bias in Investigation of Core International Crimes: Risk Factors and Quality Control Techniques, p. 519; ICC-OTP (2013). Strategic Plan June 2012-2015, 11 October 2013.
[100] ICC-OTP (2013). Strategic Plan June 2012-2015, 11 October 2013.
[101] Mettraux et al. (2015). Expert Initiative on Promoting Effectiveness at the International Criminal Court, pp. 1–254.
[102] ICC OTP (2015), Strategic Plan 2016-2018, 16 November 2015, pp. 40–41.
[103] Agirre Aranburu (2020). The Contribution of Analysis to the Quality Control in Criminal Investigation, pp. 257–259.

some potential as debiasing techniques. All three procedures are 'stress tests'[104] that challenge the investigative findings using partially overlapping mechanisms.

A Devil's Advocate is often a member of an investigate group tasked with offering critical alternative perspectives.[105] Research on Devil's Advocate procedures have shown mixed results, as the success of the procedures seem to be dependent on how 'devilish' the Devil's Advocate really is,[106] for example, whether the dissent is genuine or contrived.[107] Thus, for a Devil's Advocate to have the intended effect, rather than become a pointless ritual, the Devil's Advocate should actively research and advocate a contrary position, not just pose rhetorical questions and make insincere or unsubstantiated comments before slipping back into the mainstream of conventional thought. Specifically, research suggest that 'merely pointing out the abstract possibility of an alternative explanation may not be successful in changing people's mind, but a detailed alternative story of the suspect's point of view might be able to reduce perceived guilt of the defendant'.[108]

In fact, if the Devil's Advocate's dissent is ingenuine and/or if the Devil's Advocate presents merely a theoretical possibility of an alternative explanation, research suggests that 'the task of having to think of alternative explanations can backfire and bolster previous beliefs'.[109] Hence, there is a risk that Devil's Advocate procedures that are not conducted properly are, in fact, worse than ineffective as they might have a biasing effect, thus the opposite of the intended debiasing effect. Some suggestions on how to ensure that the assigned Devil's Advocate is 'devilish enough' to achieve a debiasing effect, are, for example, to rotate the Devil's Advocate role among the members of the group and/or assigning the role to more than one group member, so that the Devil's Advocate is not at a numerical disadvantage in relation to the rest of the group.[110]

---

[104] Agirre Aranburu (2020). The Contribution of Analysis to the Quality Control in Criminal Investigation, p. 138.

[105] Nemeth, Brown, & Rogers (2001). Devil's Advocate Versus Authentic Dissent: Stimulating Quantity and Quality, pp. 707–720.

[106] Janis (1989). Crucial Decisions, Leadership in Policymaking and Crisis Management, p. 248; Jones (1995). The Thinker's Toolkit, 14 Powerful Techniques for Problem Solving, p. 218.

[107] Schulz-Hardt, Jochims, & Frey (2002). Productive Conflict in Group Decision Making: Genuine and Contrived Dissent as Strategies to Counteract Biased Information Seeking, pp. 563–86; Nemeth, Brown, & Rogers (2001). Devil's Advocate Versus Authentic Dissent: Stimulating Quantity and Quality, pp. 707–720.

[108] Tenney, Clearly, & Spellman (2009). Unpacking the Doubt in 'Beyond a Reasonable Doubt': Plausible Alternative Stors Increase not Guilty Verdicts, pp. 1–8; Schmittat et al. (2021). Alternative Stories and the Decision to Prosecute: An Applied Approach Against Confirmation Bias in Criminal Prosecution, pp. 1–29.

[109] Schmittat et al. (2021). Alternative Stories and the Decision to Prosecute: An Applied Approach Against Confirmation Bias in Criminal Prosecution, p. 3, citing Nemeth, Brown, & Rogers (2001). Devil's Advocate Versus Authentic Dissent: Stimulating Quantity and Quality, pp. 707–720.

[110] Janis (1972). Victims of Groupthink: A Psychological Study of Foreign-Policy Decisions and Fiascoes, p. 216; Kiser (2010). Beyond Right and Wrong, The Power of Effective Decision Making for Attorneys and Clients, p. 389.

Ideally, however, the individuals assigned the task of offering alternative views should be as independent as possible in relation to the members of the investigative teams and the prosecutor.[111] In other words, they should form a separate 'Red Team' or similar unit. Stemming from the field of military intelligence, and having been used in both the security and private sectors by companies striving to achieve greater certainty and efficiency,[112] Red Teams are expected not only to challenge a proposed hypothesis but also to build an alternative argument or scenario using the same information.[113] Hence, while having a Red Team is more demanding in terms of resources,[114] they also hold greater promise than Devil's Advocate procedures as a bias mitigation measure. Yet, as with Red Teams, their success is not guaranteed but dependent on their relative independence in relation to the investigative group. Factors such as the Red Team composition will be important too.[115] Hence, just like with Devil's Advocate procedures, poorly conducted red teaming may result in false confidence and therefore, in practice, have the opposite of the intended effect since the investigative group 'may feel victorious without having been really challenged'.[116] Unless there is a designated permanent group acting as a Red Team (and this is fairly unusual),[117] it may, in practice, be difficult to ensure sufficient independence in relation to the investigative groups.[118] Also, especially in extensive investigations, Red Teams will need to start from scratch and spend lots of time and resources to be able to review the evidence critically in relevant ways.[119]

Evidence Review Boards, sometimes referred to as 'murder boards' because of the expected merciless approach from the reviewers,[120] are similar to Red Teams since they are meant to offer independent and critical review of the investigation.[121] However, an Evidence Review Board's task is framed somewhat differently,

---

[111] Agirre Aranburu (2020). The Contribution of Analysis to the Quality Control in Criminal Investigation.
[112] Agirre Aranburu (2020). The Contribution of Analysis to the Quality Control in Criminal Investigation.
[113] Zenko (2015). Red Team: How to Succeed by Thinking like the Enemy; Zenko (2015)., 'Red Team Reading List', Council on Foreign Relations; de Landa (1991). War in the Age of Intelligent Machines, Swerve Editions.
[114] Adkins (2013). Red Teaming the Red Team: Utilizing Cyber Espionage to Combat Terrorism, pp. 1–9.
[115] Agirre Aranburu, The Contribution of Analysis to the Quality Control in Criminal Investigation, p. 257.
[116] Agirre Aranburu (2020). The Contribution of Analysis to the Quality Control in Criminal Investigation, p. 257; The Commission on the Intelligence Capabilities of the United States Regarding Weapons of Mass Destruction (2005). Report to the President of the United States, pp. 1–8.
[117] Coliandris & Rogers (2014). Improving Organisational Performance—Red Team Policing and Partnerships, pp. 63–72.
[118] Agirre Aranburu (2020). The Contribution of Analysis to the Quality Control in Criminal Investigation.
[119] Agirre Aranburu (2020). The Contribution of Analysis to the Quality Control in Criminal Investigation.
[120] Agirre Aranburu, The Contribution of Analysis to the Quality Control in Criminal Investigation.
[121] Agirre Aranburu, The Contribution of Analysis to the Quality Control in Criminal Investigation.

158 CONFIRMATION BIAS IN CRIMINAL LITIGATIONS

focusing more on the applicable legal standards, since the reviewers need to conduct a prospective assessment on the likelihood of success of the case in court. In other words, the Evidence Review Board is intended to advise on whether the available evidence is sufficient to file charges or not.[122] The applicable legal standards will of course vary across different jurisdictions but, for example, in England and Wales, the standard is a 'realistic prospect of conviction'.[123] It should be noted that Evidence Review Boards have not been empirically and systematically evaluated for the purpose of bias mitigation in criminal cases. However, the debiasing potential of Evidence Review Boards is supported by social psychological findings (Chapter 2.2.2.3) as well as the research into Devil's Advocate procedures and Red Teams. It can also be noted that using Evidence Review Boards has been recommended, for example on the basis of the experiences of the five international or hybrid tribunals (International Criminal Tribunal for the Former Yugoslavia (ICTY), International Criminal Tribunal for Rwanda (ICTR), Special Court for Sierra Leone (SCSL), Extraordinary Chambers in the Courts of Cambodia (ECCC), and Special Tribunal for Lebanon (STL)).[124]

4.2.4 Conclusion

Because of prosecutors' influential roles in criminal cases, confirmation bias in their decision-making can directly impact not only the accuracy but also the legitimacy of both investigations and litigations. As leaders of criminal investigations, they may directly contribute to false positives, for example if prosecutors push forensic examiners or forensic doctors to confirm their hypothesis through their analysis, or because one, or even multiple, innocent individuals are led to confess to a crime they did not commit. Notably, since confirmation bias is a more or less subconscious bias, the intention of the prosecutor in question is not necessarily to impact on the evidence. Rather, the prosecutor may strive to ensure that the evidence confirms what the prosecutors genuinely perceives to be the truth. While such behaviours intuitively seem more strongly associated with false positives, the risk of false negatives should not be neglected. Since confirmation bias is associated with overconfidence in a given hypothesis, it is easy to see how prosecutors may perceive their cases to be stronger than outside observers, such as judges, view

---

[122] Xabier Agirre Aranburu (2020). The Contribution of Analysis to the Quality Control in Criminal Investigation.
[123] Director of Public Prosecutions of the Crown Prosecution Service (2018). The Evidential Stage, sect. 4.6.
[124] Agirre Aranburu (2020). The Contribution of Analysis to the Quality Control in Criminal Investigation, p. 150.

them to be. This is to be expected on the basis of social psychological findings pertaining to the bias blind spot and how decision-makers tend to be less critical in relation to a self-generated hypothesis than a hypothesis generated by someone else (Chapter 2.2.2.3).

While they still need more evaluation when it comes to prosecutorial decision-making specifically, bias mitigation strategies that are most likely to be effective include changing the deciding prosecutor between different decisions during the investigative and trial phases, to use Devil's Advocates procedures, Red Teams, and/or Evidence Review Boards. The relative success of these measures will depend on to what extent the reviewing individual or individuals are independent, critical enough, and genuine enough when it comes to presenting and integrating dissent and alternative viewpoints into the decision-making process.

4.3 Judges' Decision-making

4.3.1 Introduction

Given that confirmation bias has been studied and found in multiple investigative settings including interviews, crime scene investigations, forensic analysis, and also in prosecutor's decisions, there is a tangible risk that evidence presented to judges may not accurately represent a course of event. Undeniably, this will impact negatively on the risk of false positives as well as false negatives. Even if judges were immune to confirmation bias, their evaluation of evidence, careful and professional though it may be, would not protect sufficiently against false positives and false negatives simply because the foundation of their decision-making may be flawed. This emphasizes the fact that the final outcome of a criminal case is dependent on many actors, including police officers, crime scene investigators, forensic doctors, and prosecutors. To promote sufficient and accurate evidence being presented in court, bias mitigation measures need to be undertaken by all these actors.

Furthermore, since research, unsurprisingly, shows that judges are not immune to confirmation bias, it is also essential to examine how this bias can manifest in their decisions. This will be addressed in the following sections, focusing on pre-trial detention, interim decisions, and other decisions preceding the assessment of guilt (Section 4.3.2.1), story construction (Section 4.3.2.2), as well as the gravity of the crime and sentencing (Section 4.3.2.3). Bias mitigation measures will also be examined, including changing decision-maker (Section 4.3.3.1) and structured evaluations of evidence (Section 4.3.3.2).

4.3.2 Understanding Bias

4.3.2.1 Pre-trial Detention, Interim Decisions, and Other Decisions Preceding the Assessment of Guilt

He [Mr Hauschildt] did not claim that a judge in such a position would conduct himself with personal bias, but argued that the kind of decisions he would be called upon to make at the pre-trial stage would require him, under the law, to assess the strength of the evidence and the character of the accused, thereby inevitably coloring his appreciation of the evidence and issues at the subsequent trial.[125]

In 1989, the European Court of Human Rights (ECtHR) decided a case called *Hauschildt v. Denmark*[126] in which a Danish judge, who had made repeated decisions to detain Hauschildt awaiting trial, also decided about Hauschildt's guilt during the main hearing. The Court concluded that Hauschildt's right to a fair trial following Article 6 of the European Convention for the Protection of Human Rights and Fundamental Freedoms (ECHR) had been breached. Specifically, the Court decided that the judge had not been impartial when deciding about Hauschildt's guilt. In Denmark, the case resulted in new legislation, the Code of Judicial Procedure § 60 paragraph 2, read together with the Administration of Justice Act § 762 paragraph 2. These paragraphs prevent judges from deciding on both detention and guilt, when the detention is based on the standard of proof 'particularly confirmed suspicion' clarity ('*saerlig bestyrkt misstanke*' in Danish). It has been discussed whether this should apply when the detention is based on lower standards of proof as well.[127] As submitted by Mr Hauschildt, a detention decision requires judges, by law, to hypothesize about the suspect's guilt. Furthermore, this happens, by necessity, before the point in time at which the accused's guilt has been legally determined. Since early hypotheses, especially self-generated hypotheses (Chapter 2.2.2.3), can easily trigger confirmation bias, there is indeed a risk that pre-trial detention decisions will impact on judges' subsequent guilt determinations. This is likely to be the case regardless of the applicable standard of proof. Hence, while not explicitly and specifically addressed by either Hauschildt or the ECtHR, confirmation bias is, demonstrably, a good reason to avoid a situation where the same judge makes decisions regarding both pre-trial detention and guilt.[128]

---

[125] ECtHR, Case of Hauschildt v. Denmark, 10486/83, pp. 14–15.
[126] ECtHR, Case of Hauschildt v. Denmark, 10486/83.
[127] Retspolitisk forening (2016). Åbent brev till justitsministeren angående rpl. §§ 60 stk. 2 og 762 stk. 1.
[128] Lidén, Gräns, & Juslin (2018). 'Guilty, No Doubt': Detention Provoking Confirmation Bias in Judges' Guilt Assessments and Debiasing Techniques, pp. 219–247.

Outside Denmark, in for example Canada, the two decisions are also separated since Justices of Peace are the ones who decide on pre-trial motions and if a case reaches trial, judges who are more educated in the law are appointed to decide cases. In Chile, the two decisions are separated logically following the two-step criminal process.[129] However, the *Juzgado de Garantia*, who makes decisions about pre-trial detention, may also be one of three judges who decides guilt in the tribunal de juicio.[130] Similarly, in international criminal justice, there are often pre-trial judges dealing with detention and it varies between different tribunals whether those judges may also be part of the Trial Chamber deciding whether to convict or acquit.[131] In yet other jurisdictions, for example Finland,[132] Sweden,[133] and in some US states (in relation to certain crimes), no such separation of decision-making powers is made. Subsequently, judges in these jurisdictions are allowed to decide both detention and guilt and indeed they do so fairly regularly. For example, in some Swedish District Courts this happens in as many as 80 per cent of the cases.[134] The three most important factors deciding whether the same or different judges decide are organizational factors such as rotation schedules for allocating cases (79.17 per cent), work load (62.05 per cent), and the type of case to be determined (33.33 per cent).[135]

Unless there is an expectation that a suspect will be found guilty of a crime which can motivate a liberty-depriving sentence, primarily a jail sentence, it would be legally unjustified to detain a suspect. In fact, suspects who are deprived of their liberty pre-trial but who are then acquitted following the main hearing have a right to compensation in many jurisdictions.[136] As such, from a legal normative

---

[129] Hersant (2017). Patronage and Rationalization: Reform to Criminal Procedure and the Lower Courts in Chile, pp. 423–449, Diaz (2014). Tradiciones Indigenas en La Applicacion de la Ley Penal (Juzgado de Garantia de Arica).

[130] For more on the Juzgado de Garantia and the Chileans Criminal Procedure see, for example, Hersant (2017). Patronage and Rationalization: Reform to Criminal Procedure and the Lower Courts in Chile, pp. 423–449; Diaz (2014). Tradiciones Indigenas en La Applicacion de la Ley Penal (Juzgado de Garantia de Arica).

[131] See, for example, Article 2 of the Agreement and Articles 7(a) and 18 of the STL Statute, Rules of Procedure and Evidence, Explanatory Memorandum by the Tribunal's President § 11 discussed in the Separate Opinion of Judge David Re, STL Trial Chamber's Judgment in The Prosecutor v. Salim Jamil Ayyash, Hassan Habib Merhi, Husseing Hassan Oneissi, Assad Hassan Sabra, pp. 2275–2276.

[132] Lidén, Gräns, & Juslin (2019). 'Guilty, No Doubt': Detention Provoking Confirmation Bias in Judges' Guilt Assessments and Debiasing Techniques, pp. 219–247.

[133] The Swedish Code of Judicial Procedure 4 ch. 13 § and The Swedish Government Bill, Prop. 1992/93:25 p. 16.

[134] Lidén, Gräns, & Juslin (2018). 'Guilty, No Doubt!' Detention Provoking Confirmation Bias in Judges' Guilt Assessments and Debiasing Techniques, pp. 219–247.

[135] Lidén, Gräns, & Juslin (2018). 'Guilty, No Doubt!' Detention Provoking Confirmation Bias in Judges' Guilt Assessments and Debiasing Techniques, pp. 219–247.

[136] Safi (2016). Ensuring Compensation for Wrongful Imprisonment and Wrongful Detention in Afghanistan, pp. 35–80. In Sweden, the state's responsibility to compensate in such situation is strict and therefore does not require a fault or negligence; see The Swedish Office of the Chancellor of Justice, Justitiekanslern (JK) decision, 8 May 2001, registration no. 45-01-41. However, the wording of The Code of Judicial Procedure 24 ch. 24 § illustrates that detentions followed by acquittals are considered wrongful. See the Law (1998:714) on compensation after deprivation of liberty and other coercive measures.

perspective there is no doubt that hypotheses about guilt should be formed during detention hearings. Such hypotheses formation is not surprising or uncommon but is in fact entailed in a range of other pre-trial and interim decisions. In 1969, Davis remarked on the enormous consequences such decisions are likely to have on discretionary justice.[137] Today, it is known that hypothesis formation can make decision-makers such as judges emphasize and evaluate as stronger the evidence that is consistent with their hypothesis,[138] while simultaneously making them unresponsive, or at least less responsive, to hypothesis-inconsistent evidence.[139]

Although many different types of decisions entail early hypothesis formation, so far, pre-trial detention has received most attention as a trigger of confirmation bias. This makes sense, since during a detention hearing, judges are not only exposed to an explicit identification of a suspect but also to other kinds of claims regarding the suspect's character. For example, this includes claims that the suspect would relapse into crime if set free. In many jurisdictions, such as the Netherlands,[140] some US states,[141] and Sweden,[142] such risk assessments are regularly part of the pre-trial detention decision. These assessments are often based on the suspect's personal circumstances, including employment stability, education, housing/residential stability,[143] socioeconomic status, and/or criminal record.[144]

In fact, research suggests that the identification of a suspect in itself can trigger confirmation bias, since this made Dutch judges less susceptible to the knowledge of an alternative suspect in their estimations of the incriminating power of the evidence.[145] Suspect identification also made mock jurors 'hear' more incriminating information in a degraded audio recording.[146] Furthermore, when exposed to the defendant's criminal record[147] or low socio-economic

---

[137] Davis (1969). Discretionary Justice: A Preliminary Inquiry. For more on other types of interim decisions see for example Clarke & Kurtz (1983). The Importance of Interim Decisions to Felony Trial Court Dispositions, pp. 476–518.

[138] Greenwald (1980). The Totalitarian Ego, pp. 603–618; Lord, Ross & Lepper (1979). Biased Assimilation and Attitude Polarization: The Effects of Prior Theories on Subsequently Considered Evidence, pp. 2098–2109; Nickerson (1998), Confirmation Bias: A Ubiquitous Phenomenon in Many Guises.

[139] Lidén, Gräns, & Juslin (2018). 'Guilty, No Doubt!' Detention Provoking Confirmation Bias in Judges' Guilt Assessments and Debiasing Techniques, pp. 219–247; Ross, Lepper, & Hubbard (1975). Perseverance in Self-perception and Social Perception: Biased Attributional Processes in the Debriefing Paradigm, pp. 880- 892.

[140] van Wingerden, van Wilsem, & Moerings (2014). Pre-Sentence Reports and Punishment: A Quasi-Experiment Assessing the Effects of Risk-based Pre-Sentence Reports on Sentencing, pp. 723–744.

[141] Desmarais & Lowder (2019). Pretrial Risk Assessment Tools. A Primer for Judges, Prosecutors, and Defense Attorneys.

[142] Lidén (2021). 'Inter-domar reliabilitet': Är Individuella Skillnader i Domares Beslutsfattande ett Löfte eller Hot mot Rättssäkerheten?, pp. 1–18.

[143] Desmarais & Lowder (2019). Pretrial Risk Assessment Tools. A Primer for Judges, Prosecutors, and Defense Attorneys.

[144] Grommon et al. (2017). Process Evaluation of the IRAS-PAT Pilot Program Implementation.

[145] Rassin (2010). Blindness to Alternative Scenarios in Evidence Evaluation, pp. 153–163.

[146] Lange et al. (2011). Contextual Biases in the Interpretation of Auditory Evidence, pp. 178–187.

[147] Cornish & Sealy (1973). Jurors and their Verdicts, pp. 496–508; Doob & Kirshenbaum, (1972). Some Empirical Evidence on the Effect of S.12 of the Canada Evidence Act upon an Accused, pp. 88–96;

status,[148] mock jurors got less favourable impressions of the defendant and made more guilt-consistent interpretations of the evidence. On top of this, an assessment of whether there is a risk that someone might relapse into crime is in itself, strictly speaking, a premature conclusion about someone's guilt. This is because it is logically and legally impossible to relapse into a crime that has not already been committed. Several authors have acknowledged that such *risk-based justice* is likely to be associated with bias.[149]

Early research into whether, how, and to what extent pre-trial detentions may bias judges' decision-making consisted of archive studies. As a matter of fact, as early as 1932, research into cases in the US state of Oregon claimed that case outcomes were different for detained and released defendants, even if their cases did not vary in legally relevant ways.[150] Later (1964–2018), several researchers started empirically evaluating this claim. For instance, a review of court records in Florida illustrate that detained defendants were more likely to be incarcerated and to receive longer sentences than defendants who were released pending the main hearing.[151] On the basis of this and other similar data from, for instance, Philadelphia,[152] New York City,[153] New Jersey, and Pennsylvania Eastern District,[154] researchers have argued that detained defendants may be at a disadvantage during the main hearing. Other reviews of court records from the Miami-Dade county and Philadelphia county illustrate that pre-trial detentions increase the probability of guilty pleas and thereby also increase the probability of a conviction.[155] Also, data from misdemeanour cases,[156] adjudicated by the Harris County Criminal Court of Law in Texas, provides compelling evidence that pre-trial detentions

---

Hans & Doob (1975) Section 12 of the Canada Evidence Act and the Deliberation of Simulated Juries, pp. 235–253; Kalven & Zeisel (1967). The American Jury, pp. 158–175; Gordon (2004). Social Cognition and Section 12 of the Canada Evidence Act: Can Jurors 'Properly' use Criminal Record Evidence?, pp. 1–340; Wissler & Saks (1985). On the Inefficacy of Limiting Instruction: When Jurors use Prior Conviction Evidence to Decide on Guilt, pp. 37–48.

[148] Blanck, Rosenthal, & Hazzard Cordell (1985). The Appearance of Justice: Judges' Verbal and Nonverbal Behavior in Criminal Trials, pp. 89–164.

[149] Van Eijk (2020). Inclusion and Exclusion through Risk-based Justice: Analysing Combinations of Risk Assessment from Pretrial Detention to Release, pp. 1080–1097; Ballard (2011). Research Report on Remand Detention in South Africa: An Overview of the Current Law and Proposals for Reform.

[150] Morse & Beattie (1932). Survey of the Administration of Justice in Oregon.

[151] Williams (2003). The Effect of Pretrial Detention on Imprisonment Decisions, pp. 299–316.

[152] Goldkamp (1980). The Effects of Detention on Judicial Decisions: A Closer Look, pp. 234–257.

[153] Landes (1973). The Bail System: An Economic Approach, pp. 79–105; Leslie & Pope (2017). The Unintended Impact of Pretrial Detention on Case Outcomes: Evidence from New York City Arraignments, pp. 529–557; Rankin (1964). The Effect of Pretrial Detention, pp. 641–656.

[154] Oleson et al. (2016). The Effect of Pretrial Detention on Sentencing in Two Federal Districts, pp. 1–20.

[155] Dobbie, Goldin, & Yang (2018). The Effects of Pretrial Detention on Conviction, Future Crime, and Employment: Evidence from Randomly Assigned Judges, pp. 201–240.

[156] LaFountain et al. (2010). National Centre for State Courts, Examining the Work of State Courts: An Analysis of 2008 State Court Caseloads, p. 47.

exert pressure on accused individuals to plead guilty.[157] More specifically, detained defendants were 25 per cent more likely to plead guilty.[158] They were also 43 per cent more likely to be sentenced to jail, and received jail sentences that were more than twice as long on average, compared to those who were not detained.[159] Similar results have been found in Philadelphia, New York City, Pittsburgh, and Miami.[160] Certainly, the described tendencies are problematic given due process clauses found in, for example, the Fifth and Fourteenth Amendments of the US Constitution requiring that guilty pleas be 'voluntary' and 'intelligent'. This presupposes that the defendant, in practice, has a meaningful choice. It also follows from, for example, Brady v. United States,[161] holding that a plea must be a 'knowing, intelligent act … done with sufficient awareness of the relevant circumstances and likely consequences'. Arguably, pre-trial detention might render guilty pleas involuntary. Furthermore, the described tendencies shed some new light on regulations according to which detained individuals are routinely given sentences based on time served. These regulations clearly have a limited impact if the detention itself results in a longer sentence.

As a whole, this body of research suggests that detention effects exist across case types and jurisdictions. However, the mechanisms behind them have not necessarily been identified in the cited research. Although the studies did control for factors such as offence seriousness, prior criminal record, and attorney type, some of the noted differences between detained and non-detained defendants may have other explanations than a confirmation bias making judges more inclined to treat detained defendants more harshly. For example, the differences may be due to differences in the available evidence or the more specific course of event as charged.[162] While archive studies are always associated with limitations of this nature, the potential importance of the cited research should not be underestimated, particularly not when considering that similar results have been found in more recent experimental research.

Today, researchers interested in whether pre-trial detention can trigger a confirmation bias in judges are more likely to choose experimental methods. This is because experimental methods allow studying the isolated effect of pre-trial

---

[157] Euvrard & Leclerc (2017). Pre-trial Detention and Guilty Pleas: Inducement or Coercion?, pp. 525–542.
[158] Euvrard & Leclerc (2017). Pre-trial Detention and Guilty Pleas: Inducement or Coercion?, pp. 525–542.
[159] Heaton, Mayson, & Stevenson (2017). The Downstream Consequences of Misdemeanor Pretrial Detention, pp. 713 -784.
[160] Stevenson, Distortion of Justice: How the Inability to Pay Bail Affects Case Outcomes, pp. 511–542; Leslie & Pope (2016). The Unintended Impact of Pretrial Detention on Case Outcomes: Evidence from NYC Arraignments; Gupta (2016). The Heavy Costs of High Bail: Evidence from Judge Randomization, pp. 472–473; Dobbie et al. (2016). The Effects of Pre-trial Detention on Conviction, Future Crime, and Employment: Evidence from Randomly Assigned Judges.
[161] Brady v. United States, 397 U.S. 742, 748 (1970).
[162] William (2003). The Effect of Pretrial Detention on Imprisonment Decisions, p. 300.

detention, keeping all other relevant circumstances constant (*ceteris paribus*). Experimental method was also the method of choice in a study with Swedish District Court and Appellate Court judges.[163] In this study, all judges made their decisions on the basis of the same eight scenarios, which enabled isolation of the variables of interest. Specifically, in this study, the variables of interest were the detention decision and the decision-maker, that is, whether the same or different judges decided on detention and guilt during the main hearing. Since the Swedish criminal justice system does not offer the possibility of a plea bargain, the effect of the detention decision was measured in relation to judges' assessments of the evidence and whether they decided to acquit or convict during the main hearing. Overall, judges who had previously decided to detain a defendant prior to the main hearing, and who then decided about the same defendant's guilt during the main hearing, perceived the evidence as more indicative of guilt and were also more likely to convict.[164] In fact, the odds of a conviction were 2.79 times higher when judges themselves had detained compared to when a colleague had detained the defendant.[165] Furthermore, this study suggests that confirmation bias was reduced when participants were explicitly asked to evaluate the evidence piece by piece rather than to just make an overall assessment.[166] It deserves to be emphasized that the evidence, the suspect, and all other circumstances were identical in the scenarios and the only variables were whether the suspect had been detained, by whom, and, in a second experiment, how the evidence was evaluated.

Hence, the research available gives reason to believe that detentions may result in a confirmation bias in judges, which significantly impacts case outcomes. Given the number of individuals who are detained awaiting trial, this is a potential threat to the proper administration of justice. For example, in the United States, there are approximately 11 million annual admissions to local jails,[167] many because the admitted individual cannot afford their bail.[168] In many cases, these individuals cannot afford to pay for proper and effective legal counsel either and, by means of their incarceration, they are also hindered from gathering evidence themselves or in other ways prepare their defence, adding to the likelihood of a conviction.[169] For defendants with a job or apartment under threat, the chance to get out of jail

---

[163] Lidén, Gräns, & Juslin (2018). 'Guilty, No Doubt': Detention Provoking Confirmation Bias in Judges' Guilt Assessments and Debiasing Techniques, pp. 219–247.
[164] Lidén, Gräns, & Juslin (2018). 'Guilty, No Doubt': Detention Provoking Confirmation Bias in Judges' Guilt Assessments and Debiasing Techniques, pp. 219–247.
[165] Lidén, Gräns, & Juslin (2018). 'Guilty, No Doubt': Detention Provoking Confirmation Bias in Judges' Guilt Assessments and Debiasing Techniques, p. 231.
[166] Lidén, Gräns, & Juslin (2018). 'Guilty, No Doubt': Detention Provoking Confirmation Bias in Judges' Guilt Assessments and Debiasing Techniques, pp. 236–237.
[167] Bylund (1993). Tvångsmedel.
[168] N.Y.C. Criminal Justice Agency (2013). Annual Report, pp. 22, 30; Heaton, Mayson, & Stevenson (2017). The Downstream Consequences of Misdemeanor Pretrial Detention, pp. 736–737.
[169] Barker v. Wingo, 407 U.S. 514, 533 (1972).

may be impossible to pass up.[170] Hence, a detained person may plead guilty, even if innocent, simply to get out of jail.[171] Hence, the high rate of pre-trial detention in the United States is due both to widespread use of monetary bail and the limited financial resources of many defendants.[172] However, high rates of pre-trial detention have been noted also in other countries. For example, when the rate is measured per 100,000 of the general population, particularly high rates have been noted in, for example, Panama and Uruguay.[173] When the rate is instead measured as a proportion of the overall prison population, Paraguay, Bangladesh, Nigeria,[174] and China[175] come across as particularly high.[176] Canada has witnessed a steady growth in the pre-trial detention population in provincial prisons over the past several decades, although with variation across different provinces.[177] This is believed to be part of a 'tough on crime' policy.[178] Similar increases in the remand population have been noted in New South Wales in Australia.[179] The global median proportion of pretrial detainees is 27 per cent.[180]

Taken together, this suggests not only that detentions can trigger a confirmation bias in judges which increases the likelihood of a conviction, it also reinforces the fact that detentions are often associated with other disadvantages for a suspect, for example because they create pressure to accept a plea, or result in an inability to prepare one's defence properly. Given the high detention rates in many jurisdictions, as well as the many examples of detentions that have been initiated or continued despite a lack of evidence,[181] the risk of a wrongful outcome, primarily a false positive, may easily materialize.

---

[170] Gross & O'Brien (2008). Frequency and Predictors of False Conviction: Why We Know So Little, and New Data on Capital Cases, pp. 930–931.

[171] Gross & O'Brien (2008). Frequency and Predictors of False Conviction: Why We Know So Little, and New Data on Capital Cases, pp. 930–931.

[172] Dobbie, Goldin, & Yang (2018). The Effects of Pretrial Detention on Conviction, Future, Crime, and Employment: Evidence from Randomly Assigned Judges, pp. 201–240.

[173] Walmsley (2017). World Pre-trial/Remand Imprisonment List, Schönteich (2018). Global Pretrial Detention Use: A Cross-National Analysis, p. 7.

[174] Walmsley (2017). World Pre-trial/Remand Imprisonment List, Schönteich (2018). Global Pretrial Detention Use: A Cross-National Analysis, p. 7.

[175] Walmsley (2017). World Pre-trial/Remand Imprisonment List and Schönteich (2018). Global Pretrial Detention Use: A Cross-National Analysis, p. 8.

[176] Walmsley (2017). World Pre-trial/Remand Imprisonment List and Schönteich (2018). Global Pretrial Detention Use: A Cross-National Analysis, p. 8.

[177] Webster, Doob, & Myers (2009). The Parable of Ms Baker: Understanding Pre-Trial Detention in Canada, p. 83.

[178] McLellan (2010). Bail and the Diminishing Presumption of Innocence, pp. 57–74.

[179] Booth & Townsley (2009). The Process is the Punishment: The Case of Bail in New South Wales; Hucklesby & Sarre (2009). Bail in Australia, the United Kingdom and Canada: Introduction, p. 1.

[180] Booth & Townsley (2009). The Process is the Punishment: The Case of Bail in New South Wales; Hucklesby & Sarre (2009). Bail in Australia, the United Kingdom and Canada: Introduction, p. 1.

[181] See, for example, Separate Opinion of Judge David Re, STL Trial Chamber's Judgment in The Prosecutor v. Salim Jamil Ayyash, Hassan Habib Merhi, Hussein Hassan Oneissi, Assad Hassan Sabra, p. 2241 and WGAD report § 9.

4.3.2.2 Story Construction

> *When tragedy strikes and a scapegoat is required to satiate the public demand for justice, fair evidential assessments and fundamental rights are most at risk. DNA, footprints, fingerprints, and murder weapons are more easily misinterpreted, or re-arranged, to resemble guilt. Inferences, stretched to the breaking point, can become the departure point for conclusions that transform the notion of reasonable doubt into a moveable feast, with terrible consequences for the truth and the unfortunate accused.*[182]
>
> Wayne Jordash, for the Kyiv Post, 2020

Research into so-called *story construction*[183] illustrates that confirmation bias can be the glue that make even a very few or unstable building blocks not only stick together but also come across as a sound narrative. Using legal terms, this could be explained in the following way. Confirmation bias can change the perception of the evidence from circumstantial and insufficient to robust and sufficient for finding the accused guilty beyond reasonable doubt. This is what appears to have happened in the court in Pavia in Italy, in July 2019. The Pavia court convicted Ukrainian soldier Vitaliy Markiv and sentenced him to 24 years' imprisonment for killing Italian journalist Andrea Rochelli in May 2014.[184] Mr Rochelli and his interpreter had been hit and killed by mortar shelling in Donbas, and, according to the verdict, Mr Markiv was responsible.[185] The verdict was strongly opposed by multiple observers,[186] one of them Mr Jordash. The critics suggested that the conviction undermined the presumption of innocence,[187] was 'politically motivated',[188] and 'the most outrageous case … that no one has heard of'.[189] The Russian human rights organization Memorial issued a statement criticizing the approach

---

[182] Jordash (2020). How an Italian Court Undermined the Presumption of Innocence in Markiv's Conviction, the Kyiv Post.

[183] Pennington & Hastie, Evidence Evaluation in Complex Decision Making, pp. 242–258; Pennington & Hastie (1992). Explaining the Evidence: Tests of the Story model for Juror Decision Making, pp. 189–206; Pennington & Hastie (1991). A Cognitive Theory of Juror Decision Making: The Story Model, pp. 5001–5039.

[184] Tribunale di Pavia, Sezione Penale Corte D'Assise, Case No. 8065/16; Corte D´Assise di Pavia Sentenza in Nome del Popolo Italiano, No. 2/2018; Corte d'Assise di Pavia Sentenza in Nome del Popolo Italiano, Sentenza No. 1/2019.

[185] Tribunale di Pavia, Sezione Penale Corte D'Assise, Case No. 8065/16; Corte D'Assise di Pavia Sentenza in Nome del Popolo Italiano, N. 2/2018; Corte d'Assise di Pavia Sentenza in Nome del Popolo Italiano, Sentenza, N° 1/2019.

[186] Radio Free Europe Documents and Publications (2019). Kyiv Protesters Demand Freedom for Veteran Jailed in Italy for Journalist's Death.

[187] Jordash (2020). How an Italian Court Undermined the Presumption of Innocence in Markiv's Conviction, the Kyiv Post.

[188] Tokariuk (2019). The Most Outrageous Case this Summer that No One Has Heard of.

[189] Tokariuk (2019). The Most Outrageous Case this Summer that No One Has Heard of.

of the Italian court.[190] The Ukrainian Interior Minister Avakov publicly referred to the conviction as 'unfair and shameful'.[191]

Specifically, critics claimed that the Italian court had failed to approach circumstantial evidence with care and objectivity.[192] Lacking any direct evidence, the court merely presumed that Mr Markiv must have been the man responsible for leading the AK-74 attack and coordinating the deadly mortar attack.[193] This was despite the fact that, usually, there were 100 other men from the Ukrainian Army and 30 to 40 soldiers from the National Guard located on the mountain.[194] Also, Markiv's statement to other journalists[195] regarding the event was interpreted as an out-of-court confession. In fact, this statement was indeed ambiguous. Furthermore, Mr Rochelli was killed during heavy fighting in Slovyansk during the early months of Russia's war against Ukraine.[196] Neither was there any evidence suggesting that the individual who shot at Mr Rochelli intentionally killed him, nor that Mr Markiv was in fact on active duty at the relevant time. As such, the Italian court took a 'gargantuan leap of faith'[197] when it convicted Mr Markiv. The trial against Mr Markiv was resumed in the Milan Court of Appeal in October 2020.[198] Acknowledging some of the mentioned flaws, for example that Mr Markiv could not possibly have killed Mr Rochelli given the weapons he had access to at the time and the distance to the place where Mr Rochelli was,[199] the Appellate Court acquitted Mr Markiv, after he had spent more than three years in detention.[200] On 9 December 2021, the Supreme Court of Cassation in Rome upheld the Appellate Court's acquittal.

A story can originate from a range of sources, including pre-trial media reports.[201] In Mr Markiv's case, immediately after his arrest, Italian media referred

---

[190] Jordash (2020). How an Italian Court Undermined the Presumption of Innocence in Markiv's Conviction, the Kyiv Post.

[191] Avakov (2021). Twitter account: <https://twitter.com/avakovarsen/status/1149678909841170433> (accessed 20 February 2023).

[192] Coynash (2020). Baffling Denial by Italy of War in Donbas as Excuse for Trial of Ukrainian Soldier Markiv.

[193] Coynash (2020). Baffling Denial by Italy of War in Donbas as Excuse for Trial of Ukrainian Soldier Markiv.

[194] Coynash (2020). Baffling Denial by Italy of War in Donbas as Excuse for Trial of Ukrainian Soldier Markiv.

[195] Morani (2014). Ucraina, il Racconto del Capitano 'Ecco come e morte Rocchelli'.

[196] Jordash, How an Italian Court Undermined the Presumption of Innocence in Markiv's Conviction, the Kyiv Post

[197] Jordash, How an Italian Court Undermined the Presumption of Innocence in Markiv's Conviction, the Kyiv Post

[198] Radio Free Europe Documents and Publications (2020). Ukrainian Ex-Fighter Acquitted in 2014 Killing of Italian Journalist Return to Kyiv; Coynash (2020). Ukrainian Soldier Vitaly Markiv Acquitted and Freed in Italy.

[199] Tribunale Appelati di Milano. For more details on these flaws see the documentary 'Crossfire' by Cristiano Tinazzi.

[200] Tribunale Appelati di Milano.

[201] Daftary-Kapur et al. (2014). Examining Pretrial Publicity in a Shadow Jury Paradigm: Issues of Quantity, Persistence and Generalizability, pp. 462–477; Ruva & Guenther (2015). From the Shadows into the Light: How Pretrial Publicity and Deliberation Affect Mock Jurors' Decisions, Impressions, and Memory, pp. 294–310.

to him as a murderer.[202] For example, the local newspaper *Il Resto del Carlino Bologna* published an article about the case on 1 July 2017 with the following headline: 'Bologna, the killer of the Italian photojournalist arrested at the airport' ('Bologna, arrestato all'aeroporto il killer del fotoreporter italiano').[203] The next day, the nation-wide newspaper *Il Giornale* reported on Mr Rochelli's death, describing that '[t]he murderous hand is that of an Italian with a Ukrainian mother Vitaly Markiv' ('La mano omicida è quella di un italiano con madre ucraina Vitaly Markiv').[204] This early labelling of Mr Markiv, which some claim was a result of propaganda,[205] may, alone or together with other factors, have triggered a confirmation bias in the judges' evaluation of the evidence. Such potentially biasing pre-trial publicity is far from unique to Mr Markiv's case. For example, the Indian Central Bureau of Investigation's (CBI) inquiry into the suspicious death of Bollywood celebrity Sushant Singh Rajput was accompanied by months of media speculation.[206] The speculation concerned Mr Rajput's girlfriend, Mrs Chakraborty. Within a few days after Mr Rajput's death, she was not only identified as a likely perpetrator but also trolled mercilessly in the Indian media, leading to her arrest.[207] After Mrs Chakraborty was let out on bail, these circumstances were acknowledged by the Bombay High Court to constitute a threat to the proper administration of justice in the case.[208] The investigation conducted thereafter into Mr Rajput's death suggests that Mr Rajput was most likely to have committed suicide.[209] In line with the view expressed by Bombay High Court, there is a substantial risk of confirmation bias in judges who have been exposed to this kind of publicity. This is in line with the view expressed by Bennett and Feldman in 1981 that 'a good story is half the evidence'.[210]

Apart from pre-trial publicity, stories can also be implied through the context in which judges evaluate the evidence. For example, research suggests that when *the*

---

[202] Tokariuk (2019). The Most Outrageous Case this Summer that No One Has Heard of.
[203] Il Resto del Carlino Bologna (2017). Bologna, arrestato all'aeroporto il killer del fotoreporter italiano.
[204] Biloslavo (2017). Uccise Fotoreporter Italiano in Ucraina Arrestato a Bologna Miliziano Anti-Putin.
[205] See, for example, Federazione Italiana Diritti Umani (FIDU) (2019), Caso Markiv: Dalla Parte Della Verità; The New York Times (2019). How Russian Propaganda Showed Up in an Italian Murder Trial; Tokariuk (2021). Battle of Narratives: Kremlin Disinformation in the Vitaliy Markiv Case in Italy.
[206] BBC News (2020). Sushant Singh Rajput: Rhea Chakraborty on 'Media Trial' after Bollywood Star's Death; Sky News, Bollywood Producers Take Legal Action over TV Coverage Following Star's Death.
[207] BBC News (2020). Sushant Singh Rajput: Rhea Chakraborty on 'Media Trial' after Bollywood Star's Death; Sky News, Bollywood Producers Take Legal Action over TV Coverage Following Star's Death.
[208] Dodhiya (2020). Media Trial in Sushant Singh Rajput Case: Bombay High Court Says Journalists Have Lost their Neutrality.
[209] Pandey (2020). Sushant Singh Rajput Murder Completely Ruled Out, It Was Suicide: Dr Sudhir Gupta of AIIMS; Asian News International (2020). SSR Death Case: Medical Board Submitted Report Directly to CBI, Can Obtain Inputs from Bureau, Says AIIMS.
[210] Bennett & Feldman (1981). Reconstructing Reality in the Courtroom.

exact same charge against a defendant is assessed either together with other charges or separately, this impacts the evaluation of the evidence so that the odds of a conviction are higher in the former case, especially if the charges and evidence are similar.[211] Joint charges increase the risk of confirmation bias because they make the evaluation of the evidence more cognitively demanding (Chapter 2.2.2.1) and they can also create a narrative about the accused that goes beyond the evidence; for example, that the accused has a criminal lifestyle. Subsequently, judges may attend more to, remember better, and evaluate as stronger the evidence that is consistent with this narrative. This explanation gains support in the less favourable ratings of the defendant among subjects who judged joint charges.[212] It is also consistent with more recent research findings obtained on Dutch criminal trial judges ($N = 105$) who studied a case file and decided on whether to convict as well as on subsequent investigation endeavours.[213] Unknown to participants, there were two versions of the case file, *the suspect-friendly* and *the suspect-unfriendly* version, differing in, for example, the suspect's facial appearance and criminal record. All the differences between the versions were, legally speaking, irrelevant as to the question of guilt. The judges in the suspect-unfriendly condition were more conviction prone and also, to a greater extent, preferred guilt-confirming investigation endeavours. This confirms what Wagenaar and colleagues noted in 1993, namely that 'corroboration apparently is an entirely subjective concept in need of not only a logical, but also a psychological definition'.[214] When it comes to joining charges specifically, this appears to be a particularly important factor to address in detail in future research. Regularly, across jurisdictions, joining charges against the same defendant is the rule rather than the exception.[215] Furthermore, some types of crime, by their legal construction, consist of multiple acts that by themselves constitute crimes. In national jurisdictions domestic abuse laws often either require multiple acts or open up for the possibility to charge multiple acts jointly as part of the same crime. For example, in the United Kingdom, according to the Domestic Abuse Act 2021 Section 1, 'domestic abuse' is defined as either a single incident or a 'course of conduct' including, for example, physical or sexual abuse and threats. Furthermore, pursuant to the Swedish Criminal Code 4 ch. 4a §, the crime 'gross violation of integrity' requires that multiple acts (including violence, threats, violations of non-contact orders etc.) have been 'part of a repeated violation of the person's integrity and that the acts were liable to severely damage the person's self-esteem'. The inclusion of multiple criminal acts within one and the same crime is

---

[211] Tanford, Penrod, & Collins (1985). Decision Making in Joined Criminal Trials: The Influence of Charge Similarity, Evidence Similarity, and Limiting Instructions, pp. 319–337.
[212] Tanford, Penrod, & Collins (1985). Decision Making in Joined Criminal Trials: The Influence of Charge Similarity, Evidence Similarity, and Limiting Instructions, pp. 319–337.
[213] Rassin (2020). Context Effect and Confirmation Bias in Criminal Fact Finding, pp. 80–89.
[214] Wagenaar, van Koppen, & Crombag (1993). Anchored Narratives—The Psychology of Criminal Evidence, pp. 4–10.
[215] The Swedish Code of Judicial Procedure, 19 ch. 1, 6 and 45 ch. 3 §§.

also the rule rather than the exception when it comes to core international crimes. For example, a genocide can be construed through multiple killings of members of a national, ethical, racial, or religious group. As illustrated by, for example, the Rwandan genocide, processed by the ICTR, the charges often involve hundreds or even thousands of killings.[216] It is also fairly common that the courts rely heavily on oral testimony, with multiple victims and witnesses who may have experienced similar events.[217] Since such multiple acts are part of one and the same crime, they cannot possibly be severed. Needless to say, the questions of whether and how confirmation bias manifests in relation to such charges need more scientific attention.

Notably, much of the available research focuses on how confirmation bias can be disadvantageous to the accused, for example because of the risk of a false positive, yet it is essential to keep in mind that confirmation bias can also be unfairly advantageous to the accused. Certainly, following the presumption of innocence, the evaluation of the evidence shall be to the accused's advantage. Thus, a certain advantage is fair and consistent with the accused's rights. Arguably, therefore, a confirmation bias that benefits the accused is unproblematic from a legal normative perspective, yet this disregards one important aspect. If a confirmation bias is at play in relation to an innocence hypothesis, this would make judges *systematically downgrade incriminating information*. This very far-reaching advantage is not intended by the presumption of innocence. Instead, the presumption of innocence requires that the minds of judges remain open regarding whether to convict until the procedure has come to a determined end.[218] Thus, even if some advantage is expected and justified, confirmation bias can result in this advantage becoming unfair and unintended. If incriminating information is systematically downgraded, and/or exonerating information is overemphasized (Chapter 3.3.2), this constitutes a considerable risk of a false negative.

Just like with stories to the defendant's disadvantage, stories to a defendant's advantage can originate from the media or from impressions that judges get of the case early on. For example, these can be stories that the suspects are, simply, innocent (depending on the strength of the story about guilt), or that the case against them is weak and that it therefore would be unjustified, legally speaking, to convict. This question also ties back to the effect of interim or other decisions preceding the main hearing (Chapter 4.3.1.1). Just as interim decisions can create an impression that the suspect is guilty and should be convicted, they can also create the opposite impression that the suspect is innocent and the case against him or her too weak. As such, a story is constructed as the process moves along so that by the time the

---

[216] United Nations International Residual Mechanism for Criminal Tribunals, The Genocide, <https://unictr.irmct.org/en/genocide> (accessed 20 February 2023).
[217] Chlevickaite, Hola, & Biijleveld (2019). Thousands on the Stand: Exploring Trends and Patterns of International Witnesses, pp. 819–836; Lidén. 'Child Soldier or Soldier?' Estimating Age in Cases of Core International Crime.
[218] Stuckenberg (2014). Who is Presumed Innocent of What by Whom?

case reaches the main hearing, the outcome is fairly predictable from the media coverage and the previous decisions made. In this regard, it is interesting to note the statement of former ICC Judge Christine van den Wyngaert in relation to the case *The Prosecutor v. Laurent Gbagbo and Charles Blé Goude*[219] in an interview for *De Standaard* in 2019: 'I am disappointed, because the public prosecutor was once again, as so many times before, unable to prove her case. Everyone saw from the beginning that this was a weak case.'[220]

The Prosecutor had brought charges of crimes against humanity (murder, rape, etc.) allegedly committed in the context of post-electoral violence in Côte d'Ivoire between December 2010 and April 2011.[221] As in many national jurisdictions, the main proceedings at the ICC are preceded by other decisions and hearings that may give judges impressions of the case. These range from the decision to open an investigation to the hearing on confirmation of charges. In relation to Mr Gbagbo, the judges had decided to adjourn the confirmation of charges hearing and requested the Prosecutor to consider providing it with further evidence or conduct additional investigation.[222] After having received such additional submissions of evidence, Pre-Trial Chamber I, on the 12 June 2014, did confirm the charges against Mr Gbagbo.[223] Subsequently, it also confirmed the charges against Mr Blé Goudé.[224] However, both accused were acquitted from all charges of crimes against humanity by Trial Chamber I on 15 January 2019.[225] The acquittal was confirmed by the Appeals Chamber.[226]

It is possible that the first impression, that the case was 'weak' and anyone could see it, somehow transpired and impacted on the case outcome in one way or

---

[219] The Prosecutor v. Laurent Gbagbo and Charles Blé Goudé, Situation in Côte d'Ivoire, ICC-02/11-01/15

[220] De Standaard (2019). Het Strafhof moet Dringend in De Spiegel Kijken. Translation of the original words in Dutch: 'Ik ben ontgoocheld omdat het de zoveelste keer is dat de aanklager haar bewijzen niet hard wist te maken. Iedereen zag van bij het begin dat dit een zwakke zaak was.' The author extends her gratitude to Bruno Debaenst for help with the translation. For the full interview see <https://www.standaard.be/cnt/dmf20190125_04131754> (accessed 20 February 2023).

[221] Case Information Sheet, The Prosecutor v. Laurent Gbagbo and Charles Blé Goudé, Situation in Côte d'Ivoire, ICC-02/11-01/15.

[222] Case Information Sheet, The Prosecutor v. Laurent Gbagbo and Charles Blé Goudé, Situation in Côte d'Ivoire, ICC-02/11-01/15.

[223] Pre-Trial Chamber I, Decision on the Confirmation of Charges Against Laurent Gbagbo, ICC-02/11-01/11, 12 June 2014. Judges deciding: Judge Silvia Fernández de Gurmendi, Presiding Judge, Judge Hans-Peter Kaul, and Judge Christine Van den Wyngaert.

[224] Pre-Trial Chamber I, Decision on the Confirmation of Charges Against Charles Blé Goudé, ICC-02/11-02/11, 11 December 2014. Judges deciding: Judge Silvia Fernández de Gurmendi, Presiding Judge, Judge Ekaterina Trendafilova, and Judge Christine Van den Wyngaert.

[225] Trial Chamber I, Reasons for Oral Decision of 15 January 2019 on the Requete de la defense de Laurent Gbagbo afin qu'un jugement d'acquittement portant sur toues les charges soit prononcé en faveur de Laurent Gbagbo et que sa mise en liberté immediate soit ordonnée, and on the Blé Goudé Defence of No Case to Answer Motion. Judges deciding: Judge Cuno Tarfusser, Presiding Judge, Judge Olga Herrera Carbuccia, and Judge Geoffrey Henderson. <https://www.icc-cpi.int/fr/court-record/icc-02/11-01/15-1263> (accessed 20 February 2023).

[226] Appeals Chamber, Judgment in the Appeal of the Prosecutor against Trial Chamber I's Decision on the No Case to Answer Motions, ICC-02/11-01/15-1400.

another. Historically, the ICC has been criticized for being unable to properly secure the rights of the accused.[227] For this reason, Robinson argues, that some of the ICC judges apply unprecedently high standards of proof and have a 'hyper sceptical' approach to potentially incriminating evidence.[228] Specifically, the judges look at each item in isolation, scrutinizing it for any possible reason to disbelieve or downplay it.[229] This includes freely inventing alternative narratives for each item, even without any evidentiary support for such narratives. According to Robinson, this hyper scepticism in relation to potentially incriminating evidence is combined with uncritical credulity toward potentially exonerating evidence. Undeniably, the tendencies that Robinson describe are very similar to asymmetrical scepticism (see Chapter 3.3.2), but reversed. In other words, what Robinson describes in the ICC judges is that they systematically downplay incriminating information while emphasizing exonerating information. This is the opposite from how asymmetrical scepticism is usually described with downplaying of exonerating information and emphasis on incriminating information. The described tendencies also tie back to the emotional explanations of confirmation bias, and particularly primary error detection and minimization (see **Chapter 2.2.2.2**).[230] If primary error detection and minimization is at play in ICC judges, it could manifest in that they fear wrongful convictions and/or being criticized for letting a 'weak case' slip through. They may prefer not to take the risk of being criticized for not safeguarding the accused's right sufficiently. Of course this is, to a certain extent, how judges should act, from a legal normative point of view. The problem may be more that they are doing it too well. In addition, in national jurisdictions such claims are sometimes made as critics believe the judges are, in fact, applying unprecedented and unreasonably high standards of proof.[231] Importantly, in line with the theory of confirmation bias, such tendencies in judges are likely to be more or less subconscious.[232]

The research examined so far suggests that a first impression or hypothesis can bias judges' decision-making, resulting both in false positives and false negatives. It is also relevant to consider what consequences confirmation bias might have for appeal procedures and criminal case reviews after a verdict has become legally binding. If even a hypothesis formed on early and ambiguous evidence can trigger a confirmation bias, then it is reasonable to think that a verdict based on

---

[227] Robinson (2019). The Other Poisoned Chalice: Unprecedented Evidentiary Standards in the Gbagbo Case (Part I); Robinson (2019). The Other Poisoned Chalice: Unprecedented Evidentiary Standards in the Gbagbo Case (Part II).
[228] Robinson, 2019 (Part I).
[229] Robinson, 2019 (Part I).
[230] Friedrich (1993). Primary Error Detection and Minimization (PEDMIN) Strategies in Social Cognition: A Reinterpretation of Confirmation Bias Phenomena, pp. 298–319.
[231] Dagens Nyheter (DN). Polis och Åklagare efter Friande Domar: Beviskraven är för Höga.
[232] De Keijser & van Koppen (2007). Paradoxes of Proof and Punishment, pp. 189–205; Englich et al. (2005). The Last Word in Court: A Hidden Disadvantage for the Defense, pp. 705–722.

more substantial evidence could do so too. This risk has been pointed out before.[233] Prosecutors' decisions on whether to reopen inquiries, as well as judges' decisions on whether to reverse a verdict on appeal or grant a new trial, are, clearly, discretionary assessments. For example, in order to grant a new trial, it is often required that the applicant has referred to evidence that is materially 'new'. It is possible that a hypothesis, after already having stood the test in one, or even two, instances, has become very sticky. Hence, apart from the fact that legal demands to grant new trials are often high, the judges may hold a confirmation bias that makes them unlikely to consider any 'new' evidence presented in the case seriously. This has some parallels to the argument with cold cases and how knowing that a case is cold may make investigators unable to reason independently of ideas previously presented (Chapter 3.3.2). In fact, research in the Swedish setting, conducted using archive studies, suggested that there may be reason to think of a *system-level confirmation bias*.[234] This system-level confirmation bias is defined as an inability to acquit wrongfully convicted persons who appeal or petition for a new trial. While this approach has obvious similarities to an inability to change or abandon an initial hypothesis held by in individual decision-makers, it uses the theory of confirmation bias in an unconventional way, aimed at trends observed in the legal system rather than among individual decision-makers.

Specifically, evaluating the prevalence of such a system-level confirmation bias, the Swedish research tentatively assumed a very low rate of wrongful convictions (0.50 per cent) in District Courts (2010–2014).[235] Thereafter, an empirical review of appeals and petitions for new trials in the Appellate Courts and the Supreme Court between 2010 and 2014 was carried out to evaluate to what extent these legal remedies can be expected to change wrongful convictions into acquittals. Realistic assumptions and empirical estimates of real-world statistics suggested that at least 34.67 per cent of those wrongfully convicted remained convicted despite the possibility both to appeal and petition for a new trial. According to additional analyses, the odds of an acquittal were low even for appeals referring to new innocence-supportive evidence. The odds were particularly low for private individuals who applied without legal counsel and who claimed to be innocent of, for example, assault or murder.

---

[233] Edmond & Martire (2019). Just Cognition: Scientific Research on Bias and Some Implications for Legal Procedure and Decision-Making, pp. 633–664; Lidén (2018). Confirmation Bias in Criminal Cases.

[234] Lidén, Gräns, & Juslin (2019). Self-correction of Wrongful Convictions: Is there a 'System-level' Confirmation Bias in the Swedish Legal System's Appeal Procedure for Criminal Cases?—Part I; Lidén, Gräns, & Juslin (2019). Self-correction of Wrongful Convictions: is there a 'System-level' Confirmation Bias in the Swedish Legal System's Appeal Procedure for Criminal Cases?—Part II.

[235] Lidén, Gräns, & Juslin (2019). Self-correction of Wrongful Convictions: Is there a 'System-level' Confirmation Bias in the Swedish Legal System's Appeal Procedure for Criminal Cases?—Part I; Lidén, Gräns, & Juslin (2019). Self-correction of Wrongful Convictions: is there a 'System-level' Confirmation Bias in the Swedish Legal System's Appeal Procedure for Criminal Cases?—Part II.

With a first conviction in a District Court the story presented by the prosecutor is confirmed as at least somewhat likely. Hence, it is possible that a conviction, as compared to an acquittal, will make judges more inclined to believe in a guilt hypothesis than in an innocence hypothesis. From a legal normative point of view, a previous conviction should not make Appellate Court judges less critical of the guilt hypothesis. However, the theory of confirmation bias points to the risk that they might be, perhaps even more so if the conviction has not only been confirmed by one but two instances, both in the District and Appellate Court. Such system-level confirmation bias would clearly have the potential of locking erroneous verdicts into the system. If one were to address the corresponding bias mitigation measure in relation to such a system-level confirmation bias, it would be to establish procedures that enable the best quality criminal case review possible. As addressed in Section 4.3.3.1 this can also be related to the empirically evaluated debiasing technique of changing decision-maker.

4.3.2.3 Crime Gravity and Sentencing

Today, there is a substantial amount of research demonstrating the prevalence and significant impacts of biases, not least ethnicity/racial biases[236] and gender bias,[237] in judges' sentencing, yet so far, less is known about the potential importance of confirmation bias in sentencing. However, confirmation bias can help us to understand the process by which factors such as ethnicity and gender as well as other potentially hypothesis triggering circumstances may affect sentencing. Also, since decisions about sentencing are never made in a vacuum but often as one of the final steps of criminal proceedings, the potential of confirmation bias has to be understood in the appropriate context. For example, as illustrated in Section 4.3.1.1, in Swedish judges, the decision to detain a suspect seemed to generate a hypothesis that the suspect was guilty as the odds of a conviction were higher when the same judge was responsible for making decisions about both detention and guilt. The following addresses the question of whether this confirmation bias also extends to the perceived crime gravity and sentencing.

Following the principle *Iura novit curia* ('the court knows the law'), expressed in the Swedish Code of Judicial Procedure 30 ch. 3 § p. 2, judges have discretion to reclassify crimes both in terms of crime type and crime gravity as long as this fits within the description of the behaviour forming the basis for the alleged crimes charged by the prosecutor. In Sweden, sentencing happens on the basis

---

[236] Alesina & La Ferrara (2014). A Test of Racial Bias in Capital Sentencing, pp. 3397–3433; Snowball & Weatherburn (2007). Does Racial Bias in Sentencing Contribute to Indigenous Overrepresentation in Prison?, pp. 272–290; Everett & Wojtkiewics (2002). Difference, Disparity, and Race/Ethnic Bias in Federal Sentencing, pp. 189–211.

[237] Bielen & Grajzl (2020). Gender-based Judicial Ingroup Bias in Sex Crime Sentencing: Evidence from Belgium, pp. 1–13; Williams (1999). Gender and Sentencing: An Analysis of Indicators, pp. 471–490. For a somewhat opposing view, see Pluskota (2018). Petty Criminality, Gender Bias, and Judicial Practice in Nineteenth-Century Europe, pp. 717–735.

of sentencing frames laid down in law. There is also a set of aggravating circumstances, such as if the crime entails a racist motive or misuse of someone's inferior or dependent position (the Swedish Criminal Code 29 ch. 2 §). Furthermore, judges shall also consider alleviating circumstances, for example that the crime was induced by someone else's obviously offensive behaviour, or motivated by strong compassion (the Swedish Criminal Code 29 ch. 3 §).

In this experiment,[238] prior to the main hearing, there was a detention hearing where the prosecutor had presented very limited evidence and the judges had to either decide themselves whether the suspect should be detained or not, or were informed about another judges' decision in this regard. In one of the scenarios, the criminal charges allowed fairly different conclusions regarding crime type and gravity. More specifically, the prosecutor had claimed that the accused was guilty of gross violation of integrity (Criminal Code, 4 ch. 4a §), in relation to his co-habitant. As an alternative, the prosecutor had demanded that the behaviour should be legally classified as three cases of assault (Criminal Code, 3 ch. 5§), which are less severe crimes than gross violation of integrity. During the main hearing, all the evidence was presented, and judges were to decide on guilt, crime type, and sentencing.

The results of this scenario showed that whether the accused had been detained pre-trial and who had made that decision impacted significantly not only on whether the accused was found guilty or acquitted (Section 4.3.1.1), but it also significantly impacted on the chosen crime types and sentencing. For example, among judges who had themselves decided to detain the accused pre-trial, 58.30 per cent categorized the behaviour as one or multiple assaults, while 41.70 per cent instead categorized the behaviour as gross violation of integrity, the more severe crime. This is to be compared to the numbers of judges who had themselves decided to not detain the accused pre-trial (but the prosecutor still pressed charges). In this group, 100 per cent of the judges who decided to convict categorized the behaviour as one or multiple assaults, that is, the less severe crimes.

Thus, it seems that what happens before the main hearing has an impact not only on the crime classifications but also, as a consequence, the applicable sentencing frames. In this specific situation, the applicable sentencing frame for gross violation of integrity is imprisonment for nine months to six years (Criminal Code 4 ch. 4a §), while for each of the assaults the sentencing frame is a fine to imprisonment for six months, although the aggravating and alleviating circumstances mentioned above are to be taken into account as well. As illustrated in Table 4.1, following these differences in the applicable sentencing frames, as well as differences in the

---

[238] This research was conducted by Moa Lidén in 2019 with this specific data published for the first time in this book. The original experiment including methodology can be found in Lidén, Gräns, & Juslin (2019). 'Guility, No Doubt': Detention Provoking Confirmation Bias in Judges' Guilt Assessments and Debiasing Techniques, pp. 219–247.

Table 4.1 Variation in choice of sentence upon conviction (%) in the same scenario, depending on whether pre-trial detention was decided upon and by whom.

Decision	Decision-maker	Sentence upon conviction		
		Prison 4–9 months	Probation w/ wo community service or a fine	Conditional sentence w/wo community service
Detention	Self	43.30	28.30	28.30
No detention	Self	0	0	100
Detention	Colleague	42.90	28.60	28.60
No detention	Colleague	0	66.70	33.30

Note: In the table, 'w' means 'with' and 'wo' means 'without'.

perceived seriousness of the crime, the judges sentencing also varied depending on whether they themselves had decided to detain or not detain the accused pre-trial.

There was a significant association between the decision to detain or not detain pre-trial, who was the decision-maker and what sentence was decided upon during the main hearing, $\chi^2(1) = 4.56 p < 0.05$ For example, while 43.30 per cent of the judges who had themselves previously detained the accused decided on a prison sentence (six to nine months), 0 per cent of those judges who had decided to not detain pre-trial decided upon a prison sentence. Similar numbers were observed when a judge colleague had decided to detain or not detain. Also, most of the judges who thought six to nine months in prison was an appropriate sentence were all in the position where they themselves had decided to detain pre-trial, while the judge (one only) who instead wanted a four-month prison sentence was in the position where the colleague had previously decided to detain pre-trial.

While these data only refer to one scenario, and include only Swedish judges, the experiment is an indication that confirmation bias may be at play in determinations of crime gravity and sentencing.

4.3.3 Mitigating Bias

4.3.3.1 Changing Decision-maker

All other things being equal, research suggests that the odds of a conviction were 2.79 times higher when judges themselves had decided to detain a defendant prior to the main hearing (Section 4.3.1.1).[239] This has strong ties to confirmation bias as a self-enhancement bias as described in social psychology (Section 2.2.2.3). It

---

[239] Lidén, Gräns, & Juslin (2018). 'Guilty, No Doubt': Detention Provoking Confirmation Bias in Judges' Guilt Assessments and Debiasing Techniques, pp. 219–247.

furthermore suggests that changing the presiding judge between detention and main hearing may function as a debiasing technique. When judges themselves have decided to detain pre-trail, this may trigger a mindset whereby the judges want to convince others that their decision was correct, whereas a colleague's decision to detain triggers a more critical and independent stance.[240]

In practice, there may be a number of reasons why a change of decision-maker does not take place, for instance that there is a limited number of judges available, especially in courts in small communities with more limited numbers of staff. Often, keeping the same judge for both hearings is perceived as more efficient since that judge already knows the case.[241] Note that similar arguments are sometimes referred to in the choice of having one or multiple prosecutors involved in a case (Section 4.2.3.1). As suggested by estimations made by Swedish Chief Judges at the District Courts, the variation between courts in how often the same judge presides both hearings is large, ranging from 1 per cent to 80 per cent ($M = 26.39\%$, $SD = 24.40\%$) of the cases.[242] However, it is also clear that in the comparable Danish jurisdiction, rotation schedules have successfully been implemented to prevent judges from making both decisions, suggesting that such a technique is feasible. That measures are undertaken to promote separation of detention and guilt decision is all the more important given that this is the most effective debiasing technique known.

A more drastic approach is *trial bifurcation*, that is, detention hearings and main hearings are divided between separate courts.[243] While a judge would still know that a suspect is detained as well as who has made this detention decision, having different courts is likely to increase the cognitive distance from that previous decision. This possibility has not been empirically evaluated but given the available research[244] it seems like a feasible option.

The idea of changing decision-maker and/or dividing tasks between separate courts is also relevant as regards criminal case review. It seems fairly straightforward that judges who have been involved, in one way or another, in the conviction or acquittal of an individual, shall not also decide whether a petition from this individual to reopen the case shall be granted or not. It is possible that this should not even be dealt with within the same court or within the same court system that dealt

---

[240] Mercier & Sperber (2011). Why do Humans Reason? Arguments for an Argumentative Theory, pp. 57–11; Sperber et al. (2010). Epistemic Vigilance, pp. 359–393.

[241] Lidén, Gräns, & Juslin (2018). 'Guilty, No Doubt': Detention Provoking Confirmation Bias in Judges' Guilt Assessments and Debiasing Techniques, pp. 219–247.

[242] Chief Judges for Sweden's 48 District Courts were contacted and 54.17 per cent (26 out of 48) responded.

[243] Horowitz & Bordens (1990). An Experimental Investigation of Procedural Issues in Complex Tort Trials, pp. 269–285; Smith & Greene (2005). Conduct and its Consequences: Attempts at Debiasing Jury Judgments, pp. 505–526; Zeisel & Callahan (1963). Split trials and Time-saving: A Statistical Analysis, pp. 1606–1625.

[244] Lidén, Gräns, & Juslin (2018). 'Guilty, No Doubt!' Detention Provoking Confirmation Bias in Judges' Guilt Assessments and Debiasing Techniques, pp. 219–247.

with the case in ordinary procedure. However, internationally, there is much variation as to how criminal case review is structured and it is uncertain whether and to what extent different systems enable effective and critical review. Even between different Scandinavian countries the differences are pronounced. For example, Norway and Denmark both have external review commissions, the *Gjenopptakel sekommisjon*[245] and *Den Særlige Klageret*,[246] which are competent to both handle and decide on the application. However, in Sweden it is the court superior to the court that decided in the original proceedings that will decide whether to grant a new trial, and a new trial will be held in the same court that originally decided the case.[247] This is to be compared to the English Criminal Cases Review Commission (CCRC) and the Scottish Criminal Cases Review Commission (SCCRC), both external review commissions that only refer applications to the courts that have the final say.[248] In the United States, there are currently more than 40 so-called Innocence Projects operating, and these are national litigation and public policy organizations which promote, but do not decide about, reopening of criminal cases, by assisting convicted individuals who claim to be innocent.[249]

4.3.3.2 Structured Evaluations of Evidence

Since human cognitive resources are limited, and since criminal trials can sometimes entail much more information than human beings can normally process efficiently, it is desirable to find ways to reduce cognitive load (Chapter 2.2.2.1). This can be done, for example, by structuring the evaluation of evidence. Certainly, there is variation across different jurisdictions when it comes to admissibility rules,[250] for example, as well as the nature and amount of evidence which is processed during hearings, yet in most legal orders, judges and/or jurors are expected to evaluate each piece of evidence separately and only thereafter make a total assessment of the evidence. This is in accordance with the so-called *principle of evidentiary independence*.[251] It is unknown to what extent this principle is abided by in practice.

---

[245] The Norwegian Government, Ot.prp.nr 70 (2000-2001) and <https://www.gjenopptakelse.no/> (accessed 20 February 2023).

[246] Den Saerlige Klageret's Webpage, <https://domstol.dk/densaerligklageret/> (accessed 20 February 2023).

[247] Lidén, Gräns, & Juslin (2019). Self-correction of Wrongful Convictions: Is there a 'System-level' Confirmation Bias in the Swedish Legal System's Appeal Procedure for Criminal Cases?—Part I; Lidén, Gräns & Juslin (2019). Self-correction of Wrongful Convictions: Is there a 'System-level' Confirmation Bias in the Swedish Legal System's Appeal Procedure for Criminal Cases?—Part II.

[248] English Criminal Case Review Commission's Webpage, <https://ccrc.gov.uk/> (accessed 20 February 2023) and Scottish Criminal Case Review Commision's webpage, <https://www.sccrc.co.uk/> (accessed 20 February 2023).

[249] Innocence Project's webpage, <https://innocenceproject.org> (accessed 20 February 2023).

[250] Murphy (1999). The Admissibility of CCTV Evidence in Criminal Proceedings, pp. 383–404; Klamberg (2013). Evidence in International Criminal Trials: Confronting Legal Gaps and the Reconstruction of Disputed Events, Pattenden (2006) Admissibility in Criminal Proceedings of Third Party and Real Evidence Obtained by Methods Prohibited by UNCAT, pp. 1–41.

[251] The Swedish Government Bills, NJA II 1943 p. 445; The Swedish Government Official Reports, SOU 1938:44 p. 377.

However, the principle has practical relevance as a debiasing technique as structured step-by-step evaluations, compared to holistic assessments, seem to mitigate confirmation bias.[252] This is expected, based on research in Cognitive Psychology, specifically the *Divide and Conquer principle*.[253] According to this principle, decision quality is improved when complex decision problems are broken down into smaller, more manageable parts.[254] When judges evaluate the evidence item by item, it is more likely that any differences in implications of the evidence become more salient to them. Therefore, their assessments will also be more nuanced compared to more unstructured and holistic assessments of the evidence.

A seemingly important difference between national and international jurisdictions is that the evidence before international criminal tribunals and courts is regularly much more extensive, even if giant trials occasionally occur also in the national settings. Investigations and proceedings into core international crimes usually entail significantly more evidence than national cases, as an average case before the international courts and tribunals lasts 4.9 years.[255] Also, in these cases, there is often a heavy reliance on oral testimony,[256] possibly hundreds of testimonies,[257] regularly depicting horrific acts by alleged perpetrators. Even far less cognitive load would constitute a risk factor for confirmation bias.[258] The cited research ought to be an incentive for researchers to keep evaluating different ways of reducing cognitive load as a way to help mitigate confirmation bias in the evaluation of evidence. Clearly, however, it is up to the judges and jurors who are the only ones present during deliberations to implement such techniques in real cases.

4.3.4 Conclusion

Judges can help mitigate confirmation bias in two somewhat different ways. First, they can take knowledge of the risk of confirmation bias during the investigation

---

[252] Lidén, Gräns, & Juslin (2018). 'Guilty, No Doubt': Detention Provoking Confirmation Bias in Judges' Guilt Assessments and Debiasing Techniques, pp. 219–247.

[253] Kolling & Hunt (2015). Divide and Conquer: Strategic Decision Areas, pp. 616–618; Morera & Budescu (1998). A Psychometric Analysis of the 'Divide and Conquer' Principle in Multicriteria Decision Making, pp. 187–206.

[254] Kolling & Hunt (2015). Divide and Conquer: Strategic Decision Areas, pp. 616–618; Morera & Budescu (1998). A Psychometric Analysis of the 'Divide and Conquer' Principle in Multicriteria Decision Making, pp. 187–206.

[255] Smeulers, Hola, & van den Berg (2013). Sixty-five Years of International Criminal Justice: The Facts and Figures, p. 18.

[256] See, for example, Chlevickaite, Hola, & Bijleveld (2019). Thousand on the Stand: Exploring Trends and Patterns of International Witnesees, pp. 1–18.

[257] For instance, there were 434 in the ICTY case, The Prosecutor v. Karadzic, IT-95-5/18-T, 152 of which were admitted in writing.

[258] Miller (1956). The Magical Number Seven, Plus or Minus Two: Some Limits on Our Capacity for Processing Information, pp. 81–97.

actively into account when evaluating the evidence presented to them. For example, information about how a crime scene investigation has been conducted is informative as to whether important traces needed to evaluate alternative hypothesis have been left behind at the scene. Similarly, knowledge of what traces have been collected but never undergone forensic analysis will help judges evaluate whether alternative explanations have been sufficiently evaluated to enable a conviction. The same way of reasoning can be applied in relation to, for example, witness interviews. Knowledge of how an interview has been conducted can help judges understand the process by which a witness statement came about. There are many examples from a range of jurisdictions illustrating how witness as well as suspect statements are impacted by leading or confrontational interviewing techniques. In an applied setting, the ability of the judges to take such information into account can be limited by procedural rules or principles dictating whether and to what extent such information can be presented during the main hearing. From a legal normative perspective, it can also be debated to what extent judges are expected to reason in terms of alternative explanations on their own initiative. Following the evidentiary standard 'beyond all reasonable doubt', reasonable alternative explanations should at least be actively evaluated. However, there is little or no guidance as to what alternative explanations are reasonable to consider in a given case, and to what extent judges are expected to generate the alternative explanations themselves. This also highlights the important interaction between the judges' decision-making and the parties' inclinations and abilities to introduce alternative explanations during the main hearing. Whether the prosecution has any legal duty to do so varies between different jurisdictions, but, for example, in the Swedish setting, the prosecutors' duty to consider both incriminating and exonerating information extends equally also to the trial phase, pursuant to the Code of Judicial Procedure 45 ch. 3a §. When it comes to defence counsels, their duty to protect their client's interest can often entail presenting alternative explanations, at least when the client denies having committed the relevant crime(s). Yet, in practice the defence may struggle to introduce alternative explanations that seem reasonable enough to judges. This is due, for example, to limited resources and limited access to relevant evidentiary material and expertise to evaluate the material in ways that will not impact negatively on the probative value. This suggests that judges may sometimes have to take a more active role in generating alternative explanations themselves for the court proceedings to have the intended safeguarding function. Notably, any such evaluations made in writing in a verdict, particularly from the higher courts, can serve as incentives and instructions to investigators, forensic doctors, forensic analysts, and so on, to pay more attention to bias mitigation in their respective decision-making.

Secondly, judges can also help mitigate confirmation bias in their own reasoning by implementing the outlined mitigation strategies. This includes changing the decision-maker between different decisions pertaining to the accused's guilt, such as pre-trial detention and guilt determinations during main hearings. It also includes reducing cognitive load in judges' decision-making through structured evaluations of the evidence. It remains to be seen whether research can identify other debiasing techniques in this regard, yet even today, there is quite a lot that judges can do. As outlined above, this pertains first to the *content* of their evaluations; actively evaluating the risk of bias during the investigative phase. Secondly, it pertains to the *context* and *process* of their evaluations; that is, considering whether preceding decisions may have triggered a confirmation bias, and to conduct meticulous step-by-step evaluations. Such evaluations are likely to make any differences in implications of the evidence more salient to judges.

5
Overall Summary and Conclusion

5.1 Summary and Implications

Since the 1960s and Wason's famous experiments, the research into confirmation bias has become more field specific and realistic. It has also, gradually, shifted from a focus almost entirely on different problematic manifestations of confirmation bias to now also include bias mitigation. This book has provided an overview of the research available so far as regards confirmation bias in criminal investigations and litigations. It has also highlighted and exemplified manifestations and possible debiasing techniques using case studies from a wide range of jurisdictions including France, India, Israel, Italy, Kenya, Norway, Spain, Sweden, the United Kingdom, the United States, the International Criminal Court (ICC), the Special Tribunal for Lebanon (STL), the International Criminal Tribunal for Rwanda (ICTR), and the European Court of Human Rights (ECtHR). Across these jurisdictions, there is much variation when it comes to the historical roots, the contemporary challenges, the material as well as procedural law. Such variation does not, however, change the fact that all these jurisdictions depend, fundamentally, on the decision-making of the human beings operating inside the jurisdictions. This human factor is continuous and inevitable in all jurisdictions across the world. As such, jurisdictions worldwide have more in common than what is regularly acknowledged in legal science as well as in legal practice. Working with, and understanding, the human factor requires stepping outside the legal domain, primarily into the psychological field. It also requires effective integration, that is, that the problematic aspects of the human factor in the legal field are effectively addressed and countered using psychological research findings. Evidently, legal decision-making is not just about law, that is, the applicable paragraphs, principles, and so on. It is at least as much about the human decision-makers.

Confirmation bias has been identified and demonstrated to be one of the most, if not *the* most, problematic aspect of human reasoning. Its problematic nature is particularly clear in the context of criminal inquiries and litigations. This is due to the applicable objectivity demands and the major implications that criminal practitioners' decision-making has for private individuals' lives as well as for the accuracy and legitimacy of criminal law and procedure in a wider sense.

As illustrated throughout the chapters of this book, particularly Chapters 3 and 4, no-one is immune to confirmation bias. Thus, contrary to common beliefs, there is no judicial exceptionalism making legal actors or other criminal practitioners like crime scene investigators (CSIs), forensic doctors, and forensic analysts, generally better prepared than most to resist confirmation bias. In accordance with research into the bias blind spot, individuals are usually unable to detect confirmation bias in their own reasoning. Hence, without criminal practitioners necessarily noticing it, confirmation bias can influence the search for, perception, and evaluation of information at every stage of criminal investigation and litigation. In other words, it may have an impact from the beginning of the inquiry to the final verdict, and even beyond , for example when legal action is sought against a legally binding verdict.

Overall, confirmation bias may manifest itself in the search for information, that is, suspect-driven investigations, which was identified in the Dutch setting in the 1990s. This research is still valid and seemingly relevant for a range of jurisdictions. However, it does not account for the fact that investigations can also be *hypothesis driven* in a wider sense, that is, both in relation to the alleged criminal conduct and the alleged perpetrator(s). This is likely to be the case not least when it comes to investigations into more complex crimes in which, for example, hierarchical command structures need to be investigated and proven. The book has provided a few examples of such cases, including the New York Mafia case in which the RICO Act was applied as well as the ICC cases The Prosecutor v. Joseph Kony and Vincent Otti and The Prosecutor v. Ahmad Al Faqi.

Biased search for information constitutes a serious risk of errors, both false positives and false negatives, especially in combination with biased evaluations of information. The Egunkaria case and Otamendi Egiguren v. Spain illustrate how, for example, a belief that terrorism is omnipresent biased evaluations of the content of articles published by a Basque newspaper. Since the evaluators believed the newspaper had ties to terrorism, they also 'saw' signs of it in the articles. Additionally, asymmetrical scepticism means that information consistent with a hypothesis is preferred and evaluated as more reliable compared to hypothesis inconsistent information. As exemplified by the Sture Bergwall case, this can result in information inconsistent with a suspect's confession being downplayed or even disregarded. This results in an obvious risk of a wrongful conviction, not least if the verdict relies primarily on a confession which the suspect later retracts. And yet, this is far from the only possible manifestation of asymmetrical scepticism. As illustrated by the Olof Palme case, it can also manifest in individuals being prematurely dismissed as suspects and instead considered as witnesses, even though there are indeed circumstances suggesting that their involvement should be further evaluated. Hence, it is clear that confirmation bias can result in both false positives (wrongful suspicions or convictions) and false negatives (wrongful dismissals or acquittals). These errors can be traced back to the identity of the suspect as such but also to hypotheses about the course of event in a more general sense.

While bias mitigation is facilitated by knowledge of overall manifestations of confirmation bias, the research into more specific investigative settings offer a more 'hands-on' approach. This is essential as confirmation bias in specific investigative settings can contribute to different types of errors that will, on their own or in combination, make an investigation suspect or hypothesis driven. For example, CSIs may secure only or primarily traces that are expected to be present at a scene, should the investigative hypothesis be true, and leave behind traces suggesting something else. Thereafter, forensic analysts or doctors, aware of the investigative hypothesis, are more likely to confirm it. Similarly, any witness aware that the suspect's guilt has been confirmed through forensic analysis is more likely also to confirm that the suspect is, in fact, the perpetrator. If such evidence is available, it is unsurprising that prosecutors and judges consider that they have the corroboration needed to press charges and/or convict. Furthermore, should they, against all odds, be made aware of any hypothesis-inconsistent evidence, they may be overly sceptical in relation to it, as apparently everything else seems to confirm the investigative hypothesis. Hence, all the assessments and decisions made throughout the course of the criminal investigation and litigation can, in one way or another, contribute to error. Effective bias mitigation will, subsequently, have to entail all these assessments and decisions. Table 5.1 outlines how confirmation bias can manifest and be mitigated in specific investigative settings, as well as in prosecutors' and judges' decisions during the litigation phase.

Confirmation bias in suspect interviews can result in guilt-presumptive questioning and evaluation of the suspect, as exemplified by the interviews with Mr El-Sayyed in the Ayyash et al. case. Not only may interviewers feel tempted to elicit a confession, ask confrontational or even manipulative questions, contrary to best practice guidelines, but they may also perceive of the suspect as less credible. As highlighted by the existing research, such biased interviewing can occur at an early stage. This can be due, for example, to expectations of guilt that arise from apprehension decisions or other reasons such as stereotypical beliefs about specific ethnicities, and so on. Similarly, if interviewers believe that a certain suspect is guilty, and/or that the crime must have occurred in a certain way, it can impact on how they interview witnesses. So-called *police-generated witness testimony* seems to be an important source of error in applied settings. It is easy to see how witnesses may want to accommodate the police, especially if witnesses themselves are at risk of becoming suspects if they do not do so. This is clearly illustrated in the Adriano R. Cadiz case. Similarly, also other beliefs, for example that a plaintiff report is false in alleged rape cases can trigger a process of behavioural confirmation. The interviewer communicates his/her belief, more or less subtly, to the plaintiff. The plaintiff, in turn, becomes more withdrawn and less motivated to provide the information needed to press charges. For the interviewer this comes across as confirmation of his/her initial belief that the plaintiff did indeed provide a false account and therefore backed away from the initial report. For bias mitigation in interviews, adherence to best practice guidelines for investigative interviewing is essential. Also the possibility of changing decision-maker between for example

Table 5.1 Manifestations of confirmation bias and possible debiasing techniques in specific settings during investigative and litigation phases.

Settings	Manifestations	Debiasing Techniques
Investigative phase Interviews	*Suspects:* Guilt-presumptive questions, credibility perceived as low *Witness:* Leading questions, police-generated testimony *Plaintiffs:* Beliefs that plaintiff report is false can trigger process of behavioural confirmation	(1) Investigative interviewing, training, and adherence including addressing erroneous perceptions about effective interviewing (2) Changing decision-maker, e.g. between apprehension and suspect interview
Suspect Line-ups	Line-ups that can only confirm rather than critically evaluate a guilt hypothesis; identifications based on suggestion rather than the witnesses' memory	(1) Pre-testing the line-up, by establishing baseline, evaluating with naïve observers, replacing foils, and re-testing line-up if necessary (Steps 1–3)
Crime Scene Investigations	One-sidedness in the search, interpretation, and collection of traces, as well as in the prioritization of traces for forensic analysis (triage)	(1) Contextual information management (CIM) (2) Multiple CSIs (3) Structured strategies for trace collection (4) Technological Advances, e.g. rapid identification technologies, 3D laser scanning
Forensic Analysis	One-sided observations and conclusions in *forensic science*: e.g. fingerprint analysis, comparison of shoes, tools, tires, handwriting *Medicine*: e.g. determinations of e.g. cause of death or origin of injury *Anthropology*: e.g. sex, ancestry and age determinations	(1) Contextual information management (CIM) (2) Linear Sequential Unmasking (LSU) (3) Independent review 4) Technological advances e.g. software, AI
Litigation phase Prosecutors' decision-making	Overconfident leadership, one-sided investigations aimed to confirm guilt following pre-trial decision and/or the charging decision	(1) Changing decision-maker 2) Devil's Advocates, Red Teams, and Evidence Review Boards
Judges' Decision Making	More guilt-consistent evaluations of the evidence, odds of confirming investigative hypothesis greater	(1) Changing decision-maker (2) Structured evaluations of evidence

apprehension and the subsequent interviewing of a suspect should be considered. Note that the technique of changing decision-maker has been tested in relation to suspect interviews, but not with witnesses and plaintiffs. When it comes, for example, to child interviews, other considerations such as establishing sufficient rapport often motivate the use of one and the same interviewer.

In suspect line-ups, even very subtle influences can result in a line-up which was originally set up to test a guilt hypothesis being capable only of confirming the hypothesis supporting guilt. If, as in the Ivan the Terrible case, there is really only one person (the suspect) who fulfils the description as provided by witnesses, then no-one should be surprised that this individual is also identified by witnesses. This simply confirms something that was already known before the line-up was conducted, namely that the suspect resembles the perpetrator in one way or another. Pre-testing of the line-up following the three steps outlined in Chapter 3.5.2.3.1 is a fairly straightforward way of mitigating bias and ensuring that a court of law can properly evaluate the line-ups evidentiary value. These three steps entail (i) establishing the baseline for a balanced line-up, (ii) evaluation with naïve observers, and (iii) replacing foils and retesting the line-up if necessary. This will allow detection of and adjustment in relation to any bias present in the initial line-up. While requiring some police resources, this should be seen as an essential quality control mechanism. It can prevent the wrong individual being identified as the suspect and the court having to dismiss the line-up and acquit, not because the identified individual is innocent but because the line-up was biased.

Confirmation bias in crime scene investigations should be understood and evaluated with reference not only to the actual collection of traces at the scene but also the preceding and succeeding stages. The stage preceding the trace collection sets an important frame in terms of invested resources and notions of what type of traces should be collected. This follows an initial hypothesis about whether a crime has been committed and, if so, which crime. When arriving at the scene, decisions on what specific area should be taped off set tangible frames for the trace search and collection. Furthermore, even within the taped-off area, an initial hypothesis can bias how and to what extent CSIs examine the scene. This constitutes a serious risk that far from all potentially relevant traces are secured. Also in the stage succeeding the trace collection, further selection and prioritization is necessary. This is due to limited investigative resources and/or ideas about what traces are or are not relevant. This means that potentially relevant traces may never be analysed because their relevance is not understood or, once it is realized, that traces have already been destroyed following applicable rules of storage of forensic evidence. The Sabri case illustrates this point. In this case, a T-shirt used for reanalysis of blood patterns was a vital piece of evidence for Mr Sabri's granted application for a retrial and the subsequent acquittal. The T-shirt was requested from the forensic lab only after the applicable mandatory time frame for storage of evidence items had passed. Out of pure luck, the T-shirt was still being stored. Among the techniques outlined in Table 5.1, contextual information management is the one proven to be an effective debiasing technique. The other techniques, such as using structured strategies for trace collection and having more than one CSI examine the scene, still need more evaluation. When it comes to technological advances, such as 3D laser scanning and 3D point cloud technology, these help to ensure, for example, that prints taken from the scene are clear rather than ambiguous. Surely, this can promote accurate forensic analysis, but the impact that such technologies have on human decision-making processes still need to be further addressed.

The range of criminalistic, medical, and anthropological assessments in which the forensic confirmation bias may occur is indeed wide. Globally, there are many cases which illustrate how, for example, a confession can taint forensic analysis. The Tair Rada case is one such example. In this case, it is remarkable how the shoe print examiner, after having learned about the accused's confession, *suddenly saw* shoe prints in the photos from the crime scene. Furthermore, these were matched to the accused's shoes. Likewise, it is telling how, in the Therese Johanessen case, analysts who were aware of Mr Bergwall's confession confirmed that the organic material found in the Norwegian forest was human bone, yet the analysts who re-examined the same material following Mr Bergwall's retracted confession concluded that they were not human bone at all. Forensic medical assessments, for example regarding the cause of death, may indeed be influenced by what contextual information is available to the forensic doctor. This is illustrated by, for example, the Indian Struck by Lightning case and the Kenyan Homicide or Cardiac Myxoma case. Hence, for criminalistic, medical, and anthropological assessments, contextual information management is essential. It is not necessarily easy to decide in any given case whether information is relevant and/or potentially biasing, especially not if this assessment is made by the forensic analysts, forensic doctors, or forensic anthropologists themselves. Having a context manager with the specific role of conducting such assessments indeed increases the chances of effective bias mitigation. For example, the context manager can decide whether the disclosure of the contextual information should be postponed or whether independent review—maybe even from an external lab in another jurisdiction—should take place. Furthermore, technological advances such as different types of software or AI are already in use in the forensic disciplines, to a certain extent. These can help reduce cognitive load or even conduct complex cognitive tasks that humans would struggle greatly with. Yet, to get more insight regarding any debiasing potential they may have, researchers need to evaluate the concept of distributed cognition still further. So far, distributed cognition has only been properly evaluated in relation to the Automated Fingerprint Identification System (AFIS) for fingerprint examinations.

Prosecutors have often been criticized for conducting one-sided investigations. While there may be several reasons for this in an applied setting, confirmation bias is likely to contribute. Specifically, confirmation bias can manifest in overconfident leadership. This is illustrated, not least, by Mr Goodsey's observations of his own work as a prosecutor in New York City. It seems that prosecutors can sometimes be so convinced that their hypothesis is correct that they do not necessarily see any issues with requesting forensic analysts to confirm their beliefs even though forensic analysts, of course, are to conduct their own impartial examination of the forensic traces. Following different research methodologies as well as differences in prosecutors' roles across jurisdictions, it is uncertain at what more specific point in time and in which more specific situations confirmation bias may be triggered. Some research suggests that this happens by the time pre-trial decisions such as arresting/identifying a suspect are taken. Other research suggests that it happens only at the time of the decision to charge a suspect. Regardless of when and how confirmation bias is triggered, it seems its effect on prosecutorial decision-making can be far-reaching. As illustrated by, for example, the Norfolk Four case, this constitutes a risk of false positives. In this case, the guilt hypothesis was maintained despite repeated exposure to hypothesis-inconsistent evidence, such as non-matching DNA evidence. Even under these circumstances, confessions were forced not from one but from four individuals. In other words, like in many other cases, the investigative hypothesis was maintained long after it should have been abandoned, or at least seriously questioned. Furthermore, as illustrated by for example the ICC case The Prosecutor v. Laurent Gbagbo and Charles Blé Goudé, confirmation bias in prosecutors also constitutes a risk of a false negative. It is clear from the judges' opinions following their acquittal in this case that they believed the prosecutor had shown overconfidence in relation to the investigative hypothesis. This had resulted in the prosecutor failing to detect and address major evidentiary gaps. The judges themselves saw these gaps all too clearly and therefore had to acquit. While the truth in this case is unknown, it highlights how confirmation bias and overconfidence in a hypothesis may result in false negatives. One condition that is likely to contribute to confirmation bias and the associated overconfidence in prosecutors is that they often have multiple roles. Not only are they leaders of inquiries but they also act as the defendant's counterparty in court. This demands a great deal of a prosecutor, arguably too much, of their cognitive flexibility, especially given added pressure from outside and/or inside their organizations to be tough on crime and/or get convictions. While bias mitigation in prosecutors is still greatly under researched, the techniques most likely to work based on the research available today is changing decision-maker, using Devil's Advocate procedures, Red Teams, and Evidence Review Boards. This recommendation should be read in juxtaposition with the clarifications and more detailed examination outlined in Chapters 4.2.3.1 and 4.2.3.2.

Even if judges are the individuals ultimately responsible for the legitimacy and accuracy of a criminal case, the evidence presented to them may be one-sided. This is due to, for example, the risk of confirmation bias in relation to all evidence types, overconfident leadership from a prosecutor, and so on. Importantly, such shortcomings are not necessarily always visible in a court of law. This means that the very foundation of judges' decision-making be flawed. Furthermore, just like all other human beings, judges are themselves prone to confirmation bias. For judges, confirmation bias can be triggered by, for example, an interim decision or other decisions preceding the assessment of guilt. This is illustrated by Hauschildt v. Denmark and the related research using Swedish judges. Also, confirmation bias in judges can be due to external information or pressures, whether political or via the media. A story, not necessarily accurate or factual, can be constructed about the alleged criminal conduct, alleged perpetrator, and so.

It is likely that judges have difficulties abandoning such stories, even if they consciously strive to be objective. While there are many possible examples of such issues, they have been illustrated here by the Vitaliy Markiv case and the Sushant Singh Rajput case. These are two cases dealt with in jurisdictions and cultures distinctively different from one another, but both seem to reinforce story construction as a risk factor. To mitigate confirmation bias in judges, the research available today suggests that changing the presiding judge, for example between detention and a main hearing, has potential. Furthermore, there is debiasing potential in conducting structured (piece by piece) rather than unstructured (overall) evaluations of the evidence.

Table 5.1 can easily give the impression that there are clear-cut answers on how to mitigate confirmation bias in all the listed investigative settings, yet it is highly recommended that the reader also carefully reviews the chapters pertaining to each debiasing technique and is mindful of the limitations and clarifications outlined there. The debiasing techniques outlined in Table 5.1 have been included because they have been identified as *potential* rather than foolproof debiasing techniques.

Apart from the need to be aware of the research available today into bias mitigations measures, it is also essential to conduct further research into this field. The explanations of confirmation bias found in cognitive psychology (Chapter 2.2.2.1), emotion and motivation psychology (Chapter 2.2.2.2), and social and organizational psychology (Chapter 2.2.2.3) are a good starting point in any debiasing attempt. In specific settings, such as those outlined in Chapters 3 and 4, or other settings yet to be researched, they can be converted and their debiasing potential empirically evaluated. While all the mentioned psychological fields need to be further examined, the research conducted so far seems to emphasize the social and cognitive explanations. Specifically, social explanations suggest that individuals struggle more in reasoning independently in relation to hypotheses that they themselves have generated, compared to hypotheses generated by others. This information is useful and can be converted into a debiasing technique. Since the risk of confirmation bias appears to be larger in relation to self-generated hypotheses, individuals should, ideally, not make multiple related decisions pertaining to, for example, the same suspect.

Instead, the decision-maker should be changed between such decisions. So far, this has been tested and found to be effective when it comes to, for example, judges' decisions about pre-trial detention and decisions about guilt during the main hearing. Furthermore, when different police officers arrested and interviewed suspects, the interviews were less guilt presumptive, compared to when the same police officer first decided to arrest and conducted the suspect interview. Probably such a change of decision-maker could be effective in other situations, like different types of interim decisions or other types of preliminary assessments of an individual's involvement in a crime. Similarly, the cognitive explanations of confirmation bias suggest that the risk of confirmation bias is greater in relation to cognitively more demanding tasks. This information is useful in any debiasing attempt. It suggests that reducing cognitive load can be functional as a debiasing technique. What more specific measures would, in fact, reduce cognitive load needs to be scientifically evaluated, for example by asking participants to rate different types of tasks. So far, reduced cognitive load and, specifically, using standardized interviewing frameworks rather than questions generating free answers, have proven to be effective for bias mitigation in suspect interviews. These findings are in line with research into the investigative interviewing framework suggesting that investigative interviewing models are essential toolkits for interviewers. This is because these models take some of the cognitive load off. For example, rather than constantly coming up with new questions, the models suggest that interviewers instead use open-ended non-presumptive encouragement to 'tell more' about incidents of interest. Simultaneously, in suspect interviews, investigative interviewing is also beneficial for other reasons. Usually, such an interviewing style makes the interview more cognitively demanding for the suspect, leaving less cognitive resources available for successfully deceiving the interviewer.

Apart from the need to conduct more research into bias mitigation, effective bias mitigation, in practice, will of course also require proper implementation. The most appropriate and effective ways of implementing debiasing techniques will vary between different jurisdictions as well as between different police stations, forensic labs, forensic doctors units, prosecution offices, and courts. The question of appropriate implementation is therefore left to the policy-makers and practitioners in each respective field to consider.

5.2 Concluding Remarks

This book has provided a general framework for understanding what confirmation bias is and why it occurs. It has also addressed manifestations of confirmation bias as well as possible debiasing techniques relating to specific investigative settings as well as decisions by prosecutors and judges during the litigation phase. This framework includes a range of practitioners with distinct, albeit related and intertwined, decision-making tasks.

Although the police are not the final decision-makers in criminal cases, their way of conducting suspect interviews and line-ups as well as witness interviews, for example, can be the starting point of a suspect-driven investigation. If the apprehension of a suspect in itself can trigger guilt-presumptive questioning and perceptions that the suspect is not trustworthy, investigators may already have formed impressions that they will struggle to rid themselves of. Also, the risk of false confessions resulting from guilt-presumptive questioning has been mentioned throughout this book as well as how knowledge of a suspect' confession can taint other lines of evidence, illustrated not the least by forensic confirmation bias. Furthermore, an impression that the suspect is guilty can transcend into the witness interview. This can result, for example, in police-generated witness testimony, that is, testimony that fits the police's hypothesis rather than the witness' recollection. Also, it may transpire into a suspect line-up which, especially if the line-up is not pre-tested and the line-up administrator is aware of the suspect's identity, will increase the odds that the witness identifies the suspect as the perpetrator. Hence, an impression that the suspect is guilty can result in apparent corroboration of a wrongful guilt hypothesis.

Although it varies exactly at what point a crime scene investigation is conducted it is often at an early stage. This means that while there may be some information available about what might have happened, there is not yet any sound evidence. If CSIs enter a crime scene aware of such preliminary information, there is a substantial risk that they will see what they expect to see. In other words, they are more likely to search for, interpret, and secure traces which can confirm the initial piece of information. This selection process, as well as that following during the triage phase, is essential not only for what forensic analysis will be conducted. It is also essential for what evidence will be available to form decisions about prosecution and guilt. It could be that essential traces are left behind at the crime scene or that they are secured from the crime scene but never analysed because they do not, given the investigative hypothesis, seem relevant.

Thus, even if all the items that were sent off to forensic analysis were analysed in a completely bias-free way, they may still not be capable of conveying the true story of what happened at the crime scene. Needless to say, adding a forensic confirmation bias to this equation has the power to distort the true picture even more. If CSIs only or primarily focus on traces consistent with the investigative hypothesis, and forensic analysts interpret this evidence in hypothesis-consistent ways, it is unsurprising that the investigative hypothesis is 'confirmed' or 'corroborated'. This can even include multiple forensic analysis entailing forensic science, medicine, and anthropology.

When prosecutors need to decide, for example, whether the suspect shall remain in custody or whether to press charges, these decisions are of course formed on the basis of the evidence collected and/or produced at the previous stages. If this evidence is biased, it undoubtedly has the potential of completely undermining the prosecutor's ability to make fair and reasonable decisions. In fact, even when the evidence has not been biased by another practitioner's processing of it, it seems prosecutors can also themselves develop a confirmation bias. While some research suggests that this can happen with a prosecutor's decision to identify or arrest a suspect, other research suggests it only happens by the time of the decision to press charges. This bias can result in exculpatory evidence being downplayed and/or the prosecutor only rarely initiating additional investigation, and if such investigation is initiated, it is aimed primarily at confirming the suspect's guilt. Surely such a bias among prosecutors can only add to the risk of a wrongful conviction in court, since the evidence against the suspect, by now, may seem fairly persuasive. Hence, to prevent this from happening, it is essential that a change of decision-maker takes place and that the charging decision is preceded by adversarial techniques such as Devil's Advocate Procedures, Red Teaming, as well as involving an Evidence Review Board, provided that these offer real challenges and critical reviews of the case evidence, rather than superficial examination or even validation of the case at hand.

A judge's interim (preliminary) decision or decision to detain a suspect awaiting trial seems capable of triggering confirmation bias in the judge. It is also possible that certain aspects or characteristics of the cases, such as a political sensitivity, media exposure, or the accused's personal circumstances, can lead judges to subconsciously construct stories of what has happened. These stories dictate how judges perceive and evaluate the evidence. In a worst-case scenario, and particularly if the judges themselves have developed confirmation bias, this can result in a wrongful conviction (false positive). However, it is also possible that the judges are able to critically evaluate the evidence presented in court, and see through any deficiencies and alternative hypotheses that have not been evaluated. The extent to which judges will conduct such thinking into alternative scenarios will vary between different jurisdictions as well as between different judges. Notably, however, a one-sided information search can also result in the narrative being presented in court coming across as very shaky and dubious to the judge. While the investigators and prosecutors may be certain of their hypothesis, and this has resulted in them being asymmetrically sceptical in relation to the evidence, judges can see through this and consider themselves forced to acquit. This results in a risk of a wrongful acquittal (false negative). In fact, the case does not even have to go all the way to court. A confirmation bias can also result in a guilty person being dismissed from suspicions at an early stage, for example because this person is not behaving the way the investigators expect a guilty person to behave. Such a scenario constitutes a risk both of a false negative and a false positive since someone else may, wrongfully, become suspected, prosecuted, or even convicted of the crime.

In sum, confirmation bias is indeed an aspect of the 'human factor' which deserves attention by researchers and practitioners. It is directly related to the progress, outcome, and accuracy of criminal investigations and proceedings. This book has specified what this means, how it can impact negatively on the administration of justice, as well as possible ways to mitigate it. Since criminal investigations involve a range of scientific disciplines as well as a range of practitioners, bias mitigation in criminal cases requires involvement of all these actors and tailor-made mitigation measures. The human factor, including the risk of confirmation bias, is a constant in criminal investigations and litigations. Hence, effective administration of justice, inevitably, includes bias mitigation. In turn, bias mitigation requires open-mindedness and critical and nuanced thinking both in practitioners and researchers.

Glossary

Ad hoc; 'when necessary or needed'. For example, groups of investigators from different jurisdictions come together to investigate a cross-border crime where all their expertise will be needed.

Baseline; a starting point or standard against which research findings can be compared and conclusions can be drawn; for example, what the effect of introducing a variable is.

Bayesian model; a statistical model building on probability to represent uncertainty in decision-making situations; for example, how to update beliefs in the face of new data.

Ceteris paribus; 'all other things equal'. In experimental studies, all aspects of a decision-making scenario remain equal except for the variable of interest to the researcher.

Condition; research participants are divided into different conditions or groups that allow comparisons with other groups to be made, since the preconditions for the groups' performance vary in some way relevant to the research study at hand.

Core international crimes; entailing genocide, crimes against humanity, war crimes, and crimes of aggression, as defined by, for example, the Rome Statute of the International Criminal Court.

Experiment; a research method in which research participants, often unknowingly, are randomly assigned to different groups (conditions) in which the conditions vary in relevant ways. For example, police officers may be asked to evaluate the reliability of a witness either when the witness provides a hypothesis-consistent or hypothesis-inconsistent statement, which allows conclusions to be drawn about whether the implications of the witness statements significantly impact how police officers perceive the witness' reliability.

Experimental manipulation; a process researchers use intentionally to alter the presence of or type of a variable in order to test the effect of the variable on another variable. For example, a researcher can alter whether judges are to make pre-trial detention decisions themselves or simply be informed of the decision of a colleague. Then the researcher studies whether and how the decision-maker variable affects judges' decisions during the main hearing, given that all other circumstances are equal.

Foils; or fillers, are the individuals other than the suspect that are included in a line-up.

Generalizability; the extent to which findings generalize to other environments or circumstances than those specific environments or circumstances that have been studied.

Inattentional blindness; sometimes referred to as 'looking without seeing', that is, even if human are looking at something we do not necessarily see it, as in actively acknowledge that it is there, unless we also direct our attention to it.

N; abbreviation for 'number', used to indicate the number of participants or cases included in a research study.

Naïve observers; neutral individuals that participate in a research study to test whether the assessments of the neutral individuals are different from, for example, individuals that are involved in a criminal case or for other reasons have relevant knowledge about the case.

Normative; a standard found in for example applicable laws stating how decision-making should be conducted, to be distinguished from how decision-making actually is conducted.

***p*;** statistical measurement indicating whether an effect is significant (usually when $p < 0.05$) or not (usually when $p > 0.05$). The *p*-value is a critical value that decides whether a researcher should reject or keep a null hypothesis.

Rigor mortis; rigidity or stiffening of joints and muscles post-mortem.

Sample; a group of participants recruited from a wider population of, for example, prosecutors, forensic doctors, or judges.

Schema; a cognitive framework or mental structure that individuals acquire through, for example, experience, used for categorization of objects, events, or other individuals.

Significance; refers to statistical significance. If the *p*-value is less than 0.05, the result is usually considered statistically significant. This means that the probability of obtaining the results by chance, if the null hypothesis is true, is less than 5 per cent. Statistical significance is in itself no indicator of practical relevance, but for this the effect size, that is, a measurement of how much of an effect there is, needs to be known too.

Bibliography

a) European Union Sources

Treaty of Lisbon Amending the Treaty on European Union and the Treaty Establishing the European Community, 2007.

The European Parliament and Council's Directive 2012/13/EU on the right to information in criminal proceedings, 2012.

b) Committees

i) The European Committee for the Prevention of Torture (CPT)

CPT/Inf (2002) 15, 12th General Report.

CPT/Inf (2009) 34, Report to the Swedish Government on the visit to Sweden carried out by the European Committee for the Prevention of Torture and Inhuman or Degrading Treatment or Punishment.

ii) The United Nation's Subcommittee on Prevention of Torture (SPT)

SPT CAT/OP/SWE/1 (2008) Report on the visit of the subcommittee on prevention of torture and other cruel, inhuman or degrading treatment or punishment to Sweden

Security Council Resolution 1595, UN Doc.S/RES//1595 (2005), 7 April 2005.

United Nations International Residual Mechanism for Criminal Tribunals (2010). The Genocide, available at: <https://unictr.irmct.org/en/genocide> (accessed 20 February 2023).

United Nationals Office on Drugs and Crime (UNODC) (2009). Crime Scene and Physical Evidence Awareness for Non-forensic Personnel, available at: <https://www.unodc.org/documents/scientific/Crime_scene_awareness__Ebook.pdf> (accessed 20 February 2023).

c) Official Documents

i) Sweden

Swedish Government Bills (NJA and Prop.)

NJA II 1940 no 2.

NJA II 1943.

NJA II 1966.

Prop. 1986/87:89 om ett reformerat tingsrättsförfarande.

Regeringens proposition 1986/87:112 om anhållande och häktning.

NJA II 1989 Ändring i reglerna om tvångsmedel.

Regeringens proposition 1992/93:25 om handläggning av brottmål efter rättspsykiatrisk undersökning m.m.

Prop. 1996/97:133 Domstols sammansättning m.m.

Regeringens proposition 2000/01:92 7 kap. Rättegångsbalken.
Prop. 2010/11:1 Budgetpropositionen för 2011. Förslag till statsbudget för 2011, finansplan och skattefrågor m.m.
Regeringens proposition 2011/12:156. Resningsförfarandet i brottmål—återupptagande av förundersökning och rätt till bitrade.
NJA II 2012.
Regeringens proposition 2013/14:157. Misstänktas rätt till insyn vid frihetsberövanden.
Regeringens proposition 2015/16:68. Förstärkt rättssäkerhet och effektivitet i förundersökningsförfarandet.

Swedish Government Official Reports (SOU)

SOU 1926:32. Processkommissionens betänkande angående rättegångsväsendets ombildning. Andra delen, rättegången i brottmål.
SOU 1938:44 Processlagberedningens förslag till rättegångsbalk.
SOU 1977:50 Häktning och anhållande. Betänkande ang. översyn av häktningsbestämmelserna.
SOU 1985:27. Gripen—anhållen—häktad. Straffprocessuella tvångsmedel m.m. Betänkande av 1983 års häktningsutredning.
SOU 1988:18. Rapport av parlamentariska kommissionen med anledning av mordet på Olof Palme. Del 3.
SOU 1996:18. Totalförsvarspliktiga m95.
SOU 1999:98 Granskningskommissionens Betänkande, Brottsutredningen efter Mordet på Statsminister Olof Palme.
SOU 2005:84. En ny uppgifts- och ansvarsfördelning mellan polis och åklagare.
SOU 2011:45. Förundersökning—objektivitet, beslag, dokumentation m.m.
SOU 2012:13. En sammanhållen svensk polis. Betänkande av Polisorganisationskommittén.
SOU 2015:52. Rapport från Bergwallkommissionen.

The Parliamentary Ombudsman (Justitieombudsmannen, JO)

Justitieombudsmännens ämbetsberättelse 1975/76 pp. 20–38. Åtal mot polisintendent m.fl. för tagande av muta m.m.
Justitieombudsmännens ämbetsberättelse 1978/79 pp. 58–59. Medan två personer är omhändertagna hos polisen enligt 3 § lagen om tillfälligt omhändertagande (LTO) blir de misstänkta för brott. Fel att gripa och överföra dem till allmänt häkta när de inte längre kan kvarhållas hos polisen med stöd av LTO.
Justitieombudsmännens ämbetsberättelse 1983/84 pp. 56–59. Åklagares prövning av frågor om anhållande i den misstänktes utevaro och om åtgärder när beslut därom har verkställts.
Justitieombudsmännens ämbetsberättelse 1989/90 pp. 44–52. Fråga om jäv för åklagare och riksåklagarens handläggning av denna fråga: dröjsmål med åtalsbeslut.
JO decision, 30 January 2003, registration no. 194-2001. Fråga om den särskilda förutsättningen för en polisman att gripa en person, dvs. brådskande fall, var uppfylld samt dokumentationen av ingripandet.
JO decision, 16 May 2003, registration no. 2318-2002. Anmälan mot Polismyndigheten i Stockholms län med anledning av ett gripande m.m.
Justitieombudsmännens ämbetsberättelse 2003/04 p. 67. Åklagar- och polisväsendena. Fråga om den särskilda förutsättningen för en polisman att gripa en person, dvs. brådskande fall, var uppfylld samt dokumentationen av ingripandet.

JO decision, 7 July 2006, registration no. 2181-2005. 'Fallet AA'—en granskning av bl.a. objektivitetsprincipens tillämpning under förundersökning och rättegång samt av Riksåklagarens handläggning av ett ärende gällande resning.
Justitieombudsmännens ämbetsberättelse 2007/08 p. 87. 'Fallet AA'—en granskning av bl.a. objektivitetsprincipens tillämpning under förundersökning och rättegång samt av Riksåklagarens handläggning av ett ärende gällande resning.
JO decision, 27 October 2009, registration no. 2839-2008. Uttalanden om åklagares vid Åklagarmyndigheten, Riksenheten för polismål, underhandskontakter med befattningshavare som en polisanmälan avsåg.
Justitieombudsmännens ämbetsberättelse 2009/10 p. 111 Kritik mot polisen med anledning av att resultat av en fotokonfrontation inte redovisades till åklagare och inte heller i förun dersökningsprotokollet.
JO decision, 18 June 2014, registration no. 2572-2013. Information om rättigheter och verkställighetens innebörd till intagna i polisarrest.

The Office of The Chancellor of Justice (Justitiekanslern, JK)
JK decision, 8 May 2001, registration no. 45-01-41. Anspråk på skadestånd av staten på grund av ett frihetsberövande samt i anledning av en brottsutredning; fråga om tillämpning av skadeståndslagen och frihetsberövandelagen.
JK decision, 21 September 2006, registration no. 3704-04-21. Kritik mot en åklagare för underlåtenhet att iaktta objektivitetsprincipen.
Felaktigt dömda, Rapport från JK:s rättssäkerhetsprojekt 2006.

The Ministry of Justice (Justitiedepartementet)
Committee Directive, Dir. 2010:75 En ny organisation för polisen?
Letter of appropriation for 2018 concerning the Police Authority (2018). Regleringsbrev för budgetåret 2018 avseende Polismyndigheten. https://www.esv.se/statsliggaren/regleri ngsbrev/?RBID=18597 (accessed 20 February 2023).
Letter of appropriation for 2017 concerning the Courts (2017). Regleringsbrev för budgetåret 2017 avseende Sveriges Domstolar. <https://www.esv.se/statsliggaren/regleri ngsbrev/?RBID=17990> (accessed 20 February 2023).
Letter of appropriation for 2018 concerning the Prosecution Authority (2018). Regleringsbrev för budgetåret 2018 avseende Åklagarmyndigheten. <https://www.esv.se/ statsliggaren/regleringsbrev/?RBID=18904> (accessed 20 February 2023).

Committee on Justice (Justitieutskottet)
Report 2000/01: JuU23. 7 kap rättegångsbalken.

Government Offices (Regeringskansliet)
The Council on Basic Values (2014). Common basic values for central government employees—a summary.
Mål för rättsväsendet (2015). <http://www.regeringen.se/regeringens-politik/rattsvasen det/mal-for-rattsvasendet/> (accessed 20 February 2023).

The National Police Board (Rikspolisstyrelsen, RPS)
RPS Report 2005:2 Vittneskonfrontation.
Rikspolisstyrelsens utvärderingsfunktion, Rapport 2013:7. Granhag, Pär Anders, Strömwall, Leif A and Cancino Montecinos, Sebastian (Eds). Polisens förhör med misstänkta, svensk utbildning i internationell belysning.
Brott i nära relationer, Handbok 2009.

The National Police Board (Rikspolisstyrelsen, RPS) and the Prosecution Authority. Gemensamt regeringsuppdrag för Åklagarmyndigheten och Rikspolisstyrelsen, Granskning av kvaliteten i den brottsutredande verksamheten, 2013.

The Prosecution Authority

Report, Häktningstider och restriktioner, 2014. <https://www.aklagare.se/om_rattsproces sen/fran-brott-till-atal/forundersokningen/haktningstider-och-restriktioner/> (accessed 20 February 2023).

Annual Report 2016. <https://www.aklagare.se/globalassets/dokument/planering-och-uppfoljning/arsredovisningar/arsredovisning-2016.pdf> (accessed 20 February 2023).

The Prosecution Authority's webpage, Uppdrag och mål, 2018 <https://www.aklagare.se/om-oss/uppdrag-och-mal/> (accessed 20 February 2023).

The Swedish Prosecution Authority (2020). Beslut i Förundersökningen om Mordet på Sveriges Statsminister Olof Palme, see <https://www.aklagare.se/nyheter-press/press meddelanden/2020/juni/beslut-i-forundersokningen-om-mordet-pa-sveriges-statsm inister-olof-palme/> (accessed 20 February 2023).

The Police Authority

Polisens Metodstöd för Utredning av Grova Våldsbrott (PUG), available at: <https://poli sen.se/om-polisen/polisens-arbete/dodligt-vald/> (accessed 20 February 2023), and for domestic violence, see Brott i nära relationer, Handbok 2009.

The Police Authority's webpage, Polisens resultat till och med maj 2018, 2018. <https://poli sen.se/om-polisen/uppdrag-och-mal/polisens-resultat/> (accessed 20 February 2023).

Swedish Police Authority's Webpage, <https://polisen.se/aktuellt/nyheter/2020/juni/utre dningen-om-palmemordet-avslutad/>.

The National Board of Forensic Medicine (Rättsmedicinalverket, RMV)

RMV, Mall för kroppsundersökning i PDF format, Mall för yttrande i PDF format. <http://www.rmv.se/?id=208> (accessed 2 October 2014)

The National Forensic Centre (Nationellt forensiskt centrum, NFC, previously Statens Kriminaltekniska Laboratorium, SKL)

SKL (2010). Internal report, Tillförlitligheten av fingeravtrycksbevis ifrågasatt—ärenden internationellt där man yrkat på att avfärda fingeravtryck som bevis i domstol, Kemi- och Teknikenheten 2010:06.

SKL, Faktablad—Riktlinjer för tolkning av dna-jämförelser i träffrapporter och sakkunnigutlåtanden, 2015.

NFC web page, Så fungerar resultatvärdering, 2017 <http://www.nfc.polisen.se/Ostergotl and/kriminalteknik/logiska-angreppssattet/> (accessed 20 February 2023).

NFC web page, Dna-analyser, 2017 <http://www.skl.polisen.se/kriminalteknik/biologi/dna-analyser/> (acessed 20 February 2023).

NFC web page, Är fingeravtryck säkra bevis? 2018 <http://www.skl.polisen.se/krimina lteknik/kemi-och teknik/fingeravtryck/Fingeravtryck-ifragasatt/> (accessed 20 February 2023).

The Swedish National Courts Administration (Domstolsverket, DV)

DV-rapport 1989:9.
DV-rapport 1995:2.

Courts statistics 2014. Official statistics of Sweden.
Extract from Vera, Report No. 601 (2016).
Strategisk inriktning 2010–2020, <http://www.domstol.se/Publikationer/Strategisk_inriktning/strategisk_inriktning_webb.pdf> (accessed 20 February 2023).

The National Council for Crime Prevention (Brottsförebyggande rådet, BRÅ)
BRÅ Statistics (2013). Arrests, application for detention orders and detainees, 1965–2013.
BRÅ Report, En polis närmare medborgaren. Ett kunskapsstöd i arbetet med medborgarlöften. 2016. <https://polisen.se/om-polisen/medborgarloften/> (accessed 20 February 2023).
BRÅ Statistics, Correctional treatment, Table appendix, 2016.

The Bar Association
Vägledande Regler om God Advokatsed, 2016.
Swedish Agency for Health Technology Assessment and Assessment of Social Services (Statens Beredning for Medicinsk och Social Utvärdering, SBU). (2016). Skakvåld—Triadens roll vid medicinsk utredning av misstänkt skakvåld.

ii) Norway
Justis- og Beredskapsdepartementet
CEtterkontroll av kommisjonen for gjenopptakelse av straffesaker, Rapport fra arbeidsgruppe for etterkontroll av Gjenopptakelsekommisjonen 2012.

The Norwegian Government
Ot.prp.nr 70 (2000–2001).

Gjenopptakelsekommisionen
Webpge, <https://www.gjenopptakelse.no/> (accessed 20 February 2023).

iii) Denmark
Den Saerlige Klageret
Den Saerlige Klageret's Webpage, <https://domstol.dk/densaerligeklageret/> (accessed 20 February 2023).

iv) United States
The Department of Justice
Peterson, Joseph L., Mihajlovic, Steven, & Gilliland, Michael. Forensic evidence and the police: the effects of scientific evidence on criminal investigations. Washington, DC, U.S. Department of Justice: National Institute of Justice, 1984.
Feeney, Floyd (1998). German and American Prosecutions: An Approach to Statistical Comparison. US Department of Justice, 1998
Peterson, Joseph L., Mihajlovic, Steven and Gilliland, Michael (1984). Forensic Evidence and the Police: The Effects of Scientific Evidence on Criminal Investigations. US Department of Justice, 1984 pp. 1–266.

Laber, Terry, Kish, Paul, Taylor, Michael, Owens, Glynn, Osborne, Nikola, Curran, James (2014). Reliability Assessment of Current Methods in Bloodstain Pattern Analysis. Final Report for the National Institute of Justice

National Commission on Forensic Science, Ensuring That Forensic Analysis is Based Upon Task-relevant Information (2015). <https://www.justice.gov/ncfs/file/818196/download> (accessed 22 February 2023).

Police Executive Research Forum (2013). A National Survey of Eyewitness Identification Procedures in Law Enforcement Agencies. <https://www.policeforum.org/assets/docs/Free_Online_Documents/Eyewitness_Identification/a%20national%20survey%20of%20eyewitness%20identification%20procedures%20in%20law%20enforcement%20agencies%202013.pdf> (accessed 22 February 2023).

Office of the Inspector General (OIG). Oversight and Review Division U.S. Department of Justice. A Review of the FBI's Handling of the Brandon Mayfield Case, 2006.

United States

Committee on Identifying the Needs of the Forensic Science Community

Committee on Identifying the Needs of the Forensic Science Community (2009). Strengthening Forensic Science in the United States: A Path Forward.

N.Y.C. Criminal Justice Agency

N.Y.C. Criminal Justice Agency (2013). Annual Report.

Innocence Project

Innocence Project (2008). New Report. Prosecutorial Misconduct and Wrongful Convictions.

Innocence Project (2016). Prosecutorial Oversight: A National Dialogue in the Wake of Connick v. Thompson.

v) United Kingdom

Intelligence and Security Committee

Intelligence and Security Committee (2006). Report into the London Terrorist Attacks on 7 July 2005.

House of Lords

House of Lords (2019). Science and Technology Select Committee, Forensic Science and the Criminal Justice System: A Blueprint for Change.

House of Lords, Earsferry in Helow v. Home Secretary (2008) 1 WLR 2416.

National Police Chief's Council (NPCC)

NPCC (2021). Retention, Storage and Destruction of Material and Records relating to Forensic Examination.

Office for National Statistics

Office for National Statistics (2020). Coronavirus (COVID-19) Related Deaths by Ethnic Group, England and Wales: 2 March 2020 to 10 April 2020.

Crown Prosecution Service

Crown Prosecution Service (2011). Guidance for Charging Perverting the Court of Justice and Wasting Police Time in Cases Involving Allegedly False Allegations of Rape and/or Domestic Abuse.

The National Forensic Science Technology Centre (NFSTC)

The National Forensic Science Technology Centre (NFSTC).(2013). Crime Scene Investigation—A Guide for Law Enforcement.

The Association of Chief Police Officers (ACPO)

The Association of Chief Police Officers (ACPO) (2006). Murder Investigation Manual.

Home Office

Lord Devlin, Report to the Secretary of State for the Home Department of the Departmental Committee on Evidence of Identification in Criminal Cases, Home Office 1976.
Ministry of Justice
Criminal Procedure and Investigations Act 1996, section 23 (1), Code of practice, revised in accordance with section 25 (4) of the Criminal Procedure and Investigations Act 1996.

d) International Case Law

i) International Criminal Court (ICC)

The Darfur Case, ICC, ICC-02/05-1.
The Kenya Case, ICC-01/09 26.
The Prosecutor v. Ahmad Al Faqi, ICC, ICC-01/12-01/15.
The Prosecutor v. Bosco Ntaganda, ICC-01/04-02/06.
The Prosecutor v. Joseph Kony and Vincent Otti, ICC, ICC-02/04-01/05.
The Prosecutor v. Laurent Gbagbo and Charles Blé Goudé, ICC-02/11-01/15.
Office of the Prosecutor (OTP). Full Statement of the Prosecutor, Fatou Bensouda, on External Expert Review and Lessons Drawn from the Kenya Situation.

ii) Special Tribunal for Lebanon (STL)

Trial Chamber judgment, STL-11-01/T/TC, The Prosecutor v. Salim Jamil Ayyash, Hassan Habib Merhi, Hussein Hassan Oneissi, Assad Hassan Sabra.
STL Webpage, Judgment in the Ayyash et al. case postponed to 18 August 2020.
Separate Opinion of Judge David Re, STL Trial Chamber's Judgment in The Prosecutor v. Salim Jamil Ayyash, Hassan Habib Merhi, Husseing Hassan Oneissi, Assad Hassan Sabra, p. 2241 and WGAD report § 9.

iv) International Criminal Tribunal for Rwanda (ICTR)

Kabuga, Félicien, ICTR-98-44B.
Special Court of Sierra Leone (SCSL).
Brima, Kamara, & Kanu, SCSL-2004-16-A.
Norman, Fofana, & Kondewa, SCSL-04-14-A.
Sesay, Kallon, & Gbao, SCSL-04-15-A.
Taylor, SCSL-03-01-A.

v) The European Court of Human Rights (ECtHR)

Academy Trading Ltd and Others v. Greece, judgment of 4 April 2001, 30342/96.
Allan v. The United Kingdom, judgment of 5 November 2002, 48539/99.
Allenet de Ribemont v. France, judgment of 10 February 1995, 15175/89.
Grand Chamber, Armani da Silva v. the United Kingdom, judgment of 30 March 2016, 5878/08.
Butkevičius v. Lithuania, judgment of 17 January 2012, 23369/06.
Böhmer v. Germany, judgment of 15 November 2001, 37568/97.
Campbell and Fell v. United Kingdom, judgment of 28 June 1984, 7819/77.
Coyne, Cable et al. v. United Kingdom, judgment of 18 February 1999, 24436/94.
Dallos v. Hungary, judgment of 1 March 2001, 29082/95.
Dikme v. Turkey, judgment of 11 July 2002, 20869/92.
Edwards v. UK, judgment of 7 June 1998, 46477/99.
Falk v. Netherlands, judgment of 19 October 2004, 66273/01.
Ferrantelli and Santangelo v. Italy, judgment of 7 August 1996, 19874/92.
Findlay v. United Kingdom, judgment of 25 February 1997, 22107/93.
Gregory v. United Kingdom, judgment of 25 February 1997, 22299/93.
Hauschildt v. Denmark, judgment of 24 May 1989, 10486/83.
Jalloh v. Germany, judgment of 11 July 2006, 54810/00.
Konstas v. Greece, judgment of 24 May 2011, 53466/07.
Krumpholz v. Austria, judgment of 18 March 2010, 13201/05.
Marziano v. Italy, judgment of 28 November 2002, 45313/99.
Mikolajová v. Slovakia, judgment of 18 January 2011, 4479/03.
Mills v. United Kingdom, judgment of 6 May 1997, 35685/97.
Neumeister v. Austria, judgment of 27 May 1966, 1936/63.
Padovani v. Italy, judgment of 26 February 1993, 13396/87.
Pandy v. Belgium, judgment of 21 September 2006, 13583/02.
Pham Hoang v. France, judgment of 25 September 1992, 13191/87.
Phillips v. The United Kingdom, judgment of 12 December 2001, 41087/98.
Piersack v. Belgium, judgment of 26 October 1984, 8692/79.
Poppe v. The Netherlands, judgment of 24 March 2009, 32271/04.
Radio France and others v. France, judgment of 30 March 2004, 53984/00.
Remli v. France, judgment of 23 April 1996, 16838/90.
Rojas Morales v. Italy, judgment of 16 November 2000, 39676/98.
Salabiaku v. France, judgment of 7 October 1988, 10519/83.
Sander v. United Kingdom, judgment of 9 May 2000, 34129/96.
Saraiva de Carvalho v. Portugal, judgment of 25 July 2017, 17484/15.
Schwarzenberg v. Germany, judgment of 10 November 2006, 75737/01.
Sekanina v. Austria, judgment of 25 August 1993, 13126/87.
Stoimenov v. The Former Yugoslav Republic of Macedonia, judgment of 5 April 2007, 17995/02
Teixeira de Castro v. Portugal, judgment of 9 June 1998, 25829/94.
Otamendi Eguiren v. Spain, judgment of 16 October 2012, 47303/08.
Vanyan v. Russia, judgment of 13 May 2004, 53203/99.
Vostic v. Austria, judgment of 17 October 2002, 38549/97.
Grand Chamber, Armani da Silva v. the United Kingdom, Judgment, 5878/08, p. 14.
Kuopila v. Finland, judgment of 27 April 2000, ECtHR; Neumeister v. Austria, judgment of 7 May 1974.

John Murray v. United Kingdom, judgment of 8 February 1998.

e) National Case Law, Cases from the Lower Courts, Documents from Prosecution and Police Authorities, etc.

i) France

The Paris Attacks. No 84 The EU and its Counter-Terrorism Policies after the Paris Attacks. <https://www.ceeol.com/search/book-detail?id=833933> (accessed 13 July 2022).

ii) India

Struck by Lightning Case. Moorthy (2019). Suspicious Death—Crime Scene Evidence Indicated the Cause of Death: An Interesting Multiple Death Case Report, pp. 5–7.

The Sushant Singh Rajput Case, Bombay High Court, 1 July 2022. Tribune India (2022). Bombay High Court Grants Bail to Sushant Singh Rajput's Ex-Flatmate in Drugs Case. <https://www.tribuneindia.com/news/nation/bombay-high-court-grants-bail-to-sushant-singh-rajputs-ex-flatmate-in-drugs-case-409396> (accessed 13 July 2022).

India Today (2020). Sushant Singh Rajput Family vs Rhea Chakraborty Case Verdict: SC Allows CSI Probe into SSR Death. <https://www.indiatoday.in/movies/celebrities/story/sushant-singh-rajput-family-vs-rhea-chakraborty-case-verdict-sc-allows-cbi-to-take-control-of-investigation-1712765-2020-08-19> (accessed 13 July 2022).

iii) Israel

The Ivan Grozny Case, State of Israel v. Ivan (John) Demjanjuk, 347/88.

The Tair Rada Case, Nazareth District Court, February 2014, Israel Supreme Court, December 2015. The Times of Israel (2021). Supreme Court orders Retrial of Convicted Killer of 13-year Old Tair Rada.

The Jerusalem Post (2022). Criminal Law Expert: Roman Zadorov will be Acquitted in Tair Rada Murder Case. <https://www.jpost.com/israel-news/article-715131> (accessed 28 November 2022).

iv) Italy

The Vitaliy Markiv Case (Italy) Corte D´Assise di Pavia Sentenza in Nome del Popolo Italiano, N. 2/2018.

Tribunale di Pavia, Sezione Penale Corte D'Assise, Case No. 8065/16.

Corte D´Assise di Pavia Sentenza in Nome del Popolo Italiano, N. 2/2018, Corte d'Assise di Pavia Sentenza in Nome del Popolo Italiano, Sentenza No 1/2019.

Federazione Italiana Diritti Umani (FIDU), Caso Markiv: Dalla Parte Della Verità.

v) Kenya

The Westgate Shopping Mall Case, Milimani Court, Nairobi. Voice of America (2020). Kenyan Court Convicts Two in 2013 Westgate Mall Attack. <https://www.voanews.com/a/africa_kenyan-court-convicts-two-2013-westgate-mall-attack/6196842.html> (accessed 13 July 2022).

Homicide or Cardiac Myxoma (Kenya). Walong & Odour (2019). A 26-year Old Female Presenting with a Fatal Stroke due to Embolism of Cardiac Myxomatous Neoplasm Diagnosed at a kenyan Forensic Autopsy Service: A Case Report, pp. 1–4.

vi) Norway

The Breivik Case, Oslo District Court: TOSLO-2011-188627-24.

vii) Spain

The Egunkaria Case: The Spanish National High Court, 27/2010.
The Madrid Bomber Case. US Department of Justice (2005). Report on the Erroneous Fingerprint Individualization in the Madrid Train Bombing Case.

viii) Sweden

The Supreme Court

NJA 1974 p. 614.
NJA 1974 p. 221.
NJA 1975 C 125.
NJA 1979 p. 425.
NJA 1980 p. 725.
NJA 1986:470.
NJA 1986 p. 489.
NJA 1990:93.
NJA 1991 p. 56.
NJA 1992 C 119.
NJA 1993:764.
NJA 1994 p. 678.
NJA 1995 p. 3.
NJA 1998:53.
NJA 1998 p. 204.
NJA 1998 p. 228.
NJA 2006 p. 457.
NJA 2007 N 18.
NJA 2011 p. 638.
Ö 1459-12 (2012).
Ö 1860-12 (2012).
Ö 2345-12 (2012).
NJA 2014 p. 699.
NJA 2015 p. 141.

The Courts of Appeal

The Court of Appeal of Lower Norrland
Ö 889-11 (2011).

The Court of Appeal of Skåne and Blekinge
RH 1995:76 (1995).

Svea Court of Appeal
The Olof Palme Case, 1952/89:3 (1989).
The Samir Sabri Case, Ö 7110-15 (2015).
The B Case, B 2450-16 (2016).
The Adriano R. Cadiz Case, B 7958-18 (2018).
The Cyanide Woman Case, B 6615-19 (2019).
B 6328-02 (2002).

Ö 3147-09 (2009).
Ö 3293-10 (2010).
Ö 3085-11 (2011).
Ö 1375-13 (2013).
Ö 6261-14 (2014).
Ö 7110-15 (2015).
B 2450-16 (2016).
B 6615-19 (2019).
B 7958-18 (2018).

The Court of Appeal of Upper Norrland
Ö 454-12 (2012).
Ö 493-12 (2012).
Ö 880-12 (2012).

The Court of Appeal of Western Sweden
B 1402-05 (2005).
B 1132-10 (2010).
RH 2012:14 (2014).
RH 2013:8 (2008).

The District Courts
Attunda District Court
Adriano Cadiz Case, B9865-17 (2017).

Falun District Court
B 3585/10 (2010).
B 3510-12 (2012).
B 2384-14 (2014).

Hedemora District Court
The Therese Johannessen Case, B100/97 (1997).

Kalmar District Court
The Moose Case, B 2994-08 (2008).
Extract from IW's criminal record, 2008-09-09.
Autopsy Report, 20080910.
Record from the detention hearing.
Record appendix from detention hearing.
Medical opinion 20090123.

Mölndal District Court
B 1953-04 (2004).

Norrtälje District Court
The Cyanide Woman Case, B 1268-18 (2018).

Solna District Court
B 322-86 (1986).
B 3551-15 (2015).

Stockholm District Court
B 847/88 (1988).
B 21167-07 (2007).
B 4343-16 (2016).

Södertörn District Court
B 13157-13 (2013).

Västmanland District Court
The Moose Case, B 2522-01 (2001).

Kalmar Local Public Prosecution Office
The Moose Case, AM 138010-08.
Decisions to use coercion; Search of premises 2008-09-06, 2008-10-07, 2008-10-21, 2008-11-11, 2008-12-02, 2008-12-05.
Decision to use coercion; Seizure, 2008-09-06.
Decision to rescind the detention order, 2008-09-15.
Email correspondence between prosecutor and police officer, 2008-10-16 and 2008-11-19.
Prosecutor's notes, summary of investigation 2008-10-28.
E-mail correspondence prosecutor and police officer, 2008-11-17.
Directive from the prosecutor, 2008-11-28.
Directive from the prosecutor/Record from meeting, 2008-12-04.
Directive from the prosecutor, 2009-01-23.
Decision to dismiss IW as a suspect, 2009-01-28.

Kalmar Local Public Police Office
The Moose Case, 0800-K19154-08 (2008).
Detention Memo.
Interrogation 2008-09-05, 22:55-23:15.
Interrogation 2008-09-06, 00:00-00:50.

Stockholm Local Public Police Office
The Adriano Cadiz Case, Swedish Police Reference No. K1427657-17. Police interview with Trajan Popov, 22 November 2017, starting 11:47 ending 15:48.

ix) United Kingdom

R v. Silcott, R v. Braithwaite, R v. Raghip (The Tottenham Three Case). Central Criminal Court, London, March 1987 and 1991.
R v. Murphy and Maguire [1989] (The IRA Funeral Murders Case). Belfast Crime Court, Judgment, 1 June 1989, Crown Court of Northern Ireland, April, 1989, Court of Appeal in Northern Ireland [1990], NI 306.
Al Megrahi v. Her Majesty's Advocate (The Lockerbie Bomber Case), Special Panel of three Scottish Judges, Camp Zeist, Netherlands, C104/01.
Barry George and R, EWCA Crim 2722 (The Jill Dando Case). Court of Appeal of England and Wales, 15 November 2007.
R v. Kiszko (The Stefan Kiszko Case). Murder conviction quashed by Court of Appeal, 18 February 1992
Al Deghayes/Rawi and others v. The Security Services and Others (The Omar Deghayes Case). The Supreme Court, EWCA Civ 482, 13 July 201.
R v. Connor & Rollock [2004] UKHL 2.

R v. Miah [1997] 2 Cr. App. R. 12.
R v. Mirza [2002] Crim LR 921.
R v. Sally Clark [2003] EWCA Crim 1020.
R v. Ward, 1993, 96 Crim. App. 1, 68 UK.
R v. Young [1995] Q.B. 324.
R v. Quereshi [2011] EWCA Crim 1584.

x) United States

Miles v. United States, 103 US 304 (1880).
Barker v. Wingo, 407 U.S. 514, 533 (1972).
Coffin v. United States, 156 U.S. 432, 455 (1895).
Danial Williams v. Karen D. Brown, Joseph J. Dick v. Karen D. Brown, US District Court for the Eastern District of Virginia, Civil Action No. 3:09CV769, 3: 10CV505, 31 October 2016, Derek Elliot Tice v. Gene Johnson, US District Court of Virginia, Civil Action No, 3:08CV69, 14 September 2009 (The Norfolk Four Case).
United States v. Anthony Salerno and Vincent Cafaro (The New York Mafia Case). 481 US 739, Supreme Court, 26 May 1987.
The People of the State of New York against Kharey Wise, Kevin Richardson, Antron McCray, Yusef Salaam and Raymond Santana. Supreme Court of the State of New York County of New York. Affirmation in Response to Motion to Vacate Judgment of Convictions, Indictment No. 4762/89. New York, 5 December 2002 (The Central Park Five Case).
Dassey v. Dittman, United States Court of Appeals for the Seventh Circuit, No. 16-3397, 12 August 2017 (The Brendan Dassey Case).
Daubert v. Merrell Dow Pharmaceutical Inc., 509 U.S. 579, 1993.
Colorado v. Connelly, 479 U.S. 157 (1986).
Brady v. United States, 397 U.S. 742, 748 (1970).

f) Literature

i) Books, Book Chapters, and Dissertations

Abadinsky, Howard. Law and Justice, An Introduction to the American Legal System. London. Pearson Education, 1988.
Agirre Aranburu, Xabier. Prosecuting the Most Responsible for International Crimes: Dilemmas of Definition and Prosecutorial Discretion. In Gonzales, J (Ed.). *Protección Internacional de Derechos Humanos y Estado de Derecho* (pp. 381–404). Bogota: Grupo Editorial Ibanez, 2010.
Agirre Aranburu, Xabier. The Contribution of Analysis to the Quality Control in Criminal Investigation. In Agirre, Xabier, Bergsmo, Morten, De Smet, Simon & Stahn. Carsten (Eds). *Quality Control in Criminal Investigation* (pp. 117–272). Brussels: Torkel Opsahl Academic EPublisher, 2020.
Alamuddin, Amal, and Bonini, Anna. The UN Investigation of the Hariri Assassination, in Alamudding, Nabil Jurdi, and Tolbert (Eds), *The Special Tribunal for Lebanon: Law and Practice*. Oxford: Oxford University Press, 2014.
Alexy, Robert. *A Theory of Legal Argumentation: The Theory of Rational Discourse as Theory of Legal Justification*. Oxford: Oxford University Press, 2009.
Allport, Gordon W. *The Nature of Prejudice*. New York: Doubleday, 1958.

Allwood, Carl Martin. Eyewitness Confidence, in P.A. Granhag (Ed.), *Forensic Psychology in Context: Nordic and International Approaches* (pp. 281–303). London: Willan Publishing, 2010.

Alvesson, Mats and Sköldberg, Kaj. *Tolkning och reflektion: vetenskapsfilosofi och kvalitativ metod.* Lund: Studentlitteratur, 2008.

Allsop, Cheryl. *Cold Case Reviews: DNA, Detective Work, and Unsolved Major Crimes.* Oxford: Oxford University Press, 2018.

Andersson, Bruce. *'Discovery' in Legal Decision-Making.* Dordrecht: Springer, 1996.

Andersson, Håkan. Constructive Deconstruction. A Test of Postmodern Legal Reasoning: The Example of Third Party Losses on the Borderline between Tort Law and Contract Law in Anglo-Swedish Studies in Law, pp. 356–401, in Mads Andenas and Nils Jareborg (Eds), *Anglo-Swedish Studies in Law.* Uppsala: Uppsala University, 1998.

Andersson, Håkan. Postmoderna och diskursteoretiska verktyg inom rätten, pp. 343–368, in Fredric Korling and Mauro Zamboni (Eds), *Juridisk metodlära.* Lund: Studentlitteratur, 2013.

Andersson, Simon. *Skälig misstanke.* Stockholm: Norstedts Juridik, 2016.

Arendt, Hannah, and Jaspers, Karl. Correspondence: 1926-1969. United Kingdom: Hartcourt Brace, 1993.

Ashbaugh, David R. *Quantitative-Qualitative Friction Ridge Analysis—An Introduction to Basic and Advanced Ridgeology.* Boca Raton: CRC Press, 1999.

Ask, Karl. *Criminal Investigation: Motivation, Emotion and Cognition in the Processing of Evidence.* Göteborg: Göteborg University, 2006.

Ask, Karl and Granhag, Pär Anders. Psykologiska påverkansfaktorer vid utredningsarbete, pp. 161–174, in Pär Anders Granhag and Sven Å. Christianson (Eds), *Handbok i rättspsykologi.* Stockholm: Liber, 2008.

Asp, Petter. *EU & Straffrätten, Studier rörande den europeiska integrationens betydelse för den svenska straffrätten.* Uppsala: Iustus, 2002.

Asp, Petter. Om relationalistisk metod eller spridda anteckningar i jämförande rättsvetenskap, pp. 47–67, in Petter Asp and Kimmo Nuotio (Eds), *Konsten att rättsvetenskapa—den tysta kunskapen i juridisk forskning.* Uppsala: Iustus, 2004.

Asp, Petter and Nuotio, Kimmo. *Konsten att rättsvetenskapa—den tysta kunskapen i juridisk forskning.* Uppsala: Iustus, 2004

Atkinson, Richard and Shiffrin, Richard. Human Memory: A Proposed System and its Control Processes, pp. 89–195, in Kenneth Spence and Janet Taylor Spence (Eds), *The Psychology of Learning and Motivation.* London: Academic Press, 1968.

Bacon, Francis. Novum Organum, pp. 24–123, in Edwin A. Burtt (Ed.), *The English Philosophers from Bacon to Mill.* New York, NY: Random House, 1939.

Baier, Matthias and Svensson, Måns. *Om normer.* Malmö: Liber, 2009.

Ballard, Clare. Research Report on Remand Detention in South Africa: An Overview of the Current Law and Proposals for Reform. Civil Society Prison Reform Initiative (CSPRI). University of Western Cape, South Africa, 2011.

Bankowski, Zenon. The Jury and Rationality, pp. 8–26, in Mark Findlay and Peter Duff (Eds), *The Jury under Attack.* Edinburgh: Butterworths, 1988.

Bergman Blix, Stina and Wettergren, Åsa. *Professional Emotions in Court: A Sociological Perspective.* London: Routledge, 2018.

Basu, Kaushik. *Prelude to Political Economy: A Study of the Social and Political Foundations of Economics.* Oxford: Oxford University Press, 2003.

Baumeister, Roy F. *Meanings of Life.* New York, NY: Guilford Press, 1991.

Beckman, Jett and Irle, Martin. Dissonance and Action Control, pp. 129–150, in Julius Kuhl and Jürgen Beckmann (Eds), *Action Control: From Cognition to Behavior*. Berlin: Springer-Verlag, 1985.
Bengoetxea, Joxerramón. *The Legal Reasoning of The European Court of Justice: Towards a European Jurisprudence*. Oxford: Clarendon Press, 1993.
Bhaskar, Roy. Introduction, in Bhaskar, Roy (Ed.), *A Realist Theory of Science* (pp. 12–20). Brighton, Sussex: Harvester Press, 1978.
Bladini, Moa. *I objektivitetens sken—en kritisk granskning av objektivtetsideal, objektivtetsanspråk och legitimeringsstrategier i diskurser om dömande i brottmål*. Göteborg: Makadam, 2013.
Blackstock, Jodie, Spronken, Taru, Cape, Ed, Hodgson, Jacqueline. *Inside Police Custody: Training Framework on the Provisions of Suspects' Rights*. Cambridge: Intersentia, 2014.
Borg, Elisabet and Westerlund, Joakim. *Statistik för beteendevetare*. Malmö: Liber, 2012.
Boyce, Melissa, Beaudry, Jennifer and Lindsay, Roderick Cameron Lodge. Belief of Eyewitness Identification Evidence, in Lindsay, Ross, Don Read, and Toglia (Eds). *Handbook of Eyewitness Psychology* (pp. 501–525). Mahwah, NJ: Lawrence Erlbaum, 2007.
Brewer, Marilynn B. and Brown, Rupert J. Intergroup Relations, pp. 554–594, in Daniel T. Gilbert, Susan T. Fiske, and Gardner Lindzey (Eds), *The Handbook of Social Psychology*. New York, NY: McGraw-Hill, 1998.
Bring, Thomas and Diesen, Christian. *Förundersökning*. Stockholm: Norstedts Juridik, 2009.
Bruner, Jerome S. and Austin, George A. *A Study of Thinking*. New York, NY: John Wiley, 1956.
Bull, Ray. Investigative Interviewing. New York, NY: Springer, 2014.
Bull, Thomas and Sterzel, Fredrik. *Regeringsformen—en kommentar*. Stockholm: SNS Förlag, 2010.
Buratti, Sandra and Allwood, Carl Martin. *Regulating Metacognitive Processes—Support for a Meta-metacognitive Ability*.Cham: Springer International Publishing, 2014.
Bylander, Eric. *Muntlighetsprincipen: en rättsvetenskaplig studie av processuella handläggningsformer i svensk rätt*. Uppsala: Uppsala Universitet, 2006.
Bylund, Torleif. *Tvångsmedel I: Personella tvångsmedel i straffprocessen*. Uppsala: Iustus Förlag, 1993.
Cabell, Craig. *Witchfinder General*. Stroud: Sutton Publishing, 2006.
Cameron, Iain. *An Introduction to the European Convention on Human Rights*. Uppsala: Iustus, 2014.
Campbell, Donald T. Asch's Moral Epistemology for Socially Shared Knowledge, pp. 39–55, in Irvin Rock (Ed.), *The Legacy of Solomon Asch: Essays in Cognition and Social psychology*. Hillsdale, NJ: Lawrence Erlbaum Associates Inc., 1990.
Cars, Thorsten. *Om resning i rättegångsmål*. Stockholm: Nordiska bokhandeln, 1959.
Carver, Charles S. and Scheier, Michael F. *Perspectives on Personality*. Boston, MA: Pearson, 2012.
Ceci, Stephen J. and Bruck, Maggie. The Role of Interviewer Bias, pp. 87–108, in Stephen J. Ceci and Maggie Bruck (Eds), *Jeopardy in the Courtroom: A Scientific Analysis of Children's Testimony*. Washington, DC: American Psychological Association, 1995.
Chaiken, Shelly, Wood, Wendy, and Eagly Alice H. Principles of Persuasion, pp. 361–399, in E. Tory Higgins and Arie W. Kruglanski (Eds), *Social Psychology: Handbook of Basic Principles*. New York, NY: Guilford Press, 1996.
Christensen, Angi M., Passalacqua, Nicholas V., and Bartelink, Eric J. *Forensic Anthropology—Current Methods and Practice*. Amsterdam: Academic Press, 2019.

Christianson, Sven Åke and Montgomery, Henry. Kognition i ett rättspsykologiskt perspektiv, pp. 114–128, in Pär Anders Granhag and Sven Å. Christianson (Eds), *Handbok i rättspsykologi*. Stockholm: Liber, 2008.

Cole, Simon A. *Suspect Identities: A History of Fingerprinting and Criminal Identification*. Cambridge, MA: Harvard University Press, 2001.

Cooley, Craig and Turvey, Brent E. Observer Effects and Examiner Bias: Psychological Influences on the Forensic Examiner, pp. 61–68, in Jerry Chisum and Brent E. Turvey (Eds), *Crime Reconstruction*. Boston, MA: Elsevier, 2007.

Cotton, John L. Cognitive Dissonance in Selective Exposure, pp. 11–33, in Dolf Zillmann and Jennings Bryant (Eds), *Selective Exposure to Communication*. Hillsdale. NJ: Erlbaum, 1985.

Cutler, Brian L. and Penrod, Steven D. *Mistaken Identification: The Eyewitness, Psychology, and Law*. New York, NY: Cambridge University Press, 1995.

Dalberg-Larsen, JØrgen and Evald, Jens. *Rettens ansigter—en grundbog i almindelig retslaere*. Copenhagen: Jurist-og Økonomforbundet, 1998.

Damasio, Antonio. *The Strange Order of Things: Life, Feeling, and the Making of Cultures*. New York: Pantheon Books, 2018

Danelius, Hans. *Mänskliga rättigheter i europeisk praxis. En kommentar till Europakonventionen om de mänskliga rättigheterna*. Stockholm: Norstedts Juridik, 1997.

Daun, Åke. *Svensk mentalitet: Ett jämförande perspektiv*. Stockholm: Rabén Prisma, 1998.

Diesen, Christian. *Bevisprövning i brottmål*. Stockholm: Norstedts Juridik, 2002.

Diesen, Christian, Björkman, Johanna, Forsman, Fredrik, and Jonsson, Peter. *Bevis. Värdering av erkännande, konfrontationer, DNA och andra enstaka bevis*. Stockholm: Norstedts Juridik, 1997.

Diesen, Christian and Bring, Thomas. *Förundersökning*. Stockholm: Juristförlaget, 1995.

Douglas, Lawrence. *The Right Wrong Man: John Demjanjuk and the Last Great Nazi War Crimes Trial*. Princeton: Princeton University Press, 2016.

Dror, Itiel E. Land Mines and Gold Mines in Cognitive Technologies, in Dror, Itiel (Ed.) *Cognitive Technologies and the Pragmatics of Cognition* (pp. 1–7), Amsterdam, NL.: John Benjamins, 2007.

Dror, Itiel E. Cognitive Bias in Forensic Science, pp. 43–45, in David. I. Eggenberger (Ed.), *Yearbook of Science & Technology*. New York, NY: McGraw-Hill, 2012.

Dror, Itiel E. and Harnad, Stevan. Offloading Cognition onto Cognitive Technology, pp. 1–23, in Dror, Itiel E. and Harnad, Stevan (Eds), *Cognition Distributed: How Cognitive Technology Extends our Minds*. Amsterdam: John Benjamins Publishing, 2008.

Dror, Itiel E. and Harnad, Steven. *Cognition Distributed: How Cognitive Technology Extends our Minds*. Amsterdam: John Benjamins Publishing, 2008.

Dunbar, Kevin and Klahr, David. Developmental Differences in Scientific Discovery Processes, pp. 109–143, in David Klahr and Kenneth Kotovsky (Eds), *Complex Information Processing, The Impact of Herbert A. Simon*. Hillsdale. NJ: Lawrence Erlbaum Associates, 1989.

Dwyer, Christopher, Hogan, Michael, and Stewart, Ian. The Promotion of Critical Thinking Skills through Argument Mapping, pp. 97–122 in Horvarth, Christoper P. & Forte, James M. (Eds). *Critical Thinking*. New York: Nova Science Publishers, 2011.

Earman, John. *Bayes or Bust? A Critical Examination of Bayesian Confirmation Theory*. London: The MIT Press, 1996.

Edland, Anne and Svensson, Ola. Judgement and Decision Making under Time Pressure, pp. 27–40, in Ola Svensson and John Maule (Eds), *Time Pressure and Stress in Human Judgement and Decision Making*. New York, NY: Plenum Press, 1993.

Eels, Ellery. *Probabilistic Causality*. New York, NY: Cambridge University Press, 1991.
Ekelöf, Per Olof. *Är den juridiska doktrinen en teknik eller vetenskap?* Lund: Gleerup, 1951.
Ekelöf, Per Olof. *Rättegång II*. Stockholm: Norstedts Juridik, 1985.
Ekelöf, Per Olof and Edelstam, Henrik. *Rättegång I*. Stockholm: Norstedts Juridik, 2002.
Ekelöf, Per Olof and Edelstam, Henrik. *Rättsmedlen*. Uppsala: Iustus, 2008.
Ekelöf, Per Olof, Bylund, Torleif, and Edelstam, Henrik. *Rättegång III*. Visby: Norstedts Juridik, 2006.
Ekelöf, Per Olof, Edelstam, Henrik, and Heuman, Lars. *Rättegång IV*. Visby: Norstedts Juridik, 2009.
Eklycke, Lars. *Bokrecension av Björkman, Johanna, Diesen, Christian, Forsman, Fredrik & Jonsson, Peter. Bevis, Värdering av erkännande, konfrontationer, DNA och andra enstaka bevis*. Stockholm: Norstedts Juridik, 1998.
Elias, Norbert. *The Court Society*. Oxford: Basil Blackwell, 1983.
Epstein, Lee and Martin, Andrew D. Quantitative Approaches to Empirical Legal Research, pp. 901–924, in Peter Cane and Herbert M. Kritzer (Eds), *The Oxford Handbook of Empirical Legal Research*. Oxford: Oxford University Press, 2012.
Eriksson, Johan. *Handbok för försvarare*. Limhamn: Limhamnsgruppen, 2018.
Evans, Jonathan St. B.T. *Bias in Human Reasoning: Causes and Consequences*. Hillsdale, NJ: Erlbaum, 1989.
Eysenck, Michael W. and Keane, Mark T. *Cognitive Psychology—A Student's Handbook*. Hove: Psychology Press, 2015.
Fahsing, Ivar. *The Making of an Expert Detective*. Gothenburg, Gothenburg University Press, 2016.
Feldbrugge, Ferdinand J.M. *The Law's Beginning*. Leiden: Nijhoff, 2003.
Festinger, Leon. *A Theory of Cognitive Dissonance*. Stanford, CA: Stanford University Press, 1957.
Festinger, Leon. *Conflict, Decision, and Dissonance*. Stanford, CA: Stanford University Press, 1964.
Fiedler, Klaus and Juslin, Peter. Taking the Interface Between Mind and Environment Seriously, pp. 3–32, in Klaus Fiedler and Peter Juslin (Eds), *Information Sampling and Adaptive Cognition*. Cambridge: Cambridge University Press, 2010.
Fiske, Susan T. and Taylor, Shelley E. *Social Cognition*. New York, NY: McGraw-Hill, 1991.
Fitger, Peter. *Rättegångsbalken*. Stockholm: Norstedts Juridik, 2014.
Frank, Jerome. *Law and the Modern Mind*. London: Coward-McCann, 1949.
Freedman, Jonathan L. and Sears, David O. Selective Exposure, pp. 57–97, in Leonard Berkowitz (Ed.), *Advances in Experimental Social Psychology*. New York, NY: Academic Press, 1965.
Frey, Dieter. Recent Research on Selective Exposure to Information, pp. 41–80, in Leonard Berkowitz (Ed.), *Advances in Experimental Social Psychology*. New York, NY: Academic Press, 1986.
Gadelius, Bror. *Häxor och häxprocesser*. Stockholm: Prisma, 1986.
Gadelius, Bror. *Tro och öfvertro i gångna tider*. Stockholm: Geber, 1912.
Gardner, Ross M. Practical Crime Scene Processing and Investigation. Boca Raton: CRC Press, 2011
Gigerenzer, Gerd. *Adaptive Thinking—Rationality in the Real World*. New York, NY: Oxford University Press, 2000.
Gigerenzer, Gerd. *Rationality for Mortals—How People Cope with Uncertainty*. New York, NY: Oxford University Press, 2008.

Gigerenzer, Gerd and Selten, Reinhard. Rethinking Rationality, pp. 1–12, in Gerd Gigerenzer and Reinhard Selten (Eds), *Bounded Rationality: The Adaptive Toolbox*. Cambridge, MA: MIT Press, 2001.

Gilliéron, Gwladys. Public Prosecutors in the United States and Europe—A Comparative Analysis with Special Focus on Switzerland, France, and Germany. Zurich: Springer, 2014

Gleeson, Murray. The Rule of Law and the Constitution. London: ABC Books, 2000

Godsey, Mark. Blind Injustice: A Former Prosecutor Exposes the Psychology and Politics of Wrongful Convictions. Oakland, California: University of Californa Press, 2017.

Gorman, Michael E. Hypothesis Testing, pp. 243–265, in Stephen E. Newstead and Jonathan St. B.T. Evans (Eds), *Perspectives on Thinking and Reasoning. Essays in honour of Peter Wason*. Hove: Lawrence Erlbaum Associates Ltd, 1995.

Gould, Laurence, Stapley, Lionel F., and Stein, Mark. *The Systems Psychodynamics of Organizations—Integrating the Group Relations Approach, Psychoanalytic and Open Systems Perspective*. London: Routledge, 2006.

Griffin, Dale, and Brenner, Lyle. Perspectives on Probability Judgment Calibration, pp. 177–198, in Koehler, Derek J. and Harvey, Nigel (Eds). *Blackwell Handbook of Judgment and Decision Making*. Malden, MA: Blackwell Publishing, 2004.

Gross, Hans. Criminal Investigation, A Practical Handbook for Magistrates, Police Officers and Lawyers. Madras: Ramasawmy Chetty & Co., 1906.

Gudjonsson, Gisli H. Courtroom Testimony in Cases of Disputed Confessions, in Brown, Jennifer M. and Horvath, Miranda A.H. (Eds), *The Cambridge Handbook of Forensic Psychology*. Cambridge: Cambridge University Press, 2021.

Gutting, Gary. The Logic of Invention, pp. 221–234, in Thomas Nickles (Ed.), *Scientific Discovery, Logic, and Rationality*. Dordrecht: Springer, 1980.

Hacking, Ian. *Representing and Intervening: Introductory Topics in the Philosophy of Natural Sciences*. Cambridge: Cambridge University Press, 1983.

Halpern, Diane F. (2008). Is Intelligence Critical Thinking? Why We Need a New Definition of Intelligence, pp. 293–310, in Kyllonen, Patrick C., Roberts, Richard, D. and Stankov, Lazar (Eds). *Extending Intelligence: Enhancement and New Constructs*, New York, NY: Routledge, 2007.

Hammond, Kenneth R. *Human Judgment and Social Policy, Irreducible Uncertainty, Inevitable Error, Unavoidable Injustice*. New York: Oxford University Press, 1996.

Haney, Craig, Banks, Curtis, and Zimbardo, Phil. A Study of Prisoners and Guards in a Simulated Prison, pp. 19–34, in Michael Balfour (Ed.), *Theatre in Prison: Theory and Practice*. Bristol: Intellect, 2004.

Harley, Trevor. *The Psychology of Language: From Data to Theory*. Hove: Psychology Press, 2008.

Harris, David A. The Interaction and Relationship Between Prosecutors and Police Officers in the US and hos this Affects Police Reform Efforts. In Luna, Erik (Ed.). The Prosecutor in Transnational Perspective. New York: Oxford Academic, 2015.

Hasel, Lisa E. Evidentiary Independence—How Evidence Collected Early in an Investigation Influences the Collection and Interpretation of Additional Evidence, pp. 142–159, in Lynn Nadel and Walter P. Sinnott-Armstrong (Eds), *Memory and Law*. Oxford: Oxford University Press, 2013.

Hastie, Reid, Penrod, Steven D., and Pennington, Nancy. *Inside the Jury*. Cambridge, MA: Harvard University Press, 1983.

Herschel, John. *A Preliminary Discourse on the Study of Natural Philosophy*. Chicago, IL: University of Chicago Press, 2010.

Heuman, Lars. *Bevisbörda och beviskrav i tvistemål*. Stockholm: Norstedts Juridik, 2001.
Hogg, Michael A. and Vaughan, Graham M. *Essentials of Social Psychology*. Harlow: Person Education Limited, 2010.
Hogan. Michael J., Dwyer, Christopher P., Harney, Owen M., Noone, Chirs, Conway, Ronan J. Metacognitive Skill Development and Applied Systems Science: A Framework of Metacognitive Skills, Self-regulatory Functions and Real-World Applications. In Pena-Ayala, Alejandro (Ed.). Metacognition: Fundaments, Applications, and Trends (pp.75-106). Intelligent Systems Reference Library, vol 76. Cham, Springer, 2015.
Holland, Paul W. Probabilistic Causation Without Probability, pp. 257–292, in Paul Humphreys (Ed.), *Patrick Suppes: Scientific Philosopher*. Dordrecht: Kluwer, 1994.
Hollis, Martin and Lukes, Steven. *Rationality and Relativism*. Oxford: Basil Blackwell, 1982.
Hovland, Carl I. (1957). The Order of Presentation in Persuasion. New Haven
Horwich, Paul. *Probability and Evidence*. Cambridge: Cambridge University Press, 1982.
Howson, Colin and Urbach, Peter. *Scientific Reasoning: the Bayesian Approach*. La Salle, IL: Open Court Pub. Co, 1989.
Hoyningen-Huene, Paul. Context of Discovery and Context of Justification, pp. 119–131, in Jutta Schikore and Friedrich Steinle (Eds), *Revisiting Discovery and Justification: Historical and Philosophical Perspectives on the Context Distinction*. Dordrecht: Springer, 2006.
Hoyningen-Huene, Paul. On the Varieties of the Distinction between the Context of Discovery and the Context of Justification, pp. 11–16, in Jutta Schikore and Friedrich Steinle (Eds), *Revisiting Discovery and Justification*. Dordrecht: Springer, 2006.
Huber, George P. *Managerial Decision Making*. Glenview, IL: Scott, Foresman and Co, 1980.
Hull, Clark L. *A Behavior System: An Introduction to Behavior Theory Concerning the Individual Organism*. New Haven, CT: Yale University Press, 1952.
Hull, Clark L. (1951). Essentials of Behavior. New Haven: Yale University Press, 1951.
Hulley, Stephen, B. *Designing Clinical Research*, Wolters Kluwer, Philadelphia, 2007.
Hume, David. *A Treatise of Human Nature*. Cheapside: White-Hart, 1738.
Hume, David. *An Enquiry Concerning Human Understanding*. Oxford: Oxford University Press, 1999.
Hydén, Håkan. *Rättssociologi som rättsvetenskap*. Lund: Studentlitteratur, 2002.
Iskandar, Marwan. Rafiq Hariri and the Fate of Lebanon. London: Saqi, 2006.
Janis, Irving L. Crucial Decisions, Leadership in Policymaking and Crisis Managemen. New York: Free Press, 1989
Janis, Irvin L. *Groupthink*. Hopewell: Houghton Mifflin Company, 1982.
Jex, Steve M. and Britt, Thomas W. *Organizational Psychology: A Scientist-Practitioner Approach*. New York, NY: Wiley, 2014.
Jones, Morgan D. The Thinker's Toolkit, 14 Powerful Techniques for Problem Solving. New York: Three Rivers Press, 1995.
Juslin, Peter and Montgomery, Henry. *Judgment and Decision Making: Neo-Brunswikian and Process-tracing Approaches*, Mahwah, NJ: Erlbaum Associates, 1999.
Kahneman, Daniel. *Thinking, Fast and Slow*. New York, NY: Farrar, Straus and Girous, 2013.
Kahneman, Daniel and Frederick, Shane. A Model of Heuristic Judgment, pp. 267–294, in Keith Holyoak and Robert G. Morrison. *The Cambridge Handbook of Thinking and Reasoning*. Cambridge: Cambridge University Press, 2005.
Kahneman, Daniel, Sibony, Oliver, and Sunstein, Cass R. Noise—A Flaw in Human Judgment. Little, Brown Spark: Hachette Book Group. 2021
Kalat, James W. *Biological Psychology*. Wadsworth, MA: Cengage Learning, 2017.
Kaplan, Martin F., Wanshula, Tatiana and Zanna, Mark P. Time Pressure and Information Integration in Social Judgement: The Effect of Need for Structure, pp. 255–267, in Ola

Svensson and John Maule (Eds), *Time Pressure and Stress in Human Judgement and Decision Making*. New York, NY: Plenum Press, 1993.

Katz, Daniel and Kahn, Robert L. *The Social Psychology of Organizations*. New York, NY: Wiley, 1978.

Klahr, David. Designing Good Experiments to Test 'Bad' Hypotheses, pp. 355–402, in Jeffrey Shrager and Pat Langley (Eds), *Computational Models of Discovery and Theory Formation*. Berlin: Morgan Kaufmann Publishers: 2000.

Klamberg, Mark. *Evidence in International Criminal Trials: Confronting Legal Gaps and the Reconstruction of Disputed Events*. Leiden, Martinus Nijhoff Publishers, 2013.

Kleineman, Jan. Rättsdogmatisk metod, pp. 21–45, in Fredric Korling and Mauro Zamboni (Eds), *Juridisk metodlära*. Lund: Studentlitteratur, 2013.

Kolflaath, Eivind. *Bevisbedømmelse i praksis*. Bergen: Fagbokforlaget, 2013.

Koriat, Asher (2002). Metacognition Research: An Interim Report. In Perfect , Timothy, J. and Schwarts, Bennett, L. (Eds), *Applied Metacognition* (pp. 261–286). Cambridge: Cambridge University Press, 2002.

Kordig, Carl R. *Discovery and Justification*. Chicago, IL: University of Chicago Press, 1978.

Kronkvist, Ola. *Om sanningen skall fram: polisförhör med misstänkta för grova brott*. Växjö: Linnaeus University Press, 2013.

Kruglanski, Arie W. *Lay Epistemics and Human Knowledge: Cognitive and Motivational Bases*. New York, NY: Plenum Press, 1989.

Kruglanski, Arie W. Motivated Social Cognition: Principles of the Interface, pp. 493–520, in E. Tory Higgins (Ed.), *Social Psychology: Handbook of Basic Principles*. New York, NY: Guilford Press, 1996.

Kruglanski, Arie W. A Motivated Gatekeeper of Our Minds: Need-for-closure Effects on Interpersonal and Group Processes, pp. 465–496, in Richard M. Sorrentino and E. Tory Higgins (Eds), *Handbook of Motivation and Cognition: The Interpersonal Context*. New York, NY: Guilford, 2016.

Kruse, Corinna. The Social Life of Forensic Evidence. Oakland, Californa; University of California Press. 2015.

Kuhl, Julis. Volitional Aspects of Achievement Motivation and Learned Helplessness: Toward a Comprehensive Theory of Action Control, pp. 99–170, in Brendan A. Maher (Ed.), *Progress in Experimental Personality Research*. New York, NY: Academic Press, 1984.

Köehler, Hans and Subler, Jason. *The Lockerbie Trial: Documetns Related to the I.P.O. Observer Mission*. Vienna: International Progress Organization, 2002.

Leanza, Piero and Pridal, Ondrej. *The Right to a Fair Trial*. Alphen aan den Rijn: Wolters Kluver, 2014.

Leo, Richard A. *Police Interrogation and American Justice*. Cambridge, MA: Harvard University Press, 2008.

Leslie and Pope. *The Unintended Impact of Pretrial Detention on Case Outcomes: Evidence from NYC Arraignments*. 2016.

Lewicka, Maria. Is Hate Wiser than Love? Cognitive and Emotional Utilities in Decision Making, pp. 90–106, in Rob Ranyard, Ray Crozier and Ola Svenson (Eds), *Decision Making: Cognitive Models and Explanations*. London: Routledge & Kegan Paul, 1997.

Lewicka, Maria. Confirmation Bias, Cognitive Error or Adaptive Strategy of Action Control? pp. 233–258, in Miroslaw Kofta, Gifford Weary, and Grzegorz Sedek (Eds), *Personal Control in Action, Cognitive and Motivational Mechanism*. New York, NY: Plenum Press, 1998.

Lidén, Moa (2020). Child Soldier or Soldier? Estimating Age in Cases of Core International Crimes: Challenges and Opportunities, pp. 323–460, in Agirre, Xabier, Bergsmo, Morten, de Smet, Simon and Stahn, Carsten (Eds), *Quality Control in Criminal Investigations.* Torkel Opsahl Academic EPublisher, <https://www.legal-tools.org/doc/mty6cj/>.

Lidén, Moa (2020). Confirmation Bias in Investigations of Core International Crimes: Risk Factors and Quality Control Techniques, pp. 461–528, in Agirre, Xabier, Bergsmo, Morten, de Smet, Simon and Stahn, Carsten (Eds), *Quality Control in Criminal Investigation.* Torkel Opsahl Academic EPublisher, <https://www.legal-tools.org/doc/mty6cj/>.

Lidén, Moa (2022). 'That's Him!' Evaluating a Guilt Hypothesis in the Context of a Suspect Lineup, pp. 49–78, in Bystranowski, Piotr, Janik, Bartosz, and Próchnicki, Maciej (Eds). *Judicial Decision-making: Integrating Empirical and Theoretical Perspectives.* Springer, 2022.

Lidén, Moa (2023). The Time Variable in Relation to Insider Witnesses: Quantitative and Qualitative Analysis of ICC Cases, pp. 1–43, in Bergsmo, Morten (Ed.) *Using Old Evidence in Core International Crimes.* In press.

Lieberman, Matthew. Reflexive and Reflective Judgment Processes: A Social Cognitive Neuroscience Approach, pp. 44–60, in Joseph P. Forgas, Kipling D. Williams, and William von Hippel (Eds), *Social Judgments: Implicit and Explicit Processes.* Cambridge: Cambridge University Press, 2003

Lindberg, Gunnel. *Straffprocessuella tvångsmedel—när och hur får de användas?* Stockholm: Karnov Group, 2012.

Lindberg, Gunnel. *Rättegångsbalk* 1942:740. Stockholm: Karnov Group, 2018.

Lindblom, Per Henrik. *Process och exekution.* Uppsala: Iustus, 1990.

Lindblom, Per Henrik. Straffprocessens samhällsfunktioner, pp. 418–420, in Arne Fliflet (Ed.), *Festskrift till Hans Gammeltoft-Hansen.* Copenhagen, Jurist-og Okonomforbundets Forlag, 2004.

Lindell, Bengt. Ett rättsfall om resning och beviskravet i brottmål, pp. 431– 441, in Torbjörn Andersson and Bengt Lindell (Eds), *Festskrift till Per Henrik Lindblom.* Stockholm: Norstedts Juridik, 1992.

Lindell, Bengt. *Sakfrågor och rättsfrågor: en studie av gränser, skillnader och förhållanden mellan faktum och rätt.* Uppsala: Iustus Förlag, 1987.

Lindell, Bengt. *Multi-Criteria Analysis in Legal Reasoning.* Northampton: Edward Elgar Publishing, 2017.

Lindell, Bengt, Eklund, Hans, Asp, Petter, and Andersson, Torbjörn, *Straffprocessen.* Uppsala: Iustus Förlag, 2005.

Llewelyn, Karl. *Jurisprudence: Realism in Theory and Practice.* Chicago, IL: University of Chicago Press, 1962.

Luhmann, Niklas. *Rechtssoziologie.* Opladen: Westdeutscher Verlag, 1983.

Lundh, Lars-Gunnar, Montgomery, Henry, and Waern, Yvonne. *Kognitiv psykologi.* Lund: Studentlitteratur, 1992.

Lundstedt, Anders V. *Die Unwissenschaftlichkeit der Rechtswissenschaft.* Berlin: Grunewald, 1932.

Lushbaugh, Charles and Weston, Paul. *Criminal Investigation: Basic Perspectives.* London: Pearson, 2015

Luthans, Fred and Kreitner, Robert. *Organizational Behavior Modification and Beyond: an Operant and Social Learning Approach.* London: Scott Foresman & Co, 1984.

Luus, Elizabeth. *Eyewitness Confidence: Social Influence and Belief Perseverance.* Retrospective Theses and Dissertations, Iowa State University, 1991.

MacCormick, Neil. *Legal Reasoning and Legal Theory*. Oxford: Clarendon Press, 1978.
Mackay, Charles. *Extraordinary Popular Delusions and the Madness of Crowds*. Boston, MA: Page, 1932.
Magnani, Lorenzo, Carnielli, Walter, and Pizzi, Claudio. *Model-Based Reasoning in Science and Technology—Abduction, Logic, and Computation Discovery*. Berlin: Springer-Verlag, 2010.
Manzini, Vincenzo. *Trattato di Diritto Processuale penale*. Torino: *Unione tipografico-editrice torinese*, 1972.
Maslow, Abraham H. *A Theory of Human Motivation*. New York, NY: Merchant Books, 2013.
McGrath, Joseph E. *Groups: Interaction and Performance*. Englewood Cliffs, NJ: Prentice-Hall, 1984.
Meissner, Christian and Kassin, Saul M. You're Guilty, So Just Confess! Cognitive and Behavioral Confirmation Biases in the Interrogation Room. In G D Lassiter (Ed.). Interrogations, confessions and entrapment (pp. 85–106). Boston, MA: Springer, 2004.
Milne, Rebecca and Bull, Ray. Investigative Interviewing: Psychology and Practice. London: Wiley, 1999
Milgram, Stanley. *The Individual in a Social world: Essays and Experiments*. New York, NJ: McGraw-Hill, 1992.
Milikan, Robert A. *The Autobiography of Robert Milikan*. Whitefish: Literary Licensing, 2013.
Mill, John S. *A System of Logic: Ratiocinative and Inductive*. Cambridge: Cambridge University Press, 2011.
Miller, Neal E. *Selected Papers on Conflict, Displacement, Learning Drives & Theory*. Chicago: Aldine Atherton, 1971.
Miller, George A. Project Grammarama, pp. 190–197, in George A. Miller (Ed.), , *The Psychology of Communication: Seven Essays*. New York, NY: Basic Books, 1967.
Mitroff, Ian. *The Subjective Side of Science*. Amsterdam: Elsevier Scientific Publishing Co, 1974.
Mohr, Lawrence B. Rationality and Fitness: Two Broad Theories of Intentional Behavior, pp. 152–165, in Lawrence B. Mohr (Ed.), *The Causes of Human Behavior: Implications for Theory and Method in the Social Sciences*. Michigan, MI: University of Michigan Press, 1996.
Montgomery, Henry. From Cognition to Action: the Search for Dominance in Decision Making, pp. 23–49, in Henry Montgomery and Ola Svensson (Eds), *Process and Structure in Decision Making*. Oxford: John Wiley & Sons, 1989.
Nemeth, Charlan & Brown, Jeffrey. Three Images of the Trial: Their Implications for Psychological Research, pp. 19–38 in Sales, Bruce Dennis (Ed.), *Psychology in the Legal Process*. New York, NY: Pocket Books, 1977.
Nordh, Roberth. *Praktisk process, Tvångsmedel, kvarstad, häktning, beslag, husrannsakan m.m.* Uppsala: Iustus Förlag, 2007.
Nordh, Roberth and Lindblom, Per Henrik. *Kommentar till RB*. Uppsala: Iustus, 2001.
Nowak, Karol. *Oskyldighetspresumtionen*. Stockholm: Norstedts Juridik, 2003.
Nussbaum, Martha C. *Love's Knowledge: Essays on Philosophy and Literature*. New York, NY: Oxford University Press, 1990.
Oaksford, Mike and Chater, Nick. *Bayesian Rationality: The Probabilistic Approach to Human Reasoning*. Oxford: Oxford University Press, 2007.
Okasha, Samir. *Philosophy of Science: Very Short Introduction*. Oxford: Oxford University Press, 2016.
Osborne, Nikola K.P., Zajac, Rachel and Taylor, Michael C. (2014). Bloodstain Pattern Analysis and Contextual Bias, pp. 1–8 in Jamieson, Allan and Moenssens, Andre (Eds), *Wiley Encyclopedia of Forensic Science*. John Wiley & Sons, 2015.

Packer, Herbert L. *The Limits of the Criminal Sanction*. Stanford, CA: Stanford University Press, 1968.

Passer, Michael W. and Smith, Ronald E. *Psychology, the Science of Mind and Behavior*. New York, NY: McGraw-Hill Higher Education, 2011.

Payne-James, Jason and Simpson, Keith (2011). *Simpson's Forensic Medicine*. London: Hodder Arnold. 2011.

Pearson, Stephen and Watson, Richard (2010). *Digital Triage Forensics: Processing the Digital Crime Scene*. Rockland, Mass: Syngress, 2010.

Peczenik, Alexander. *Rätten och förnuftet: en lärobok i allmän rättslära*. Stockholm: Norstedts, 1986.

Peczenik, Alexander. *Vad är rätt? Om demokrati, rättssäkerhet, etik och juridisk argumentation*. Stockholm: Fritzes Förlag, 1995.

Pennington, Nancy and Hastie, Reid. The Story Model for Juror Decision Making, pp. 192–221, in R. Hastie (Ed.), *Inside the Juror: The Psychology of Juror Decision Making*. New York, NY: Cambridge University, 1993.

Peterson, Joseph L., Mihajlovic, Steven, and Gilliland, Michael. *Forensic Evidence and the Police: The Effects of Scientific Evidence*. Washington, DC: National Institute of Justice, 1984.

Pettersson, *Den Osannolika Mördaren—Skandiamannen och Mordet på Olof Palme*. Stockholm: Offside Press, 2018.

Pietrusewsky, Michael. Metric Analysis of Skeletal Remains: Methods and Applications. In Katzenberg, Anne and Saunders, Shelly R. *Biological Anthropology of the Human Skeleton* (pp. 487–533). Hoboken, New Jersey, 2008.

Plichta, Stacey Beth, Kelvin, Elizabeth A, Munro Barbara Hazard. *Munro's Statistical Methods for Health Care Research*. Philadelphia, PA: Wolters Kluwer, 2005.

Popper, Karl. *Conjectures and Refutations: the Growth of Scientific Knowledge*. London: Routledge, 2002.

Popper, Karl. *The Logic of Scientific Discovery*. New York, NY: Basic Books, 1968.

Posner, Richard. *How Judges Think*. London: Harvard University Press, 2008.

Powell, Martine B., Garry, Maryanne, and Brewer, Neil. Eyewitness Testimony, pp. 1–42, in Ian Freckelton and Hugh Selby (Eds), *Expert Evidence*. Sydney: Thompson Reuters, 2009.

Pratkanis, Anthony R. *Attitude Structure and Function*. London: Psychology Press, 1989.

Prislin, Radmila and Wood, Wendy. Social Influence in Attitudes and Attitude Change, pp. 671–706, in Dolores Albaraccín, Blair T. Johnson, and Mark P. Zanna (Eds), *The Handbook of Attitudes*. Hillsdale, NJ: Erlbaum, 2005.

Proctor, Robert W. and Capaldi, Elisabeth. *Why Science Matters: Understanding the Methods of Psychological Research*. Malden: Blackwell Publishing, 2005.

Pyszczynski, Tom and Greenberg, Jeff. Toward an Integration of Cognitive and Motivational Perspectives on Social Inference: A Biased Hypothesis-Testing Model, pp. 297–340, in Leonard Berkowitz (Ed.), *Advances in Experimental Social Psychology*. New York, NY: Academic Press, 1987.

Rebelius, Anna. *Investigator Bias: Contextual Influences on the Assessment of Criminal Evidence*. Gothenburg: University of Gothenburg, 2011.

Reeve, John M. *Understanding Motivation and Emotion*. Hoboken, New Jersey: John Wiley & Sons Inc, 2015.

Reichenbach, Hans. *Experience and Prediction: an Analysis of the Foundations and Structure of Knowledge*. Chicago, IL: University of Chicago Press, 1938.

Richardson, Virginia. The Role of Attitudes and Beliefs in Learning to Teach, pp. 102–119. In Sikula, John (Ed.), *Handbook of Research on Teacher Education*. New York: McMillan, 2016.

Roach, Jason and Pease, Ken. Necropsies and the Cold Case, pp. 327–348, in Rossmo, Kim D. (Ed.), *Criminal Investigative Failures*. Boca Raton, FL: CRC Press, 2006.
Ross, Alf. *Om ret og retferdighed*. Copenhagen: Nyt nordisk Forlag, 1971.
Rossmo, D. Kim. *Criminal Investigative Failures*. London: Taylor and Francis Group, 2009.
Rothstein, Hannah R., Sutton, Alexander J., and Borenstein, Michael. *Publication Bias in Meta-Analysis: Prevention, Assessment and Adjustments*. West Sussex: John Wiley & Sons 2005
Russo, J. Edward and Schoemaker, Paul J.H. *Decision Traps: Ten Barriers to Brilliant Decision-Making and How to Overcome Them*. New York, NY: Simon & Schutzer, 1998.
Sachs, Albie. *The Strange Alchemy of Life and Law*. Oxford: Oxford University Press, 2011.
Samuelsson, Joel. Hermeneutik, pp. 371–392, in Fredric Korling and Mauro Zamboni (Eds), *Juridisk metodlära*. Lund: Studentlitteratur, 2013.
Schaffner, Kenneth F. *Discovery and Explanation in Biology and Medicine*. Chicago, IL: University of Chicago Press, 1993.
Schelin, Lena. *Bevisvärdering av utsagor i brottmål*, Stockholm: Norstedts juridik, 2007.
Schultheiss. Oliver C. and Pang, Joyce S. (2007). Measuring Implicit Motives. In Robins, Richard W., Fraley, Chirs R., & Krueger, Robert F. (Eds), Handbook of Research Methods in Personality Psychology (pp. 322–344). New York: The Guilford Press, 2007
Scheck, Barry, Neufeld, Peter J, and Dwyer, Jim (2000). Actual Innocence: Five Days to Execution and other Dispatches from the Wrongly Convicted. New York: Doubleday, 2000
Schmidgen, Henning and Custance, Gloria. *Bruno Latour in Pieces: An Intellectual Biography*. New York, NY: Fordham University Press, 2015.
Schnurbush, Kim E (2012). *Wrongful Convictions: A Conceptual Framework for Understanding Police and Prosecutor Misconduct*. Doctor of Philosophy, College of Criminal Justice, May 2012, Houston State University. Huntsville, Texas.
Schönteich, Martin. *Global Pretrial Detention Use: A Cross-National Analysis*. 2018. CUNY Academic works. <https://academicworks.cuny.edu/gc_etds/2918>.
Schultheiss, Oliver C. and Pang, Joyce S. Measuring Implicit Motives, pp. 322–344, in Richard W. Robins, R. Chris Fraley, and Robert F. Krueger (Eds), *Handbook of Research Methods in Personality Psychology*. New York, NY: Guilford Press, 2007.
Schum, David A. Argument Structuring and Evidence Evaluation, pp. 175–191, in Reid Hastie (Ed.), *Inside the Juror: The Psychology of Juror Decision Making*. New York, NY: Cambridge University Press, 1993.
Schunn, Christian D. and Klahr, David. Other vs. Self-generated Hypotheses in Scientific Discovery, pp. 365–378, in Walter Kintsch (Ed.). *Proceedings of the 15th Annual Conference of the Cognitive Science Society*. Colorado, CO: Psychology Press, 1993.
Schneider, Stephen. *Racketeer Influenced and Corrupt Organizations Act (RICO)*. Encyclopedia Britannica, 2015.
Schönteich, Martin (2018). *Global Pretrial Detention Use: A Cross-National Analysis*. City University of New York, 2018.
Sekuler, Robert and Blake, Randolph. (2002). *Perception*. New York, NY: McGraw-Hill, 2002.
Shadish, William R., Cook, Thomas D., and Campbell, Donald T. *Experimental and Quasi-Experimental Designs for Generalized Causal Inference*. Wadsworth, MA: Cengage Learning, 2002.
Sherif, Muzafer. *The Psychology of Social Norms*. New York, NY: Harper and Brothers, 1936.
Sherif, Muzafer and Hovland, Carl. *Social Judgment. Assimilation and contrast effects in communication and attitude change*. New Haven, CT: Yale University Press, 1961.

Simon, Herbert. From Substantive to Procedural Rationality, pp. 129–148, in Timothy J. Kastelein, Simon Kuipers, and Willem Nijenhuis (Eds), *25 Years of Economic Theory: Retrospect and Prospect*. Leiden: Wolters-Noordhoof, 1976.

Simon, Herbert. *Models of Man: Social and Rational-Mathematical Essays on Rational Human Behavior in a Social Setting*. New York. NY: Wiley, 1957.

Simpson, John A. *The Oxford Dictionary of Quotations*. Oxford: Oxford University Press, 1979.

Slife, Brent D. and Williams, Richard N. *What's Behind the Research? Discovering Hidden Assumptions in the Behavioral Sciences*. London: Sage Publications 1995.

Smith, Peter, Bond, Michael H., and Kagitçibaşi, Çigdem. *Understanding Social Psychology Across Cultures: Living and Working in a Changing World*. London: Sage, 2006.

Smits, Jan. *The Mind and Method of the Legal Academic*. Cheltenham: Edward Elgar Publishing, 2012.

Snyder, Mark. When Belief Creates Reality, pp. 247–305, in L. Berkowitz (Ed.), *Advances in Experimental Social Psychology*. San Diego, CA: Academic Press, 1984.

Söderberg, Boel. *Svartalf och sotpacka, folktro och häxjakt i 1600-talets Sverige*. Lidköping: Ekelunds Förlag 1999.

Strömholm, Stig. *Rätt, rättskällor och rättstillämpning: En lärobok i allmän rättslära*. Stockholm: Norstedts Juridik, 1996.

Strömwall, Leif, Granhag, Pär Anders and Hartwig, Maria. *Practitioners' Beliefs about Deception*, pp. 229–250, in Pär Anders Granhag and Leif Strömwall, *The Detection of Deception in Forensic Contexts*, Cambridge: Cambridge University Press, 2004.

Ställvik, Olof. *Domarrollen, Rättsregler, yrkeskultur och ideal*. Uppsala: Uppsala Universitet, 2009.

Sutto, Raul, Trueman, Keith, and Moran, Christopher. *Crime Scene Management: Scene Specific Methods*. Oxford: Wiley- Blackwell, 2017.

Svensson, Ola. Values, Affect, and Processes in Human Decision Making: A Differentiation and Consolidation Theory Perspective, pp. 287–326, in Sandra L. Schneider and James Schanteu (Eds), *Emerging Perspectives on Judgment and Decision Research*. Cambridge: Cambridge University Press, 2003.

Svensson, Ola. Pre-and Post-Decision Construction of Preferences: Differentiation and Consolidation, pp. 356–371, in Sarah Lichtenstein and Paul Slovic (Eds), *The Construction of Preference*. New York, NY: Cambridge University Press, 2006.

Svensson, Ola and Hill, Teci. Turning Prior Disadvantages into Advantages, Differentiation and Consolidation in Real-Life Decision Making, pp. 218–235, in Rob Ranyard, W. Ray Crozier, and Ola Svensson (Eds), *Decision Making: Cognitive Models and Explanations*. London: Routledge, 1998.

Swanson. Lee H. (2015). Intelligence, Working Memory, and Learning Disabilities, pp. 175–196. In Papadopoulos, Timothy, Parrila, Rauno, Kirby, John R. (Eds), *Cognition, Intelligence, and Achievement: A Tribute to J*. London: Elsevier Academic Press, 2015.

Tajfel, Henri. Interpersonal Behaviour and Intergroup Behaviour, pp. 27–60, in Henri Tajfel (Ed.), *Differentiation Between Social Groups: Studies in the Social Psychology of Intergroup Relations*. London: Academic Press, 1978.

Tajfel, Henri. *Human Groups and Social Categories: Studies in Social Psychology*. Cambridge: Cambridge University Press, 1981.

Tajfel, Henri and Turner, John. An Integrative Theory of Intergroup Conflict, pp. 33–47, in William G. Austin and Stephen Worchel (Eds), *The Social Psychology of Intergroup Relations*. Monterey, CA: Brooks/Cole, 1979.

Tajfel, Henri and Turner, John. An Integrative Theory of Intergroup Conflict, pp. 33–47, in Michael A. Hogg and Dominic Abrams (Eds), *Key Readings in Social Psychology. Intergroup Relations: Essential Readings*. New York, NY: Psychology Press, 2001.

Tak, Peter J. (2012). The Dutch Prosecutor, in Luna, Erik & Wade, Marianne (Eds), The Prosecutor in Transnational Perspective. New York: Oxford Academic, 2012.

Taylor, Shelley E., Peplau, Letitie A., and Sears, David O. *Social Psychology*. Upper Saddle River, NJ: Prentice Hall, 2003.

Tegler Jerselius, Kristina. *Den stora häxdansen, vidskepelse, väckelse och vetande i Gagnef 1858*. Uppsala: Acta Universitatis Upsaliensis, 2003.

Thiblin, Ingemar. *Rättsmedicin i teori och praktik—en guide för läkare och jurister*. Lund: Studentlitteratur, 2014.

Tindale, Scott. Decision Errors Made by Individuals and Groups, pp. 109–124, in John N. Castellan (Ed.), *Individual and Group Decision Making: Current Issues*. Hillsdale, NJ: Lawrence Erlbaum Associates, 1993.

Tokariuk, Olga. *Battle of Narratives: Kremlin Disinformation in the Vitaliy Markiv Case in Italy*. Ukraine Crisis Media Center, 2021.

Todd, Peter M. and Gigerenzer, Gerd. *Ecological Rationality: Intelligence in the World*. Oxford: Oxford University Press, 2012.

Triandis, Harry C. Cross-Cultural Studies of Individualism and Collectivism, pp. 41–133, in John J. Berman (Ed.), *Nebraska Symposium on Motivation 1989: Cross Cultural Perspective*. Lincoln, NE: University of Nebraska Press, 1990.

Tuerkheimer, Deborah. *Flawed Convictions: 'Shaken Baby Syndrome' and the Inertia of Injustice*. Oxford: Oxford University Press, 2014.

Turner, John C. Social Categorization and the Self-Concept: A Social Cognitive Theory of Group Behavior, pp. 77–122, in Edward J. Lawler (Ed.), *Advances in Group Processes*. Greenwich: JAI Press, 1985.

Twining, William. *Karl Llewelyn and The Realist Movement*. Cambridge: Cambridge University Press, 2012.

van Koppen, Peter J. Blundering Justice, pp. 207–228, in Richard N. Kocsis (Ed.), *Serial Murder and the Psychology of Violent Crimes*. Totowa, New Jersey: Humana Press, 2008.

Vernon Gordon, Rose (2004). Social Cognition and Section 12 of the Canada Evidence Act: Can Jurors 'Properly' use Criminal Record Evidence? Simon Fraser University, 2013

Vinchur, Andrew J. and Koppes, Laura. A Historical Survey of Research and Practice in Industrial and Organizational Psychology, pp. 3–36, in Sheldon, Zedeck (Ed.), *APA Handbook of Industrial and Organizational Psychology. Building and Developing the Organization*. Washington, DC: American Psychological Association, 2011.

Visholm, Steen. *Organisationspsykologi och psykodynamisk systemteori*. Copenhagen: Hans Reitzels FØrlag, 2004.

Vrij, Aldert. *Detecting Lies and Deceit, Pitfalls and Oppurtunities*. Chichester: John Wiley & Sons, 2008.

Wagenaar, Willem Albert. *Identifying Ivan—A Case Study in Legal Psychology*, London: Harvester Wheatsheaf, 1988.

Wagenaar, Willem A. Anchored Narratives: A Theory of Judicial Reasoning, and its Consequences, pp. 267–286, in G. Davies (Ed.), *Psychology, Law, and Criminal Justice: International Developments in Research and Practice*. Oxford: Walter De Gruyter, 1995.

Wagenaar, Willem A., van Koppen, Peter J., and Crombag, Hans F. M. *Anchored Narratives: the Psychology of Criminal Evidence*. New York, NY: St. Martin's Press, 1993.

Wahlgren, Peter. *Automatiserade juridiska beslut*, pp. 395–420, in Fredric Korling and Mauro Zamboni (Eds), *Juridisk metodlära*. Lund: Studentlitteratur 2013.
Wason, Peter C. and Johnson-Laird, Philip N. *Psychology of Reasoning: Structure and Content*. Cambridge, MA: Harvard University Press, 1972.
Wasserstrom, Richard A. *The Judicial Decision: Toward a Theory of Legal Justification*. Stanford, CA: Stanford University Press, 1961.
Waterhouse, Genevieve, Ridley, Anne, Wilcock, Rachel, and Bull, Ray (2016). Investigative Interviewing in England and Wales: Adults, Children and the Provision of Support for Child Witnesses. In Walsh, David, Oburgh, Gavin, Redlich, Allison, Myklebust, Trond (Eds), International Developments and Practices in Investigative Interviewing and Interogation (pp. 112–129). London: Routledge, 2015.
Weigend, Thomas (2019). The Potential to Secure a Fair Trial Through Evidence Exclusion: A German Perspective. In Gless Richter (Eds). Do Exclusionary Rules Ensure a Fair Trial? (pp. 61–92). Cham: Ius Gentium: Comparative Perspectives on Law and Justice, 2019.
Welamson. Lars and Munck, Johan. *Rättegång VI: Processen i hovrätt och Högsta domstolen*. Stockholm: Wolters Kluwer, 2016.
Wickens, Thomas D. *Elementary Signal Detection Theory*. Oxford: Oxford University Press, 2001.
Winburn, Allysha Powanda, Boyd, C., Clifford, Boyd, Donna C. (2018). Subjective with a Capital S? Issues of Objectivity in Forensic Anthropology. In Boyd, Donna C. and Boyd, Clifford (Eds) *Forensic Anthropology: Theoretical Framework and Scientific Basis* (pp. 21–37). London: Wiley, 2018.
White, Peter. Crime Scene to Court, The Essentials of Forensic Science. Cambridge: Royal Society of Chemistry, 1949.
van Dijk and van Hoof. Theory and Practice of the European Convention on Human Rights. Antwerpen: Intersentia, 2006.
Winter, Steven L. *A Clearing in the Forest: Law, Life and Mind*. Chicago, IL: University of Chicago Press, 2003.
Wróblewski, Jerzy. *Meaning and Truth in Judicial Decision Making*. Helsinki: Kluwer Academic Publishers, 1983.
Wroblewski, Jerzy. *The Judicial Application of Law*. Dordrecht: Kluwer Academic Publishers, 1992.
Wróblewski, Jerzy. *Ontology, Epistemology and Methodology of Law*. Dordrecht: Kluwer Academic Publishers, 1992.
Wyer, Robert S. and Albaraccín, Dolores, The Origins and Structure of Beliefs and Goals, pp. 273–322, in Dolores Albaraccín, Blair T. Johnson, and Mark P. Zanna (Eds), *Handbook of Attitudes*. Hillsdale, NJ: Erlbaum, 2005.
Zamboni, Mauro. *Law and Politics, a Dilemma for Contemporary Legal Theory*. Berlin: Springer-Verlag, 2008.
Zamboni, Mauro. *The Policy of Law: a Legal Theoretical Framework*. Stockholm: Stockholm University, 2004.
Zimbardo, Philip, Haney, Craig, Banks, William, and Jaffe, Adi. The Psychology of Imprisonment, pp. 230–235, in John C. Brigham (Ed.), *Contemporary Issues in Social Psychology*. Monterey, CA: Brooks/Cole, 1982.
Zimbardo, Philip, Maslach, Christina, and Haney, Craig. Reflections on the Stanford Prison Experiment: Genesis, Transformations, Consequences, pp. 193–237, in Thomas Blass (Ed.), *Obedience to Authority: Current Perspectives on the Milgram Paradigm*. Mahwah, NJ: Erlbaum, 2000.

Zuckerman, Adrian A.S. Bias and Suggestibility: Is There an Alternative to the Right to Silence?, pp. 117–140, in Derek Morgan and Geoffrey M. Stephenson (Eds), *Suspicion and Silence–The Right to Silence in Criminal Investigations*. London: Blackstone Press Ltd, 1994.

ii) Articles

Abdullah, Fizan, Nuernberg, Amy, and Rabinovici, Reuven. Self-inflicted Abdominal Stab Wounds. *International Journal of the Care of the Injured*, 34 (2003), 35–39.

Abtahi, Hirad, Ogwuma, Odo, and Young, Rebecca. The Composition of Judicial Benches, Disqualification and Excusal of Judges at the International Criminal Court. *Journal of International Criminal Justice*, 11(2) (2013): pp. 379–398.

Adams-Quackenbush, Nicole M., Horselenberg, Robert, and van Koppen, Peter J. Where Bias Begins: A Snapshot of Police Officers' Beliefs About Factors that Influence the Investigative Interview with Suspects. *Journal of Police and Criminal Psychology*, 34(4) (2018), pp. 373–380.

Adelman, James S., Marquis, Suzanne J., and Sabatos-DeVito, Maura G. Letters in Words are Read Simultaneously, not in Left-to-Rights Sequence. *Psychological Science*, 21(12) (2010): pp. 1799–1801.

Adelson, Beth. When Novices Surpass Experts: The Difficulty of a Task May Increase with Expertise. *Journal of Experimental Psychology*, 10(3) (1984): pp. 483–495.

Agirre Aranburu, Xabier. Sexual Violence beyond Reasonable Doubt: Using Pattern Evidence and Analysis for International Cases. *Leiden Journal of International Law*, 23 (2010): pp. 609–627.

Alceste, Fabiana, Jones, Kristyn A., Kassin, Saul M, and McAuliff, Bradley D. Facts Only the Perpetrator Could Have Known? A Study of Contamination in Mock Crime Interrogations. *Law and Human Behavior*, 44(2) (2020): pp. 128–142.

Alesina, Alberto and La Ferrara, Eliana. A Test of Racial Bias in Capital Sentencing. *The American Economic Review*, 104(11) (2014): pp. 3397–3433.

Alison, Laurence, Smith, Matthew D., and Morgan, Keith. Intepreting the Accuracy of Offender Profiles. *Psychology, Crime, and Law*, 9 (2003): pp. 185–195.

Alladio, Eugenio, Omedei, Monica, Sisana, Selena, D'Amico, Giuseppina, Caneparo, Denise, Vicenti, Marco & Garofano, Paolo. DNA Mixtures Interpretation—A Proof of Concept Multi-software Comparison Highlighting Different Probabilistic Methods' Performances on Challenging Samples. *Forensic Science International: Genetics*, 37 (2018): pp. 143–150.

Andersson, Jacob and Thiblin, Ingemar. National Study Shows that Abusive Head Trauma in Sweden was at least 10 Times Lower than in Other Western Countries. *Acta Pediatrica*, 107 (2018): pp. 477–483.

Andersson, Simon and Hopman, Suus. Rätt till försvarare före polisförhöret. Nya domar från Europadomstolen kräver lagändringar i Sverige. *Juridisk Tidsskrift*, 4 (2010/2011): pp. 795–820.

Andreassen, Nancy C. Brain Imaging: Applications in Psychiatry. *Science*, 239 (1998): pp. 1381–1388.

Antrobus, Emma and Pilotto, Andrew. Improving Forensic Responses to Residential Burglaries: Results of a Randomized Controlled Field Trial. *Journal of Experimental Criminology*, 12 (2016): pp. 319–345.

Appleby, Sara C., Hasel, Lisa E., and Kassin, Saul, M. Police-induced Confessions: An Empirical Analysis of their Content and Impact. *Psychology, Crime & Law*, 19(2) (2013), pp. 111–128.

Arkes, Hal, R. The Psychology of Waste. *Journal of Behavioral Decision Making, 9* (1996): pp. 213–224.
Arkes, Hal R. and Blumer, Catherine. The Psychology of Sunk Cost. *Organizational Behavior and Human Decision Processes, 35* (1985): pp. 125–140.
Asch, Solomon. Opinions and Social Pressure. *Scientific American, 19* (1955): pp. 31–35.
Ashton, Michael C., Lee, Kibeom, Vernon, Philip A., & Jang, Kerry L. Fluid Intelligence, Crystallized Intelligence, and the Openness/Intellect Factor, *Journal of Research in Personality, 34*(2) (2000): pp. 198–207.
Ask, Karl and Granhag, Pär Anders. Motivational Sources of Confirmation Bias in Criminal Investigations: The Need for Cognitive Closure. *Journal of Investigative Psychology and Offender Profiling, 2* (2005): pp. 43–63.
Ask, Karl and Granhag, Pär Anders. Hot Cognition in Investigative Judgments: The Differential Influence of Anger and Sadness. *Law and Human Behavior, 31* (2007): pp. 537–551.
Ask, Karl and Granhag, Pär Anders. Motivational Bias in Criminal Investigators' Judgments of Witness Reliability. *Journal of Applied Social Psychology, 37* (2007): pp. 561–591.
Ask, Karl and Landström, Sara. Why Emotions Matter: Expectancy Violation and Affective Response Mediate the Emotional Victim Effect. *Law and Human Behavior, 34*(5) (2010): pp. 392–401.
Ask, Karl, Granhag, Pär Anders, and Rebelius, Anna. Investigators under Influence: How Social Norms Activate Goal-Directed Processing of Criminal Evidence. *Applied Cognitive Psychology, 25* (2011): pp. 548–553.
Ask, Karl, Rebelius, Anna, and Granhag, Pär Anders. The Elasticity of Criminal Evidence: a Moderator of Investigator bias. *Applied Cognitive Psychology, 22* (2008): pp. 1245–1259.
Arkes, Hal R. The Psychology of Waste. *Journal of Behavioral Decision Making, 9* (1996): pp. 213–224.
Arkes, Hal R. and Ayton, Peter. The Sunk Cost and Concorde Effects: Are Humans Less Rational than Lower Animals? *Psychological Bulletin, 125* (1999): pp. 591–600.
Arkes, Hal R. and Blumer, Catherine. The Psychology of Sunk Cost. *Organizational Behavior and Human Decision Processes, 35* (1985): pp. 125–140.
Atkinson, Richard C. and Shiffrin, Richard M. Human Memory: a Proposed System and Its Control Processes. *Psychology of Learning and Motivation, 2* (1968): pp. 89–195.
Austin, James T. and Vancouver, Jeffrey B. Goal-Setting Theory, Goal Constructs in Psychology: Structure, Process, and Content. *Psychological Bulletin, 120* (1996): pp. 338–375.
Awan, Imran. 'I Never Did Anything Wrong'—Trojan Horse: A Qualitative Study Uncovering the impact in Birmingham. *British Journal of Sociology of Education*, 39 (2018), pp. 197–211.
Babcock, Linda and Loewenstein, George. Explaining Bargaining Impasse: The Role of Self-Serving Biases. *Journal of Economic Perspectives, 11*(1) (1997), pp. 109–126.
Baddeley, Alan D. Is Working Memory Still Working? *European Psychologist, 7* (2002): pp. 851–864.
Baechler, Simon. Study of Criteria Influencing the Success Rate of DNA Swabs in Operational Conditions: A Contribution to an Evidence-based Approach to Crime Scene Investigation and Triage. *Forensic Science International: Genetics, 20* (2016): pp. 130–139.
Baldwin, Fletcher N. Racketeer Influenced and Corrupt Organizations Act (RICO) and the Mafia Must Now Welcome Organizational Crime. *Journal of Financial Crime, 17*(4) (2010): pp. 404–416.

Bales, Scott. Turning the Microscope Back on Forensic Scientists. *Litigation*, 26(2) (2000): pp. 51–58.

Balzan, Ryan, Delfabbro, Paul, Galletly, Cherrie, and Woodward, Todd. Confirmation Biases across the Psychosis Continuum: The Contribution of Hypersalient Evidence-Hypothesis Matches. *British Journal of Clinical Psychology*, 52 (2013): pp. 53–69.

Baron, Robert S., Vandello, Joseph A., and Brunsman, Bethany. The Forgotten Variable in Conformity Research: Impact of Task Importance on Social Influence. *Journal of Personality and Social Psychology*, 71 (1996): pp. 915–927.

Barros, Gustavo. Herbert A. Simon and the Concept of Rationality: Boundaries and Procedures. *Brazilian Journal of Political Economy*, 30 (2010): pp. 455–472.

Barry, Carly and Halfmann, Kameko. The Effect of Mindset on Decision-making. *Journal of Integrated Social Sciences*, 6(1) (2016): pp. 49–74

Bates, Timothy C. and Shieles, Alexandra. Crystallized Intelligence as a Product of Speed and Drive for Experience: The Relationship of Inspection Time and Openness to G and Gc. *Intelligence*, 31(3) (2003): pp. 275–287.

Batson, Daniel C. Rational Processing or Rationalization? The Effect of Disconfirming Information on a Stated Religious Belief. *Journal of Personality and Social Psychology*, 32(1) (1975): pp. 176–184.

Batts, Anthony W., deLone, Maddy, and Stephens, Darrel W. Policing and Wrongful Convictions. *New Perspectives in Policing*, August (2014): pp. 1–31.

Bayen, Ute J., Nakamura, Glenn, V., Dupuis, Susan & Yang, Chin-Lung (2000). The Use of Schematic Knowledge about Sources in Source Monitoring. *Memory & Cognition*, 28(3), pp. 480–500.

Bechara, Antoine and Damasio, Antonio R. The Somatic Marker Hypothesis: A Neural Theory of Economic Decision. *Games and Economic Behavior*, 52 (2005): pp. 336–372.

Bedau, Hugo Adam and Radelet, Michael L. Miscarriages of Justice in Potentially Capital Cases. *Stanford Law Review*, 40(1) (1987): pp. 21–179.

Beeler, Jesse D. and Hunton, James E. The Influence of Compensation Method and Disclosure Level on Information Search Strategy and Escalation of Commitment. *Journal of Behavioral Decision Making*, 10 (1997): pp. 77–91.

Behrman, Bruce W. and Richards, Regina E. Suspect/Foil Identification in Actual Crimes and in the Laboratory: A Reality Monitoring Analysis. *Law and Human Behavior*, 29 (2005): pp. 279–301.

Ben-Ezra, Menachem, Mahat-samir, Michal, Leshem, Elazar, Goodwin, Robin & Kaniasty, Krzysztof. Psychological Reactions Following the November 2015 Paris Attacks: Perceiving the World as Unjust and Unsafe. *The Journal of Clinical Psychiatry*, 78(3) (2017): pp. 360–361.

Benforado, Adam. The Body of the Mind: Embodied Cognition, Law and Justice. *Saint Louis University Law Journal*, 54 (2010): pp. 1185–1216.

Bengtsson, Bertil. Om rättsvetenskapen som rättskälla. *Tidskrift for Rettsvitenskap*, 115 (2002): pp. 14–32.

Bentall, Richard P. and Young, Heather F. Sensible Hypothesis Testing in Deluded, Depressed and Normal Subjects. *The British Journal of Psychiatry*, 168 (1996): pp. 372–375.

Benton, Tanja Rapus, Ross, David F, Bradshaw, Emily, Thomas, W. Neil. Bradshaw, Gregory S. Eyewitness Memory is Still Not Common Sense: Comparing Jurors, Judges and Law Enforcement to Eyewitness Experts. *Applied Cognitive Psychology*, 20(1) (2006): pp. 115–129.

Berkowitz, Leonard. Evil is More than Banal: Situationism and the Concept of Evil. *Personality and Social Psychology Review*, 3 (1999): pp. 246–253.

Bernstein, David E. Junk Science in the United States and the Commonwealth. *The Yale Journal of International Law*, 21(1) (1996): p. 123.
Berridge, Kent C. Evolving Concepts of Emotion and Motivation. *Frontiers in Psychology*, 9 (2018): p. 1647.
Betz, Peter, Tutsch-Bauer, Edith and Eisenmenger, Wolfgang. Tentative Injuries in a Homicide. *American Journal of Medical Pathology*, 16(3) (1995): pp. 246–248.
Bielen, Samantha and Grajzl, Peter. Gender-based Judicial Ingroup Bias in Sex Crime Sentencing: Evidence from Belgium. *International Journal of Law, Crime and Justice*, 62 (2020): pp. 1–13.
Blanck, Peter David, Rosenthal, Robert and Hazzard Cordell, LaDoris. The Appearance of Justice: Judges' Verbal and Nonverbal Behavior in Criminal Trials, pp. 89–164. *Stanford Law Review*, 38(1) (1985), pp. 89–164.
Blanford, Nicholas. Killing Mr Lebanon: The Assassination of Rafik Hariri and its Impact of the Middle East. *Journal of Peace Research*, 44(4) (2006): pp. 178–179.
Blakey, Robert. RICO: The Genesis of an Idea. *Trends in Organized Crime*, 9(4) (2006), pp. 8–34.
Bodenhausen, Galen V. Stereotypes as Judgmental Heuristics: Evidence of Circadian Variations in Discrimination. *Psychological Science*, 1 (1990): pp. 319–322
Bond, Charles F. and DePaulo, Bella M. Accuracy of Deception Judgments. *Personality and Social Psychology Review*, 10 (2006): pp. 214–234.
Bond, Rod and Smith, Peter B. Culture and Conformity: A Meta-Analysis of Studies Using Asch's (1952b, 1956) Line Judgment Task. *Psychological Bulletin*, 119 (1996): pp. 111–137.
Bogaard, Glynis, Meijer, Ewout H, Vrij, Aldert, Broers, Nick J. and Merkelbach, Harald. Contextual Bias in Verbal Credibility Assessment: Criteria-Based Content Analysis, Reality Monitoring and Scientific Content Analysis. *Applied Cognitive Psychology*, 28(1) (2014): pp. 79–90.
Booth, Tracey and Townsley, Lesley. The Process is the Punishment: The Case of Bail in New South Wales. *Current Issues in Criminal Justice*, 21(1) (2009): pp. 41–58.
Borden, Kenneth S. and Horowitz, Irwin. Information Processing in Joined and Severed Trials. *Journal of Applied Social Psychology*, 13 (1983): pp. 351–370.
Bosco, Robert M. The Assassination of Rafik Hariri: Foreign Policy Perspectives. *International Political Science Review*, 30(4) (2009): pp. 349–361.
Bowling, Benjamin. How Police Stop Defines Race and Citizenship. *Policing and Society*, 28 (2018): pp. 1–4.
Brainerd, Charles J. and Reyna, Valerie F. Mere Memory Testing Creates False Memories in Children. *Developmental Psychology*, 32 (1996): pp. 467–478.
Brett, Allan S., Phillips, M., and Beary, John F. Psychophysiology: Predictive Power of the Polygraph: Can the 'Lie Detector' Really Detect Liars? *The Lancet*, 327 (1986): pp. 544–547.
Brown, Donald R. Stimulus-Similarity and the Anchoring of Subjective Scales. *The American Journal of Psychology*, 66 (1953): pp. 199–214.
Brunelle, Erica, Huynh, Crystal, Alin, Eden, Eldridge, Morgan, Minh Le, Anh, Halámková, Lenka, and Halámek, Jan. Fingerprint Analysis: Moving Toward Multiattribute Determination via Individual Markers. *Analytical Chemistry*, 90 (2018): pp. 980–987.
Bruner, Jerome S. and Goodman, Cecile C. Value and Need as Organizing Factors in Perception. *Journal of Abnormal and Social Psychology*, 42 (1947): pp. 33–44.
Bruun, Niklas and Wilhelmsson, Thomas. Rätten, moralen och det juridiska paradigmet. *Svensk Juristidning* 68 (1983): pp. 701–713.

Brycz, Hanna, Wyszomirksa-Góra, Magdalena, Bar-Tal, Yoram, and Wisniewski, Piotr. The Effect of Metacognitive Self on Confirmation bias Revealed in Relation to Community and Competence. *Polish Psychological Bulletin, 45* (2014): pp. 306–311.

Buchy, Lisa, Woodward, Todd S., and Liotti, Mario. A Cognitive Bias Against Disconfirmatory Evidence (BADE) is Associated with Schizotypy. *Schizophrenia Research, 90* (2007): pp. 334–337.

Buratti, Sandra and Allwood, Carl Martin. The Accuracy of Meta-metacognitive Judgments: Regulating the Realism of Confidence. *Cognitive Processing, 13*(3) (2012): pp. 243–253.

Buratti, Sandra, Allwood, Carl Martin, and Kleitman, Sabine. First-and Second-order Metacognitive Judgments of Semantic Memory Reports: The Influence of Personality Traits and Cognitive Styles. *Metacognition and Learning, 8*(1) (2013): pp. 79–102.

Burger, Jerry M. Replicating Milgram: Would People Still Obey Today? *American Psychologist, 61* (2009): pp. 1–11.

Burger, Jerry M., Girgis, Zackary, M., and Manning, Caroline C. In Their Own Words: Explaining the Obedience to Authority Through an Examination of the Participants' Comments. *Social Psychological and Personality Science, 2* (2011): pp. 460–466.

Burke, Alafair. Improving Prosecutorial Decision Making: Some Lessons of Cognitive Science. *William and Mary Law Review, 47*(5) (2006): pp. 1588–1631.

Burns, Bruce D. Heuristics as Beliefs and as Behaviors: The Adaptiveness of the 'Hot Hand'. *Cognitive Psychology, 48*(3) (2004): pp. 208–216.

Burns, Kylie. Judges 'Common Sense' and Judicial Cognition. *Griffith Law Review, 25* (2016): pp. 319–351.

Busby, Lindsay, Courtier, Jesse L. Glastonbury, Christine M.Bias in Radiology: The How and Why of Misses and Misinterpretations. *Radiographics, 38*(1) (2017): pp. 236–247.

Byard, Roger W. Unexpected Infant Death: Lessons From the Sally Clark Case. *The Medical Journal of Australia, 181* (2004): pp. 52–54.

Bylander, Eric. Om jävsprövningen i TPB-målet. *Juridisk Publikation, 2* (2009): pp. 175–198.

Berner, Eta and Graber, Mark L., Overconfidence as a Cause of Diagnostic Error in Medicine. *The American Journal of Medicine, 121*(5) (2008): pp. 22–23.

Chen, Weo. Applications of 3D Laser Scanning Technology in Reconstruction of Criminal Scene. *Image Technology*, (2011): pp. 51–54.

Camden, Matt C., Price, Virgina A., and Ludwig, Timothy D. Reducing Absenteeism and Rescheduling among Grocery Store Employees with Point-Contingent Rewards. *Journal of Organizational Behavior Management, 31* (2011): pp. 140–149.

Campbell, Bradley A., Menaker, Tasha A., and King, William R. The Determination of Victim Credibility by Adult and Juvenile Sexual Assault Investigators. *Journal of Criminal Jsutice, 43*(1) (2015): pp. 29–39.

Canter, David, Hammond, Laura, and Youngs, Donna. Cognitive Bias in Line-Up Identifications: The Impact of Administrator Knowledge. *Science and Justice, 53* (2013): pp. 83–88.

Carew, Rachael M., Morgan, Ruth M. & Rando, Carolyn. A Preliminary Investigation into the Accuracy of 3D Modelling and 3D Printing in Forensic Anthropology Evidence Reconstruction. *Journal of Forensic Sciences, 64*(2) (2019): pp. 342–352.

Carrasco, Marisa. Visual Attention: The Past 25 Years. *Vision Research, 51* (2011): pp. 1484–1525.

Ceci, Stephen J. and Bruck, Maggie. Suggestibility of the Child Witness: A Historical Review and Synthesis. *Psychological Bulletin, 113* (1993): pp. 403–439.

Chaplin, Chloe and Shaw, Julia. Confidently Wrong: Police Endorsement of Psych-Legal Misconceptions. *Journal of Police and Criminal Psychology*, 31(3) (2016): pp. 208–216.

Chapman, Gretchen B. and Johnson, E.J. (1994). The Limits of Anchoring. *Journal of Behavioral Decision Making*, 7 (1994): pp. 223–242.

Charlton, David, Fraser-Mackenzie, Peter A.F., and Dror, Itiel E. Emotional Experiences and Motivating Factors Associated with Fingerprint Analysis. *Journal of Forensic Sciences*, 55 (2010): pp. 385–393.

Charman, Steve D, Gregory, Amy H., and Carlucci, Marianna. Exploring the Diagnostic Utility of Facial Composites: Beliefs of Guilt Can Bias Perceived Similarity between Composite and Suspect. *Journal of Experimental Psychology: Applied*, 15 (2009): pp. 76–90.

Charman, Steve D., Kavetski, Melissa, and Hirn Mueller, Dana. Cognitive Bias in the Legal System: Police Officers Evaluate Ambiguous Evidence in a Belief-Consistent Manner. *Journal of Applied Research in Memory and Cognition*, 6 (2017): pp. 193–202.

Cherubini, Paulo, Castelvecchio, Elena, and Cherubini, Anna Maria. Generation of Hypotheses in Wason's 2-4-6 Task: An Information Theory Approach. *Quarterly Journal of Experimental Psychology*, 58 (2005): pp. 309–332.

Chiam, Sher-Lin, Dror, Itiel E., Huber, Christian D., and Higgins, Denice. The Biasing Impact of Irrelevant Contextual Information on Forensic Odontology Radiograph Matching Decisions. *Forensic Science International*, 327 (2021): pp. 110997–110997.

Chlevickaite, Gabriele and Holá, Barbora. Empirical Study of Insider Witnesses' Assessments at the International Criminal Court. *International Criminal Law Review*, 16(4) (2016): pp. 673–702.

Chlevickaite, Gabriele, Hola, Barbora, and Bijleveld, Catrien. Thousands on the Stand: Exploring Trends and Patterns of International Witnesses. *Leiden Journal of International Law*, 32 (2019): pp. 819–836.

Christensen, David Steward, Heckerling, Caryn, Mackesy, Paul S., Bernstein, Mary E., and Elsten, Arthur S. Framing Bias among Expert and Novice Physicians. *Academic Medicine*, 66 (1991): pp. 76–78.

Clark, Steven. A Re-Examination of the Effects of Biased Lineup Instructions in Eyewitness Identifications. *Law and Human Behavior*, 29 (2005): pp. 575–604.

Clark, Steven E, Marshall, Tanya E., and Rosenthal, Robert. Line-up Administrator Influences on Eyewitness Identification Decisions. *Journal of Experimental Psychology: Applied*, 15 (2009): pp. 63–75.

Clarke, Colin, Milne, Rebecca, Bull, Ray. Interviewing Suspects of Crime: The Impact of PEACE Training, Supervision and the Presence of a Legal Advisor: Interviewing Suspects. *Journal of Investigative Psychology and Offender Profiling*, 8(2) (2011): pp. 149–162.

Cole, Simon. A Surfeit of Science: The 'CSI Effect' and the Media Appropriation of the Public Understanding of Science. *Public Understanding of Science*, 24 (2015): pp. 130–146.

Cole, Simon and Dioso-Villa, Rachel. CSI and Its Effects: Media, Juries and the Burden of Proof. *New England Law Review*, 41(3) (2007), pp. 435–469.

Conlon, Edward and Parks, Judi McLean. Information Requests in the Context of Escalation. *Journal of Applied Psychology*, 72 (1987): pp. 344–350.

Cook, Gabriel I., Marsh, Richard L., and Hicks, Jason. Halo and Devil Effects Demonstrate Valence-Based Influences on Source-Monitoring Decisions. *Consciousness and Cognition*, 12 (2003): pp. 257–258.

Cooper, Arnold C., Woo, Carolyn, Y., and Dunkelberg, William C. Entrepreneurs' Perceived Chance of Success. *Journal of Business Venturing*, 3 (1988): pp. 97–108.

Cornish, William R. and Sealy, Thomas. Jurors and their Verdicts. *Modern Law Review*, 36(5) (1973), pp. 496–508.

Correll, Joshua, Park, Bernadette, Judd, Charles, Wittenbrink, Bernd, Sadler, Melody, and Keesee, Tracie. Across the Thin Blue Line: Police Officers and Racial Bias in the Decision to Shoot. *Journal of Personality and Social Psychology*, 92 (2007): pp. 1006–1023.

Cosmelli, Diego, David, Oliver, Lachaux, Jean-Phillipe, Martinerie, Jacques, Garnero, Line., Renault, Bernard, and Varela, Francisco. Waves of Consciousness: Ongoing Cortical Patterns During Binocular Rivalry. *NeuroImage*, 23 (2004): pp. 128–140.

Crawford, Matthew, T. and Skowronski, John J. When Motivated Thought Leads to Heightened Bias: High Need for Cognition can Enhance the Impact of Stereotypes on Memory. *Personality and Social Psychology Bulletin*, 24 (1998): pp. 1075–1089.

Cronin, Patrick and Reicher, Steven. A Study of the Factors that Influence How Senior Officers Police Crowd Events: On SIDE Outside the Laboratory. *British Journal of Social Psychology*, 45 (2006): pp. 175–196.

Cuddy, Amy, Fiske, Susan, and Glick, Peter. The BIAS map: Behaviors from Intergroup Affect and Stereotypes. *Journal of Personality and Social Psychology*, 92 (2007): pp. 631–648. doi:10.1037/0022-3514.92.4.631.

Cutler, Brian L. and Penrod, Steven D. Improving the Reliability of Eyewitness identification: Lineup Construction and Presentation. *Journal of Applied Psychology*, 73 (1988): pp. 281–290.

Cutler, Brian L. and Penrod, Steven, Stuve, Thomas, Roesch, Ronald. Juror Decision Making in Eyewitness Identification Cases. *Law and Human Behavior*, 12(1) (1988), pp. 41–55.

Daftary-Kapur, Tarika, Dumas, Rafaele, and Penrod, Steven D. Jury Decision Making Biases and Methods to Counter Them. *Legal and Criminological Psychology*, 15 (2010): pp. 133–154.

Daftary-Kapur, Tarika, Penrod, Steven D., O´Connor, Maureen, and Wallace, Brian. Examining Pretrial Publicity in a Shadow Jury Paradigm: Issues of Quantity, Persistence and Generalizability. *Law and Human Behavior*, 38 (2014): pp. 462–477.

Dahlman, Christian. Determining the Base Rate for Guilt. *Law, Probability & Risk*, 17 (2017): pp. 15–28.

Dahlman. De-Biasing Legal Fact-Finders With Bayesian Thinking (2019): pp. 1115–1131.

Dahlman, Christian, Zenker, Frank, and Sarwar, Farhan. Miss Rate Neglect in Legal Evidence. *Law, Probability & Risk*, 15 (2016): pp. 239–250.

Daly, Gillian. Jury Secrecy: R v. Mirza; R v. Connor and Rollock. *The International Journal of Evidence & Proof*, 8 (2004): pp. 186–190.

Darley, John M. and Gross, Paget H. A Hypothesis-confirming Bias in Labelling Effects. *Journal of Personality and Social Psychology*, 44 (1) (1983): pp. 20–33.

Dascal, Marcelo and Dror, Itiel E. The Impact of Cognitive Technologies—Towards a Pragmatic Approach. *Pragmatics & Cognition*, 13(3) (2005), pp. 451–457.

Davelaar, Eddy J., Goshen-Gottstein, Y., Ashkenazi, Amir, Haarmann, Henk J., and Usher, Marius. The Demise of Short-Term Memory Revisited: Empirical and Computational Investigations of Recency Effects. *Psychological Review*, 112 (2005): pp. 3–42.

Davis, Angela. The American Prosecutor: Independence, Power, and the Threat of Tyranny. *Iowa Law Review*, 86(2), pp. 393–465.

Davis, Daniel P., Campbell, Colleen J., Poste, Jennifer C., and Ma, Gene. The Association between Operator Confidence and Accuracy of Ultrasonography Performed by Novice Emergency Physicians. *Journal of Emergency Medicine*, 29(3) (2005): pp. 259–64.

Davis, Robert C., Jensen, Carl J., Burgette, Lane, and Burnett, Kathry. Working Smarter on Cold Cases: Identifying Factors Associated with Successful Cold Case Investigations. *Journal of Forensic Sciences*, 59(2) (2014): pp. 375–382.

De Gruijter, Madeleine and de Poot, Christianne. The Use of Rapid Identification Information at the Crime Scene: Similarities and Differences between English and Dutch CSIs. *Policing & Society*, 29(7) (2018): pp. 848–868.

De Gruijter, Madeleine, de Poot, Christianne J., and Elffers, Henk. Reconstructing with Trace Information: Does Rapid Identification Information Lead to Better Crime Reconstructions? *Journal of Investigative Psychology and Offender Profiling, 14(1)* (2016): pp. 88–103.

De Gruijter, Madeleine, Nee, Claire, and de Poot, Christianne J. Identification at the Crime Scene: The Sooner, the Better? The Interpretation of Rapid Identification Information by CSIs at the Crime Scene. *Science and Justice, 57* (2017): pp. 296–306.

Dehaene, Stanislas. Conscious and Nonconscious Processes, Distinct Forms of Evidence Accumulation? *Biological Physicals*, (2007): pp. 141–168.

Dehaene, Stanislas and Naccache, Lionel. Towards a Cognitive Neuroscience of Consciousness: Basic Evidence and a Workspace Framework. *Cognition, 79*(1) (2001): pp. 1–37.

De Jong, Peter J., Haenen, Marie-Anne, Schmidt, Anton, and Mayer, Birgit. Hypochondriasis: The Role of Fear-Confirming Reasoning. *Behaviour Research and Therapy, 36* (1998): pp. 65–74.

De Jong, Peter J., Mayer, Birgit, and van den Hout, Marcel. Conditional Reasoning and Phobic Fear: Evidence for a Fear-Confirming Reasoning Pattern. *Behaviour Research and Therapy, 3* (1997): pp. 507–516.

De Keijser, Jan W. and van Koppen, Peter J. Paradoxes of Proof and Punishment: Psychological Pitfalls in Judical Decision Making. *Legal and Criminological Psychology*, 12(1) (2007): pp. 189–205.

De Neys, Wim. Dual Processing in Reasoning: Two Systems but One Reasoner. *Psychological Science, 17* (2006): pp. 428–433.

De Neys, Wim. Bias and Conflict: A Case for Logical Intuitions. *Perspectives on Psychological Science*, 7(1) (2011): pp. 23–38.

De Neys, Wim and Glumicic, Tamara. Conflict Monitoring in Dual Process Theories of Thinking. *Cognition, 106*(3) (2008): pp. 1248–1299.

De Paulo, Bella M., Lindsay, James J., Malone, Brian E., Muhlenbruck, Laura, Charlton, Kelly, and Cooper Harris. Cues to Deception. *Psychological Bulletin, 129* (2003): pp. 74–118.

Devine, Patricia. Stereotypes and Prejudice: Their Automatic and Controlled Components. *Journal of Personality and Social Psychology*, 56 (1989): pp. 5–18.

Dewey, John. Logical Method and Law. *Cornell Law Quarterly, 10* (1925): pp. 17–26.

Dhami, Mandeep K., Lundrigan, Samantha, and Thomas, Sian. Police Discretion in Rape Cases. *Journal of Police and Criminal Psychology*, 35(2) (2018): pp. 157–169.

Diaz, Alvaro. Tradiciones Indigenas en La Applicacion de la Ley Penal (Juzgado de Garantia de Arica). *Revista de Derecho, 27*(2) (2014): pp. 271–276.

Dibbets, Pauline, Fliek, Lorraine, and Meesters, Cor. Fear-Related Confirmation Bias in Children: A Comparison Between Neutral-and Dangerous- Looking Animals. *Child Psychiatry & Human Development, 46* (2015): pp. 418–425.

Ditto, Peter H. and Lopez, David F. Motivated Skepticism: Use of Differential Decision Criteria for Preferred and Nonpreferred Conclusions. *Journal of Personality and Social Psychology, 63* (1992): pp. 568–584.

Ditto, Peter H., Munro, Geoffrey D., Apanovitch, Anne Marie, Scepansky, James A., and Lockhart, Lisa K. Spontaneous Skepticism: The Interplay of Motivation and Expectation in Responses to Favorable and Unfavorable Medical Diagnoses. *Personality and Social Psychology Bulletin, 29* (2003): pp. 1120–1132.

Dobbie, Will, Goldin, Jacob, and Yang, Crystal S. The Effects of Pretrial Detention on Conviction, Future, Crime, and Employent: Evidence from Randomly Assigned Judges. *The American Economic Review, 108*(2) (2018): pp. 201–240.

Doherty, Michael E. and Mynatt, Clifford R. (1990). Inattention to P (H) and to P (D\ ~ H): A Converging Operation. *Acta Psychologica, 75* (1990): pp. 1–11.

Doherty, Michael E., Mynatt, Clifford R., Tweney, Ryan D., and Schiavo, Michael D. Pseudodiagnosticity. *Acta Psychologica, 43* (1979): pp. 111–121.

Doll, Bradley B., Hutchison, Kent E., and Frank, Michael, J. Dopaminergic Genes Predict Individual Differences in Susceptibility to Confirmation Bias. *The Journal of Neuroscience, 31* (2011): pp. 6188–6198.

Doll, Bradley B., Waltz, James, Cockburn, Jeffrey, Brown, Jaime K., Frank, Michael J., and Gold, James M. Reduced Susceptibility to Confirmation Bias in Schizophrenia, *Cognitive, Affective, & Behavioral Neuroscience, 14* (2014): pp. 715–728.

Doob, Anthony N. and Kirshenbaum, Hershi M. Some Empirical Evidence on the Effect of S.12 of the Canada Evidence Act upon an Accused. *Criminal Law Quarterly, 15* (1972): pp. 88–96.

Drew, Trafton, Vo, Melissa, and Wolfe, Jeremy M. The Invisible Gorilla Strikes Again: Sustained Inattentional Blindness in Expert Observers. *Psychological Science, 24*(9) (2013), pp. 1848–1853.

Drizin, Steven A. and Leo, Richard A. The Problem of False Confessions in the post-DNA World. *North Carolina Law Review, 82*(3) (2004), pp. 891–1007.

Dror, Itiel E. A Novel Approach to Minimize Error in the Medical Domain: Cognitive Neuroscientific Insights into Training. *Medical Teacher, 33* (2011): pp. 34–38.

Dror, Itiel E. Practical Solutions to Cognitive and Human Factor Challenges in Forensic Science. *Forensic Science Policy & Management, 4* (2013): pp. 1–9.

Dror, Itiel E. What is (or Will Be) Happening to the Cognitive Abilities of Forensic Experts in the New Technological Age. *Journal of Forensic Sciences, 58* (2013): pp. 563.

Dror, Itiel E. Cognitive Neuroscience in Forensic Science: Understanding and Utilizing the Human Element. *Philosophical Transactions B, 370* (2015): pp. 1–8.

Dror, Itiel E. A Hierarchy of Expert Performance. *Journal of Applied Research in Memory and Cognition, 5* (2016): pp. 121–127.

Dror, Itiel E. Biases in Forensic Experts. *Science, 360* (2017): p. 243.

Dror, Itiel E. and Charlton, David. Why Experts Make Errors. *Journal of Forensic Identification, 51* (2006): pp. 600–616.

Dror, Itiel E. and Cole, Simon A. The Vision in Blind Justice: Expert Perception, Judgment, and Visual Cognition in Forensic Pattern Recognition. *Psychonomic Bulletin & Review, 17* (2010): pp. 161–167.

Dror, Itiel E. and Hampikian, Greg. Subjectivity and Bias in Forensic DNA Mixture Interpretation. *Science & Justice, 51* (2011): pp. 204–208.

Dror, Itiel E. and Kukucka, Jeff. Linear Sequential Unmasking—Expanded (LSU-E): A General Approach for Improving Decision Making as well as Minimizing Noise and Bias. *Forensic Science International: Synergy, 3* (2021): pp. 1–5.

Dror, Itiel E. and Mnookin, Jennifer L. The Use of Technology in Human Expert Domains: Challenges and Risks Arising from the Use of Automated Fingerprint Identifications Systems in Forensics. *Law, Probability & Risk, 9*(1) (2019): pp. 8–9.

Dror, Itiel E., and Rosenthal, Robert. Meta-analytically Quantifying the Reliability and Biasability of Forensic Experts. *Journal of Forensic Sciences, 53* (2008): pp. 900–903.

Dror, Itiel E., Charlton, David, and Péron, Ailsa E. Contextual Information Renders Experts Vulnerable to Making Erroneous Identifications. *Forensic Science International, 156* (2006): pp. 74–78.

Dror, Itiel E., Wertheim, Kasey, Fraser-Mackenzie, Peter, Walatys, Jeff. The Impact of Human-Technology Cooperation and Distributed Cognition in Forensic Science: Biasing Effects of AFIS Contextual Information on Human Experts. *Journal of Forensic Sciences, 57*(2) (2012): pp. 343–352.

Dror, Itiel E., Kukucka, Jeff, Kassin, Saul M., and Zapf, Patricia A. No One is Immune to Contexual Bias—Not Even Forensic Pathologists. *Journal of Applied Research in Memory and Cognition, 7* (2018): pp. 316–317.

Dror, Itiel E., Kukucka, Jeff, Kassin, Saul M., and Zapf, Patricia A. When Expert Decision Making Goes Wrong: Consensus, Bias, the Role of Experts, and Accuracy. *Journal of Applied Research in Memory and Cognition, 7* (2018): pp. 162–163.

Dror, Itiel E., Morgan, Ruth, Rando, Carolyn, and Nakhaeazadeh, Sherry. The Bias Snowball and the Bias Cascade Effects: Two Distinct Biases that May Impact Forensic Decision Making. *Journal of Forensic Sciences, 62* (2017): pp. 832–833.

Dror, Itiel E., Péron, Alisa. E., Hind, Sara-Lynn, and Charlton, David. When Emotions Get the Better of Us: The Effect of Contextual Top-down Processing on Matching Fingerprints. *Applied Cognitive Psychology, 19* (2005): pp. 799–809.

Dunbar, Kevin. Concept Discovery in a Scientific Domain. *Cognitive Science, 17* (1993): pp. 397–434.

Dwyer, Christopher P., Hogan, Michael J., and Stewart, Ian. An Integrated Critical Thinking Framework for the 21st Century. *Thinking Skills and Creativity, 12* (2014): pp. 43–52.

Eadie, Tanya, Sroka, Alicia, Wright, Derek R, and Merati, Albert. Does Knowledge of Medical Diagnosis Bias Auditory-Perceptual Judgments of Dysphonia? *Journal of Voice, 25*(4) (2011): pp. 420–429.

Eagly, Alice H., Chaiken, Serena, Chen, Shelly, and Shaw-Barnes, Kelly. The Impact of Attitudes on Memory: An Affair to Remember. *Psychological Bulletin, 125* (1999): pp. 64–89.

Ebbinghaus, Hermann. Memory: A Contribution to Experimental Psychology. *Annals of Neurosciences, 20* (4) (2013): pp 155–156.

Edmond, Gary and Martire, Kristy A. Just Cognition: Scientific Research on Bias and Some Implications for Legal Procedure and Decision-making. *Modern Law Review, 82*(4) (2019): pp. 633–664.

Edwards, Kari and Smith Edward E. A Disconfirmation Bias in the Evaluation of Arguments. *Journal of Personality and Social Psychology, 71* (1996): pp. 5–24.

Engel, Christoph and Glöckner, Andreas. Role-Induced Bias in Court: an Experimental Analysis. *Journal of Behavioral Decision Making, 26* (2012): pp. 272–284.

Englich, Birte, Mussweiler, Thomas, Strack, Fritz, Wiener, Richard L. The Last Word in Court: A Hidden Disadvantage for the Defense. *Law and Human Behavior, 29*(6) (2005): pp. 705–722.

Ernberg, Emelie, Tidefors, Inga, and Landström, Sara. Prosecutors' Reflections on Sexually Abused Preschoolers and their Ability to Stand trial. *Child Abuse & Neglect, 57* (2016): pp. 21–29.

Evans, Jonathan St. B.T. The Heuristic-Analytic Theory of Reasoning: Extension and Evaluation. *Psychonomic Bulletin & Review, 13* (2006): pp. 378–395.

Evans, Jonathan St. B.T. Dual-Processing Accounts of Reasoning, Judgment and Social Cognition. *Annual Review of Psychology, 59* (2008): pp. 255–278.

Evans, Jonathan St. B.T. and Stanovich, Keith E. Dual-Process Theories of Higher Cognition: Advancing the Debate. *Perspectives on Psychological Science, 8* (2013): pp. 223–241.

Everett, Ronald S. and Wojtkiewics, Roger A. Difference, Disparity, and Race/Ethnic Bias in Federal Sentencing. *Journal of Quantitative Criminology, 18*(2) (2002): pp. 189–211.

Fahsing, Ivar and Ask, Karl. Decision Making and Decisional Tipping Points in Homicide Investigations: An Interview Study of British and Norwegian Detectives. *Investigative Psychology and Offender Profiling, 10* (2013): pp. 155–165.

Faulconer, James E. and Williams, Richard N. Temporality in Human Action: An Alternative to Positivism and Historicism. *American Psychologist, 40* (1985): pp. 1179–1188.

Feeser, Henry R. and Willard, Gary E. Founding Strategy and Performance: A Comparison of High and Low Growth High Tech Firms. *Strategic Management Journal, 11* (1990): pp. 87–98.

Fehr, Beverley and Russell, James A. Concept of Emotion Viewed from a Prototype Perspective. *Journal of Experimental Psychology General, 113* (1984): pp. 464–486.

Fernandes, Myra A. and Moscovitch, Morris. Divided Attention and Memory: Evidence of Substantial Interference Effects at Retrieval and Encoding. *Journal of Experimental Psychology: General, 129* (2000): pp. 155–176.

Festinger, Leon. A Theory of Social Comparison Processes. *Human Relations, 5* (1954): pp. 327–346.

Fiedler, Klaus. Beware of Samples! A Cognitive-Ecological Sampling Approach to Judgment Biases. *Psychological Review, 107* (2000): pp. 659–676.

Fiedler, Klaus. Meta-Cognitive Myopia and the Dilemmas of Inductive-Statistical Inference. *Psychology of Learning and Motivation, 57* (2012): pp. 1–55.

Fiedler, Klaus, Hofferbert, Joscha, and Wöllert, Franz. Metacognitive Myopia in Hidden-Profile Tasks: The Failure to Control for Repetition Biases. *Frontiers in Psychology, 9* (2012): pp. 1–13.

Findley, Keith. Tunnel Vision, Conviction of the Innocent: Lessons from Psychological Research. *University of Wisconsin Legal Studies Research Paper, 11161* (2010): pp. 1–31.

Findley, Keith and Scott, Michael. The Multiple Dimensions of Tunnel Vision in Criminal Cases. *Wisconsin Law Review, 2* (2006): p. 291.

Fischhoff, Baruch and Beyth-Marom, Ruth. Hypothesis Evaluation from a Bayesian Perspective. *Psychological Review, 90* (1983): pp. 239–260.

Fisher, Stanley Z. In Search of the Virtuous Prosecutor: A Conceptual Framework. *American Journal of Criminal Law, 15*(3) (1988), pp. 197–261.

Flavell, John H. Metacognition and Cognitive Monitoring: A New Area of Cognitive-developmental Inquiry. *The American Psychologist, 34*(10) (1979), pp. 906–911.

Fletcher, George P. The Presumption of Innocence in the Soviet Union. *University of California at Los Angeles Law Review, 15* (1968): pp. 1203–1225.

Folkman, Judah. Fighting Cancer by Attacking its Blood Supply. *Scientific American, 275* (1996): pp. 150–154.

Forsberg, Moa. Rätt utan Sanning? En reflektion över sanningens roll i straffprocessen idag. *Nordisk Tidsskrift for Kriminalvidenskab, 95* (2008): pp. 243–258.

Frank, Jerome. Say it with Music. *Harvard Law Review, 61* (1948): pp. 921–957

Frank, Jerome. Modern and Ancient Legal Pragmatism - John Dewey & Co. Vs. Aristotele: I & II. *Notre Dame Lawyer, 25* (1950): pp. 250–257.

Fraser, Ian, Houlihan, Michael, Bond-Fraser, Louise, Eliis, Charlotte. Is the Accuracy of Eyewitness Testimony Common Knowledge? *Criminal Law Quarterly*, 59, (2013): pp. 498-510.
Freedman, Eric M. Innocence, Federalism, and the Capital Jury: Two Legislative Proposals for Evaluating Post-trial Evidence of Innocence in Death Penalty Cases. *Review of Law & Social Change, XVIII:315*, (1990): pp. 315-323.
Friedrich, James. Primary Error Detection and Minimization (PEDMIN) Strategies in Social Cognition: A Reinterpretation of Confirmation Bias Phenomena. *Psychological Review*, 100(2) (1993): pp. 298-319.
Fugelsang, Jonathan A., Stein, Courtney B., Green, Adam E., and Dunbar, Kevin N. Theory and Data Interactions of the Scientific Mind: Evidence from the Molecular and the Cognitive Laboratory. *Canadian Journal of Experimental Psychology*, 58 (2004): pp. 86-95.
Fukuda, Keisuke and Vogel, Edward K. Human Variation in Overriding Attentional Capture. *The Journal of Neuroscience*, 29 (2009): pp. 8276-8733.
Friedman, Charles, Gatti, Guido, Elstein, Arthur, Frans, Timothy, Murphy, Gwendolyn, Wolf, Fredric Are Clinicians Correct When They Believe they are Correct? Implications for Medical Decision Support. *Studies in Health Technology and Informatics*, 84(1) (2001): pp. 454-458.
Friedman, Charles, Gatti, Guido, Franz, Timothy M., Murhpy, Gwendolyn,, Wolf, Fredric M, Hecerling, Paul S, Fine Paul L, Miller Thomas and Elstein Arthur S. Do Physicians Know When Their Diagnoses are Correct? Implications for Decision Support and Error Reduction? *Journal of General Internal Medicine*, 20(4) (2005): pp. 334-339.
Gabr, Ahmed, Kallini, Joseph R., Desai, Kush, Hickey, Ryan, Thornburg, Bartley, Kulik, Laura, Lewandowki, Robert J., and Salem, Riad. Types of Research Bias Encountered in IR. *Journal of Vascular and Interventional Radiology*, 27 (2016): pp. 546-550.
Gale, Maggie and Ball, Linden. Exploring the Determinants of Dual Goal Facilitation in a Rule Discovery Task. *Thinking & Reasoning*, 15 (2009): pp. 294-315.
Gallimore, Paul. Confirmation Bias in the Valuation Process: A Test for Corroborating Evidence. *Journal of Property Research*, 13 (1996): pp. 261-273.
Gergen, Kenneth J. Toward a Postmodern Psychology. *The Humanist Psychologist*, 18 (1990): pp. 23-24.
Gershman, Bennett L. The Prosecutor's Duty to Truth. *The Georgetown Journal of Legal Ethics*, 14(2) (2001): pp. 309-354.
Gianelli, Paul C. Independent Crime Laboratories: The Problem of Motivational and Cognitive Bias. *Utah Law Review*, 2 (1993): p. 247.
Giannelli, Paul C. Confirmation Bias in Forensic Testing. *Trial Practice*, 25 (2008): pp. 22-23.
Giannelli, Paul C. Cognitive Bias in Forensic Science. *Criminal Justice*, 25 (2010): pp. 61-64.
Gibson, Stephen. Milgram's Obedience Experiments: a Rhetorical Analysis. *British Journal of Social Psychology*, 52 (2013): pp. 290-309.
Gigerenzer, Gerd. Mindless Statistics. *The Journal of Socio-Economics*, 33 (2004): pp. 587-606
Gilbey, Andrew and Hill, Stephen. Confirmation Bias in General Aviation Lost Procedures. *Applied Cognitive Psychology*, 26 (2012): pp. 785-795.
Gill, James R., Pinneri, Kathryn, Denton, John Scott, and Aiken, Sally S. Letter to the Editor, Commentary on; Dror, Melinek, Arden, Kukucka, Hawkins, Carter et al. Cognitive bias in Forensic Pathology Decisions. *Jounral of Forensic Sciences*, 66(6) (2021): p. 2554.
Gilovich, Thomas. Biased Evaluation and Persistence in Gambling. *Journal of Personality and Social Psychology*, 44 (1983): pp. 1110-1126.

Glanzer, Murray. Storage Mechanisms in Free Recall. *Psychology of Learning and Motivation,* 5 (1972): pp. 129–153.

Glöckner, Anders and Engel, Cristoph. Can We Trust Intuitive Jurors? Standards of Proof and the Probative Value of Evidence in Coherence Based Reasoning. *Journal of Empirical Legal Studies, 10* (2013): pp. 230–255.

Goldberg, Lewis R. The Development of Markers for the Big Five Structure. *Psychological Assessment, 4*(1) (1992): pp. 26–42.

Goldkamp, John S. The Effects of Detention on Judicial Decisions: A Closer Look. *The Justice System Journal, 5*(3) (1980): pp. 234–257.

Goodman-Delahunty, Jane and Graham, Kelly. The Influence of Victim Intoxication and Victim Attire on Police Responses to Sexual Assault. *Journal of Investigative Psychology and Offender Profiling, 8*(1) (2010): pp. 22–40.

Götz, Frank M., Schönborg, Holger, Borsdorf, Viktoria, Pflugbeil, Anne-marie, Labudde, Dirk. GenoProof Mixture 3—New Software and Process to Resolve Complex DNA Mixtures. *Forensic Science International, Genetics Supplement Series,* 6 (2017), e549–e551.

Granhag, Pär Anders, Strömwall, Leif A., and Hartwig, Maria. Eyewitness Testimony: Tracing the Beliefs of Swedish Legal Professionals. *Behavioral Sciences & the Law, 23*(5) (2005): pp. 709–727.

Grear, Anna. Learning Legal Reasoning While Rejecting the Oxymoronic Status of Feminist Judicial Rationalities: A View from the Law Classroom. *The Law Teacher,* 46 (2012): pp. 239–254.

Greathouse, Sarah M. and Kovera, Margaret B. Instruction Bias and Line-Up Presentation Moderate the Effects of Administrator Knowledge on Eyewitness Identifications. *Law and Human Behavior, 33* (2009): pp. 70–82.

Green, Bruce A. Prosecutorial Ethics as Usual. *University of Illinois Law Review,* 5 (2003): p. 1573.

Griffin, Leslie C. The Prudent Prosecutor. *The Georgetown Journal of Legal Ethics,* 14 (2001): p. 259.

Green, Bruce A. and Roiphe, Rebecca. Rethinking Prosecutor's Conflicts of Interest. *Boston College Law Review, 58*(2) (2017), pp. 464–5387.

Greene, Edith and Loftus, Elizabeth F. When Crimes Are Joined at Trial. *Law and Human Behavior, 9* (1985): pp. 193–207.

Greenland, Sander. Accounting for Uncertainty About Investigator Bias: Disclosure is Informative. *Journal of Epidemiology and Community Health, 63* (1979): pp. 593–598.

Greenwald, Anthony G. The Totalitarian Ego—Fabrication and Revision of Personal History. *American Psychologist, 35* (1980): pp. 603–618.

Griffiths, Thomas L. Understanding Human Intelligence through Human Limitations. *Trends in cognitive Science, 24*(11) (2020): pp. 873–883.

Gross, Samuel R. and O'Brien, Barbara. Frequency and Predictors of False Conviction: Why We Know So Little, and New Data on Capital Cases. *Journal of Emrpical Legal Studies, 5*(4) (2008): pp. 930–931.

Gross, Samuel R., Jacoby, Kristen, Matheson, Daniel J., Montgomery, Nicholas, and Patel, Sujata. Exonerations in the United States, 1989 through 2003. *The Journal of Criminal Law & Criminology, 95*(2) (2005): pp. 523–560.

Guastini, Riccardo. A Realistic View on Law and Legal Cognition. *Journal for Constitutional Theory and Philosophy of Law,* 27 (2015): pp. 1–9.

Gudjonsson. Gisli H. The IRA Funeral Murders: The Confession of PK and the Expert Psychological Testimony. *Legal and Criminological Psychology, 4*(1) (1999): pp. 45–50.

Guerra Thompson, Sandra. Judicial Gatekeeping of Police-Generated Witness Testimony. *The Journal of Criminal Law & Criminology*, 102(2) (2012): pp. 329–395.

Gunderman, Richard B. Biases in Radiologic Reasoning. *American Journal of Roentgenology*, 192(3) (2009): pp. 561–564.

Gupta, Jatinder N.D., Kalaimannan, Ezhil, and Yoo, Seong-Moo. A Heuristic for Maximizing Investigation Effectiveness of Digital Forensic Cases involving Multiple Investigators. *Computers & Opertaions Research*, 69 (2016): pp. 1–9.

Gupta, Arpit, Hansman, Christopher, and Frenchman, Ethan. The Heavy Costs of High Bail: Evidence from Judge Randomization. *The Journal of Legal Studies*, 45(2) (2016): pp. 472–473.

Hadwin, Julie A., Garner, Matthew, and Perez-Olivas, Gisela. The Development of Information Processing Biases in Childhood Anxiety: A Review and Exploration of its Origins in Parenting. *Clinical Psychology Review*, 26 (2006): pp. 876–894.

Hall, Alison, Hall, Erika, and Perry, Jamie. Black and Blue: Exploring Racial Bias and Law Enforcement in the Killings of Unarmed Black Male Civilians. *American Psychologist*, 71 (2016): pp. 175–186.

Halpern, Diane F. Teaching Critical Thinking for Transfer Across Domains: Disposition, Skills, Structure Training, and Metacognitive Monitoring. *The American Psychologist*, 53(4) (1998): pp. 449–455.

Handley, Ian M., Fowler, Stephanie L., Rasinski, Heather M., Helfer, Suzanne G., and Geers, Andrew L. Beliefs About Expectations Moderate the Influence of Expectations on Pain Perception. *International Journal of Behavioral Medicine*, 20 (2013): pp. 52–58.

Hans, Valerie P. and Doob, Anthony N. Section 12 of the Canada Evidence Act and the Deliberation of Simulated Juries. *Criminal Law Quarterly*, 18(2) (1975): pp. 235–253.

Harman, Gilbert H. The Inference to the Best Explanation. *The Philosophical Review*, 74 (1965): pp. 88–95.

Hart, William, Albarracin, Dolores, Eagly, Alice H., Brechan, Inge, Lindberg, Matthew J., and Merrill, Lisa. Feeling Validated Versus Being Correct: A Meta-Analysis of Selective Exposure to Information. *Psychological Bulletin*, 135 (2009): pp. 555–588.

Harris, William. Investigating Lebanon's Political Murders: International Idelaism in the Realist Middle East. *The Middle East Journal*, 67(1) (2013): pp. 9–27.

Hartley, Stephanie, Winburn, Allysha Powanda and Dror, Itiel E. Metric Forensic Anthropology Decisions: Reliability and Biasability of Sectioning-Point-Based Sex Estimates. *Journal of Forensic Sciences*, 67(1) (2021): pp. 68–79.

Hasel, Lisa E. and Kassin, Saul M. On the Presumption of Evidentiary Independence: Can Confessions Corrupt Eyewitness Identifications? *Psychological Science*, 20 (2009): pp. 122–126.

Haslam, S. Alexander and Reicher, Stephen D. Contesting the 'Nature' of Conformity: What Milgram and Zimbardo's studies Really Show. *PLoS Biology*, 10 (2012): e1001426.

Haverkamp, Beth E. Confirmatory Bias in Hypothesis Testing for Client-Identified and Counselor Self-Generated Hypotheses. *Journal of Counseling Psychology*, 40 (1993): pp. 303–315.

Haw, Ryann M. and Fisher, Ronald. Effects of Administrator-Witness Contact on Eyewitness Identification Accuracy. *Journal of Applied Psychology*, 89 (2004): pp. 1106–1112.

Heaton, Paul, Mayson, Sandra, and Stevenson, Megan. The Downstream Consequences of Misdemeanor Pretrial Detention. *Stanford Law Review*, 69(3) (2017): pp. 713–784.

Helm, Rebecca K., Wistrich, Andrew J., and Rachlinski, Jeffrey J. Are Arbitrators Human? *Journal of Empirical Legal Studies*, 13 (2016): pp. 666–692.

Henrion, Max and Fischoff, Baruch. Assessing Uncertainty in Physical Constants. *American Journal of Physics, 54* (1986): pp. 791–798.

Hergovich, Andreas, Schott, Reinhard, and Burger, Christoph. Biased Evaluation of Abstracts Depending on Topic and Conclusion: Further Evidence of a Confirmation Bias within Scientific Psychology. *Current Psychology, 29*(3) (2010): pp. 188–209.

Hersant, Jeanne. Patronage and Rationalization: Reform to Criminal Procedure and the Lower Courts in Chile, *Law & Social Inquiry, 42*(2) (2017): pp. 423–449.

Heuman, Lars. Domarens och åklagarens skyldighet att vara objektiva. *Juridisk Tidsskrift* (2004): pp. 42–52,

Hobbs, Sam Earle. Prosecutor's Bias, An Occupational Disease. *Alabama Law Review, 2*(1) (1950): p. 40.

Hobbs, Harry. Towards a Principled Justification for the Mixed Composition of Hybrid International Criminal Tribunals. *Leiden Journal of International Law, 30*(1) (2016): pp. 177–197.

Hodges, Bert H. and Geyer, Anne L. A Nonconformist Account of the Asch Experiments: Values, Pragmatics, and Moral Dilemmas. *Personality and Social Psychology, 1* (2006): pp. 2–19.

Hofmann, Wilhelm, Schmeichel, Brandon J and Baddeley, Alan D. Executive Functions and Self-regulation. *Trends in Cognitive Science, 16*(3) (2012): pp. 174–180.

Holyoak, Keith J. and Simon, D. Bidirectional Reasoning in Decision Making by Constraint Satisfaction. *Journal of Experimental Psychology: General, 3* (1999): pp. 3–31.

Hon H. Lloyd, King. Why Prosecutors are Permitted to Offer Witness Inducements: A Matter of Constitutional Authority. *Stetson Law Review, 29* (1999): pp. 155–181.

Horowitz, I.A. and Bordens, Kenneth S. An Experimental Investigation of Procedural Issues in Complex Tort Trials. *Law and Human Behavior, 14* (1990): pp. 269–285.

Horry, Ruth, Memon, Amina, Wright, Daniel, and Milne, Rebecca. Predictors of Eyewitness Identification Decisions From Video Lineups in England: A Field Study. *Law and Human Behavior, 36* (2012): pp. 257–265.

Horsman, Graeme, and Sunde, Nina. Part 1: The Need for Peer Review in Digital Forensics. *Forensic Science International: Digital Investigation, 35* (2020): p. 301062.

Houghton, Susan M., Simon, Mark, Aquino, Karl, and Goldberg, Caren B. No Safety in Numbers: Persistence of Biases and Their Effects of Team Risk Perception and Team Decision making. *Group & Organization Management, 25* (2000): pp. 325–353.

Asche, Solomon E. (1964). Forming Impressions of Personality. The Journal of Abnormal and Social Psychology, 41 (3), pp. 258–290.

Huang, Ching-Yu, and Shih, Chih-Hung. The Good, the Bad and the Ugly of Eyewitness Identification Practice in Police Officers—A Self-Report Survey Study. *Psychology, Crime & Law, 26*(10) (2020): pp. 1–22.

Hucklesby, Anthea and Sarre, Rick. Bail in Australia, the United Kingdom and Canada: Introduction. *Current Issues in Criminal Justice, 21*(1) (2009): pp. 1–2.

Hughes, Brent L. and Zaki, Jamil. The Neuroscience of Motivated Cognition. *Trends in Cognitive Science, 19* (2015): pp. 62–63.

Hulland, John S. and Kleinmuntz, Dan N. Factors Influencing the Use of Internal Summary Evaluations Versus External Information in Choice. *Journal of Behavioral Decision Making, 7* (1994): pp. 79–102.

Hutcheson, Joseph. The Judgment Intuitive: the Function of the 'Hunch' in Judicial Decisions. *The Cornell Law Quarterly, 14* (1929): pp. 274–288.

Hwa, Hsiao-Lin, Wu, Ming-Yih, Chung, Wan-Chia, Ko, Tsang-Ming, Lin, Chih-Peng, Yin, Hsiang-I, Lee, Tsui-Ting, Lee, James Chun-I. Massively Parallel Sequencing

Analysis of Nondegraded and Degraded DNA Mixtures using the ForenSeq System in Combination with EuroForMix Software. *International Journal of Legal Medicine, 133*(1) (2019): pp. 25–37.

Isenberg, Daniel J., Group Polarization: A Critical Review and Meta-Analysis. *Journal of Personality and Social Psychology, 6* (1986): pp. 1141–1151.

Izard, Carroll E. Four Systems for Emotion Activation: Cognitive and Noncognitive Development. *Psychological Review, 100* (1993): pp. 68–90

Jacobson, Katarina. 'We Can't Just Do It Any Which Way'—Objectivity Work among Swedish prosecutors. *Qualitative Sociology Review, 4*(1) (2008): pp. 46–68.

Jacoby, Joan E. The American Prosecutor, A Search for Identity. Lexington, Mass: Heath, 1980.

Janis, Irving L. Crucial Decisions, Leadership in Policymaking and Crisis Managemen. New York: Free Press, 1989.

Jelliffe, Derrick B. Age Assessment in Field Surveys of Children of the Tropics. *The Journal of Pediatrics, 69*(1) (1966): pp. 826–828.

Jiang, Lina, Luo, Dahua & Dang, Yong-hui. Legal Professionals' Knowledge of Eyewitness Testimony in China: A Cross-Sectional Survey. *PLoS One, 11*(2) (2016): pp. e0148116–e0148116.

Johnson, Blair and Eagly, Alice H. Effects of Involvement on Persuasion: A Meta-Analysis. *Psychological Bulletin, 106* (1989): pp. 375–384.

Johnson, Marcia K., Hastroudi, Shahin, and Lindsay, Stephen D. Source Monitoring. *Psychological Bulletin, 114*(1) (1993): pp. 3–28.

Johnson-Laird, Philip, Legrenzi, Paolo, and Legrenzi, Maria S. Reasoning and a Sense of Reality. *British Journal of Psychology, 63* (1972): pp. 395–400.

Jonakait, Randolph, N. The Ethical Prosecutor's Misconduct. *Criminal Law Bulletin, 550* (1987): pp. 550–567.

Jonas, Eva, Graupmann, Verena, and Frey, Dieter. The Influence of Mood on the Search for Supporting Versus Conflicting Information: Dissonance Reduction as a Means of Mood Regulation. *Personality and Social Psychology Bulletin, 32* (2006): pp. 3–15.

Jones, Helen, Brookman, Fiona, Williams, Robin, and Fraser, Jim. We Need to Talk about Dialogue: Accomplishing Collaborative Sensemaking in Homicide Investigations. *Police Journal, 94*(4) (2020): pp. 1–18.

Jordan, Sarah, Brimbal, Larue, Wallace, Brian D., Kassin, Saul M, Hartwig, Maria, Street, Chris N.H. A Test of the Micro-Expressions Training Tool: Does it Improve Lie Detection? *Journal of Investigative Psychology and Offender Profiling, 16*(3) (2019): pp. 222–235.

Joselow, Margaux. Promise-Induced False Confessions: Lessons from Promises in Another Context. *Boston College Law Review, 60*(6) (2019): pp. 1641–1687.

Joy, Peter A. The Relationship Between Prosecutorial Misconduct and Wrongful Convictions: Shaping Remedies for a Broken System. *Wisconsin Law Review, 2* (2006): pp. 399–405.

Jupe, Louise Marie and Keatley, David Adam. Airport Artificial Intelligence Can Detect Deception—Or am I Lying? *Security Journal, 33*(4) (2020): pp. 622–635.

Kahan, Dan M. Laws of Cognition and the Cognition of Law. *Cognition, 135* (2015): pp. 56–60

Kahneman, Daniel, Anderson, Norman B. A Perspective on Judgment and Choice: Mapping Bounded Rationality- *The American Psychologist, 58*(9) (2003): pp. 697–720.

Kaplan, John. Decision Theory and the Factfinding Process. *Stanford Law Review, 20* (1968): pp. 1065–1092.

Karlsson, Jan. C.H. Does Swedishness exist? A Scrutiny of Theories About the Swedish National Character and Mentality. *Sociologisk Forskning, 31* (1994). pp. 41–57.

Karlsson, Thore. Multivariate Analysis ('Forensiometrics')—A New Tool in Forensic Medicine. Differentiation between Firearm-related Homicides and Suicides. *Forensic Science International, 101*(2): pp. 131–140.

Kassin, Saul M. On the Psychology of Confessions: Does Innocence Put Innocent at Risk? *American Psychologist, 60* (2005): pp. 215–218.

Kassin, Saul M. False Confessions: Causes, Consequences, and Implications for Reform. *Current Directions in Psychological Science: A Journal of the American Psychological Society, 17*(4) (2008): pp. 112–121.

Kassin, Saul M. Why Confessions Trump Innocence. *American Psychologist, 67* (2012): pp. 431–445.

Kassin, Saul M., Neumann, Katherine & Wiener, Richard L. On the Power of Confession Evidence: An Experimental Test of the Fundamental Difference Hypothesis. *Law and Human Behavior, 21*(5) (1997): pp. 469–484.

Kassin, Saul M, Sukel, Holly & Wiener, Richard L. Coerced Confessions and the Jury: An Experimental Test of the 'Harmless Error' Rule. *Law and Human Behavior, 21*(1) (1997): pp. 27–46,

Kassin, Saul M., Bogart, Daniel, and Kerner, Jacqueline. Confessions that Corrupt: Evidence from the DNA Exoneration Case Files. *Psychological Science, 23* (2012): pp. 41–45.

Karger, B, Niemeyer, J. Brinkmann, B. Suicides by Sharp Force: Typical and Atypical Features. *International Journal of Legal Medicine, 113* (2000): pp. 259–262.

Kassin, Saul M., Goldstein, Christine C., and Savitsky, Kenneth. Behavioral Confirmation in the Interrogation Room: On the Dangers of Presuming Guilt. *Law and Human Behavior, 27/2* (2003): pp. 187–203.

Kassin, Saul M., Leo, Richard A., Meissner, Christian A., Richman, Kimberly D. Colwell, Lri H, Leach Amy-May, La Fon, Dana, and Cutler, Brian. Police Interviewing and Interrogation: A Self-Report Survey of Police Practices and Beliefs. *Law and Human Behavior, 31*(4) (2007): pp. 381–400.

Kassin, Saul M., Drizin, Steven, Grisso, Thomas, Gudjonsson, Gisli H. Leo, Richard A., and Redlich, Alison D. Police-Induced Confessions: Risk Factors and Recommendations. *Law and Human Behavior, 34* (2010): pp. 3–34.

Kassin, Saul M., Dror, Itiel E., and Kukucka, Jeff. The Forensic Confirmation Bias: Problems, Perspectives, and Proposed Solutions. *Journal of Applied Research in Memory and Cognition 2* (2013): pp. 42–52.

Kassin, Saul M., Goldstein, Christine C., and Savitsky, Kenneth. Behavioral Confirmation in the Interrogation Room: On the Dangers of Presuming Guilt. *Law and Human Behavior, 27* (2003): pp. 187–203.

Kebbell, Mark R. and Milne, Rebecca. Police Officers' Perception of Eyewitness Performance in Forensic Investigations. *The Journal of Social Psychology, 138*(3) (1998): pp. 323–330.

Keinan, Giora. Decision Making under Stress: Scanning of Alternatives under Controllable and Uncontrollable Threats. *Journal of Personality and Social Psychology, 52*(3) (1987): pp. 639–644.

Kelley, Harold H. The Warm-Cold Variable in First Impressions of Persons. *Journal of Personality, 18* (1950): pp. 431–439.

Kelley, Matthew R., Neath, Ian, and Surprenant, Aimée M. Serial Position Functions in General Knowledge. *Journal of Experimental Psychology: Learning, Memory, and Cognition, 41* (2015): pp. 1715–1727.

Kelman, Herbert C. The Policy Context of Torture: A Social-Psychological Analysis. *International Review of the Red Cross, 87* (2006): pp. 123–134.

Kennedy, Duncan. Freedom and Constraint in Adjudication: A Critical Phenomenology. *Journal of Legal Education, 36* (1986): pp. 518–562.
Keren, Gideon and Schul, Yaacov. Two is Not Always Better Than One: A Critical Evaluation of Two-System Theories. *Perspectives on Psychological Sciences, 4* (2009): pp. 533–550.
Kerr, Norbert L. and Tindale, R. Scott. Group Performance and Decision Making. *Annual Review of Psychology, 55* (2004): pp. 623–655.
Kerstholt, José, Eikelboom, Aletta, Dijkman, Tjisse, Stoel, Reinoud, Hermsen, Rob, and van Leuven, Bert. Does Suggestive Information Cause a Confirmation bias in Bullet Comparisons. *Forensic Science International, 198* (2010): pp. 138–142.
Kerstholt, José, Passhuis, Rose, and Sjerps, Marjan. Shoe Print Examinations: Effects of Expectation, Complexity and Experience. *Forensic Science International, 165* (2007): pp. 30–34.
Klayman, Joshua and Ha, Young-Won. Confirmation, Disconfirmation, and Information in Hypothesis Testing. *Psychological Review, 94* (1987): pp. 211–228.
Klein, William M. and Kunda, Ziva. Motivated Person Perception: Constructing Justifications for Desired Beliefs. *Journal of Experimental Social Psychology, 28* (1992): pp. 145–168.
Kloosterman, Ate, Sjerps, Marjan J., and Quak, Astrid. Error Rates in Forensic DNA Analysis: Definition, Numbers, Impact and Communication. *Forensic Science International: Genetics, 12* (2014): pp. 77–85.
Knobe, Joshua. Philosophers are Doing Something Different Now: Quantitative Data. *Cognition, 135* (2015): pp. 36–38.
Koehler, Jonathan J. The Base Rate Fallacy Reconsidered: Descriptive, Normative, and Methodological Challenges. *Behavioral & Brain Sciences, 19* (1996): pp. 1–17.
Kolflaath, Eivind. Sannsynlighetsovervekt og kumulering av tvil. *Lov og Rett, 47* (2008): pp. 149–164.
Kondo, Toshikazu and Ohshima, Takashi. Retrospective Investigation of Medico-legal Autopsy Cases involving Mentally Handicapped Individuals. *The Japanese Journal of Legal Medicine*, 49(6) (1995): pp. 478–483.
Konopka, Tomasz, Bolechała, Filip, and Strona, Marcin. Chest Stab Wound Comparison in Suicidal and Homicidal Cases. *Archives of Forensic Medicine and Criminology*, 53(2) (2003): pp. 117–128.
Koppelaar, Leendert, Lange, Alfred, and van de Velde, Jan-Willem. The Influence of Positive and Negative Victim Credibility on the Assessment of Rape Victims: An Experimental Study of Expectancy—Confirmation Bias. *International Review of Victimology*, 5(1) (1997): pp. 61–85.
Koriat, Asher and Goldsmith, Morris. Monitoring and Control Processes in the Strategic Regulation of Memory Accuracy. *Psychological Review*, 103(3) (1996), pp. 490–517.
Koriat, Asher, Lichtenstein, Sarah, and Fischhoff, Baruch. Reasons for Confidence. *Journal of Experimental Psychology: Human Learning and Memory, 2* (1980): pp. 107–118.
Kozhevnikov, Maria and Hegarty, Mary (2001). Impetus Beliefs as Default Heuristics: Dissociation Between Explicit and Implicit Knowledge about Motion. *Psychonomic Bulletin & Review*, 8(3), pp. 439–453.
Kozlov, Mikhail V. and Zvereva, Elena L. Confirmation Bias in Studies of Fluctuating Asymmetry. *Ecological Indicators, 57* (2015): pp. 293–297.
Krane, Dan E., Ford, Simon, Gilder, Jason R., Inman, Keith, Jamieson, Allen, Koppl, Rogger, Kornfield, Irving, Risinger, Michael D., Rudin, Norah. Taylor, Marc S., and William C. Thompson. Sequential Unmasking: A Means of Minimizing Observer Effects in Forensic DNA Interpretation. *Journal of Forensic Sciences, 53* (2008): pp. 1006–1007.

Kruglanski, Arie W. and Webster, Donna M. Motivated Closing of the Mind: 'Seizing' and 'Freezing'. *Psychological Review, 103* (1996): pp. 263–268.

Kruglanski, Arie W., Webster, Donna M., and Klem, Adena M. Motivated Resistance and Openness to Persuasion in the Presence or Absence of Prior Information. *Journal of Personality and Social Psychology, 65* (1993): pp. 861–876.

Kruse, Corinna. Swedish Crime Scene Technicians: Facilitations, Epistemic Frictions and Professionalization from the Outside. *Nordic Journal of Criminology, 21*(1) (2020): pp. 67–83.

Ku, Kelly Y.L. Assessing Student's Critical Thinking Performance: Urging for Measurements using Multiple-response Format. *Thinking Skills and Creativity, 4*(1) (2009): pp. 70–76.

Kuhl, Julius. Volitional Aspects of Achievement Motivation and Learned Helplessness: Toward a Comprehensive Theory of Action Control. *Progress in Experimental Personality Research, 13* (1984): pp. 99–170.

Kukucka, Jeff and Kassin, Saul M. Do Confessions Taint Perceptions of Handwriting Evidence? An Empirical Test of the Forensic Confirmation Bias. *Law and Human Behavior, 38* (2013): pp. 1–15.

Kukucka, Jeff, Kassin, Saul M., Zapf, Patricia A., and Dror, Itiel E. Cognitive Bias and Blindness: A Global Survey of Forensic Examiners. *Journal of Applied Research in Memory and Cognition, 6* (2017): pp. 452–459.

Kunda, Ziva. Motivated Inference: Self-Serving Generation and Evaluation of Causal Theories. *Journal of Personality and Social Psychology, 53* (1987): pp. 636–647.

Kunda, Ziva, The Case for Motivated Reasoning. *Psychological Bulletin, 108* (1990): pp. 480–498.

Köhnken, Günther. Training Police Officers to Detect Deceptive Eyewitness Statements. Does it Work? *Social Behavior, 2* (2018): pp. 1–17.

Lamm, Helmut and Myers, David G. Myers. Group-Induced Polarization of Attitudes and Behavior. *Advances in Experimental Social* Psychology, 11 (2008): pp. 145–187.

Lammers, Joris and Stapel, Diederik. Retracted: Racist Biases in Legal Decisions are Reduced by a Justice Focus. *European Journal of Social Psychology, 41* (2011): pp. 375–387.

Lange, Nick D., Thomas, Rick P., Dana, Jason and Dawes, Robyn, M. Contextual Biases in the Interpretation of Auditory Evidence. *Law and Human Behavior, 35*(3) (2011): pp. 178–187.

Landes, William M. The Bail System: An Economic Approach. *The Journal of legal Studies, 2*(1) (1973): pp. 79–105.

Lankford, Adam. Promoting Aggression and Violence at Abu Ghraib: The US Military's Transformation of Ordinary People into Torturers. *Aggression and Violent Behavior, 14* (2009): pp. 388–395.

Lee, HweeLing, Devlin, Joseph T., Shakeshaft, Clare, Brennan, Amanda, Glensman, Jen, Pitcher, Katherine et al., Anatomical Traces of Vocabulary Acquisition in the Adolescent Brain. *Journal of Neuroscience, 27* (2007): pp. 1184–1189.

Lee, Cindy S., Nagy, Paul G., Weaver, Sallie J., Newman-Toker, David, E. Cognitive and System Factors Contributing to Diagnostic Errors in Radiology. *American Journal or Roentgenology, 201*(3) (2013): pp. 611–617.

Lemaigre, Charlotte, Taylor, Emily, and Gittoes, Claire. Barriers and Facilitators to Disclosing Sexual Abuse in Childhood and Adolescence: A Systematic Review. *Child Abuse & Neglect, 70* (2017): pp. 39–52.

Leo, Richard A. and Davis, Deborah. From False Confession to Wrongful Conviction: Seven Psychological Processes. *Journal of Psychiatry & Law, 38*(1-2) (2010): pp. 9–56.

Leo, Richard A. and Ofshe, Richard J. The Consequences of False Confessions: Deprivation of Liberty and Miscarriages of Justice in the Age of Psychological Interrogation. *The Journal of Criminal Law & Criminology*, 88 (2) (1998), pp. 429–496.

Leslie. Emily and Pope, Nolan G. The Unintended Impact of Pretrial Detention on Case Outcomes: Evidence from New York City Arraignments. *The Journal of Law & Economics*, 60 (3) (2017): pp. 529–557.

Levin, Emma A., Morgan Ruth M., Griffin, Lewis D., Jones, Vivienne, J. A Comparison of Thresholding Methods for Forensic Reconstruction Studies Using Fluorescent Powder Proxies for Trace Materials. *Journal of Forensic Sciences*, 64 (2) (2019): pp. 431–442.

Levine, Murray. Do Standards of Proof Affect Decision Making in Child Protection Investigations? *Law and Human Behavior*, 22 (1998): pp. 341–347.

Levinson, Justin D. and Young, Danielle. Different Shades of Bias: Skin Tone, Implicit Racial Bias and Judgments of Ambiguous Evidence. *West Virgina Law Review*, 112(2) (2010): pp. 307–350.

Lewis, David. Causation. *Journal of Philosophy*, 70 (1973): pp. 556–567.

Lidén, Moa. Emotions and Cognition in International Criminal Justice: An Exploration from Cognitive Biases to Emotional Intelligence. *Forensic Science International: Mind and Law*, 1 (2020): pp. 1–10.

Lidén, Moa. 'Inter-domar reliabilitet': Är Individuella Skillnader i Domares Beslutsfattande ett Löfte eller Hot mot Rättssäkerheten? *Ny Juridik*, 2(21) (2021): pp. 1–18.

Lidén, Moa and Almazrouei, Mohammed A. 'Blood, Bucks and Bias': Reliability and Biasability of Crime Scene Investigators' Selection and Prioritization of Blood Traces. *Science & Justice*, 63(2) (2021): pp. 276–293.

Lidén, Moa, Gräns, Minna and Juslin, Peter. 'Guilty, No Doubt': Detention Provoking Confirmation Bias in Judges' Guilt Assessments and Debiasing Techniques. *Psychology, Crime & Law*, 25(3) (2019): pp. 219–247.

Lidén, Moa, Gräns, Minna and Juslin, Peter (2018). The Presumption of Guilt in Suspect Interrogations: Apprehension as a Trigger of Confirmation Bias and Debiasing Techniques. *Law and Human Behavior*, 42(4): pp. 336–354.

Lidén, Moa, Gräns, Minna, and Juslin, Peter. Self-correction of Wrongful Convictions: Is there a 'System-level' Confirmation Bias in the Swedish Legal System's Appeal Procedure for Criminal Cases?—Part II. *Law, Probability & Risk*, 17 (4) (2019): pp. 337–356.

Lilienfeld, Scott O. and Landfield, Kristin. Science and Pseudoscience in Law Enforcement: A User-friendly Primer. *Criminal Justice and Behavior*, 35 (10) (2008):, pp. 1215–1230.

Lindberg, Gunnel. Om åklagaretik. *Svensk Juristtidning* (1997): pp. 197–221.

Lindblom, Per Henrik. Tvekamp eller inkvisition—reflektioner om straffprocessens samhällsfunktion och grundstruktur. *Svensk Juristtidning* (1999): pp. 617–655.

Lindblom, Per Henrik. Rättegångssalens väggar—om domstolsprocessen i tid och rum. *Svensk Juristtidning* (2002) pp. 1–11.

Lindblom, Per Henrik. Domstolarnas växande samhällsroll och processens förändrade funktioner—floskler eller fakta? *Svensk Juristtidning* (2004): pp. 229–262.

Lindsay, Rod and Wells, Gary L. What Price Justice? Exploring the Relationship Between Lineup Fairness and Identification Accuracy. *Law and Human Behavior*, 4 (4) (1980): pp. 303–314.

Lindsay, Rod, Wallbridge, Harold, and Drennan, Daphne. Do Clothes Make the Man? An Exploration of the Effect of Lineup Attire on Eyewitness Identification Accuracy. *Canadian Journal of Behavioural Science*, 19 (1987): pp. 463–478.

Lindsay, Roderick Cameron, Wells, Gary L. and Rumpel, Carolyn M. Can People Detect Eyewitness-identification Accuracy Within and Across Situations? *Journal of Applied Psychology*, 66(1) (1981): pp. 79–89.

Lindskog, Marcus, Winman, Anders, and Juslin, Peter. Calculate or Wait: Is Man an Eager or a Lazy Intuitive Statistician? *Journal of Cognitive Psychology, 25* (2013): pp. 994–1014.

Liu, Shuxia. Three-dimension Point Cloud Technology and Intelligent Extraction of Trace Evidence at the Scene of Crime. *Journal of Physics, 1237*(4) (2019): pp. 1–8.

Liu, JIn, Yu, Peng, Bai, Junxuan, Fu, Huanzhang, and Pan, Junjun. A Survey of Crime Scene Reconstruction Based on 3D Laser Scanning Technology. *Forensic Science and Technology, 42*(6) (2017): pp. 476–481.

Llewelyn, Karl. Franks' 'Law and The Modern Mind'. *Columbia Law Review, 31* (1931): pp. 82–90.

Lloyd, Eric. Making Civil RICO 'Suave': Congress Must Act to Ensure Consistent Judicial Interpretations of the Racketeer-influenced and Corrupt Organizations Act. *Santa Clara Review, 47*(1) (2007): p. 123.

Loftus, Elizabeth F. Eyewitness Testimony in the Lockerbie Bombing Case. *Memory, 21*(5) (2013): pp. 584–590.

Lord, Charles G., Ross, Lee, and Lepper, Mark R. Biased Assimilation and Attitude Polarization: The Effects of Prior Theories on Subsequently Considered Evidence. *Journal of Personality and Social Psychology, 37* (1979): pp. 2098–2109.

Ludwig, Timothy D., Geller, Scott E., and Clarke, Steven W. The Additive Impact of Group and Individual Publicly Displayed Feedback: Examining Individual Response Patterns and Response Generalization in a Safe-Driving Occupational Intervention. *Behavior Modification, 8* (2010): pp. 338–366.

Lush, Christopher. Remli v. France, Part One: European Court of Human Rights: Summaries of Judgments. *Human Rights Case Digest, 6* (1995): p. 57.

Luus, Elizabeth and Wells, Gary L. Eyewitness Identification and the Selection of Distracters for Lineups. *Law and Human Behavior, 15* (1991): pp. 43–57.

Lynch, Michael. God's Signature: DNA profiling, the New Gold Standard in Forensic Evidence. *Endeavour, 27* (2003): pp. 93–97.

Lynoe, Niels, Elinder, Göran, Hallberg, Boubou, Rosén, Måns, Sundgren, Pia and Eriksson, Anders. Insufficient Evidence for 'Shaken Baby Syndrome'—A Systematic Review. *Acta Paediatrica, 106*(7) (2016): pp. 1021–1027.

MacDonald, Stuart K. Constructing a Framework for Criminal Justice Research: Learning from Packer's Mistakes. *New Criminal Law Review, 11* (2008): pp. 257–311.

Mackie, John L. Causes and Conditions. *American Philosophical Quarterly, 2* (1965): pp. 245–264.

Mackie, John L. The Paradox of Confirmation. *British Journal for the Philosophy of Science, 38* (1963): pp. 265–277.

Magnusson, Mikaela, Ernberg, Emelie, and Landström, Sara. Preschoolers' Disclosures of Child Sexual Abuse: Examining Corroborated Cases from Swedish Courts. *Child Abuse & Neglect, 70* (2017): pp. 199–209.

Magnusson, Mikaela, Ernberg, Emelie, Landström, Sara, and Granhag, Pär Anders. Taking the stand: Defendant Statements in Court Cases of Alleged Sexual Abuse Against Infants, Toddlers and Preschoolers. *Psychology, Crime & Law, 24* (2018): pp. 1–16.

Marion, Stéphanie B., Kukucka, Jeff, Collins, Carisa, Kassin, Saul M., and Burke, Tara. Lost Proof of Innocence: The Impact of Confessions on Alibi Witnesses. *Law and Human Behavior, 40* (2016): pp. 65–71.

Marietta, Morgan and Barker, David C. Values as Heuristics: Core Beliefs and Voter Sophistication in the 2000 Republican Nomination Contest. *Journal of Elections, Public Opinion and Parties, 17*(1) (2007): pp. 49–78.

Mastroberardino, Serena and Marucci, Francesco S. Interrogative Suggestibility: Was it Just Compliance or a Genuine False Memory?: Interrrogative Suggestibility and Source Monitoring. *Legal and Criminological Psychology*, 18(2) (2013): pp. 274–286.

Ma, Xiaoye, Nie, Lei, Cole, Stephen R., Chu, Haitao, lee, Duncan, MacNab, Ying, and Lawson, Andrew B. Statistical Methods for Multivariate Meta-Analysis of Diagnostic Tests: An Overview and Tutorial. *Statistical Methods in Medical Research*, 25(4) (2016): pp. 1596–619.

Mayseless, Ofra and Kruglanski, Arie W. What Makes You So Sure? Effects of Epistemic Motivations on Judgmental Confidence. *Organizational Behavior and Human Decision Processes*, 39 (1987): pp. 162–183.

McCarthy, Anne M., Schoorman, David F., and Cooper, Arnold C. Reinvestment Decisions by Entrepreneurs: Rational Decision-Making or Escalation of Commitment. *Journal of Business Venturing*, 8 (1993): pp. 9–24.

McCloskey, James, Convicting the Innocent. *Criminal Justice Ethics*, 8(1) (1989): pp. 140–141.

McDermott, Yvonne, Koenig, Alexa, and Murray, Daragh. Open Source Information's Blind Spot: Human and Machine Bias in International Criminal Investigations. *Journal of International Criminal Justice*, 19(1) (2021): pp. 1–21.

McGarthy, Craig, Turner, John C., Hogg, Michael A., and David, Barbara. Group Polarization as Conformity to the Most Prototypical Group Member. *British Journal of Social Psychology*, 31 (1992): pp. 1–20.

McLean, Iain, Roberts, Stephen A.,White, Cath, and Paul, Sheila. Female Genital Injuries Resulting From Consensual and Non Consensual Vaginal Intercourse. *Forensic Science International*, 204 (2011): pp. 27–33.

McLellan, Myles F. Bail and the Diminishing Presumption of Innocence. *Canadian Criminal Law Review*, 15(1) (2010): pp. 57–74.

McMillan, Lesley. Police Officers' Perceptions of False Allegations of Rape. *Journal of Gender Studies*, 27(1) (2015): pp. 9–21.

Medwed, Daniel S. The Zeal Deal: Prosecutorial Resistance to Post-conviction Claims of Innocence. *Boston University Law Review*, 84(1) (2004): pp. 125–183.

Meeus, Wim. H.J. and Raaijmakers, Quinten A.W. Obedience in Modern Society: The Utrecht Studies. *Journal of Social Issues*, 51 (1995): pp. 155–175.

Meissner, Christian A. and Brigham, John C. Thirty Years of Investigating the Own-Race Bias in Memory for Faces: A Meta-Analytic Review. *Psychology, Public Policy and Law*, 7 (2001): pp. 3–35.

Meissner, Christian A. and Kassin, Saul M. 'He's Guilty!': Investigator Bias in Judgments of Truth and Deception. *Law and Human Behavior*, 26 (2002): pp. 469–480.

Melinder, Annika, Brennan, Tim, Husby, Mikael Falkhaugen, Vassend, Olav. Personality, Confirmation Bias, and Forensic Interviewing Performance. *Applied Cognitive Psychology*, 34(5) (2020): pp. 961–971.

Mellqvist, Mikael. Om empatisk rättstillämpning. *Svensk Juristtidning* (2013): pp. 493–501.

Mendel, Rosmarie, Traut-Mattausch, Eva, Jonas, Eva, Leucht, Stefan, Kane, John M., Maino, Katja, Kissling, Werner, and Hamann, Johannes. Confirmation Bias: Why Psychiatrists Stick to Wrong Preliminary Diagnoses. *Psychological Medicine*, 41 (2011): pp. 2651–2659.

Mercier, Hugo. The Argumentative Theory: Predictions and Empirical Evidence. *Trends in Cognitive Science*, 20 (2016): pp. 689–700.

Mercier, Hugo and Sperber, Dan. Why Do Humans Reason? Arguments for an Argumentative Theory. *Behavioral and Brain Sciences*, 34 (2011): pp. 57–74.

Mermillod, Martial, Marchand, Victorien, Lepage, Johan, Begue, Laurent, and Dambrun, Michael. Destructive Obedience Without Pressure. *Social Psychology, 46* (2015): pp. 345–351.

Merton, Robert K. The Self-Fulfilling Prophecy. *The Antioch Review, 8* (1948): pp. 193–210.

Milgram, Stanley. Behavioral Study of Obedience. *The Journal of Abnormal and Social Psychology, 67* (1963): pp. 371–378.

Miller, George A. The Magical Number Seven, Plus or Minus Two: Some Limits on Our Capacity for Processing Information. *Psychological Review, 63* (1956): pp. 81–97.

Miller, Larry S. Bias Among Forensic Document Examiners: A Need for Procedural Change. *Journal of Police Science & Administration, 12* (1984): pp. 407–411.

Minhas, Rashid and Walsh, Dave. Influence of Racial Stereotypes on Investigative Decision Making in Criminal Investigations: A Qualitative Comparative Analysis, *Cogent Social Sciences,* 4 (2018), 1538588.

Minhas, Rashid and Walsh, Dave. Prejudicial Stereotyping and Police Interviewing Practices in England: An Exploration of Legal Representatives' Perceptions. *Journal of Policing, Intelligence and Counter Terrorism, 16*(3) (2021): pp. 1–16.

Miyake, Akira, Friedman, Naomi P., Emerson, Michael J., Witzki, Alexander H., Howerter, Amy, and Wager, Tor D. The Unity and Diversity of Executive Functions and Their Contributions to Complex 'Frontal Lobe' Tasks: A Latent Variable Analysis. *Cognitive Psychology, 41* (2000): pp. 49–100.

Monteith, Margo, Sherman, Jeffrey, and Devine, Patricia. Suppression as a Stereotype Control Strategy. *Personality and Social Psychology Review* (1998): pp. 63–82.

Montgomery, Henry. Decision Rules and the Search for a Dominance Structure: Towards a Process Model of Decision Making. *Advances in Psychology, 14* (1983): pp. 343–369.

Moorthy, Nataraja T. Suspicious Death—Crime Scene Evidence Indicated the Cause of Death: An Interesting Multiple Death Case Report. *International Journal of Medical Toxicology and Legal Medicine, 22*(1-2) (2019): pp. 5–7.

Morse, Wayne L. and Beattie, Ronald H. Survey of the Administration of Criminal Justice in Oregon. *Oregon Law Review, 11* (1932): pp. 173–174.

Moscovici, Serge and Zavalloni, Marisa. The Group as a Polarizer of Attitudes. *Journal of Personality and Social Psychology, 12* (1969): pp. 124–135.

Mostad, Petter and Tamsen, Fredrik. Error Rates for Unvalidated Medical Age Assessment Procedures. *International Journal of Legal Medicine, 133*(2) (2019): pp. 613–623.

Mrevlje, Pavsic (2018). Police Trauma and Rorscach Indicators: An Exploratory Study. *Rorschachiana, 39*(1): pp. 1–19.

Muir-Broaddus, Jacqueline, King, Tamara, Downey, Dinah, and Petersen, Mark. Conservation as a Predictor of Individual Differences in Children's Susceptibility to Leading Questions. *Psychonomic Bulletin & Review, 5* (1998): pp. 454–458.

Mullen, Brian, Anthony, Tara, Salas, Eduardo, and Driskell, James E. Group Cohesiveness and Quality of Decision Making: An Integration of Tests of the Groupthink Hypothesis. *Small Group Research, 24* (1994): pp. 189–204.

Munro, Geoffrey D. and Ditto, Peter H. Biased Assimilation, Attitude Polarization, and Affect in Reactions to Stereotype-Relevant Scientific Information. *Personality and Social Psychology Bulletin, 23* (1997): pp. 636–653.

Munro, Geoffrey D. and Stansbury, Jessica A. The Dark Side of Self-Affirmation: Confirmation Bias and Illusory Correlation in Response to Threatening Information. *Personality and Social Psychology Bulletin, 35* (2009): pp.1143–1153.

Muris, Peter, Debipersad, Suradj, and Mayer, Birgit. Searching for Danger: On the Link Between Worry and Threat-Related Confirmation Bias in Children. *Journal of Child and Family Studies, 23* (2013): pp. 604–609.

Muris, Peter and Field, Andy P. Distorted Cognition and Pathological Anxiety in Children and Adolescents. *Cognition and Emotion, 22* (2008): pp. 395–421.

Muris, Peter, Rassin, Eric, Mayer, Birgit, Smeets, Guus, Huijding, Jorg, Remmerswaal, Danielle, and Field, Andy. Effects of Verbal Information on Fear-Related Reasoning Biases in Children. *Behaviour Research and Therapy, 47* (2009): pp. 206–214.

Murphy, Thomas. The Admissibility of CCTV Evidence in Criminal Proceedings. *International Review of Law, Computers & Technology, 13*(3) (1999): pp. 383–404.

Murphy, Gillian and Greene, Ciara M. Perceptual Load Affects Eyewitness Accuracy and Susceptibility to Leading Questions. *Frontiers in Psychology, 7* (2016): pp. 1–10.

Myers, David G. and Lamm, Helmut. The Group Polarization Phenomenon. *Psychological Bulletin, 83* (1976): pp. 602–627.

Mynatt, Clifford R., Doherty, Michael E., and Tweney, Ryan D. Confirmation Bias in a Simulated Research Environment: An Experimental Study of Scientific Inference. *The Quarterly Journal of Experimental Psychology, 29*(1) (1977): pp. 85–95.

Mynatt, Clifford R., Doherty, Michael E., and Dragan, William. Information Relevance, Working Memory, and the Consideration of Alternatives. *The Quarterly Journal of Experimental Psychology, 46* (1993): pp. 759–778.

Mynatt, Clifford R., Doherty, Michael E., and Sullivan, James A. Data Selection in a Minimal Hypothesis Testing Task. *Acta Psychologica, 76* (1991): pp. 293–305.

Podbregar, Matej, Voga, Gorazd, Krivec, Bojan, Skale, Rafael, Pareznik, Roman, Gabrscek, Lucija. 'Should we Confirm Our Clinical Diagnosis Certainty by Autopsies? *Intensive Care Medicine 27*(11) (2001): pp. 1750–55.

Mazzolo, Gionata M. and Desinan, Lorenzo. Sharp Force Fatalities: Suicide, Homicide or Accident? A Series of 21 Cases. *Forensic Science International, 147* (2005), pp. S33–S35.

Narchet, Fadia M., Meissner, Christian A., and Russano, Melissa B. Modeling the Influence of Investigator Bias on the Elicitation of True and False Confessions. *Law and Human Behavior, 35*(6) (2011): pp. 452–465.

Nakhaeizadeh, Sherry, Hanson, Ian, and Dozzi, Nathalie. The Power of Contextual Effects in Forensic Anthropology: A Study of Biasability in the Visual Interpretations of Trauma Analysis on Skeletal Remains. *Journal of Forensic Sciences, 59*(5) (2014): pp. 1177–1183.

Nakhaeizadeh, Sherry, Dror, Itiel E., and Morgan, Ruth M. Cognitive Bias in Forensic Anthropology: Visual Assessment of Skeletal Remains is Susceptible to Confirmation Bias. *Science & Justice, 54* (2014): pp. 208–214.

Nakhaeizadeh, Sherry, Morgan, Ruth M., Rando, Carolyn, and Dror, Itiel E. Cascading Bias of Initial Exposure to Information at the Crime Scene to the Subsequent Evaluation of Skeletal Remains. *Journal of Forensic Sciences 63*(3) (2017): pp. 403–411.

Narang, Sandeep K., Estrada, Cynthia., Greenberg, Sarah, and Lindberg, Daniel. Acceptance of Shaken Baby Syndrome and Abusive Head Trauma as Medical Diagnoses. *The Journal of Pediatrics, 177* (2016): pp. 273–278.

Narchet, Fadia M., Meissner, Christian A., and Russano, Melissa B. Modeling the Influence of Investigator Bias on the Elicitation of True and False Confessions. *Law and Human Behavior, 35* (2011): pp. 452–465.

Nelson, Eric L. If You Want to Convict a Domestic Violence Batterer, List Multiple Charges in the Police Report. *SAGE Open, 4* (2014): pp. 1–12.

Nelson, Thomas O. Consciousness and Metacognition. *American Psychologist, 51* (1996): pp. 102–116.

Newell, Allen, Shaw, John C., and Simon, Herbert A. Elements of a Theory of Human Problem Solving. *Psychological Review, 65* (1958): pp. 151–166.

Newell, Ben R. and Shanks, David R. Take-the-Best or Look at the Rest? Factors Influencing 'One-reason' Decision Making. *Journal of Experimental Psychology: Learning, Memory, and Cognition, 29* (2003): pp. 53–65.

Nho, Seon and Kim, Eun A. Factors Influencing Post-Traumatic Stress Disorder in Crime Scene Investigators. *Journal of Korea Academy of Nursing*, 47(1) (2017): pp. 39–48.

Nickerson, Raymond. Confirmation Bias: A Ubiquitous Phenomenon in Many Guises. *Review of General Psychology*, 2 (1998): pp. 175–220.

Nisbett, Richard E. and Wilson, Timothy D. The Halo Effect: Evidence for Unconscious Alteration of Judgments. *Journal of Personality and Social Psychology*, 4 (1977): pp. 250–256.

Nuzzo, Regina L. Statistical Errors, P values, the 'Gold Standard' of Statistical Validity, are Not as Reliable as Many Scientists Assume. *Nature*, 506 (2014): pp. 150–152.

Nysse-Carris, Kari L., Bottoms, Bette L., and Salerno, Jessica M. Experts' and Novices' Abilities to Detect Children's High Stakes Lie of Omission. *Psychology, Public Policy, and Law*, 17 (2011): pp. 76–98.

Oaksford, Mike and Chater, Nick. Précis of Bayesian Rationality: The Probabilistic Approach to Human Reasoning. *Behavioral and Brain Sciences*, 32 (2009): pp. 69–120.

O'Brien, Barbara. A Recipe for Bias: An Empirical Look at the Interplay Between Institutional Incentives and Bounded Rationality in Prosecutorial Decision Making. *Missouri Law Review*, 74(4) (2009): pp. 1000–1049.

Ogilvie, James. Cognitive Coherence. *Trends in Cognitive Science*, 3(5) (1999): p. 171.

O'Hara, Jane. Dead Wrong: How the Faulty Findings of an Eminent Pathologist Led to Erroneous Murder Charges and Ruined Lives (Dr. Charles Randall Smith). *Maclean's*, 114(20) (2001): p. 54.

Ohlin, Elisabeth. Svårt att definiera beprövad erfarenhet. *Läkartidningen*, 4 (2004): pp. 198–199.

Olivers, Christian, N.L. What Drives Memory-Driven Attentional Capture? The Effects of Memory Type, Display Type, and Search Type. *Journal of Experimental Psychology: Human Perception and Performance*, 35 (2009): pp. 1275–1291.

Oliver, William R. Effects of History and Context on Forensic Pathologist Interpretation of Photographs of Patterned Injury of the Skin. *Journal of Forensic Sciences*, 6 (2017): pp. 1500–1505.

Oliver, William R. Comment on Kukucka, Kassin, Zapf, and Dror (2017) 'Cognitive Bias and Blindness: A Global Survey of Forensic Science Examiners'. *Journal of Applied Research in Memory and Cognition*, 7 (2018): p. 161.

Oliver, William R. Comment on Dror, Kukucka, Kassin, and Zapf 'When Expert Decision Making Goes Wrong'. *Journal of Applied Research in Memory and Cognition*, 7 (2018): pp. 314–315.

Olsen, Lena. Rättsvetenskapliga perspektiv. *Svensk Juristtidning* (2004): pp. 105–143.

Olson, Elizabeth A. 'You Don't Expect Me to Believe that, Do You?': Expectations Influence Recall and Belief of Alibi Information. *Journal of Applied Social Psychology*, 43(6) (2013): pp. 1238–1247.

Ormstad, Kari, Karlsson, Thore, Enkler, Ludovic, Law, Barbara & Rajs, Jovan. Patterns in Sharp Force Fatalities—A Comprehensive Forensic Medical Study. *Journal of Forensic Science*, 31(2) (1986): pp. 529–542.

Osborne, Nikola K.P. and Taylor, Michael C. Contextual Information Management: An Example of Independent Checking in the Review of Laboratory-based Bloodstain Pattern Analysis. *Science & Justice*, 58(3) (2018): pp. 226–231.

Osborne, Nikola K.P., Taylor, Michael C., and Zajac, Rachel. Exploring the Role of Contextual Information in Bloodstain Pattern Analysis: A Qualitative Approach. *Forensic Science International*, 260 (2016): pp. 1–8.

Osborne, Nikola K. P., Woods, Sally, Kieser, Jules, and Zajac, Rachel. Does Contextual Information Bias Bitemark Comparisons? *Science & Justice, 54* (2014): pp. 267–273.

Osborne, Nikola K.P. and Zajac, Rachel. An Imperfect Match? Crime-related Context Influences Fingerprint Decisions. *Applied Cognitive Psychology, 30* (2015): pp. 126–134.

Osman, Magda. An Evaluation of Dual-Process Theories of Reasoning. *Psychonomic Bulletin & Review, 11* (2005): pp. 988–1010.

Page Dellinger, Amy. Gateway to Reform: Policy Implications of Police Officers' Attitudes towards Rape. *American Journal of Criminal Justice, 33*(1) (2008): pp. 44–58.

Page Dellinger, Amy. Judging Women and Defining Crime: Police Officers' Attitudes Towards Women and Rape. *Sociological Spectrum, 28*(4) (2008): pp. 389–411.

Page Dellinger, Amy. True Colours: Police Officers and Rape Myth Acceptance. *Feminist Criminology, 5*(4) (2010): pp. 315–334.

Parry, Nicola M.A. Keeping an Open Mind at Autopsy: Perspective from Veterinary Pathology. *Forensic Science International, Reports, 1* (2019), pp. 1–5.

Pattenden, Rosemary. Admissibility in Criminal Proceedings of Third Party and Real Evidence Obtained by Methods Prohibited by UNCAT. *The International Journal of Evidence & Proof, 10*(1) (2006): pp. 1–41.

Pennington, Nancy and Hastie, Reid. Evidence Evaluation in Complex Decision Making. *Journal of Personality and Social Psychology, 51* (1986): pp. 242–258.

Pennington, Nancy and Hastie, Reid. Explanation-Based Decision Making: Effects of Memory Structure on Judgment. *Journal of Experimental Psychology: Learning, Memory and Cognition, 14* (1988): pp. 521–533.

Pennington, Nancy and Hastie, Reid. A Cognitive Theory of Juror Decision Making—The Story Model. *Cardozo Law Review, 13* (1991): pp. 5001–5039.

Pennington, Nancy and Hastie, Reid. Explaining the Evidence: Tests of the Story Model for Juror Decision Making. *Journal of Personality and Social Psychology, 62* (1992): pp. 189–206.

Pessiglione, Mathias, Schmidt, Line, Draganski, Bogdan, Kalisch, Raffael, Lau, Hakwan. Dolan, Ray J., and Frith. Chris D. How the Brain Translates Money into Force: A Neuroimaging Study of Subliminal Motivation. *Science, 316* (2007): pp. 904–906.

Pessoa, Luiz. On the Relationship between Emotion and Cognition. *Nature Reviews, Neuroscience, 9*(2) (2008): pp. 148–158.

Peters, Emmanuelle R. Peters, Thornton, Patricia, Siksou, Lea, Linney, Yvonne and MacCabe, James H. Specificity of the 'Jump-to-conclusions' Bias in Deluded Patients. *British Journal of Clinical Psychology, 47* (2008): pp. 239–244.

Peterson, Brian L., Arnall, Michael, Avedschmidt, Sarah, Beers, Dean, Bell. Michael, Burton, Stephanie, Case, Mary, Catellier, Michele, Cina, Stephen. Cohle, Stephen, Collins, Kim, Covach, Adam, Downs, Jamie, Ely, Erin. Ely, Susan. Fajardo, Mark, fierro, Marcella, Fowler, Dave, Frost, Randy, Fudenberg, John, Fusaru. Aldo. Gill, James, Gilson, Thomas, Glenn, Chalres, Goldfogel, Gary, Graham. Stuart, Greenwell, Patrick, Grossberg, Lee Ann, Gulledge, Christopher, handler, Michael, Hansma, Patrick, Harschbarger, Kent, Hawes, Amy, Hellman, Fredric, Heninger, Michael, Hlavaty, leigh, Hoyer, Paul, Johnsson Deborah, Jorden, Michella, Kelley, Douglas, Kesha, Kilak, Kohr, Roland, Krywanczyk, Alison, Lehman, lee, Lochmuller, Christopher, Luzi, Scott, Ashley, Mathew, cDonough, Edward, Mileusnic, Darinka, Miller, Eliabeth, Milroy, Chris, Morrow, Paul, Oliver, William, orvik, Andrea, Pandey, Maneesha, parsons, Thomas, Pfalzgraf, Robert, Abraham, Philip. Poulos, Christopher, Prahlow, Joe, Pustilnik, Steven, Radisch, Deborah, Rao, Valerie, Raven, Katherine, Resk, Tom, Ross, Karen, Rudd, Tom, Schmidt, Carl,

Schmunk, Gregory, Sens, Mary Ann, Shelly, Mark, Snell, Kenneth, Sperry, Kris, Stables, Simon, Stahl-Herz, Jay, Steckbauer, Michael, Super, Mark, Tarau, Marius, Thogmartin, Jon, Tormos, Lee, Tse, Rexson, Utley, Suzanne, Vega, Russell, Williams, Karl, Wolf, Barbara, and Wright, Ron. Letter to the Editor, Commentary on: Dror, Melinek, Arden, Kukucka, Hawkins & Carter. Cognitive Bias in Forensic Pathology Decisions. *Journal of Forensic Sciences*, (2021): pp. 1–2.

Phillips, Mark R., McAuliff, Bradley D, Kovera, Margaret B., and Cutler, Brian L. Double-blind Photoarray Administration as a Safeguard Against Investigator Bias. *Journal of Applied Psychology*, 84 (1999): pp. 940–951.

Phillips, Victoria L., Saks, Michael J., and Peterson, Joseph L. The Application of Signal Detection Theory to Decision–Making in Forensic Science. *Journal of Forensic Sciences*, 46 (2001): pp. 294–308.

Pieters, Rik, Warlop, Luk, and Hartog, Michel. The Effect of Time Pressure and Task Motivation on Visual Attention to Brands. *Advances in Consumer Research*, 24 (1993): pp. 281–287.

Pincus, Jennifer, Lathrop, Sarah L., Briones, Alice J., Andrews, Sam W., Aurelius, Michelle B. Lightning Deaths: A Retrospective Review of New Mexico's Cases, 1977–2009. *Journal of Forensic Sciences*, 60(1) (2015): pp. 66–71.

Plucker, Jonathan & Shelton, Amy L. General Intelligence (g): Overview of a Complex Construct and Its Implications for Genetics Research. *The Hastings Center Report*, 45(1) (2015): pp. 21–24.

Pluskota, Marion. Petty Criminality, Gender Bias, and Judicial Practice in Nineteenth-Century Europe. *Journal of Social History*, 51(4) (2018): pp. 717–735

Poletiek, Fenna H. Paradoxes of falsification. *Quarterly Journal of Experimental Psychology*, 49 (1996): pp. 447–462.

Pope, Kenneth S. Pseudoscience, Cross-examination, and Scientific Evidence in the Recovered Memory Controversy. *Psychology, Public Policy, and Law*, 4 (1998): pp. 1160–1181.

Porter, Devon, Moss, Alexa, and Reisberg, Daniel. The Appearance-Change Instruction Does Not Improve Line-up Identification Accuracy. *Applied Cognitive Psychology*, 28 (2013): pp. 51–160.

Portwood, Sharon G. and Reppucci, N. Dickon. Adults' Impact on the Suggestibility of Preschooler's Recollections. *Journal of Applied Developmental Psychology*, 17 (1996): pp. 175–198.

Posner, Richard A. Pragmatic Adjudication. *Cardozo Law Review*, 18 (1996): pp. 1–20.

Powell, Martine B. Specialist Training in Investigative and Evidential Interviewing: Is It Having any Effect on the Behavior of Professionals in the Field. *Psychiatry, Psychology, and Law*, 9(1) (2002): pp. 44–55.

Powell, Martine B., Hughes-Scholes, Carolyn H., and Sharman, Stefanie J. Skill in Interviewing Reduces Confirmation Bias. *Journal of Investigative Psychology and Offender Profiling*, 9 (2012): pp. 126–134.

Powell, Martine B., and Snow, Pamela C. Guide to Questioning Children During the Free-Narrative Phase of an Investigative Interview. *Australian Psychologist*, 42 (2007): pp. 57–65.

Prohaska, Vincent and DelValle, Debbie, Toglia, Michael P., and Pittman, Anne E. Reported Serial Positions of True and Illusory Memories in the Deese/Roediger/McDermott Paradigm. *Memory*, 24 (2016): pp. 865–883.

Pronin, Emily, Gilovich, Thomas, and Ross, Lee. Objectivity in the Eye of the Beholder: Divergent Perceptions of Bias in Self Versus Others. *Psychological Review*, 111 (2004): pp. 781–799.

Puentes, Katerina, Taveira, Francisco, Madureira, Antonio J., Santos, Agostinho. Three-dimensional Reconstitution of Bullet Trajectory in Gunshot Wounds: A Case Report. *Journal of Forensic and Legal Medicine*, 16(7) (2009): pp. 407–410.

Rachlinski, Jeffrey. Evidence-Based Law. *Cornell Law Review*, 96 (2011): pp. 901–924.

Rachlinski, Jeffrey J., Wistrich, Andrew, J. and Guthrie, Chris. Can Judges Make Reliable Numeric Judgments? Distorted Damages and Skewed Sentences. *Indiana Law Journal*, 90(2) (2015): pp. 696–739.

Rachlinski, Jeffrey, Guthrie, Chris, and Wistrich, Andrew J. Heuristics and Biases in Bankruptcy Judges. *Cornell Law Faculty Publications*, 1081 (2007): pp. 167–186.

Rachlinski, Jeffrey, Guthrie, Chris, and Wistrich, Andrew J. Inside the Bankruptcy Judge's Mind. *Boston University Law Review*, 86 (2006): pp. 1227–1265.

Rajsic, Jason, Taylor, Eric, and Pratt, Jay. Out of Sight, Out of Mind: Matching Bias Underlies Confirmatory Visual Search. *Attention, Perception, & Psychophysics*, 79 (2017): pp. 498–507.

Rajsic, Jason, Wilson. Daryl E., and Pratt, Jay. Confirmation Bias in Visual Search. *Journal of Experimental Psychology: Human Perception and Performance*, 5 (2015): pp. 1353–1364.

Rajsic, Jason, Wilson, Daryl E., and Pratt, Jay. The Price of Information: Increased Inspection Costs Reduce the Confirmation Bias in Visual Search. *The Quarterly Journal of Experimental Psychology*, 71 (2017): pp. 1–20.

Ramsey, Carolyn B. The Discretionary Power of 'Public' Prosecutors in Historical Perspective. *The American Criminal Law Review*, 39(4) (2002): pp. 1309–1393.

Rassin, Eric. Individual Differences in the Susceptibility to Confirmation Bias. *Netherlands Journal of Psychology*, 64 (2008): pp. 87–93.

Rassin, Eric. Blindness to Alternative Scenarios in Evidence Evaluation. *Journal of Investigative Psychology and Offender Profiling*, 7(2) (2010): pp. 153–163.

Rassin, Eric. Context Effect and Confirmation Bias in Criminal Fact Finding. *Legal and Criminological Psychology*, 25(2) (2020): pp. 80–89.

Rassin, Eric, Eerland, Anita, and Kuijpers, Ilse. Let's Find the Evidence: An Analogue Study of Confirmation Bias in Criminal Investigations. *Journal of Investigative Psychology and Offender Profiling*, 7 (2010): pp. 231–246.

Ratner, Steven R. and Slaughter, Anne-Marie. Symposium on Method in International Law, Appraising the Methods of International Law: A Prospectus for Readers. *The American Journal of International Law*, 93 (1999): p. 291.

Rayner, Keith, White, Sarah J., Johnson, Rebecca L., and Liversedge, Simon P. Raeding Wrods with Jubmled Lettres: There's a Cost. *Psychological Science*, 17(3) (2006), pp. 192–193.

Reeves, Francis M. An Application of Bloom's Taxonomy to the Teaching of Business Ethics. *Journal of Business Ethics*, 9(7) (1990), pp. 609–616.

Reicher, Stephen and Haslam, S. Alexander. Rethinking the Psychology of Tyranny: The BBC Prison Study. *British Journal of Social Psychology*, 45 (2006): pp. 1–40.

Reichenbach, Hans. On Probability and Induction. *Philosophy of Science*, 5 (1938): pp. 21–45.

Remmerswaal, Danielle, Huijding, Jorg, Bouwmeester, Samantha, Brouwer, Marlies, and Muris, Peter. Cognitive Bias in Action: Evidence for a Reciprocal Relation Between Confirmation Bias and Fear in Children. *Journal of Behavior Therapy and Experimental Psychiatry*, 45 (2014): pp. 26–32.

Remmerswaal, Danielle, Muris, Peter, Mayer, Birgit, and Smeets, Guus. 'Will a Cuscus Bite You, If He Shows His Teeth?' Inducing a Fear-related Confirmation Bias in Children by Providing Verbal Threat Information to Their Mothers. *Journal of Anxiety Disorders*, 24 (2010): pp. 540–546.

Richardson, Robert D. *The Heart of William James*. *Persepctives on Psychological Science*, 8(3) (2013): pp. 314–315.

Rossner, Meredith. *Storytelling Rituals in Jury Deliberations. Onati Socio-Legal Series*, 9(5) (2018): pp. 747–770.

Risinger, Michael D., Saks, Michael J., Thompson, William C., and Rosenthal, Robert. The Daubert/Kumho Implications of Observer Effects in Forensic Science: Hidden Problems of Expectation and Suggestion. *California Law Review*, 90 (2002): pp. 1–56.

Roach, Kent and Trotter, Gary. Miscarriages of Justice in the War against Terror. Penn State Dickinson Law Review, 109 (2004), pp. 1–71.

Roberts, Andrew. The Perils and Possibilities of Qualified Identification: R v. George, The International Journal of Evidence & proof, 7(2) (2003): pp. 130–136.

Robinson, Edward S. and Brown, Martha A. Effects of Serial Position on Memorization. *The American Journal of Psychology*, 37 (1926): pp. 538–552.

Rodriguez, Dario N. and Berry, Melissa. The Effect of Line-up Administrator Blindness on the Recording of Eyewitness Identification Decisions. *Legal and Criminological Psychology*, 19 (2012): pp. 69–79.

Nemeth, Charlan, Brown, Keith, Rogers, John. Devil's Advocate Versus Authentic Dissent: Stimulating Quantity and Quality. *European Journal of Social Psychology*, 31 (2001): pp. 707–720.

Rolls, Edmund, Grabenhorst, Fabian and Deco, Gustavo. Choice, Difficulty, and Confidence in the Brain. *NeuroImage*, 53(2) (2010): pp. 694–706.

Roman, John K., Reid, Shannon E., Chalfin, Aaron, and Knight, Carly R. The DNA Field Experiment: A Randomized Trial of the Cost-Effectiveness of Using DNA to Solve Property Crimes. *Journal of Experimental Criminology*, 5 (2009): pp. 345–369.

Rosansky, Joseph A., Cook, Jeffrey, Rosenberg, Harold, Sprague, Jon E. PTSD Symptoms Experienced and Coping Tactics Used by Crime Scene Investigators in the United States. *Journal of Forensic Sciences*, 64(5) (2019): pp. 1444–1450.

Rosenthal, Robert. The 'File Drawer Problem' and Tolerance for Null Results. *Psychological Bulletin*, 86 (1979): pp. 638–641.

Ross, Lee, Lepper, Mark, and Hubbard, Michael. Perseverance in Self-Perception and Social Perception: Biased Attributional Processes in the Debriefing Paradigm. *Journal of Personality and Social Psychology*, 32 (1975): pp. 880–892.

Rossi, Sandrine, Caverni, Jean Paul, and Girotto, Vittoria. Hypothesis Testing in a Rule Discovery Problem: When a Focused Procedure is Effective. *The Quarterly Journal of Experimental Psychology*, 54 (2001): pp. 263–267.

Rowe, Paul M. What is All the Hullabaloo About Endostatin? *Lancet*, 353 (1999): p. 732.

Russo, Laura. *Date Rape: A Hidden Crime. Trends & Issues in Crime and Criminal Justice*, 157 (2000): pp. 1–6.

Ruva, Christine L. and Guenther, Christina C. Keep Your Bias to Yourself: How Deliberating With Differently Biased Others Affects Mock-Jurors' Guilt Decisions, Perceptions of the Defendant, Memories, and Evidence Interpretation. *Law and Human Behavior*, 41 (2017): pp. 478–493.

Ruva, Christine L. and Guenther, Christine C. From the Shadows Into the Light: how Pretrial Publicity and Deliberation Affect Mock Jurors' Decisions, Impressions, and Memory. *Law and Human Behavior*, 39 (2015): pp. 294–310.

Saks, Michael J., Risinger, Michael, Rosenthal, Robert, and Thompson, William C. Context Effects in Forensic Science: a Review and Application of the Science of Science to Crime Laboratory Practice in the United States. *Science & Justice*, 43 (2003): pp. 77–90.

Saks, Michael J. and Koehler, Jonathan J. The Coming Paradigm Shift in Forensic Identification Science. *Science*, 309 (2005): pp. 892–895.

Sandgren, Claes. Om empiri och rättsvetenskap. Del I. *Juridisk Tidsskrift* (1995/96): p. 726.
Sandgren, Claes. Om empiri och rättsvetenskap. Del II. *Juridisk Tidsskrift* (1995/96): p. 1035.
Santos, Laurie R. and Rosati, Alexandra. The Evolutionary Roots of Human Decision Making. *Annual Review of Psychology, 66* (2015): pp. 321–347.
Saunders, Candida Leigh. Rape as 'One Person's Word against Another's': Challenging the Conventional Wisdom. *The International Journal of Evidence & Proof, 22*(2) (2018): pp. 161–181.
Schoorman, David F. Escalation Bias in Performance Appraisals: An Unintended Consequence of Supervisor Participation in Hiring Decisions. *Journal of Applied Psychology, 73* (1988): pp. 58–62.
Schuller, Regina A., Stewart, Anna, Wiener, Richard L. Police Responses to Sexual Assault Complaints: The Role of Perpetrator/Complainant Intoxication. *Law and Human Behavior, 24*(5) (2000): pp. 535–551.
Schuller, Regina A. and Wall, Anne-Marie. The Effects of Defendant and Complainant Intoxication on Mock Jurors' Judgments of Sexual Assault. *Psychology of Women Quarterly, 22*(4) (1998): pp. 555–573.
Schulz-Hardt, Stefan, Frey, Dieter, Lüthgens, Carsten, and Moscovici, Serge. Biased Information Search in Group Decision Making. *Journal of Personality and Social Psychology, 78* (2000): pp. 655–669.
Schnider, Jasmin, Thali, Michael J., Ross, Stefan G., Oesterhelweg, Lars, Spendlove, Danny, Bolliger ,Stephen A. Injuries Due to Sharp Trauma Detected by Post-mortem Multislice Computed Tomography (MSCT): A Feasibility Study. *Journal of Legal Medicine, 11*(1) (2009): pp. 4–9.
Schulz-Hardt, Stefan, Jochims, Marc, and Frey, Dieter. Productive Conflict in Group Decision Making: Genuine and Contrived Dissent as Strategies to Counteract Biased Information Seeking. *Organizational Behavior and Human Decision Processes*, 88 (2002): pp. 563–586.
Schwartz, Barry, Ward, Andrew, Monterosso, John, Lyubomirsky, Sonja, White, Katherine, and Lehman, Darrin R. Maximising Versus Satisficing: Happiness is a Matter of Choice. *Journal of Personality and Social Psychology, 83* (2002): pp. 1178–1197.
Schweigher, David M., Sandberg, William R., and Ragan, James W. Group Approaches for Improving Strategic Decision making: a Comparative Analysis of Dialectical Inquiry, Devil's Advocacy, and Consensus. *Academy of Management Journal, 29* (1986): pp. 51–71.
Schweiger, David M., Sandberg, William R., and Rechner, Paula L. Experiental Effects of Dialectical Inquiry, Devil's Advocacy, and Consensus Approaches to Strategic Decision Making. *Academy of Management Journal, 32* (1989): pp. 745–772.
Schwenk, Charles R. Devil's Advocacy in Managerial Decision Making. *Journal of Management Studies, 21* (1984): pp. 153–168.
Schwenk, Charles R. Effects of Devil's Advocacy and Dialectical Inquiry on Decision Making: A Meta Analysis. *Organizational Behavior and Human Decision Processes, 47* (1990): pp. 161–176.
Schwenk, Charles R. and Cosier, Richard A. The Effects of Consensus and Devil's Advocacy on Strategic Decision-Making. *Journal of Applied Social Psychology, 23* (1993): pp. 126–139.
Schwenk, Charles R. and Valacich, Joseph S. Effects of Devil's Advocacy and Dialectical Inquiry on Individuals Versus Groups. *Organizational Behavior and Human Decision Processes, 59* (1994): pp. 210–222.
Schwind, Christina and Buder, Jürgen. Reducing Confirmation Bias and Evaluation Bias: When are Preference-inconsistent Recommendations Effective—and When Not? *Computers in Human Behavior, 28* (2012): pp. 2280–2290.

Schwind, Christina, Buder, Jűrgen, Cress, Ulrike, and Hesse, Friedrich W. Preference-inconsistent Recommendations: An Effective Approach for Reducing Confirmation Bias and Stimulating Divergent thinking? *Computers & Education,* 58 (2012): pp. 787–796.

Sells, Christina Mijalski and Feske, Steven K. Stroke in Pregnancy. *Seminars in Neurology,* 37(6) (2017): pp. 669–678.

Sergent, Claire and Dehaene, Stanislas. Is Consciousness a Gradual Phenomenon? Evidence for an All-or-None Bifurcation During the Attentional Blink. *Psychological Science,* 15 (2004): pp. 720–728.

Shafir, Eldar. Compatibility in Cognition and Decision. *Psychology of Learning and Motivation,* 32 (1995): pp. 257–274.

Shah, Anuj K., and Oppenheimer, Daniel M. Heuristics made Easy: An Effort-Reduction Framework. *Psychological Bulletin,* 134(2) (2008), pp. 207–222.

Sheldon, Kennon, Turban, Daniel B., Kenneth G. Brown, Barrick, Murray, and Judge, Timothy. Applying Self-determination Theory to Organizational Research. *Research in Personnel and Human Resources Management,* 22 (2003): pp. 357–393.

Sherman, Jeffrey W., Groom, Carla J. Ehrenberg, Katja and Klauer, Karl Cristoph. Bearing False Witness under Pressure: Implicit and Explicit Components of Stereotype-Driven Memory Distortions. *Social Cognition,* 21(3) (2003), pp. 213–246.

Shillcock, Richard. The Concrete Universal and Cognitive Science. *Axiomathes,* 24 (2014): pp. 63–80.

Sia, Choon-Ling, Tan, Bernard C.Y., and Wei, Kwok-Kee. Group Polarization and Computed Mediated Communication: Effects of Communication Cues, Social Presence, and Anonymity. *Information Systems Research,* 13 (2002): pp. 70–90.

Siegel-Jacobs, Karen and Yates, Frank J. Effects of Procedural and Outcome Accountability on Judgment Quality. *Organizational Behavior and Human Decision Processes,* 65 (1996): pp. 1–17.

Singh, Veena D. and Lathrop, Sarah L. Youth Suicide in New Mexico: A 26-year Retrospective Review. *Journal of Forensic Sciences,* 53(3) (2008): pp. 703–708.

Simon, Dan, Snow, Chadwick, and Read, Stephen J. The Redux of Cognitive Consistency Theories: Evidence Judgments by Constraint Satisfaction. *Journal of Personality and Social Psychology,* 86 (2004): pp. 814–837.

Simon, Dan, Stenstrom, Douglas M., and Read, Stephen J. The Coherence Effect: Blending Cold and Hot Cognitions. *Journal of Personality and Social Psychology,* 3 (2015): pp. 369–394.

Simons, Daniel J. and Chabris, Christopher F. Gorillas in our Midst: Sustained Inattentional Blindness for Dynamic Events. *Perception,* 28 (1999): pp. 1059–1074.

Slack, Donia P. Trauma and Coping Mechanisms Exhibited by Forensic Science Practitioners: A Literature Review. *Forensic Science International: Synergy,* 2 (2020): pp. 310–316.

Slovic, Paul. The Relative Influence of Probabilities and Payoffs Upon Perceived Risk of a Gamble. *Psychonomic Science,* 9 (1967): pp. 233–224.

Smeets, Guus, de Jong, Peter J., and Mayer, Birgit. 'If you Suffer From a Headache, Then You Have a Brain Tumour': Domain-specific Reasoning 'Bias' and Hypochondrias. *Behaviour Research and Therapy,* 38 (2000): pp. 763–777.

Smeulers, Alette, Hola, Barbora, and van den Berg, Tom. Sixty-five Years of International Criminal Justice: The Facts and Figures. *International Criminal Law Review,* 13(1) (2013): pp. 7–41.

Smith, Michael and Alpert, Geoffrey. Explaining Police Bias: A Theory of Social Conditioning and Illusory Correlation. *Criminal Justice and Behavior,* 34 (2007), pp. 1262–1283.

Start, Roger D., Milroy, Christopher M., Green, Michael Alan. Suicide by Self-stabbing. *Forensic Science International* 56(1) (1992): pp. 89–94.

Durham, Deborah. Youth and the Social Imagination in Africa. *Anthropological Quarterly*, 73(3) (2000): pp. 113–120.

Smith, Alison C, Greene, Edith, Wiener, Richard L. Conduct and its Consequences: Attempts at Debiasing Jury Judgments. *Law and Human Behavior*, 29(5) (2005): pp. 505–526.

Smit, Nadine M., Morgan, Ruth M., and Lagnado, David A. A Systemic Analysis of Misleading Evidence in Unsafe Ruling in England and Wales. *Science & Justice*, 58 (2018): pp. 128–137.

Snook; Brent and Cullen, Richard M. Bounded Rationality and Criminal Investigations: Has Tunnel Vision been Wrongfully Convicted? In Rossmo, Kim (Ed.). Criminal Investigative Failures (pp. 71–89). London: CRC Press, 2016.

Snowball, Lucy and Weatherburn, Don. Does Racial Bias in Sentencing Contribute to Indigenous Overrepresentation in Prison? *Australian & New Zealand Journal of Criminology*, 40(3) (2007): pp. 272–290.

Snyder, Mark. When Belief Creates Reality. *Advances in Experimental Social Psychology, 18* (1984): pp. 247–305.

Sollie, Henk, Kop, Nicolien, and Euwema, Martin C. Mental Resilience of Crime Scene Investigators: How Police Officers Perceive and Cope With the Impact of Demaning Work Situations. *Criminal Justice Behavior, 4* (2017): pp. 1580–1603.

Soto, David, Hodsoll, John, Rotshtein, Pia, and Humphreys, Glyn W. Automatic Guidance of Attention from Working Memory. *Trends in Cognitive Sciences, 12* (2008): pp. 342–348.

Speechley, William J., Whitman, Jennifer C., and Woodwards, Todd. The Contribution of Hypersalience to the 'Jumping to Conclusions' Bias Associated with Delusions in Schizophrenia. *Journal of Psychiatry & Neuroscience, 35* (2010): pp. 7–17.

Spencer, John R. Did the Jury Misbehave? Don't Ask, Because We Do Not Want to Know. *The Cambridge Law Journal, 291* (2002): pp. 291–293.

Sperber, Dan, Clement, Fabrice, Heintz, Christophe, Mascaro, Olivier, Mercier, Hugo, Origgi, Gloria, and Wilson, Deirdre. Epistemic Vigilance. *Mind & Language, 25* (2010): pp. 359–393.

Sporer, Siegfried L., Penrod, Steven D., Read, Don J., and Cutler, Brian. Choosing, Confidence, and Accuracy: A Meta-Analysis of the Confidence-Accuracy Relation in Eyewitness Identification Studies. *Psychological Bulletin, 118* (1995): pp. 315–327.

Stacey, Robert B. A Report on the Erroneous Fingerprint Individualization in the Madrid Train Bombing Case. *Journal of Forensic Identification, 54* (2005): pp. 709–711.

Stafford Smith, Clive. From Brighton to Camp Delta. *Index on Censorship*, 34(3) (2005): pp. 19–24.

Stasser, Garold and Stewart, Dennis. Discovery of Hidden Profiles by Decision-making Groups: Solving a Problem Versus Making a Judgment. *Journal of Personality and Social Psychology, 63* (1992): pp. 426–434.

Staw, Barry M. Knee-deep in the Big Muddy: A Study of Escalating Commitment to a Chosen Course of Action. *Organizational Behavior and Human Performance, 16* (1976): pp. 27–44.

Staw, Barry M., Barsade, Sigal G., and Koput, Kenneth W. Escalation at the Credit Window: A Longitudinal Study of Bank Executives' Recognition and Write-off Problem Loans. *Journal of Applied Psychology, 82* (1997): pp. 130–142.

Steblay, Nancy M. Social Influence in Eyewitness Recall: A Meta-Analytic Review of Lineup Instruction Effects. *Law and Human Behavior, 21 (3)* (1997): pp. 283–298.

Steblay, Nancy, Dysart, Jennifer. E., and Wells, Gary L. Seventy-two Tests of the Sequential Lineup Superiority Effect: A Meta-Analysis and Policy Discussion. *Psychology, Public Policy, and Law, 17 (1)* (2011): pp. 99–139.

Steblay, Nancy, Dysart, Jennifer, Fulero, Solomon, and Lindsay, Roderick C.L. Eyewitness Accuracy Rates in Sequential and Simultaneous Lineup Presentations: A Meta-Analytic Comparison. *Law and Human Behavior, 25 (5)* (2001): pp. 459–447.

Stevens, Laura E. and Fiske, Susan T. Motivated Impressions of a Power Holder: Accuracy under task dependency and misperception under evaluation dependency. *Personality and Social Psychology Bulletin, 26* (2000): pp. 907–922.

Stevenson, Megan J. Distortion of Justice: How the Inability to Pay Bail Affects Case Outcomes. *Journal of Law, Economics & Organization, 34*(4) (2018): pp. 511–542.

Stoel, Reinoud D., Dror, Itiel E., and Miller, Larry S. Bias Among Forensic Document Examiners: Still a Need for Procedural Changes. *Australian Journal of Forensic Sciences 46* (2014): pp. 91–97.

Stokes, Jim. Technical Note: Next Generation Identification—A Powerful Tool in Cold Case Investigations. *Forensic Science International, 299* (2019): pp. 74–49.

Strack, Fritz and Mussweiler, Thomas. Explaining the Enigmatic Anchoring Effect: Mechanisms of Selective Accessibility. *Journal of Personality and Social Psychology, 73* (1997): pp. 437–446.

Stroebe, Wolfgang and Diehl, Michael. Why Groups are Less Effective Than Their Members: On Productivity Losses in Idea-generating Groups. *European Review of Social Psychology, 5 (1)* (1994): pp. 271–303.

Stuckenberg, Carl-Friedrich. Who is Presumed Innocent of What by Whom? *Criminal Law and Philosophy, 8 (2)* (2014): pp. 301–316.

Studebaker, Christina A., Robbennolt, Jennifer K., Penrod, Steven D., Pathak-Sharma, Maithilee, Groscup, Jennifer L., and Devenport, Jennifer L. Studying Pretrial Publicity Effects: New Methods for Improving Ecological Validity and Testing External Validity. *Law and Human Behavior, 24 (3)* (2002): pp. 19–41.

Suarez-Moralez, Lourdes and Bell, Debora. The Relationship of Child Worry to Cognitive Biases: Threat Interpretation and Likelihood of Event Occurrence. *Behavior Therapy, 32 (3)* (2001): pp. 425–442.

Subke, Jörg, Haase, Sibylle, and Wehner, Heinz-Dieter, Wehner, Frank. Computer Aided Shot Reconstructions by Means of Individualized Animated Three Dimensional Victims Models. *Forensic Science International, 124*(2) (2002): pp. 245–249.

Sullivan, Thomas and Possley, Maurice. The Chronic Failure to Discipline Prosecutors for Misconduct: Proposals for Reform. *The Journal of Criminal Law and Criminology, 105* (4) (2015), pp. 881–945.

Summers, Robert S. Two Types of Substantive Reasoning. *Cornell Law Review, 63*(5) (1977): pp. 707–786.

Sunde, Nina and Dror, Itiel E. Cognitive and Human Factors in Digital Forensics: Problems, Challenges, and the Way Forward. *Digital Investigation, 29* (2019): pp. 101–108.

Sunde, Nina and Dror, Itiel E. A Hierarchy of Expert Performance (HEP) Applied to Digital Forensics: Reliability and Biasability in Digital Forensics Decision Making. *Forensic Science International: Digital Investigation, 37* (2021): pp. 1–11.

Svensson, Ola. Decision Making and the Search for Fundamental Psychological Regularities: What can be Learned from a Process Perspective? *Organizational Behavior and Human Decision Processes, 65* (1996): pp. 252–267.

Swarts, Richard H, Cayley, Megan L, Foley, Norine, Ladhani, Noor Niyar N. Leffert, Lisa, Bushnell, Cheryl, McClure Ja, and Lindsay, M Patrice. The Incidence of Pregnancy-related

Stroke: A Systematic Review and Meta-Analysis. *International Journal of Stroke*, *12*(7) (2017), pp. 687–697.

Taber, Charles S. and Lodge, Milton. Motivated Skepticism in the Evaluation of Political Beliefs. *Critical Review: A Journal of Politics and Society, 24* (2012): pp. 157–184.

Tajfel, Henri. Cognitive Aspects of Prejudice. *Journal of Social Issues, 25* (1969): pp. 79–97.

Tajfel, Henri. Experiments in Intergroup Discrimination. *Scientific American, 223* (1970): pp. 96–102.

Tallman, Sean D., Kincer, Caroline D., Plemons, Eric D. Centering Transgender Individuals in Forensic Anthropology and Expanding Binary Sex Estimation in Casework and Research. *Forensic Anthropology, Special Issue; Diversity and Inclusion, 5*(2) (2021): pp. 1–8.

Tanford, Sarah and Penrod, Steven D. Biases in Trials Involving Defendants Charged with Multiple Offenses. *Journal of Applied Social Psychology, 12*(6) (1982): pp. 453–480.

Tanford, Sarah, Penrod, Steven D., and Collins, Rebecca. Decision Making in Joined Criminal Trials: The Influence of Charge Similarity, Evidence Similarity and Limiting Instructions. *Law and Human Behavior, 9*(4) (1985): pp. 319–337.

Tesser, Abraham and Conlee, Mary C. Some Effects of Time and Thought on Attitude Polarization. *Journal of Personality and Social Psychology, 31(2)* (1975): pp. 262–270.

Thames, Elmer A., The Sunk Cost Effect: The Importance of Context. *Journal of Social Behavior & Personality, 11* (1996): pp. 817–826.

Thomson, Malcolm. Bias and Quality Control in Forensic Science: A Cause for Concern. *Journal of Forensic Sciences, 19*(3) (1974): pp. 504–517.

Thompson, Valerie A., Prowse Turner, Jamie A., and Pennycook, Gordon. Intuition, Reason and Metacognition. *Cognitive Psychology, 63 (3)* (2011): pp. 107–140.

Thompson, William C., Clarke-Stewart, Alison, and Lepore, Stephen J. What Did the Janitor Do? Suggestive Interviewing and the Accuracy of Children's Accounts. *Law and Human Behavior, 21* (1997): pp. 405–426.

Thorndike, Edward L. A Constant Error on Psychological Rating. *Journal of Applied Psychology, 4* (1920): pp. 25–29.

Thorngate, Warren and Tavakoli, Mahin. In the Long Run: Biological Versus Economic Rationality. *Simulation & Gaming, 36* (2005): pp. 9–26.

Thurzo, Andrej, svobodova Kosnacova, Helena, Kurilove, Veronika, Kosmel, Silvester, Benus, Radoslav, Moravansky Norbert, Kovac, Peter, Mikus Kuracinova, Kristina, Palkovic, Michal, and Varga, Ivan. Use of Advanced Artificial Intelligence in Forensic Medicine, Forensic Anthropology, and Clinical Anatomy. *Healthcare, 12*(9) (2021): p. 1545.

Träskman, Per Ole. Omvänt eller bakvänt: Om konstycket att lägga bevisbördan i brottmål på den tilltalade, utan att det kommer bak på människorättigheterna. *Nordisk tidsskrift for kriminalvidenskab, 4* (1998): pp. 352–386.

Trippas, Dries, Handley, Simon J., and Verde, Michael F. The SDT Model of Belief Bias: Complexity, Time and Cognitive Ability Mediate the Effects of Believability. *Journal of Experimental Psychology, 39*(5) (2013): pp. 1393–1402.

Tschan, Franziska, Semmer, Norbert K., Gurtner, Andrea, Bizzari, Lara, Spychiger, Martin, Breuer, Marc, and Marsch, Stephen U. Explicit Reasoning, Confirmation Bias, and Illusory Transactive Memory: A Simulation Study of Group Medical Decision Making. *Small Group Research, 40* (2009): pp. 271–300.

Tsujii, Takeo and Watanabe, Shigeru. Neural Correlates of Belief-bias Reasoning under Time Pressure: A Near-infrared Spectroscopy Study. *Neuroimage, 50* (2010): pp. 1320–1326.

Tuckey Rae, Michelle and Brewer, Neil. How Schemas Affect Eyewitness Memory over Repeated Retrieval Attempts. *Applied Cognitive Psychology, 17*(7) (2003): pp. 785–800.

Turner, John C., Oakes, Penelope J., Haslam, S. Alexander, and McGarty, Craig. Self and Collective: Cognition and Social context. *Personality and Social Psychology Bulletin, 20* (1994): pp. 454–463.

Tversky, Amos and Kahneman, Daniel. Judgment under Uncertainty: Heuristics and Biases. *Science, 185* (1974): pp. 1124–1131.

Tweney, Ryan D., Doherty, Michael E., Worner, Winifred J., Pliske, Daniel B., Mynatt, Clifford R., Gross, Kimberley A., and Arkkelin, Daniel L. Strategies of Rule Discovery in an Inference task. *Quarterly Journal of Experimental Psychology, 32* (1980): pp. 109–123.

Tydgat, Ilse & Grainger, Jonathan. Serial Position Effects in the Identification of Letters, Digits and Symbols. *Journal of Experimentl Psychology, 35*(2) (2009), pp. 480–498.

Ubasart-Gonzáles, Gemma. ETA and State Action; The Development of Spanish Antiterrorism. *Crime, Law and Social Change, 72*(5) (2019): pp. 569–586.

Valacich, Joseph S. and Schwenk, Charles. Devil's Advocacy and Dialectical Inquiry Effects on Face-to Face and Computer-mediated Group Decision Making. *Organizational Behavior and Human Decision Processes, 63*(2) (1995): pp. 158–173.

Valentine, Tim and Heaton, Pamela. An Evaluation of the Fairness of Police Line-ups and Video Identifications. *Applied Cognitive Psychology 13*(1) (1999): pp. 59–72.

Vallée-Tourangeau, Frederic and Payton, Teresa. Graphical Representation Fosters Discovery in the 2-4-6 Task. *Quarterly Journal of Experimental Psychology, 61*(4) (2008): pp. 625–640.

van den Eeden, Claire A. J., de Poot, Christianne J., and van Koppen, Peter J. Forensic Expectations: Investigating a Crime Scene with Prior Information. *Science and Justice, 56*(6) (2016): pp. 475–481.

van den Eeden, Claire A.J., de Poot, Christianne J., and van Koppen, Peter J. From Emergency Call to Crime Scene: Information Transference in the Criminal Investigation. *Forensic Science Policy & Management: An International Journal, 8*(3-4) (2017): pp. 79–89.

van den Eeden, Claire, de Poot, Christianne J and van Koppen, Peter J. The Forensic Confirmation Bias: A Comparison Between Experts and Novices. *Journal of Forensic Sciences, 64*(1) (2019): pp. 120–126.

Vanezis, Peter and West, Iain E. Tentative Injuries in Self-stabbing. *Forensic Science International, 21*(1) (1983), pp. 65–70.

Van Eijk, Gwen. Inclusion and Exclusion through Risk-based Justice: Analysing Combinations of Risk Assessment from Pretrial Detention to Release. *British Journal of Criminology, 60*(4) (2020), pp. 1080–1097.

van Veldhuizen, Tanja S., Horselenberg, Robert, Landström, Sara, Granhag, Pär Anders, and van Koppen, Peter J. Interviewing Asylum Seekers: A Vignette Study on the Questions Asked to Assess Credibility of Claims about Origin and Persecution. *Journal of Investigative Psychology and Offender Profiling, 14*(1) (2016): pp. 3–22.

van Wingerden, Sigrid, van Wilsem, Johan, and Moerings, Martin. Pre-Sentence Reports and Punishment: A Quasi-Experiment Assessing the Effects of Risk-based Pre-Sentence Reports on Sentencing. *European Journal of Criminology, 11*(6) (2014): pp. 723–744.

Victor, Dag. HD ger vägledning om skakvåld. *Svensk Juristtidning* (2015): pp. 73–79.

Vrij, Aldert and Granhag, Pär Anders. Eliciting Information and Detecting Lies in Intelligence Interviewing: An Overview of Recent Research. *Applied Cognitive Psychology, 28*(6) (2014): pp. 936–944.

Walker, Phillip L. Greater Sciatic Notch Morphology: Sex, Age, and Population Differences. *American Journal of Physical Anthropology, 127*(4) (2005): pp. 385–391.

Wallach, Michael A. and Kogan, Nathan. The Roles of Information, Discussion, and Concensus in Group Risk Taking. *Journal of Experimental Social Psychology, 1*(2) (1965): pp. 1–19.

Walong, Edwin and Oduor, Johansen. A 26-year-old Female Presenting with a Fatal Stroke Due to Embolism of Cardiac Myxomatous Neoplasm Diagnosed at Forensic Autopsy Service: A Case Report. *Forensic Science International*, 1 (2019): pp. 1–4.

Walter, Jorge and Kellermanns, Frans W., and Lechner Christoph. Decision Making Within and Between Organizations, Rationality, Politics, and Alliance Performance. *Journal of Management, 38*(5) (2012): pp. 1582–1610.

Walther, Eva, Nagengast, Benjamin, and Trasselli, Claudia. Evaluative Conditioning in Social Psychology: Facts and Speculations. *Cognition & Emotion, 19*(2) (2005): pp. 175–196.

Warach, Steven. Mapping Brain Pathophysiology and Higher Cortical Function with Magnetic Resonance Imaging. *The Neuroscientist, 1*(4) (1995): pp. 221–235.

Wason, Peter C. On the Failure to Eliminate Hypotheses in a Conceptual Task. *The Quarterly Journal of Experimental Psychology, 12*(3) (1960): pp. 129–140.

Wason, Peter C. Reasoning about a Rule. *Quarterly Journal of Experimental Psychology*, *20*(3) (1968): pp. 273–281.

Wastell, Colin, Weeks, Nicole, Wearing, Alexander, Duncan, Piers. Identifying Hypothesis Confirmation Behaviors in a Simulated Murder Investigation: Implications for Practice. *Journal of Investigative Psychology and Offender Profiling, 9*(2) (2012): pp. 184–198.

Waugh, Nancy C. and Norman, Donald A. Primary Memory. *Psychological Review, 72*(2) (1965): pp. 89–104.

Webster, Donna M. Motivated Augmentation and Reduction of the Overattribution Bias. *Journal of Personality and Social Psychology,* 65 (1993): pp. 261–271.

Webster, Donna M. and Kruglanski, Arie W. Individual Differences in Need for Cognitive Closure. *Journal of Personality and Social Psychology, 67*(6) (1994): pp. 1049–1062.

Webster Nelson, Donna, Klein, Cynthia, and Irvin, Jennifer E. Motivational Antecedents of Empathy: Inhibiting Effects of Fatigue. *Basic and Applied Social Psychology, 25*(1) (1993): pp. 37–50.

Webster, Cheryl Marie, Doob, Anthony N. and Myers, Nicole M. The Parable of Ms Baker: Understanding Pre-Trial Detention in Canada. *Current Issues in Criminal Justice*, *21*(1) (2009): pp. 79–102.

Weiner, Saul J. and Schwartz, Alan. Contextual Errors in Medical Decision Making: Overlooked and Understudied. *Academic Medicine*, *91* (5) (2016): pp. 657–662.

Weisburd, David, Hinkle, Joshua, Famega, Christine, and Ready, Justin. The Possible 'Backfire' Effects of Hot Spots Policing: An Experimental Assessment of Impacts on Legitimacy, Fear and Collective Efficacy. *Journal of Experimental Criminology, 7*(4) (2011): pp. 297–320.

Wells, Gary, Ferguson, Tamara, and Lindsay, R.C. The Tractability of Eyewitness Confidence and its Implications for Triers of Fact. *Journal of Applied Psychology, 66*(6) (1981): pp. 688–696.

Wells, Gary L., Leippe, Michael R., Ostrom, Thomas M., Sales, Bruce, D. Guidelines for Empirically Assessing the Fairness of a Lineup. *Law and Human Behavior, 3*(4) (1979): pp. 285–293.

Wells, Gary L., Malpass, Roy S., Lindsay, Roderick C.L., Fisher, Ronald P., Turtle, John W., and Fulero, Solomon. From the Lab to a Police Station: a Successful Application of Eyewitness Research. *American Psychologist, 55*(6) (2000): pp. 581–598.

Wells, Gary L. Small, Mark, Penrod, Steven D., Malpass, Roy S., Fulero, Solomon, and Elizabeth C.A. Brimacombe. Eyewitness Identification Procedures: Recommendations for Line-ups and Photo-spreads. *Law and Human Behavior, 22*(6), (1998): pp. 603–647.

Wetherick, Norman E. Eliminative and Enumerative Behavior in a Conceptual Task. *Quarterly Journal of Experimental Psychology, 14*(4) (1962): pp. 246–249.

Wettergren, Åsa and Bergman Blix, Stina. Empathy and Objectivity in the Legal Procedure; The Case of Swedish Prosecutors. *Journal of Scandinavian Studies in Criminology and Crime Prevention*, 17(1) (2016): pp. 19–35.

Wilczynski, Nancy L. and Haynes, Brian R. Developing Optimal Search Strategies for Detecting Clinically Relevant Qualitative Studies in MEDLINE. *Studies in Health Technology and Informatics*, 107(1) (2004): pp. 311–316.

Williams, Marian R. (1999). Gender and Sentencing: An Analysis of Indicators. *Criminal Justice Policy Review*, 10(4): pp. 471–490.

Williams, Marian R. (2003). The Effect of Pretrial Detention on Imprisonment Decisions. *Criminal Justice Review*, 28(2): pp. 299–316.

Williams, Mark A., Morris, Adam P., McGlone, Francis, Abbott, David F., and Mattingley, Jason B. Amygdala Responses to Fearful and Happy Facial Expression under Conditions of Binocular Suppression. *Journal of Neuroscience*, 24(12) (2004): pp. 2898–2904.

Willmott, Dominic and Sherretts, Nicole. Individual Differences in Eyewitness Identification Accuracy Between Sequential and Simultaneous Line-ups: Consequences for Police Practice and Jury Decision. *Current Issues in Personality Psychology*, 4(4) (2016): pp. 228–239.

Winterdyk, John. Canadian Police Officers and Eyewitness Evidence: A Time for Reform. *Canadian Police College Journal*, 12(3) (1988): pp. 175–191.

Wise, Richard A., Safer, Martin A., and Maro, Christina M. What US Law Enforcement Officers Know and Believe about Eyewitness Factors, Eyewitness Interviews and Identification Procedures. *Applied Cognitive Psychology*, 25(3) (2011), pp. 488–500.

Wissler, Roselle, Saks, Michael, Sales, Bruce D. On the Inefficacy of Limiting Instruction: When Jurors use Prior Conviction Evidence to Decide on Guilt. *Law and Human Behavior*, 9(1) (1985), pp. 37–48.

Wistrich, Andrew J., Rachlinski, Jeffrey J., and Guthrie, Chris. Heart Versus Head: Do Judges Follow the Law or Follow their Feelings? *Texas Law Review*, 93 (4) (2015): pp. 856–911.

Wistrich, Andrew J. and Rachlinksi, Jeffrey J. Implicit Bias in Judicial Decisions Making—How it Affects Judgment and What Judges Can Do About It. *Cornell Legal Studies Research Paper, No. 17-16* (2017): pp. 1–44.

Wogalter, Michael S., Malpass, Roy S., and McQuiston, Dawn E. A National Survey of US Police on Preparation and Conduct of Identification Lineups. *Psychology, Crime & Law*, (2004): pp. 69–82.

Wyer, Robert S. and Albarracín, Dolores. The Origins and Structure of Beliefs and Goals. *Journal of Personality and Social Psychology*, 79 (2000): pp. 5–22.

Yaroshefsky, Ellen. Cooperation with Federal Prosecutors: Experiences of Truth Telling and Embellishment. *Fordham Law Review*, 68(3) (1999): pp. 917–964.

Yazbek, Joseph, Ameye, Lieveke, Testa, Carla, Valentin, Lil, Timmerman, Dirk, Holland, Christy, van Holsbeke, Caroline, and Jurkovic, Davor. Confidence of Expert Ultrasound Operators in Making a Diagnosis of Adnexal Tumor: Effect on Diagnostic Accuracy and Interobserver Agreement. *Ultrasound in Obstetrics and Gynaecology*, 35(1) (2010): pp. 89–93

Yoo, Yang-Sook, Cho, Ok-Hee, Cha, Kyeong-Sook, Boo, Yun-Jeong. Factors Influencing Post-Traumatic Stress on Korean Forensic Science Investigators. *Asian Nursing Research*, 7(3) (2013): pp. 136–141.

Young, Maia J., Tiedens, Larissa Z., Jung, Heajung, and Tsai, Ming-Hong. Mad Enough to See the Other Side: Anger and the Search for Disconfirming Information. *Cognition and Emotion*, 1 (2011): pp. 10–21.

Zahar, Elie. Logic of Discovery or Psychology of Invention? *The British Journal for the Philosophy of Science*, 34 (1984): pp. 243–261.

Zamboni. Mauro. Legal Realisms: on Law and Politics. *Res Publica*, 12 (2006): pp. 295–317.

Zapf, Patricia A. and Dror, Itiel E. Understanding and Mitigating Bias in Forensic Evaluation: Lessons from Forensic Science. *International Journal of Forensic Mental Health*, 16(3) (2017): pp. 227–238.

Zeisel, Hans and Callahan, Thomas. Split Trials and Time-saving: A Statistical Analysis. *Harvard Law Review*, 76(8) (1963): pp. 1606–1625.

Research reports and master theses

Clarke, Colin and Milne, Rebecca Jane. National Evaluation of the PEACE Investigative Interviewing Course, Report No. PRAS/149. London: Home Office, 2001.

Dittrich, Viviane E., Lingen, Kerstin von, and Osten, Philipp. *The Tokyo Tribunal: Perspectives on Law, History and Memory*. Brussels: Torkel Opsahl Academic Epublisher, 2020.

Dror, Itiel E. *Cognitive Technologies and the Pragmatics of Cognition*. Amsterdam: John Benjamins Publishing Company, 2007.

Dror, Itiel E. (2011). The Paradox of Human Expertise: Why Experts Get it Wrong. In Narinder, Kapur (Ed.) The Paradoxical Brain (pp. 177–188). Cambridge: Cambridge University Press, 2011.

Hill, Stephen, Gilbey, Andrew, and Stichbury, Charles. On Getting 'Un-lost': Using Eye-Gaze as an Index of Hypothesis-Testing Strategies in Spatial Reasoning Scenarios. *Paper presented at the 38th Australasian Experimental Psychology Conference*, 28–30 April 2011, Auckland, New Zealand.

Lidén, Moa. Är felaktigt dömda chanslösa? En studie om enskilda individers möjligheter att driva resningsärenden framgångsrikt. *Uppsala: Juridiska institutionen* (2011): pp. 1–99.

Lovett, Jo and Kelly, Liz. Different Systems, Similar Outcomes? Tracking Attrition in Reported Rape Cases across Europe. Final Research Report, Child and Women Abuse Studies Unit London Metropolitan University, London, 2009.

Scientific Working Group on Digital Evidence (SWGDE). Establishing Confidence in Digital Forensic Results by Error Mitigating Analysis, 20 November 2018.

The Technical Working Group for Eyewitness Evidence (TWGEYEE) Eyewitness Evidence: A Guide For Law Enforcement, 1999.

McGurk, Barry. Investigative Interviewing Courses for Police Officers: An Evaluation. London: Home Office Police Department, 1993.

Smith, Terry and Brownless, Laura (2011). Age Assessment Practices: A Literature Review and Annotated Bibliography. End Immigartaion Detention oc Children. <https://endchilddetention.org/research/age-assessment-practices-literature-review/> (accessed 22 February 2023).

Sunde, Nina (2017). Non-Technical Sources of Errors When Handling Digital Evidence within a Criminal Investigation. Master thesis, Norwegian Univeristy of Science and Technology, Faculty of Technology and Electrical Engineering. <https://phs.brage.unit.no/phs-xmlui/bitstream/handle/11250/2446090/masters_Sunde.pdf?sequence=1&isAllowed=y> (accessed 22 February 2023).

Walmsley, Roy. World Pre-trial/Remand Imprisonment List. Institute for Crime & Justice Policy Research. <https://www.prisonstudies.org/sites/default/files/resources/downloads/world_pre-trial_list_4th_edn_final.pdf> (accessed 23 February 2023).

Conference proceedings

Williamson, Tom. (2006). Investigative Interviewing: Rights, Research, Regulation. International Conference on Police Interviewing.

Cavagnini, Gianluca, Sansoni, Giovanna, and Trebeschi, Marco (2009). Using 3D Range Cameras for Crime Scene Documentation and Legal Medicine. Proceedings of SPIE, 7239(1) (2009), pp. 72390Ö–7230L-10.

Edelman, Gerda, van Leeuwen, Ton, and Aalders, Maurice (2013). Hyperspectral Imaging of the Crime Scene for Detection and Identification of Blood Stains. Proceedings Volume 8743. Algorithms and Technologies for Multispectral, Hyperspectral and Ultraspectral Imagery XIX. Baltimore, Maryland, United States.

Granér, Rolf and Kronkvist, Ola (2015). The Past, the Present and the Future of Police Research: Proceedings from the Fifth Nordic Police Research Seminar. Växjö: Linneuniversitet, 2015.

Klales, Alexandra, Lesciotto, Kate M. (2016). The 'Science of Science': Examining Bias in Forensic Anthropology. The 68th Annual Meeting of the American Academy of Forensic Sciences. Las Vegas.

Pettit, Gregory S, Fegan, Greg, and Howie, Pauline. Interviewer Effects on Children's Testimony. *Paper presented at the International Congress on Child Abuse and Neglect*, Hamburg, Germany, September, 1990.

Roach, Jason. *The Retrospective Detective: Cognitive Bias and the Cold Case Investigation. British Society of Criminology Annual Conference*. Sheffield Hallam University, 2017.

iii) Other Sources

News Articles and other online material

Africa News (2020). Congolese Ex-warlord 'Sheka' sentenced to life in prison. <https://www.africanews.com/2020/11/24/congolese-ex-warlord-sheka-sentenced-to-life-in-prison//> (accessed 23 February 2023).

Andersson, Carl V. Quicks erkännande—en kopia av 'Efterlyst'. <http://www.expressen.se/nyheter/quicks-erkannande---en-kopia-av-efterlyst/> (accessed 23 February 2023).

Asian News International (2020). SSR Death Case: Medical Board Submitted Report Directly to CBI, Can Obtain Inputs from Bureau, Says AIIMS. <https://www.aninews.in/news/national/general-news/ssr-death-case-medical-board-submitted-report-directly-to-cbi-can-obtain-inputs-from-bureau-says-aiims20201005210812/> (accessed 23 February 2023).

Associated Press (2016). A Timeline of Events in the Brendan Dassey Case. <https://web.archive.org/web/20160924153606/http://bigstory.ap.org/article/3ab0384d21704517b7daf97a485f1416/timeline-events-brendan-dassey-case> (accessed 23 February 2023).

Baas, David. 'Glasögonmannen: Thomas Quick är oskyldig'. 9 February 2014. <http://www.expressen.se/nyheter/glasogonmannen-thomas-quick-ar-oskyldig/> (accessed 23 February 2023).

BBC. Kenya Westgate Mall Attack: What We Know, 21 October 2013. <https://www.bbc.co.uk/news/av/world-africa-24617763> (accessed 23 February 2023).

Coynash, Hayla (2020). Baffling Denial by Italy of War in Donbas as Excuse for Trial of Ukrainian Soldier Markiv. <https://twitter.com/halyapuff/status/1130201631503654912> (accessed 21 February 2023).

Voice of America. The Milimani Court in Nairobi, see <https://www.voanews.com/africa/3-stand-trial-alleged-role-kenyas-westgate-mall-attack> (accessed 4 February 2022).

Vredeveldt, Annelies. *Beyond WEIRD Witnesses: Eyewitness Memory in Cross-Cultural Contexts*, 2020. <https://www.narcis.nl/research/RecordID/OND1367668/Language/en> (accessed 23 February 2023).

BBC News (2019). Conviction against Barry George quashed by Court of Appeal 15 November 2007. BBC News (2019). Jill Dando Murder Case Will Never be Solved. <https://www.bbc.co.uk/news/uk-47742654.amp> (accessed 13 July 2022).

BBC News (2007). Guantanamo Detainees Out on Bail. <http://news.bbc.co.uk/2/hi/uk_news/7153146.stm> (accessed 13 July 2022).

BBC News (2020). Sushant Singh Rajput: Rhea Chakraborty on 'Media Trial' after Bollywood Star's Death. <https://www.bbc.co.uk/news/world-asia-india-53932725> (accessed 23 February 2023).

Biloslavo, Fausto (2017). Uccise Fotoreporter Italiano in Ucraina Arrestato a Bologna Miliziano Anti-Putin. <https://www.ilgiornale.it/news/politica/uccise-fotoreporter-italiano-ucraina-arrestato-bologna-1415426.html> (accessed 23 February 2023).

Bob, Yonah Jeremy (2022). Prosecution Retrial of Zadorov may be on the Ropes. The Jerusalem Post. <https://www.jpost.com/israel-news/article-700793> (accessed 9 March 2022).

CBC (2009). Dr. Charles Smith: The Man Behind the Public Inquiry. <https://www.cbc.ca/news/canada/dr-charles-smith-the-man-behind-the-public-inquiry-1.864004> (accessed 23 February 2023).

CNN. Derek Chauvin is on trial for George Floyd's Death. Medical Examiner: I 'intentionally chose not' to view videos of Floyd's death before conducting autopsy, 2021. <https://edition.cnn.com/us/live-news/derek-chauvin-trial-04-09-21/h_03cda59afac6532a0fb8ed48244e44a0> (accessed 23 February 2023).

Dagens Juridik. Hård kritik mot NFCs statistiska sannolikhetskalkyler som fällande bevisning. 17 November 2016. <http://www.dagensjuridik.se/2016/11/jag-ryser-om-nfcs-statistiska-sannolikhetskalkyler-som-fallande-bevisning> (accessed 30 July 2018).

Dagens Juridik. Jag försöker tänka som en polis—och hitta rimligt tvivel genom egna undersökningar, 23 March 2018. <http://www.dagensjuridik.se/2018/03/jag-forsoker-tanka-som-en-polis> (accessed 30 July 2018).

Dagens Juridik. Stefan Lindskog: Resningsärendena hör inte hemma i Högsta Domstolen, 12 October 2017. <http://www.dagensjuridik.se/2015/11/stefan-lindskog-resningsarendena-hor-inte-hemma-i-hogsta-domstolen> (accessed 30 July 2018).

Dagens Nyheter (DN). Polis och Åklagare efter Friande Domar: Beviskraven är för Höga, 19 February 2019. <https://www.dn.se/sthlm/polis-och-aklagare-efter-friande-domar-beviskraven-ar-for-hoga/> (accessed 23 February 2023).

Davenport, David. International Criminal Court: 12 years, $ 1 Billion, 2 Convictions, *Forbes*, 12 March 2014. <https://www.forbes.com/sites/daviddavenport/2014/03/12/international-criminal-court-12-years-1-billion-2-convictions-2> (accessed 23 February 2023).

De Standaard. Het Strafhof moet Dringend in De Spiegel Kijken, 26 January 2019.<https://www.standaard.be/cnt/dmf20190125_04131754> (accessed 23 February 2023).

Desmarais, Sarah L. and Lowder, Evan M. (2019). Pretrial Risk Assessment Tools: A Primer for Judges, Prosecutors, and Defense Attorneys. Safety and Justice Challenge, Executive Summary. <https://safetyandjusticechallenge.org/wp-content/uploads/2021/06/Desmarais-Lowder-Pretrial-Risk-Assessment-Primer-Executive-Summary.pdf> (accessed 23 February 2023).

Facione, Peter A (1990). The Delphi Report. Critical Thinking: A Statement of Expert Consensus for Purposes of Educational Assessment and Instruction. Committee on Pre-college Philosophy. Cuny.

Federazione Italiana Diritti Umani (FIDU), Caso Markiv: Dalla Parte Della Verità. <https://fidu.it/language/it/caso-markiv-dalla-parte-della-verita/> (accessed 22 February 2023).

Grissom, Brandi (2017). Death Row Inmate Seeks to Halt Execution for Dallas-area Murders, Alleges Prosecutor Misconduct, Forensic Magazine. <http://ezproxy.its.uu.se/login> (accessed 19 July 2022).

Guillou, Jan. 'Klockan tickar om de riktiga mördarna ska kunna dömas', 11 March 2011. <http://www.aftonbladet.se/nyheter/article11593647.ab> (accessed 11 February 2014)

Human Rights Watch (2008) Coercion and Intimidation of Child Soldiers to Participate in Violence. <https://www.hrw.org/news/2008/04/16/coercion-and-intimidation-child-soldiers-participate-violence> (accessed 22 February 2023).

International Investigative Interviewing Research Group (iIIRG). <https://www.iiirg.org/research/collaboration/> (accessed 23 February 2023).

Il Resto del Carlino Bologna (2017). Bologna, arrestato all'aeroporto il killer del fotoreporter italiano. <https://www.ilrestodelcarlino.it/bologna/cronaca/andrea-rocchelli-1.3239138> (accessed 22 February 2023

Jackman, Tom (2017). Norfolk 4, Wrongly Convicted of Rape and Murder: Pardoned by Gov. McAuliffe. <https://www.washingtonpost.com/news/true-crime/wp/2017/03/21/norfolk-4-wrongly-convicted-of-rape-and-murder-pardoned-by-gov-mcauliffe/> (accessed 13 July 2022).

Jordash, Wayne (2020). How an Italian Court Undermined the Presumption of Innocence in Markiv's Conviction. The Kyiv Post, 9 October 2020. <https://archive.kyivpost.com/article/opinion/op-ed/wayne-jordash-how-an-italian-court-undermined-the-presumption-of-innocence-in-markivs-conviction.html> (accessed 23 February 2023).

Karlsson, Susanne. Önskan att få fast den skyldige kan leda till tankefel, 25 August 2017. <http://nfc.polisen.se/Start/Nyheter/Onskan-att-fa-fast-den-skyldige-kan-leda-till-tankefel/> (accessed 30 July 2018).

Lindström (2018) Lisbet Palme var Säker på vem Mördaren var, 18 october 2018. <https://www.expressen.se/nyheter/lisbet-palme-var-saker-pa-vem-mordaren-var/> (accessed 23 February 2023).

Lidén, Moa. (2016).Felaktiga brottmålsdomar är rättsstatens Akilleshäl—en genomgång av 2078 resningsansökningar. <http://www.dagensjuridik.se/2016/10/analys-kronika-moa-liden-1> (accessed 30 July 2018).

MacDonald, Neil. (2010). CBC Investigation: Who Killed Lebanon's Rafik Hariri?.CBC News. <https://www.cbc.ca/news/world/cbc-investigation-who-killed-lebanon-s-rafik-hariri-1.874820> (accessed 20 February 2023).

Mills, Steve, McRoberts, Flynn and Possley, Maurice (2004). When Labs Falter, Defendants Pay: Bias Toward Prosecution Cited in Illinois Cases. Chicago Tribune

Monahan, Jerald and Polk, Sheila (2023). The Effect of Cultural Bias on the Investigation and Prosecution of Sexual Assault. IACP. Police Chief. <https://www.policechiefmagazine.org/the-effect-of-cultural-bias-on-the-investigation/?ref=2b0c8e11fa9b1f2db265fa2e4f71658c> (accessed 22 February 2023).

Morani, Ilaria (2014). Ucraina, il Racconto del Capitano 'Ecco come e morte Rocchelli'. <https://www.corriere.it/esteri/14_maggio_25/ucraina-racconto-capitano-7bf53c06-e40a-11e3-8e3e-8f5de4ddd12f.shtml> (accessed 22 February 2023).

Mutahi, Basillioh (2020). Rwanda Genocide: How Félicien Kabuga evaded capture for 26 years. <https://www.bbc.co.uk/news/world-africa-52758693> (accessed 23 February 2023).

Mbakwe, Tom (2012). 'ICC Gets First Conviction after 10 Years in Existence', New African, 1 April 2012. <https://newafricanmagazine.com/3072/> (accessed 22 February 2023).

Nordqvist, Linn. Björn Hurtigs byrå anställer egen polis: 'här i Sverige är advokatbyråerna naiva', 23 November 2012. <http://www.dagensjuridik.se/2012/11/bjorn-hurtigs-byra-anstaller-egen-polis-har-i-sverige-ar-advokatbyraerna-naiva> (accessed 30 July 2018).

Oliver, Mark (2007). Libyan Granted New Appeal over Lockerbie Conviction and Adams, How the Trial of the Century Ended as our Worst Embarrassment. The Guardian. <https://www.theguardian.com/uk/2007/jun/28/lockerbie.world> (accessed 22 February 2023).

Pandey, Munish and Kashyap, Anjana Om (2020). Sushant Singh Rajput Murder Completely Ruled Out, It Was Suicide: Dr Sudhir Gupta of AIIMS. India Today. <https://www.indiatoday.in/movies/celebrities/story/sushant-singh-rajput-murder-completely-ruled-out-it-was-suicide-dr-sudhir-gupta-of-aiims-1727920-2020-10-03> (accessed 11 July 2022).

Radio Free Europe Documents and Publications (2019). Kyiv Protesters Demand Freedom for Veteran Jailed in Italy for Journalist's Death. 15 October 2019. <https://www.rferl.org/a/kyiv-protesters-demand-freedom-for-veteran-jailed-in-italy-for-journalist-s-death/30217122.html> (accessed 23 February 2023).

Robinson, Darryl (2019). The Other Poisoned Chalice: Unprecedented Evidentiary Standards in the Gbagbo Case (Part I). <https://www.ejiltalk.org/the-other-poisoned-chalice-unprecedented-evidentiary-standards-in-the-gbagbo-case-part-1/> (accessed 23 February 2023).

Robinson, Darryl (2019). The Other Poisoned Chalice: Unprecedented Evidentiary Standards in the Gbagbo Case (Part II). <https://www.ejiltalk.org/the-other-poisoned-chalice-unprecedented-evidentiary-standards-in-the-gbagbo-case-part-2/.> (accessed 23 February 2023).

Råstam, Hannes. Material som kunde fria Quick gömdes av polisen. 17 March 2010. <http://www.dn.se/debatt/material-som-kunde-fria-quick-gomdes-av-polisen/> (accessed 11 February 2014).

Sandgren, Claes. Klagoinstans för felaktiga domar—här har 80 procent av de nya rättegångarna lett till frikännande, 14 November 2012. <https://www.dagensjuridik.se/nyheter/klagoinstans-felaktiga-domar-har-har-80-procent-av-de-nya-rattegangarna-lett-till-frikannand/> (accessed 30 July 2018).

Sandgren, Claes. RÅ blandar bort korten istället för att lägga dem på bordet—hur är det med statistiken för resning? 25 February 2013. http://www.dagensjuridik.se/2013/02/ra-blandar-bort-korten-i-stallet-att-lagga-dem-pa-bordet (accessed 30 July 2018).

Schickore, Jutta. 'Scientific Discovery', The Stanford Encyclopedia of Philosophy. 2014. <http://plato.stanford.edu/archives/spr2014/entries/scientific-discovery> (accessed 30 July 2018).

Shaik, Thair (2003). Sally Clark, mother wrongly convicted of killing her sons, found dead at home. <https://www.theguardian.com/society/2007/mar/17/childrensservices.uknews> (accessed 30 July 2018).

Sveriges Radio. JK: Felaktigt dömda sitter i fängelse, 25 November 2004. https://sverigesradio.se/sida/artikel.aspx?programid=83&artikel=510450 (accessed 30 July 2018).

SVT Online News. Forskaren: Det är väldigt svårt att beviljas resning, 11 April 2018. <https://www.svt.se/nyheter/lokalt/stockholm/forskaren-om-resningsansokningar-det-ar-valdigt-svart-att-beviljas-resning> (accessed 30 July 2018).

SVT Play. Hör Leif GW kommentera kritiserade domen i Solna tingsrätt, 6 March 2018. <https://www.svt.se/nyheter/lokalt/stockholm/hor-leif-gw-kommentera-kritiserad-dom-i-solnatingsratt> (accessed 30 July 2018).

SVT Play, Brottsjournalen, 21 January 2020. <https://www.svtplay.se/kanaler?date=2020-01-21&program=TT-402516363> (accessed 23 February 2023).

Svärdkrona, Zendry. Oskyldiga döms till fängelse, 15 advokater i öppet brev till justitieminister Thomas Bodström, 8 March 2011. <https://www.aftonbladet.se/debatt/a/gPwmyB/oskyldiga-doms-till-fangelse> (accessed 30 July 2018).

The Guardian (2008). The July 21 failed bombings, Timeline of events before and after the attempted bomb attacks in London on July 20 2005. <https://www.theguardian.com/uk/2008/feb/04/terrorism.world1> (accessed 23 February 2023).

The New York Times (2020). Appeal in Lockerbie Bombing Reaches Scotland's Highest Court, 21 December 2020. <https://www.nytimes.com/2020/11/24/world/europe/lockerbie-bombing-megrahi-appeal-scotland.html> (accessed 23 February 2023).

The New York Times (2022). A Crime Revisited: The Decision: 13 Years Later. Official Reversal in Jogger Attack, 6 December 2002. <https://www.nytimes.com/2002/12/06/nyregion/a-crime-revisited-the-decision-13-years-later-official-reversal-in-jogger-attack.html> (accessed 23 February 2023).

The New York Times (2019). How Russian Propaganda Showed Up in an Italian Murder Trial, Tokariuk, Battle of Narratives: Kremlin Disinformation in the Vitaliy Markiv Case in Italy, 17 December 2019. <https://www.nytimes.com/2019/12/17/world/europe/russia-italy-propaganda.html> (accessed 23 February 2023).

The Innocence Project (2013). Eyewitness Misidentification. <https://www.innocenceproject.org/causes/eyewitness-misidentification/> (accessed 30 July 2018).

The Innocence Project (2013). Misapplication of Forensic Science. <https://www.innocenceproject.org/causes/misapplication-forensic-science/> (accessed 30 July 2018).

Tinazzi, Christiano (2022). 'Crossfire'. <https://www.imdb.com/title/tt15085124/> (accessed 23 February 2023).

Tokariuk, Olga (2019). The Most Outrageous Case this Summer that No one Has Heard of, <https://www.atlanticcouncil.org/blogs/ukrainealert/the-most-outrageous-case-this-summer-that-no-one-has-heard-of/> (accessed 23 February 2023).

Verini, James (2016). *The Prosecutor and the President*. The New York Times Magazine.

Wahlberg, Stefan (2015). Jätterättegångarna kan strida mot Europakonventionen—'svårt att få en överblick'. <https://www.bgplay.se/video/jatterattegangarna-kan-strida-mot-europakonventionen-svart-att-fa-en-overblick> (accessed 12 February 2018).

Zimbardo, Philip (1992). Quiet rage: The Stanford prison study video. <http://www.youtube.com/watch?v=760lwYmpXbc> (accessed 26 February 2014).

Öster, Ulrika (2015). Riskabelt att göra egna undersökningar. <https://www.advokaten.se/Tidningsnummer/2015/Nr-9-2015-argang-81/Riskabelt-att-gora-egna-undersokningar/> (accessed 30 July 2018).

Podcasts

Dahlman, Christian (2020). Öppet Fall—Palmemordet. <https://podcasts.apple.com/us/podcast/palmemordet-del-2-7/id1478626548?i=1000477418957> (accessed 23 February 2023).

Index

For the benefit of digital users, indexed terms that span two pages (e.g., 52–53) may, on occasion, appear on only one of those pages.
Tables and figures are indicated by *t* and *f* following the page number

Adriano Cadiz case 60–66
age estimation 65–66, 118–19, 136
Al Faqi case 54–55, 184
arson investigation 104–5, 109–11
artificial intelligence (AI) 1–2, 137–38
Automated Fingerprint Identification System (AFIS) 138, 139, 188
Ayyash et al case 39–40, 41–42, 92–93, 185–87

Bergwall case 32, 47–51, 120–23, 145, 184
bias blind spot 29–31, 35–36, 139, 145, 155, 158–59, 183–84
bias snowball effect 109–11
Bitemark comparisons 104–5
bloodstain pattern analysis (BPA) 96–97, 104–5
Brandon Mayfield case 105–6
Breivik case 21–23, 88–89
Brendan Dassey case 108–9
Bullet comparisons 101, 104–5

cause of death 21, 112–13, 114, 118, 126, 133–34, 188
Central Park Five case 55–56, 108–9
child interview 64–65, 185–87
child soldier 26, 65–66, 118–19
closed-circuit television (CCTV) 38–39
cognitive load 18–19, 28, 68–69, 71–72, 136–38, 139, 179–80, 181–82, 188, 190–91
cognitive technologies 136–37
coherence driven cognition 21
Cold case 50–51, 53–54, 120–21
corroboration inflation 109–11
crime pattern analysis 111

Darfur case 149–50
debiasing technique 18–34, 68–73, 82–86, 98–102, 123–38, 154–58, 177–80, 184–85, 186*t*
defense 58–59, 60, 61–62, 108, 114, 118, 165–66, 174
diagnostic accuracy 51–53, 54–55
diagnostic calibration 52, 147–48
digital evidence 104–5, 111, 133–34, 136–37
distributed cognition 136–37, 138, 188

DNA 1–2, 88–89, 90–92, 104–5, 106–8, 133–34, 139, 143–44, 188–89

Egunkaria case 44–46, 184
Engin Raghip case 108–9
evidence submission form 125*f*, 125, 129–30, 131–32

false confession 56–60, 62–63, 108–9, 143–44, 192
fear 23, 25, 26, 27, 31, 42
fingerprint 104–6, 109–11, 118–19, 130–31, 133–34, 138
forensic confirmation bias 21, 103, 104–5, 107, 111, 123–24, 130

Gbagbo and Blé Goudé case 146–47, 171–72, 188–89

Hauschildt case 18, 160–66
hypothesis leakage 80–82, 86–87

International Criminal Court (ICC) 111, 143, 147–48, 154–55, 171–73
investigation plan 43, 149–57
IRA funeral murders 108–9
Ivan the Terrible case 75–82, 187

Jill Dando case 79
judicial exceptionalism 6–7, 35–36, 183–84

Kabuga case 54–55
Kenya case 149–50
Kony and Otti case 54–55, 184

laser scanning 100–2, 187–88
Lockerbie case 77–78
London bombings 4–5, 37–43
Lorenzo Montoya case 108–9
Lubanga case 65–66

Madrid bomber case 138
most responsible perpetrator 31–32, 54–55, 150

motivated reasoning 25–26, 171

New York mafia case 54–55, 184
Norfolk Four case 143–44, 188–89
Ntaganda case 21–23

offence driven investigation 41–42
Olof Palme case 49–50, 78–79, 184

Paris attack 23, 88–89
pathologist 112–19, 134–35
poison 118, 126
post-traumatic stress disorder (PTSD) 23–24
pre-trial publicity 167–75
primary error detecting and minimization 26, 172–73
pseudoscientific beliefs 70–72

Racketeer Influenced and Corrupt Organizations (RICO) act 54–55, 184
Randal Smith case 134–35
risk-based justice 162–63

Samir Sabri case 97, 108–9

self-enhancement 18–19, 29–30
sensitivity 51–55
Shaken baby syndrome 112–14
Sheka case 21–23
shoe print 101, 107–9, 188
Singh Rajput case 168–69, 190
somatic state 27
Special Court of Sierra Leone (SCSL) 23–24, 65–66, 157–58
Special Tribunal of Lebanon (STL) 39–42, 56–57
specificity 51–55
Stefan Kiszko case 108–9

Tair Rada case 107–9, 188
Taylor case 65–66
Therese Johanessen case 120
trace funnel 99–100

verdict driven juries 32
Vitaliy Markiv case 167–75, 190

Westgate shopping mall attack 23, 88–89
Westlund case 127–28
working memory 20–21